'*Each carefully crafted chapter illustrates the reader with unflinching empathy. The impact brought to bear on the family and loved ones of these men's tragic demise, wrenches you back through time and gives you a unique insight into the past. It is written with deep compassion, energy and devotion. Combined with impeccable research of the era, this is a must read for today's generation and the generations to follow. A fitting tribute to those who suffered these horrors can only be in the telling of their stories.*'

John Dean is a specialist collector of medals of the Great War, a hobby and passion he has followed for over forty years, he is also a respected former book dealer.

'*This is a very readable book reminding us of the horrors of the Great War. The author goes into great detail about the social history of the time, provides details of various medals awarded, many for gallantry and has visited the numerous war graves and memorials. There is no doubt that the book was written with a great deal of compassion by someone who fully understands the suffering caused by the loss to a family and in such tragic circumstances. Any person who has an interest in the Great War would find this book interesting. They will also be impressed by the in-depth research carried out to encourage others to do likewise.*'

Ian Hall worked as a senior official in a government department for thirty years. He has been a keen and enthusiastic collector of British war medals since 1979.

INKY DINKY PARLEZ VOUS

Charles Sandbach
with
Robert Jackson

© 2018 Charles Sandbach and Rob Jackson.
Published by Great War Exhibitions Ltd.

1st Edition 2018.

ISBN: 978-1-5272-1131-5

British Library Cataloguing in Publication Data A catalogue record for this book is available from the British Library.

Typeset by Beamreach Printing (www.beamreachuk.co.uk)
Printed and bound by Beamreach Printing (www.beamreachuk.co.uk)

CONTENTS

PROFILES

Charles Sandbach – Author

CHARLES is a student, lecturer and writer of history, he is also an award-winning campaigner for military welfare and social justice. Having made numerous appearances on radio, television and in the mainstream media he is acknowledged on the IMDb as the Director of the accredited dual-film documentary, 'A War to End All Wars'.

Bolton-born Charles has held memberships of well-respected organisations that have included the Chartered Institute of Journalists, United Services Veterans Association and the Jullundur Brigade Association. Always keen to play an active role within the specialist field of mental health care he has particularly assisted sufferers of PTSD. With passionate empathy and understanding Charles has raised hundreds of thousands of pounds to help pay for specialist treatment facilities.

Rob Jackson – Military Consultant & Project Director

ROB has demonstrated a high degree of enthusiasm and effort to ensure this book has reached you the reader. He has provided his invaluable experience as a former Army Warrant Officer with twenty-two years of military service behind him, to corroborate many aspects of factual relevance within this publication. Over four decades Rob has become a highly skilled and knowledgeable collector of British war medals.

Leeds-born ex-Coldstream Guardsman Rob has presented indicative opinions and essential facts to assist with the actual construction of the formatted chapters. The utilisation of medals from his own personal collection have provided the essential foundations for all of the stories within this book.

PREFACE

IF the title of this book intrigues you that is the intention, so we may as well start as we go on. Let us therefore surprise you and do a few more things as well. Here we have a totally unique and inspirational publication. We cross-examine many elements of a historical period as never done before and hope to make a mark upon everyone who happens to read what we have to say. This is a work of collaboration, it simply had to be.

I am a historian and proud of it, not of the conventional sort at all as I am unrepentant, unforgiving and bloody hard work, my passion spurs me on. Rob Jackson my collaborator ensures that common sense prevails. He is a distinguished former serviceman with twenty-two years in the colours. 'Raised in the Guards', Rob also went on to serve in other branches of the army. As a vastly experienced former Warrant Officer his task is to 'reign me in'.

The twenty-first century in which we live presents all kinds of expectations and different challenges from those experienced by our forefathers. No matter who we are, where we come from, what colour, religion, perceived social class or background we may have, we are all human beings. So let's make it perfectly clear, this is a totally humanistic work reaching back across the generations.

History can be one of those subjects easily dodged at school, simply because it can be looked upon as boring. So now it is our job to make sure it isn't, to a degree anyway! Rob and I bring you this publication to enlighten days gone by, you don't have to be a student of history to read this book. The pictures we will paint in your mind of ordinary people all-be-they from a different time we hope will inspire you.

I started to study the Great War as a subject at Grammar school many, many years ago. Guided and mentored by my charismatic and totally dedicated history master Robert Dearden. Bob was a former games teacher who wore the baggiest tracksuit bottoms you could imagine with numerous fag packets bulging from the pockets. How he ended up as a history teacher I will never know. He was and still is a total inspiration to me. Having travelled all over the former Western Front with my work in film documentaries, I never found the time to appreciate a sense of personal reflection relating to my inner feelings, until now.

Rob and I came together because of our mutual interest in collecting medals from servicemen of all ranks who participated and fought in WW1. Sounds boring to some, but not at all. The research potential for us both was and still is incredible and gives us a remarkable insight not always appreciated by traditional historians. Every one of the subjects profiled were awarded service medals, some additionally received further awards for bravery and gallantry. As the stories unfold the symbolic significances of their medals provide a continuous and interesting backdrop that complements the whole of this publication.

History is conjectural, formed upon opinions that often don't possess complete information, how could they? None of us lived in those times, we rely upon written statements, diaries and official records. So, how much of what was written indeed represents the actual truth? How do we proceed? We often morally challenge academic perceptions laid down by a pompous colony of privileged 'metropolitan historians'. Should we be allowed to superimpose our own opinions with direct reference to the subjects in this book? You will find the answers of that we are sure.

I was born and raised at the end of the old world order in the terraced streets of Bolton through the later part of the 1960's, then the 70's and 80's. The socially respectful community that I grew up in still harboured the good old men who had fought in the Great War. I would take my scrap book with me when I spoke to them to write everything down. At the time I was eight or nine years old whilst they were in their eighties and nineties. The old veterans gave me their time and were enthused at the fact that I had taken an interest in them. I had seen them wearing their medals so proudly at our local war memorial on Armistice Day parades. From there I went on to spend my life-time to date expanding a huge passion for the entire subject of the Great War, a conflict that tragically affected my own family. Rob was born and raised in an area of Leeds where you called 'A spade a spade' if you didn't you would be clobbered by one. He followed in the footsteps of family tradition and became a career soldier.

We proceed through the guys we have the medals for, it is as simple as that. Neither of us are Oxbridge graduates or grey haired bespectacled academics. The totally dedicated research behind everything we say has been done so with complete diligence and with special respect to ordinary people. We hope to raise more questions than answers for you the reader. As the chapters unfold we are sure you will see what we are trying to do.

This publication is presented to you the reader in order for you to share some of the real life experiences of the fifty servicemen chronicled. We embark upon a journey together to seek out their very beginnings to where destiny took them. See them, feel them, touch them in your soul, they are closer to you than you may think.

Charles Sandbach

INTRODUCTION

ALMOST every morning many of us go through a daily routine that often starts by rolling out of bed and heading for the bathroom. During the course of our visits to the WC we go through the usual procedures and a fair old few of us look at ourselves in the mirror. Sometimes, we take closer personal inspections and can easily be disappointed, on other occasions we may be pleasantly surprised. How many times have you asked yourself within the ordinary situation of the morning visit to the bathroom - Where am I going in my life? What does it all mean? How often have you wished simply just to be appreciated?

Okay, so you are just one person, maybe you work in a bank, drive a bus, toil on a building-site or in a factory. Then again you could be a lawyer, a stockbroker, a heart surgeon or even a politician! You have all been in that mirror and many of you have asked yourselves the questions I raised, you know you have.

Try to imagine one day somewhere in the distant future that someone does appreciate you and makes sure that many others do also. Your ordinary legacy could represent an amazing gesture. You never know your future great-grandchildren may just read the appreciative comments about you, even better!

The guys you will meet in this publication are all long gone, all but two of them sacrificed their lives in the Great War of 1914-18. Just like us, they were regular people, no two of them the same. Many of them had families, close friends, active social lives, hobbies, interests, hopes and fears. Now, for the first time ever the untold stories of their lives unfold, often with sprinklings of history never before spoken or written about. We hope you will relate to them, some of them may bring a tear to your eye whilst others will make you smile. Once upon a time they also looked in the mirror and asked themselves the same questions as you do now.

Astonishingly, millions of men from the British Isles enlisted into the forces during the Great War, more commonly known as the First World War. This was the first conflict on an industrialised scale with devastating effects that changed the course of our history. Many consequences of those effects of change have a bearing on the way we all live today. This is not a historical reference or text book, you won't see detailed strategic records or be bombarded with tactical planning. Invariably and inevitably certain points of fact, conjecture and opinion relating to the actions in which the subjects of this book were involved will manifest and become apparent.

We represent here a varied cross-section from our society that at the time [WW1] was more than a third smaller of what it is today, in itself making the enlistment figures even more incredible. The vast majority of those who served were not experienced soldiers, sailors or airmen, they were volunteers and as the war moved on, conscripted men. Women played more than an essential role upon the home front and especially within the medical establishments close to the battle zones. These ladies were wives, girlfriends, mothers and sisters who endured enormous suffering and grief that remained with them for the rest of their lives.

First of all we have to explain the title of this publication, only a few people may have a rough idea of where it actually comes from. Our stories often relate to comradeship and nothing bound these guys together better than when they were singing on a march either to or from the front. Almost every one of the men in here would have known the words to the first verse of this popular and risqué song from WW1. Its title is – 'Mademoiselle from Armentieres' – originally a nineteenth century French marching song about the daughter of an inn-keeper. She lived in a small town that is close to what is now the Belgian border. The words were frequently changed, as were the spellings, the lads got away with what they could. Rob tells me they wouldn't sing this particular verse when marching through a village or anywhere near a General on horseback! Our title comes from the final line of the first verse.

'Mademoiselle from Armentieres'
First Verse

Mademoiselle from Armentieres, Parlez-Vous
Mademoiselle from Armentieres, Parlez-Vous
*Mademoiselle from Armentieres, she hasn't been ****** for forty years*
'Inky-Dinky Parlez-Vous

The final dedication here is a simple one, Rob and I bring to you fifty mini-biographies relating to the conflict that was supposed to be the 'War to End All Wars'. This book is dedicated to the 704,803 servicemen of the British Isles who lost their lives and to the brave 251,900 others who fought alongside them and also perished. These men came from; India, Australia, Canada, New Zealand, South Africa, Newfoundland, the West Indies and a small number of other nations. Almost a MILLION souls lost, nearly half of whom have no known grave. Finally, to their loved ones, their families, children and descendants, in their millions more. God bless you all.

BOYS TO MEN

THE Great War of 1914-18 cast a long shadow over almost every family in this country. Regardless of their social status or class, from every town, city, village and shire parish, millions of people were affected. The vast majority of those who served were volunteers representing our largest citizen army of all time. A relatively small professional regular army was supported by the Territorial Force and former soldiers recalled from the army reserve list. These men could not be expected to defeat an aggressive and ruthless German army many times larger and better equipped than themselves. The conscripts came later as desperation grew to replace the continual losses.

By the end of 1914 and with the war having raged for less than five months over a million recruits had enlisted in Britain, the actual figure being, 1,174,000. A further 1,278,000 men joined up in 1915, the year enlistment figures peaked. Many more came afterwards, whether they chose to serve or not.

Officially a new recruit had to be between the ages of 19 and 38 to be considered for overseas service, the figure rose to 45-years old for ex-soldiers who wished to re-enlist. A man had to be medically fit and at least 5'3" tall, around three inches shorter than the average height of a male at the time. Hundreds of thousands of under-age recruits lied about how old they actually were and made it to the fronts with very often tragic consequences for themselves and their families.

Tradition was different in the Royal Navy, boys could legally enlist at 14. Tragically several 15-year old boys were killed at the Battle of Jutland in 1916, one of whom was actually awarded a Victoria Cross. The very fact that we sent young teenage boys to their deaths on a huge scale seems somewhat unthinkable and to a point deplorable today, some would go as far as to say it was criminal.

There is no question the authorities knew that many of their new recruits were under-age. Recruitment teams often turned a 'blind-eye' and in many cases encouraged the boys to lie about their ages. Despite their innocence of youth exactly the same was expected of these boys, they were to be transformed into ruthless killers. These were the days when the age of majority was 21. Many of the legitimate recruits were not legally old enough to marry without parental consent.

Boys had to become men very quickly, some succeeded but many didn't and paid with their lives in unimaginable circumstances. Through sheer terror some of them hesitated in battle. The youngsters were literally butchered by strapping professional German, Turkish or Bulgarian soldiers, sometimes at very close quarters. An actual figure of under-19's who perished for their King and country doesn't appear to have been published anywhere. You will discover as you read on there are certain other disturbing pieces of information regarding teenage soldiers that do not seem to have found their way into the public domain.

Duncan McDonald
Killed in Action
August 13th 1914
Aged 16.

ACCORDING to some official sources young Duncan was the very first British Expeditionary Force casualty of the war and he is commemorated in France. Apparently this is a very little known claim that we are stating. Why has the information relating to our revelation never been properly publicised? Are there too many people willing to accept that official records are incorrect? Or could it be that certain individuals from another time didn't want the facts to be known? We are the custodians of Duncan's 1914 Star medal, commonly known as the Mons Star. Both Rob and I have had many sleepless nights after investigating the tragic and somewhat mysterious and controversial circumstances surrounding the death of this boy. Before we go into further detail, let's talk about Duncan and his family, the boy, the son, the brother, the friend and finally the soldier.

Duncan entered the world on Monday April 18th 1898. He was born at the Hill of Fortrose Farm, Fortrose, about six miles north-east of Inverness in the Scottish highlands. It must have been a very difficult birth for his mother, Jane. She had been 46-years old at that time. Duncan was her eighth child, and the fifth to his father, William. He was the youngest of all their children. Jane Ann McDonald had lived at the farm for a number of years. After giving birth to a daughter and namesake, Jane, seemingly out-of-wedlock, she married for the first time in 1887 to the farmer of the sprawling 36-acre farm. Roderick McKenzie was a man astonishingly thirty-years her senior when he became her husband. The couple went on to have two sons, Hector and Roderick junior.

William McDonald, Duncan's father, was several years younger than his mother and was originally employed on the farm as a plough-hand. When the old farmer died it wasn't long before Jane married again, this time to the lowly paid employee William. The McDonald's went on to have five children with the former ploughman taking upon the mantle of master of the household and of course, resident farmer.

Life was harsh and somewhat rudimentary on the wind-swept farm, especially during the winter months. With the howling gales blowing in from the North Sea simply maintaining the arable land and livestock was very much a case of hard work. The isolated farmhouse wouldn't have had any utilities such as gas and electricity. Heating was provided by a large wood burning facility with the fuel sourced from the land and water drawn from a well. In addition to having to cope with those hardships, Jane, the mother of so many children also had to make many of their clothes by hand.

Almost certainly the family feuded amongst themselves and young Duncan would have been caught in the cross-fire. Eventually they lost the farm and moved to a terraced house in Jane's native Inverness. William was very bitter about relinquishing his status and consequently was forced to take a low paid job as an agricultural labourer. Tensions grew, the two older boys by Jane's first marriage, the original farmer's sons had moved out. Their departure begs the question if they had anything to do with their step-father's removal from the farm? The former ploughman, once employed by their own father would have found life difficult as the two lads grew older. His step-sons may possibly have declared the farm and all of the land associated with it as their own rightful inheritance.

Duncan made his escape as soon as he was confident and able enough to do so. At 15-years old he walked into the recruiting station of the local army regiment, the Queen's Cameron Highlanders in Inverness during the late spring-time of 1913. Duncan lied about his age and added on another three years. The false declaration was accepted by the regiment and also by his family as obviously he became one less mouth to feed.

Assigned to the 1ˢᵗ Battalion and given the service number of 9518, Duncan became a regular soldier obviously starting out at the lowest rank of Private. He settled down to army life and would have been very familiar with all aspects of discipline and routines by the time war broke out over a year later. There were no doubts as to his abilities as a soldier and his conduct had been very good. Duncan's battalion went on to become one of the first to be posted for war duty, initially as 'Army Troops' or reserves, prior to being assigned to a division. The 1ˢᵗ Battalion Cameron Highlanders were all set and ready to embark at Southampton Docks on the afternoon of Thursday August 13ᵗʰ 1914 for the trip to Le Havre in northern France. Could it have been that one of them went missing on the quayside? A relatively long and slow sailing would last for many hours on a crowded troop-ship, in their case the 'SS Gando'. Eventually they arrived at their destination on the following day, Friday August 14ᵗʰ.

So why is Duncan commemorated on the La Ferte-Sous-Jouarre Memorial, forty-five or so miles east of Paris? This magnificent memorial is dedicated to the missing 3,740 officers and men who fell at Mons, Le Cateau, the Marne and the Aisne, between August and October 1914. The first major battle in which the British were involved was at Mons, over a week after Duncan's 'death'. His battalion did not see action at Mons and it wasn't until mid-September after they had been assigned to a brigade that

The Cameron Highlanders march off to war in 1914, is Duncan amongst them?

confrontation first came their way. So is this a simple clerical error? Was it possible Duncan was killed-in-action as reported on another date? Perhaps a later one?

When Duncan signed-up he had lied about his age. The returns of Warrant Officers, NCO's and men stated within the Scottish statutory records declare that he was 19-years old at the time of his 'disappearance' and subsequent death. These documents also state his death as being 'Presumed' on August 13th 1914. The bereavement was further recorded by the same body as…'Accepted for Official Purposes'. On his statement of effects form, the date of death once again corresponds, it also does so on the Commonwealth War Graves Commission records and upon 'Soldiers Died in the Great War'. The date is further confirmed by the official Scottish National War Memorial and his official Medals Index Card. Could it be they all followed a false original declaration regarding the date of death? One thing is for certain, almost all of these documents, where applicable, correctly amended his age. His Medals Index Card suggests the army knew him by the name 'MacDonald' and not 'McDonald'. I suspect Duncan gave the former identity in an attempt to conceal his age. The later award of his 1914 star is named correctly to Duncan McDonald – for all of the amendments – it has to be noted the date of his death has NEVER been amended.

How can this date be possible? It was indeed recorded by the returns as having taken place in France, but the battalion did not arrive until the following day, so what do we think? Rob is convinced the date is genuine and that a professional regular army battalion had to file an official casualty report. That particular document would have been officially corroborated before being picked up on by the rest of the subsequent documentation, hence no amendments to the date. Another mysterious death occurred seemingly either aboard ship or just after it docked and was indeed correctly recorded. One of Duncan's comrades, 31-year-old John Cameron 'died' on August 14th. He is buried at Le Havre, so there is no doubt with regard to his particular fate. Duncan is not buried and has no grave. What we do know is that he went 'missing', he literally vanished.

The returns of the men suggest there were no witnesses to his disappearance. How could it be possible upon a crowded troop-ship no one saw anything untoward happen to young Duncan?

Some people aboard that vessel knew his real age, of that we are convinced and those said persons also knew he really shouldn't have been there. Certain men of influence would have felt extremely uncomfortable had it been reported that an under-age soldier had gone missing without trace. One or two officers of senior rank within the battalion I am convinced ensured that Duncan's misfortune was kept a secret, especially as they had not even arrived in France at the time, this was in my opinion selfishly done to protect their own positions.

If as it has been suggested by those who express their opinions upon war forums via the internet that Duncan had 'gone over the side' of the ship, surely someone on the packed little steamer would have seen that occur? But no one did, or did they? Personally, I believe he did board the ship after answering a roll-call. Rob doesn't agree with me, he thinks Duncan never made it on to the 'Gando' and that somehow he was lost before the men actually embarked.

Imagine the chaotic scenes in and around Southampton Docks. The masses of soldiers, tons of equipment and supplies as well as horses all had to be marshalled very quickly simply to contain a sense of order. Rob concludes that Duncan never even made the roll call, however, he does not believe that Duncan absconded into the dimly streets of Southampton. If the youngster had gone absent he would have been picked up very quickly. So what did happen to the boy?

Considering all of the circumstances outlined we have to allow you to form your own opinion. One thing is certain, official historical documentation of any sort cannot always be fully relied upon. There are public records that suggest a certain Private George Gooch of the Northamptonshire Regiment was killed in action on August 11th 1914. This implies that Duncan was not the first casualty of the war relating to the Western Front. Further research here by Rob conclusively proves that George was stationed in England on the date of his death.

Incidentally, the war diaries of Duncan's battalion that probably could have shed more light upon any 'misfortune' that occurred on that fateful day also went missing. These documents were apparently destroyed in battle a few weeks after August 13th 1914, how incredibly convenient that was for some. Let's not forget we are making these revelations regarding the completely unexplained disappearance of a 16-year old boy. Chillingly, I have to add that the utterly appalling way in which Duncan's demise was handled can only mean his tragic soul can't rest in peace. For the sake of reputations, in my opinion Duncan has been violated.

Our final thoughts consider what Duncan's family would have gone through, especially his mother who was back home in Scotland. She would have been devastated at the loss of the youngest of her eight children. Jane and her husband were beset with grief and guilt having knowingly seen off their young son to what they trusted would be the making of him – a life in the army. The parents knew in their hearts and minds that Duncan should never have met his fate at such a tender age. There are more questions than answers regarding Duncan's untimely end, surely it is now time to have those questions answered? The whole truth has yet to be revealed, for nothing but the truth is the very least this tragic young boy, lost forever, really does deserve.

Cyril Tawney
Killed in Action
Jutland, May 31st 1916
Aged 15.

NOW to a compelling story from the opposite end of Britain, the life and times of Cyril Vernon Tawney whose British War Medal and Victory Medal representing his full entitlement are with us. Cyril, we believe, was and still remains the youngest ever Royal Marine killed in action. He lost his life not long after his fifteenth birthday.

Cyril was born at 32 Landport Street, Portsmouth on Monday April 29th 1901. He became the youngest of three sons to his Royal Navy sailor father Stephen and mother Lily, whom had married six years earlier. His parents later went on to have three daughters and another son, David, who was born two years after Cyril was killed at the battle of Jutland in 1916.

Stephen Tawney left operational duties after serving on 'HMS St. Vincent' and 'HMS Victory(I)' to take upon a role as a telephone operator at the naval dockyard. The family moved to nearby Gosport and settled into perfectly normal everyday routines of life. Cyril, his parents and siblings all resided in a small house along an alley connected to the wide open Clarence Square in the heart of the town. Life was good with social conditions rapidly improving. New tramlines connecting people all around the district had been laid as the infant Cyril began his studies just a mere stones' throw from his home. He became a pupil at Gosport's first council educational facility, Clarence Square School.

Cyril was a popular scholar and well thought of by his tutors. Despite leaving school with a third-class certificate of education he was a bright lad. A look at some of the letters that Cyril wrote to his parents whilst he was serving demonstrate his remarkable level of literacy. As 1915 gave way to 1916, Great Britain's mighty Grand Fleet and the equally impressive Imperial German High Seas Fleet had at that point not really seen any major action. A confrontation was upon the horizon, it simply had to happen.

Young Cyril was itching to get involved in the war, but how could he? The Royal Navy legally practiced the recruitment of boys. Despite the navy's policies regarding enlistment, parental permission had to be officially received. It was his mother Lily who signed the official

The letters young Cyril wrote home to his parents whilst serving aboard HMS Black Prince, his medals are also featured.

papers, confirming Cyril's attestation into the Portsmouth Division of the Royal Marine Light Infantry at Forton Barracks, near Gosport. The excited and enthusiastic youngster became a bugler and was allocated the service number PO/18659.

Normally a father would be responsible for signing such a deed. Rob is of the opinion that his father would not have approved had he been able to sign the forms. Further investigation actually revealed that his dad who had been on the Royal Navy reserve list was indeed recalled in 1915. Stephen Tawney could well have been deployed to war himself, offering an explanation as to why Lily signed the papers.

In the spring of 1916, the inevitable 'show-down' between the two mighty fleets was brewing. Way up in the Orkneys at Scapa Flow, Admiral Jellicoe's Grand Fleet was preparing to enter the fray. Rear-Admiral Beatty's Battlecruisers were ready in support further south positioned close to Edinburgh in the Firth of Forth. Cyril was stationed aboard 'HMS Black Prince' an ageing Armoured Cruiser, one of four ships within the 1st Cruiser

Squadron under the command of Rear-Admiral Arbuthnot. The squadron's role was pretty clear, to screen and support a flank of the Grand Fleet and provide a form of escorting role. In reality older British Cruisers were not equipped to deal directly with their huge German counterparts and would be severely out-gunned if they had the misfortune to cross their bows.

The Orkneys would have seemed somewhat exotic to young Cyril. He was hundreds of miles from his home aboard the 'Black Prince' and was no doubt totally awe-inspired at the sight of the Grand Fleet. As an RMLI bugler he was part of a detachment of marines whose principal role was to 'police' the ship and its crew of over 800 men. Cyril was in good company, another 15-year old lad, Eddie Mulrooney, also assigned as a bugler was aboard and alongside him.

Designated basic 'dogs-body' tasks in addition to their minor musical roles, Cyril and Eddie were looked after by the older men on the ship and would have felt very comfortable in their roles. Cyril himself endorsed a feeling of relative comfort in his letters home. On more than one occasion he expressed to his parents that he felt 'very safe' aboard the 'Black Prince'. If only history had taken a slightly different course he would and really should have been. Fate and unfortunately some reckless tactical decisions would lead to tragedy. Command strategies taken were very distant from young Cyril's active and furtive mind as he watched the seabirds fly freely across the Orkneys.

Late in the evening of May 30th 1916, the Grand Fleet including the 1st Cruiser Squadron steamed out of Scapa Flow. The destination for this impressive armada was a wide open area of the North Sea off the western coast of Denmark, known as Jutland. Their task was to give the 'German High Seas Fleet' a nasty surprise, aided and abetted by Beatty's Battlecruisers who had already left the Firth of Forth.

Rear-Admiral Sir Robert Arbuthnot, 4th Baronet, KCB, MVO was a very ambitious and highly motivated naval commander. His 1st Cruiser Squadron consisted of his flagship, 'HMS Defence' and also 'HMS Warrior', 'HMS Duke of Edinburgh' and 'HMS Black Prince'. The squadron had a clearly defined role as a flanking escort. Arbuthnot was a ruthlessly tough and uncompromising type, a former champion boxer as well as an ex-combined services rugby player, he was desperate and hungry for action. It was his own ambition and his alone to track down the enemy with his near obsolete squadron. Further conjecture and rumour had it that he wished to further a career and increase his command to that of a higher level with more modern and powerful ships.

Less than twenty-four hours after this flanking squadron had left Scapa Flow, Arbuthnot seized upon what he thought was a golden opportunity for glory, in doing so he split up his squadron. On board his flagship the 'Defence' he raced towards a stricken German Cruiser having watched from a distance the actions of the 3rd British Battlecruiser squadron. He decided in hypothetical terms to embark upon a kind of 'maritime fox-hunt' and directly engage the enemy. 'Defence' and 'Warrior' recklessly stormed ahead followed by 'Duke of Edinburgh'. Chaos ensued as they almost collided with Beatty's 1st Battlecruiser squadron heading in the opposite direction and themselves under hostile fire.

Arbuthnot continued to brazenly steam ahead in his lightly armed flagship. He was completely oblivious to the fact that huge vessels of the German High Seas Fleet were prowling in close proximity. It wasn't long before the swashbuckling Rear-Admiral was trapped. The powerfully venomous German Battleships wasted no time in destroying the 'Defence'. Arbuthnot took over 900 men with him to their deaths, the entire crew of his flagship. Close by, 'Warrior' although mortally damaged escaped as another ship had drawn fire, she still took casualties and eventually went to the bottom of the sea the following day. 'Duke of Edinburgh' escaped, but what of the 'Black Prince' and young Cyril?

Thomas Bonham the Captain of 'Black Prince' had been holding up the rear of the squadron as Arbuthnot ruthlessly steamed into the crowded battle zone. Bonham found himself unable to communicate or keep up. Undeterred the Rear-Admiral raced ahead anyway leaving the 'Black Prince' isolated and very vulnerable. Captain Bonham would have known that his ship and the entire crew were now sitting ducks or more like 'rats in a barrel'. Less than twenty-four hours into his first ever voyage Cyril would have been reassured by senior members of the crew that everything was fine. He watched the sun set across the inky dark waters, tragically it was the last time the boy would witness the sun go down.

Darkness quickly descended and 'Black Prince' was by then lost. Bonham and his officers knew they had to at least find another British squadron or the Grand Fleet itself so as not to be 'picked off'. At last, they finally had hope, in the distance a line of ships was spotted silhouetted against the dark horizon. Cyril heard a commotion upon deck and joined his mates to view the magnificent ships. The Captain proceeded to head straight for the line as midnight approached. It would be a long night ahead without the reassurances of friendly vessels to protect his ship.

Close to the midnight hour 'Black Prince' came within sighting range of the line of huge warships at around 8,000 yards when suddenly one of those very ships signalled. Bonham momentarily froze in horror. The call-sign identified the signaller as German and one of four huge enemy vessels that had 'Black Prince' in full view at point-blank range. Desperately the Captain ordered his ship to turn in an attempt to escape. Sailors were jumping around and now for the first time Cyril began to be overcome by a sense of fear. What happened in the immediate aftermath was utterly shocking and completely horrendous.

I don't mind saying that I had been moved to tears as Rob and I discussed how to describe young Cyril's last moments, however, we believe it's important to illustrate what happened.

As Captain Bonham launched his stricken ship's escape bid, the enormous German Battleship 'Thuringen' focused six huge spotlights directly upon the 'Black Prince'. Snared like a rabbit in headlights there was no opportunity of escape. We think Cyril would have raced up to the deck, his young mind would associate bright light with a sense of well-being. 'Black Prince' now sailed squarely and directly along the line of four huge monsters of the German High Seas Fleet. She was grotesquely illuminated and well within reach of their huge arsenals of guns.

All four of the huge German vessels opened fire, the 'Ostreisland', 'Nassau' and flagship 'Friedrich der Grosse' alongside the 'Thuringen' pounded the weakly armed 'Black Prince'. The mighty Battleships proceeded to bombard the doomed British Cruiser with numerous salvos of high explosive shells. Men and boys were mutilated, decapitated and vaporised in seconds. Cyril would have witnessed some of the horrors unfolding before he succumbed to his own fate. We just hope it all went very quickly for the boy.

Every one of the crew members of over 800 aboard 'Black Prince' were lost, she was, just like Arbuthnot's flagship, obliterated. The squadron lost three of its four ships and over 1800 souls perished because of the actions of one man. A dispersed squadron failed to adhere to a basic strategy based upon common-sense. Three generations of men and boys died because of the narcissistic ego of a man who thought he was invincible. There are of course a number of sanctimonious, lily-livered 'metropolitan historians' who feel that it is wrong to criticise or condemn certain actions of high ranking officers. I wonder how any one of them would feel if they lost a child in an accident that could have been prevented?

Cyril's legacy did not fade away with him in the murky depths of the North Sea. In 1930 his elder brother Archie, who had also been involved in the battle of Jutland, had a son whom he named Cyril in honour of his lost brother. Cyril Francis Tawney became a well-known folk singer in southern England and his profile is still very prominent upon the internet even though he passed away in 2005.

In 1918, Cyril's parents Stephen and Lily were blessed with another son, David. In a desperately sad irony, he was killed whilst serving aboard 'HMS Hood' in 1941, aged 22 during the Second World War. Consequently, Stephen and Lily lost both of their youngest sons in two infamous naval actions during two world wars. The pair were married for over sixty-five years until Stephen's death in 1961. Lily made it to the grand old age of 95 before she passed away in 1970. Cyril as we know was tragically just 15, he is commemorated on the Portsmouth Naval Memorial.

John Hutcheson
Killed in Action
Belgium, Sept. 8th 1915
Aged 18.

Jack Hutcheson, the well-loved young officer, shot and killed by a sniper.

TO become an officer and a gentleman granted certain privileges, respect and honour. For many young junior officers it also represented unprecedented responsibility fraught with constant danger. John Hutcheson, better known as Jack, was one such young and aspiring officer. It is quite true to state that almost every candidate commissioned in the early stages of the war came from a wealthy background and had been well educated. Jack was no exception, however, he came from a family whose reasonable wealth was 'self-made.' He wasn't from titled heritage stock, no blue blood ran through his veins.

Jack's father was an entrepreneur, taught by his own father on how to make his way in life by brokering commodities. Robert Hutcheson moved from his native Greenock on the west coast of Scotland, not too far from Glasgow, to make his fortune in London. The canny Scotsman set up home within lodgings in Islington and became a sugar broker. It was the later Victorian period when sugar, once a luxury to the working classes, became a popular every-day ingredient in many of the treats the masses could afford themselves. Examples included bottled lemonade, cocoa and of course sweets and confectionery. Robert knew there was money to be made by trading one way or another in the sugar industry.

On March 29th 1896 Robert married Scots lady Jane Symington Downes, a native of Glasgow, at St. Mary's church in Islington. The sugar broker had progressed to merchant and was employing local people. As the money rolled in the newly-weds could even afford to employ a domestic servant when they moved into their first home. Ten months later on Sunday January 31st 1897, Jack was born at 32 Sotheby Road, Islington.

The hustle and bustle of life in the capital and continued prosperity for the Hutcheson's was complemented by the birth of a second son, and brother to young Jack, Andrew was born in 1901. Life improved further for the Hutcheson clan as they decided to move away from London. The family took up residence twenty-five miles to the north in Berkhamsted, Hertfordshire, moving to a rather splendid detached nine roomed house. Jack was enrolled at the private Berkhamsted School in 1906, life was looking good for the family and a cook was engaged to service their needs as well as a housekeeper.

A third son, William arrived in 1908, a surprise I would have thought to his mother Jane, who was at that time approaching her fortieth birthday. Sadness was to follow as tragedy befell upon the family early in 1910. Jack was just entering his teenage years when his mother Jane passed away at the early age of just 41. The success and prosperity the family had known and taken for granted was shattered. Jack, alongside his father and younger brothers attended his mother's funeral at the nearby Rectory Lane cemetery.

The two household servant girls, 18-year old Caroline Munger and 24-year old Esther White would have in their own special ways taken upon extra care and responsibility for the boys. I suppose in a tragic aspect this brought some comfort to their father, Robert. Having made himself a good nest-egg the widower embarked upon a change of career and became a market clerk and canvasser. The new role would have given him an element of control over others. He was still able to trade in his sugar interests and in the sale of other commodities and goods. Money wasn't an issue for the family as they moved house once more, perhaps in the wake of the tragedy, to another desirable residence within Berkhamsted.

Jack was doing well at the private school he had attended since he was nine-years old. In 1911 and just a year after the tragic death of his mother, he was selected to attend the school's Officer Training Corps at the age of fourteen. This placement provided the opportunity to progress a potential career as an army officer. The training was thorough and very well organised. Jack completed his three-year course in 1914, before the outbreak of war. By choice Jack decided to put any potential military career upon hold and entered the London commercial sector, probably upon the advice of his father. He was 17-years old when he started his employment as a clerk with the Clerical, Medical and General Life Assurance Society. This position would also have provided a pre-cursory opportunity to open up possibilities of future work for the Colonial Service.

The world was at Jack's feet, he had been guided by his shrewd and wealthy businessman father and became a well-educated young gentleman. Jack had prospects of becoming what we would now describe as a 'whizz-kid'. There were added opportunities on the horizon for him to possibly take up a role as an important and well paid colonial civil servant.

It was very soon realised that a huge procurement of officers would be required to complement and organise the masses of volunteers of the new armies. Quite appropriately, Jack was recalled to Berkhamsted less than two months after war had been declared. He wouldn't have complained at all and understood that he had an important role to play. Jack was immediately commissioned as a 2nd Lieutenant, the lowest of all officer rank posts at the Inns of Court Officer Training Corps.

His previous training dictated that only one further month of instruction was required. Jack was assessed for certain physical and leadership qualities that would determine his allocation. It was decided to post Jack to the 10th (Service) Battalion of the Nottinghamshire and Derbyshire Regiment (The Sherwood Foresters). He became a platoon commander with responsibility of leadership over at least five non-commissioned officers, including his platoon Sergeant and around fifty men. As a subaltern he was immediately answerable to his company commander, a Captain.

We can only imagine the excitement that Jack experienced when he went to purchase his own uniforms as an officer was required to do. Tailor-made outfits more than likely bought at a west-end store would have distinguished this young man. Jack was assigned an orderly, a personal man-servant. We know from looking at documents that his orderly thought the world of him and was deeply affected by his death, as we will later explain.

Jack must have had a lot of respect as he was trusted to take charge of men all of whom were civilian volunteers. Most of the men he was to lead came from the Derby area. The guys under his command were railway workers, coal miners, textile operatives and engineers, rough and ready working class lads. We also know from records the men took the young officer to their hearts, he was a popular and well liked leader.

After some intensive training at Winchester in the spring of 1915, Jack and his men sailed to France and landed at Boulogne on the morning of Thursday July 15th 1915. Still only 18-years old, Jack controlled many men all of whom would have been older than himself. He was still three years short of being officially recognised as an adult in Britain at that time.

The British had been having a tough time of it in France and the western Flanders areas, particularly at Ypres in Belgium. Known to the British soldiers as 'Wipers' it was the scene of a number of very hostile and bloody engagements with the Germans. Three major battles took place there. The first in 1914 was followed by another in the spring of 1915 and the largest confrontation in the late summer and autumn of 1917. Despite concerted efforts by the Germans who almost encircled Ypres on three sides the British doggedly hung on to it throughout the war.

Jack and his Sherwood Foresters were to reinforce a line of protection just to the east of Ypres. It took some time for them to get organised then proceed to embark upon their journey. The battalion had to adapt to familiarisation before moving into their strategic position. Their position as it became, I know well, just off the Menin Road close to a hamlet called Zillebeke. The Sherwood Foresters were situated in and around Sanctuary Wood the scene of previous vicious hand-to-hand fighting. Regular and some territorial British soldiers had been clinging on to the ground for weeks. The Germans occupied the eastern fringes of the smashed-up and blood-soaked tangled remains of the wood.

This particular area was extremely hazardous, not far to the left and back towards Ypres was an infamous road junction known as 'Hellfire Corner'. On more than one occasion this area was described as the 'most dangerous place in the world'. These days as you walk through 'Hellfire Corner' down the Menin Road towards Hooge the most dangerous elements of the immediate area are the cycle lanes. I know from personal experience, Belgian cyclists don't move out of the way for pedestrians and I have had more than one close shave. Another very poignant and somewhat eerie experience is driving down the deserted Menin Road at night time.

I have passed by Sanctuary Wood many times, the sense of tragedy can sometimes be enveloping. History in this part of Belgium is engrained, it doesn't and quite rightly refuses to fade away.

As you turn to the right across from Hooge and the museum you head towards Zillebeke, Sanctuary Wood is a little further east, with Maple Copse slightly to the south. Trying to pin-point the exact location of where Jack actually was, is impossible. My assumption is that he was in shallow trenches either within the wood or deeper positions to the west of it close to the smaller Zouave Wood. Jack was a conscientious young man and was held in great respect not only by his men but also his senior officers. We know that he hadn't been in direct action with the enemy when he was tragically killed. After much consultation with Rob, our opinion of how he met his end and the circumstances that led up to it are tragic to say the least. I, for one, will always think of him as a young man who had much to offer to society and a chap who demonstrated above all his care and commitment. His men trusted him with their welfare and their lives.

Jack relied very much upon his platoon Sergeant, effectively his second-in-command. The Sergeant would have been older and more familiar with the attitudes and feelings of the men and certainly more street-wise. The date was Wednesday September 8th 1915. All around Sanctuary Wood the stench of rotting corpses from those unfortunate souls who had not been recovered after months of bitter fighting filled the air. Jack was aware of the constant danger, the safety of his men was paramount.

A key role that Jack played was to inspect his front line fire-trench, at this point of the war in 1915 British soldiers hadn't been equipped with steel helmets. His concern for them was to 'keep their heads down' at all times. The lads had not yet seen action, however they were certainly about to do so, they were nervous, frightened and anxious. Jack reassured them on his inspections with a maturity beyond his years.

At the far eastern end of Sanctuary Wood the Germans held their line, at the closest point within a mere sixty metres of the British line. 'No-man's land' was narrow with broken tree stumps and shell holes also providing excellent cover for a sniper. A sniper was a particular type of soldier who would have been highly experienced with his weapon and very conscious for his own safety. These men had no regard whatsoever for their prey. For the sniper, shooting and killing a human-being was just like blasting a rabbit in a field.

The inexperienced young officer had a routine and one particular German sniper knew it. A distinction between his officers' cap and the trench caps of his men was noticeable. Snipers wanted to take out officers to reduce the morale of the men under their command, the sniper got Jack.

In an instant the blow was swift and to the head, as Jack encouraged his lads, death came to him almost instantaneously. Nothing significantly strategic was achieved by the Germans except the sniper had the prize of an officer. The killer knew nothing of Jack and didn't care, to be honest he completed a gruesome task that he was very familiar with. It was all in a day's work for the German marksman. For Jack's men, the slaying of their young officer before they had even fought any action would have been extremely disturbing.

Jack's company commander, battalion commander and more poignantly his orderly were all very upset at his tragic and untimely death, 2nd Lieutenant Hutcheson was the very first officer of the battalion to be killed. In the aftermath of this tragedy his immediate superior was one of a number of people who wrote letters to his father and brothers.

His Captain's comments were:

> 'It is the first life lost among our officers and it is one of the best that has gone... He was absolutely clean and honourable, frank, sincere and fearless'.

The company medical officer (Doctor) also wrote:

> 'A more unselfish boy one could not find, always thinking of the well-being of others... I chose his resting place. A plain wood cross has been erected that says in loving memory of 2Lt. J. Hutcheson, killed in action - and the motto to live in hearts we leave behind, is not to die'.

Even his Colonel had something to say:

> 'He was a keen and energetic officer of considerable promise and popular with all ranks'.

The final words go to Jack's orderly:

> 'I write this short letter out of respect for my esteemed officer, your son. It is a sincere blow to me to lose him, for he was the very best friend I had out here, and

although I was only a Tommy he showed every consideration for me as well as the other men in the platoon, he was very much esteemed. He is buried with full honours and his grave is in a wood with others. There is a cross at the head and I shall do my best to keep his grave clean'.

Jack was originally buried in Sanctuary Wood, his body was later exhumed and reinterred within the Hooge Crater Cemetery just across the other side of the Menin Road. It is plainly obvious that his original makeshift grave had to be identified, the orderly kept his promise. Rob saw something special in the one medal we have to Jack, the Victory Medal. The whereabouts of his other medals, the 1914-15 Star and the British War Medal are unknown, this really doesn't matter. Just one medal brought along this wonderful story.

Fred Gregory
Killed in Action
France, July 1st 1916
Aged 19.

The innocence of youth, Fred Gregory looked younger than his actual nineteen years.

THE remarkable and tragic story of young Fred would not so much be out of place within a television period drama as we hope you will conclude. This young man with the very boyish face began his short life as Frederick Covey Gregory on Saturday February 6th 1897 in Eastleigh, Hampshire. Fred's days would end upon another Saturday, over nineteen years later, on the bloodiest day in British military history.

His parents I am pretty sure knew each other for a while before they were married, both George Fisher Gregory and Eliza Caroline Covey were originally from Oxfordshire. Their vocation within the world of domestic service took them in separate directions. George, the dashing footman who caught the eyes of titled ladies and chambermaids alike ended up in Hampshire. Eliza had to go as far Sussex to find work as a housemaid.

The trysts between them continued and as a result in 1893 they were married in Hampshire. I rather assume they had to have done so, for not long afterwards their first child was born. Elsie Selina Bessie Gregory arrived on Wednesday October 4th of that very year. Life wasn't easy for a married couple working as servants. George and Eliza would have had to put their domestic duties first and I suspect they could have left service by the time Fred was born. The family appear to 'disappear' for a while, before returning upon public records some time later in rather dramatic circumstances.

One of George's siblings, Alfred Gregory, over four years his junior, entered the lives of all concerned within the family. What is known is that George Fisher Gregory and Eliza Covey Gregory had separated. The stresses and strains of trying to bring up a young family whilst being tied to domestic servitude had a bearing upon that. What is more likely is the relationship between George's brother – Fred's uncle – and Eliza caused the disintegration of the marriage. Fred and his sister Elsie had to live with the stigma more profound in Edwardian times of actually having to leave a broken home.

Both Fred and his sibling followed in their parents' footsteps and entered domestic service, Fred doing so literally as soon as he had finished his schooling. He made off to seek his fortune as his sister had done so before him and sought out the bright lights of London. The pair of them both ended up in fashionable parts of west London and without doubt would have remained in close contact with each other.

Down in Hampshire, their mother had by that time had a child by Alfred, also named Alfred, his father's namesake. The pair lived as a married couple with the same surname, Eliza retaining the Covey-Gregory version. This effectively gave her secret away during the course of my research. Eventually they settled and made their home in Basingstoke as did her estranged husband George, family tensions would have been almost unbearable. Fred and Elsie were certainly better off out of those situations as they began their lives as servants to the gentry.

Elsie lived and worked in Kensington as a housemaid and probably was only able to have one half-day off a week and one full-day per month. Fred was over in a large gentleman's club in Piccadilly working as the lowest ranking servant in the kitchen and scullery. He was persuaded that he could escape to a better life by joining the army. When war broke out he didn't hesitate.

Fred broke free of his servitude chains by enlisting into the 2nd (City of London) Battalion, Royal Fusiliers, a Territorial Force unit that was to become part of the famous 56th (First London Division). He was allocated the service number of 3640 and in accordance with the regulations of the time that followed his period of training, he was posted to France after his nineteenth birthday. Fred eventually arrived there on Tuesday April 18th 1916.

After a short period of acclimatisation, Fred joined his battalion in readiness for a major offensive. The strategic objective was at the most westerly point of the German position on the front at Gommecourt, northern France. Nine battalions of the London Regiment from the 56th Division were grouped around the area in May. A number of further territorial battalions from the 46th (North Midland) Division and the 5th Cheshire's with a volunteer service battalion, the 11th Royal Warwickshire's, lined up alongside them.

Many of the Londoners and the Midlands lads had no previous military experience prior to the war in terms of combat roles. Some of the territorials had attended camps and were familiar with drill. All were volunteers and very naive with regard to what real warfare actually entailed. These men came to face one of the strongest and formidably fortified German positions on the entire front.

The Somme offensive had been well planned in advance, at Gommecourt the two British divisions trained in almost full view of their German counterparts, as ridiculous as that may seem. An assault upon the little French village on the extreme north of the offensive line was, in my opinion, sheer bloody-minded lunacy. Against the advice of two sub-ordinate Generals, namely, Allenby and Snow the commander of the British Expeditionary Force, Sir Douglas Haig insisted it went ahead exactly as he wanted. Haig is revered by many, especially so by cosy self-assured 'metropolitan historians'. He is also loathed in equal measure for his conduct during the Great War. I don't think it takes a genius to work out exactly what my opinions are regarding countless decisions made by senior British Generals during the First World War. Rob tries very hard to 'reign me in', he has to.

As for Fred the young soldier, Rob makes an interesting and very relevant point here. He had by that time suffered more than his share of misfortune in life. His disjointed and dysfunctional family background and subsequent experiences of a lowly servant boy would to a degree have toughened him up. He wouldn't have a shed a tear when leaving his homeland for the front. Despite his choir-boy childish looks he was probably slightly more mature than the other teenage volunteers who fought and died by his side on that fateful day.

One hundred years after Fred perished at Gommecourt, Chris Turner, a colleague of mine alongside myself made a pilgrimage in honour of the young soldier. We visited the village to film part of a short promotional film. Driving across the former Somme battlefields region of today is an unforgettable experience, I have had the privilege of doing so on a number of occasions. Of course the landscape has evolved to one of peaceful serenity, yet, many things have not changed. The remote villages where hardly anyone seems to be around don't look much different today as to what they would have done so a century ago. It is the unique atmosphere that only those who visit the area will understand that seems to prevail in the air. Peace and tranquillity dampens the enveloping fire of a blood soaked history that lingers across a sprawling mass of open green countryside. So very different is the location at night time, uncomfortable, eerie and still to a degree today, pretty damn frightening.

Driving through Gommecourt in the middle of the afternoon didn't take long. Winding along a curving more or less flat deserted road gave good visual reference to the Gommecourt Park area and the Quadrangle. This is where the former 'Nameless Farm' once used to stand. Each of these separate locations bore witness to butchery, slaughter and suffering on an unimaginable scale that happened so long ago. Despite the passage of time a profoundly chilling atmosphere hovers all around like an invisible mist.

On Saturday July 1st 1916, Fred Covey Gregory became one of almost 60,000 British casualties, of whom 20,000 were actually killed. Let me repeat that figure, 20,000 killed in one single day. The devastation on a front that extended from north to south on a scale of just a few miles is hard to contemplate but it actually happened. Zero-Hour was 07.30am when thousands of civilian volunteer soldiers went 'over the top' for the very first time.

Fred wasn't actually involved from the outset as his battalion was held in reserve, this in effect made his experiences all the more worse. Very much on stand-by, Fred and his comrades were served with hot pea soup at five o'clock in the morning. Having had very little sleep and with heavy equipment at the ready the trepidation, expectation, fear and anxieties he must have felt cannot really be understood. This young man had to stand back at Zero-Hour in reserve, others plundered their way across several hundred yards of 'no-man's land' towards the German trenches. Courageously, the volunteer Londoners initially gained successes by storming three German trench positions.

The single battalions of the regiment of whom included the London Rifle Brigade, Queen Victoria's Rifles, the Rangers and the Queens Westminster Rifles took the initiative. Even from the reserve position Fred would have seen the carnage unfolding before his very eyes. Slowly but surely the Germans began to recover their lost ground, machine-gun fire was coming from all sides, along with unceasingly deafening continuous bombardments. Casualties mounted on both sides, some prisoners being led out of the line reported seeing human carcasses, many with missing limbs, piled in multiples on top of each other.

It was becoming pretty clear as the wounded desperately tried to crawl back to safety that reinforcements were required. The men of Queen Victoria's Rifles were by then getting particularly mauled. Fred's turn eventually came and I can't for one second begin to contemplate what was going through his mind. He had been waiting for over six hours amongst scenes of slaughter and devastation. Did he think one last time of his mother and father or of his sister back in London? Did he wonder if he would survive? One thing is for sure, Fred would have been terrified.

A command was issued for the reserves to move forward and just after 13.30hrs, Fred was out in 'no man's land'. The rattling of machine-guns and crashing of high explosive shells were accompanied by the moaning of the mortally wounded. Highly pitched screams of those whose bodies were being lashed and torn apart by red hot metal fragments echoed all around. It is not known exactly how far Fred actually got or how long he lasted in battle, for his body was never found. We can only pray his end was swift and that he was spared prolonged suffering.

In an astonishing act of chivalry the Germans hoisted the flag of the Red Cross to allow the British and themselves to bring in their huge numbers of wounded. Gommecourt was a disaster, no ground was gained and thousands of casualties were grotesquely received on both sides.

British VII Corps Commander, Lieutenant-General Sir Thomas D'Oyly Snow, an absurd buffoon who oversaw the catastrophe, later issued a truly astonishing comment that makes any decent person feel sick to the stomach. He referred directly to two of the Midlands battalions, the 5th and 7th Sherwood Foresters – 2,000 of his own men - involved in the action. These men suffered some of the highest casualties of all on that fateful day.

Snow arrogantly accused them of - 'lack of offensive spirit'. A shocking short statement delivered by a 'Donkey General' who had no empathy at all with the working class volunteers. General Snow effectively described them as cowards, what an utterly disgraceful and appalling reference to their ultimate sacrifice.

The last words however would go to Haig, the architect of the whole disaster of the Battle of the Somme when he ridiculously proclaimed the 'diversion at Gommecourt had fulfilled its objectives'. Rob, who is not as scathing of the military leaders as I am explains the mentality of these Generals. None of them had anything whatsoever in common with the men who served under them. A large number of these narrow-minded cossetted Generals, Haig and Allenby being prime examples had been former cavalry officers who still believed that outdated 'gung-ho' methods of warfare would prevail. Their arrogance borne of privilege and wealth would not be accepted today.

Haig, later in his years tried to justify his tactics of complete attrition stating that lessons learned from it helped to eventually defeat the enemy. Absolutely none of the tactics used on the first day of the Battle of the Somme back up that claim. Subsequent repeated deliberate acts of using men as 'cannon-fodder' in the later stages of that campaign, had no real positive effects. Haig would have continued slaughtering his men like cattle in an abattoir on the Somme had the weather not prevented it in mid-November of 1916.

As for our Fred, the only realistic way that any descendants of him would be around today surely derive from his half-brother, Alfred. His sister Elsie married Leslie Fullbrook later in life at the age of 46 in the war torn London of 1940. It is highly unlikely she would have produced any off-spring, she died aged 78 in Basingstoke back in 1972.

Fred's full medals entitlement of the British War Medal and the Victory Medal as well as his Death Plaque are with us, along with a baby-faced picture of him in uniform. In another bizarre twist to this story, his uncle and stepfather, Alfred, also served during the war. He first entered the Gallipoli theatre in 1915 with the Army Service Corps. Alf was still serving in 1918 as he approached his 50th birthday. Alfred's medals came with Fred's, they had obviously been released or sold together some time ago by his mother Eliza or a relative. As for Fred's dad George, he ended up working in the same railway depot as Alfred before the war, what a story!

John Wixted

Killed in Action
France, July 1st 1916
Aged 19.

IF the previous story had the makings of a period drama, the tale that follows of young John and his family could create several episodes of a soap opera. From internal family scandal to the harsh living conditions endured by a large family with Irish ancestral origins, this story leads to the famous 'Accrington Pals' and beyond.

John was the fourth of eight children, all of whom crammed into a tiny two-up, two-down terraced house in the village of Church, a mile or so to the west of Accrington in Lancashire. Three boys and five girls, along with their parents had to share just the two bedrooms. There was

PTE. JOHN WIXTED
(MISSING).

Private John Wixted, son of Mrs. Wixted, 12, Bradshaw-street, Church, is reported missing since the 'big push' on July 1st. Private Wixted enlisted in the "Pals" soon

after the outbreak of war and was later transferred to a trench mortar team connected with his battalion. Only 19 years of age he previously worked at Messrs. Steiner's and attended the Sacred Heart Church. Another brother of the missing soldier is in hospital at Bristol suffering from wounds, and a cousin, also of the name of Wixted, died of sunstroke while on a ship bound for

The local newspaper reports the death of Accrington Pal, John Wixted.

a seventeen-year age range between the siblings that further complicated matters. It is difficult to imagine adolescents growing up extremely quickly whilst at the same time going through puberty. For good measure, throw-in one or two babies crying and wailing all night as well!

John was of Irish descent, his paternal grandparents Michael and Ann hailed from Tipperary as did his father James. The Wixted clan, Mick, Ann and others from the family including Mick's brother all settled in Lancashire after arriving at the port of Liverpool, they came to England in the aftermath of the Irish potato famine. Hundreds of thousands of their compatriots had also made the same journey principally to escape absolute poverty. The north-west of England offered many opportunities of employment as they settled into their new lives in Lancashire. All of the men found work at the large iron foundry in Accrington after first trying their luck in Bury. John's father who was just a small boy when he moved to the red rose county from Ireland followed suit and also found work in the foundry. The family eventually set up home in the rather exotic sounding, Clayton-Le-Moors. I can assure you there was nothing 'exotic' about the rough and ready little Lancashire town.

On John's maternal side we again see a huge Irish connection, his mother, Ellen Ryan was the daughter of another Irish emigre, Peter Ryan. Mr Ryan married a local girl from the small Lancashire mill town of Oswaldtwistle. With a strong Roman Catholic background the Wixted family branches in the region I have to say would have been subjected to elements of bigotry. I can declare this with assurance despite having no Irish ancestry whatsoever.

I was born and grew up only fifteen miles or so from where the Wixted family planted their roots. My upbringing albeit seventy years later, was similar in so many ways. I come from the traditionally working-class town of Bolton and lived in a small terraced house within a maze of other back-to-back terraces. Cobbled streets, 'rag and bone men', pubs and little shops on every corner was the order of the day. People left their doors unlocked, dogs roamed freely and all of us kids played together outdoors whenever we got the opportunity.

Many of my childhood friends had Irish parents and grandparents which in itself never mattered to me, we were all kids together. We kicked lumps out of each other in back-street football games but we were all the same. If my friends were called Riley, Murphy or O'Neill so what? We looked after each other no matter what of our 'heritage', a word we wouldn't have understood anyway. The same can't be said for the attitudes of my elders at the time of the early 1970's.

I am ashamed to say that even older members of my own family would look down upon Catholic people, especially those of Irish descent. Unfortunately they did not hide their feelings to the impressionable young boy that I was, it really did disturb me. I can't begin to imagine what the Wixted clan went through.

For James Wixted and Ellen Ryan, John's parents, life was difficult from the start. Thank goodness I have Rob with me as we have spent many hours discussing how this particular story is put together. Ellen Ryan was living in lodgings and working in a local cotton mill, heavily pregnant she gave birth to a daughter, Elizabeth Ellen Ryan in January of 1891. James was at that time living with his parents. The two of them married in Ellen's parish of Oswaldtwistle on September 19th 1891.

I studied the marriage certificate and those of others who were married in the same church upon the day. It could be seen that both the witnesses to their marriage were themselves a married couple and not related to either the bride or groom. On the other certificates from that date at least one of the witnesses to each of those marriages was a family member. This suggests to us that James and Ellen's respective families were not present at the service. The wedding also took place in an Anglican church and for some reason James was not honest about his true age.

Both Rob and I think the union was, at least in the beginning not approved of by the Catholic Irish families, Ellen had a child out of wedlock, we both agree that James was the father of young Lizzie, who took the surname of Wixted. A year later it would appear the young family were living with James' parents in Clayton-Le-Moors when their second daughter Annie was born. Soon afterwards the family moved to the nearby village of Church. Two sons followed, William in 1895 and then John in 1897. The family was completed by 1908 with a further three daughters and another son. Around this time, the father James seems to 'disappear'. Analysis of the Wixted family tree posted online by people claiming to be living relatives is confusing and I believe inaccurate.

There were two men by the name James Wixted born in Tipperary in 1868 and incredibly both of them married a spouse with the surname Ryan. According to the family tree James died in Tipperary in 1908. I believe this was not the James Wixted who lived in Lancashire. An unskilled manual worker with eight children was a poor man, the man who died in Ireland left a considerable sum of money to a relative by the name of Ryan and nothing to any children. Curiously by 1911 there was a Mr. Wixted and a female living in Accrington. On the 1911 Census for the Wixted family of Church a Mrs. Wixted is mentioned as married. There is no head of family stipulated and the document was signed by the eldest daughter Lizzie. James wasn't present, perhaps he and Ellen were living away from their family to give them more space? It is a mystery and one that I believe somewhere spiritually has been concocted by James to throw me 'off the trail'. More questions than answers, however, we know the father was absent from his eight children as the First World War approached.

The two elder girls worked as cotton spinners in a local mill whilst Billy and John were employed by Accrington's largest employer at the iron foundry of 'Howard and Bullough'. This local enterprise and its huge industrial works employed 5,000 men including their grandfather Mick and their father James. Billy and John were very close with less than two years between them, they lived together, worked together and would have both dealt with any bigotry and abuse together. Their cousins of the Wixted family lived in close proximity to them, all were well known in the district.

There was a lot of civil unrest at the huge iron foundry in Accrington, workers had demanded a minimum wage of between 36 and 37 shillings a week. The men also insisted upon being allowed to apply for trades' union membership. Both requests were denied resulting in strike action. Men who wanted to work were locked out and tensions in the town and district were running high with tempers frayed. John took upon another job at Steiner's Dye works and was more than likely joined by his brother Billy. The lads simply could not afford to have any time off work as they had to contribute heavily to the upkeep of the family. With at least three of their young siblings still at school there were still many mouths to feed, life was tough.

John's life was dictated by work and helping to look after his family. He found some recreation as a regular attendee of the Sacred Heart church in Accrington in accordance with his Catholic faith. John was a decent lad awaiting an opportunity to better himself, then war broke out.

In a bold and highly ambitious enterprise the Mayor of Accrington, a certain Captain John Harwood, wanted to follow examples set by the large Lancashire cities of Liverpool and Manchester. Each had recruited volunteer battalions from their boundaries, known as 'Pals Battalions'. Men who joined these localised battalions included neighbours, friends, work colleagues and family members recruited from the immediate areas.

Captain Harwood called upon local men to volunteer from the small Lancashire town and the surrounding districts, he needed 1,100 recruits. In September 1914 the 'Accrington Pals' were formed as the 11th (Service) Battalion of the East Lancashire Regiment. Of all the 'Pals Battalions' recruited throughout the country it is the Accrington lads who became the most famous. The audacity of a little town having its own 'Pals' will forever be tinged with tragedy associated to that terrible day of Saturday July 1st 1916.

John and Billy must have examined their consciences before they both decided to join up together, they had five sisters and an infant brother at home. We believe the girls gave them their blessing as the two intrepid brothers made off to the recruitment centre at nearby Rishton on Monday September 21st 1914. The day after their cousin James also enlisted into the 'Pals'. Together the three Wixted lads would embark upon an adventure they knew would take them far away from their day to day drudgery.

The four companies of the 'Accrington Pals' were as follows – 'W-Coy' Accrington, men from the town. 'X-Coy' District, men from neighbouring towns such as Great Harwood, Oswaldtwistle, Rishton and Blackburn. 'Y-Coy' Chorley, also known as the 'Chorley Pals' and 'Z-Coy' Burnley. John and his brother remained in and around the town for the next five months carrying out drill and training before their emotional send off in February 1915.

All the companies of the 'Accrington Pals' were given a rapturous send-off from the railway station in the centre of the town as they headed for Caernarvon for further training. Lizzie, Annie, Mary, Clara, Ceicy and young James would have been joined by their cousins to see the lads off. Tragically, only one of the three Wixted lads would ever make it back to Accrington. The march through the town was witnessed by thousands of friends, relatives and associates of the men going off to fight. At those enthralling moments in time the scene would have been one of a carnival atmosphere. Happy smiling faces, cheering voices and flag-waving children against the backdrop of a marching band.

Lieutenant-Colonel Rickman formerly of the Northumberland Fusiliers took command of the battalion at Caernarvon, he would also lose his life on the first day of the Somme battle. In May 1915 the Lancashire lads moved to Penkridge Camp near Rugeley and were amalgamated into the 94th Brigade. Joining them were three other battalions of the York and Lancaster Regiment. Just like the Accrington men these units were 'Pals Battalions' and came from Yorkshire, they were the Sheffield City Battalion and the 1st and 2nd 'Barnsley Pals'. The friendly banter and rivalry between the outnumbered Lancashire lads and the Yorkshire steelworkers and coal miners would have been good humoured. These young men from the two rival counties would go on to fight and die beside each other. Their brotherhood and spirit of comradeship was unbreakable.

After two more moves to Ripon in July and then on to Salisbury the 'Pals' were ready for war. A Turkish threat to the Suez Canal meant their first destination was to be Egypt. The Wixted lads held a great excitement at the prospect of travelling to a far-off mysterious land of pyramids and pharaohs. All of the 'Accrington Pals' boarded the Troopship 'Ionic' and set sail from Devonport on December 19th 1915.

The lads made a brief stop at Gibraltar two days before Christmas as the battalion was catching up with mail. We have no doubt the Wixted's sent their letters back home. The girls would have been so proud of them telling their work mates all about their brothers and cousin off on the big adventure to sunny climes. Sadly it was to be the sun that claimed the first of the Wixted boys. Being from the dull and rainy environment of Accrington, the last thing upon their minds would have concerned taking protection from the damaging rays of the sun. The closest they had ever been to catching a sun tan was when they had lazed around in the local park.

Back at sea the journey went on towards Malta where the lads arrived on December 27th. After two days they were off again heading through the Mediterranean, the weather being reported as extremely hot. The cousin Jimmy developed sunstroke and was confined to bed with all the effects of the horrendous condition. He died shortly afterwards. At 06.30am his body was given to the sea in a service on-board that was accompanied with full military honours. This occurred within an area somewhere south-west of Crete. John and Billy arm-in-arm mourned the loss of their beloved cousin. James Clarence Wixted was later commemorated on the closest war memorial to those who have no grave, the Helles Memorial. This monument bears the names of so many who were lost at Gallipoli, a conflict that was still raging at the time of his death. It would be so easy for researchers therefore to assume he was lost at Gallipoli, obviously he wasn't.

On January 5th 1916 after running the gauntlet of German U-Boats the men landed at Port Said in Egypt and took upon defence duties at El Fardan and El Kantara. By March the threat from the Turks had subsided and the 'Pals' were off to France. 'The Accrington Pals' alongside the 'Sheffield City Pals' and the 'Barnsley Pals' suffered horrendous casualties on the very first day of the Battle of the Somme. Yet again lives were given away cheaply under the staff command of Generals who were completely out of touch with reality.

Haig had appointed Rawlinson to command the Fourth Army upon the Somme front. On the actual first day of the great battle General Rawlinson was safely four miles behind the front line as his men went 'over the top'. Lieutenant-General Hunter-Weston, under Rawlinson's command, controlled the northern sector via VIII Army Corps. The Lancashire and Yorkshire lads were attached to this formation. All of the four 'Pals' battalions were designated to take an area around the German-held French hilltop fortress of Serre within the battle zone. Hunter-Weston arguably the worst 'Donkey General' of the First World War was also known as 'Hunter-Bunter'. His reckless actions at Gallipoli the year before when he 'bloodied the pups' saw huge numbers of young Scotsmen massacred. Hunter-Weston's ludicrous lack of tactical prowess that completely lacked any form of military competence resulted in the horrific decimation of his own men. A year later this 'Donkey' then oversaw what became the worst slaughter zone on that fateful Saturday of July 1st 1916.

Even Haig himself described Hunter-Weston as a 'Rank Amateur'. Despite that the man had astonishingly been knighted after his debacle at Gallipoli. He was then placed in charge of the men on the front at Serre. Moreover, he went on to hold his position as a senior military staff commander for the rest of the war. After the catastrophe of the first day of the Somme, the butcher 'Hunter-Bunter' wrote a directive to his men congratulating them upon their bravery. He also actively encouraged them to continue with their assaults in the days to come no matter what the consequences. I have a vision of him sealing this directive as he puffed away on a cigar and swigged vintage port from a crystal glass in a chateau miles behind the lines.

The Accrington lads went over in four waves, the first of which climbed over the parapets of their trenches ten minutes before Zero-Hour. These brave boys were ripped to pieces by heavy machine-gun fire from the north of their starting-off points, ironically from the direction of Gommecourt. The German artillery did the rest. Many of the Sheffield and Barnsley lads suffered a similar fate, civilian soldiers who had been together for nearly two years were gone in a very short space of time. The Accrington commanders in the field lost contact with all of their waves within half an hour. It took four days and nights to bring in the wounded. The stretcher bearers also paid a heavy price as they toiled, unarmed, to bring in their suffering 'brothers'. These brave men spent over 96-hours retrieving their wounded comrades.

John Wixted had acquired a special skill, he had been attached to a specialist mobile trench mortar section that in theory would support the forward attacking infantry. Eighty or so courageous Accrington lads actually managed to get into Serre with the trench mortar men behind them, they didn't come back. John's body was never found, like so many of his comrades he has no known grave. The teenage lad from 'Accy' was lost forever. His brother Billy went across 'no man's land' and was badly wounded. He was evacuated to a field hospital and eventually repatriated to a general hospital in Bristol. Billy recovered and lived to fight again and again.

Without his beloved brother and cousin, Billy Wixted moved to the 5th battalion of the East Lancashire Regiment, the famous 'Burnley Mashers'. He fought bravely at Passchendaele with the 'Mashers' and despite offers of promotion within the ranks, he always refused. I sometimes wonder if he took out violent revenge upon the enemy at close quarters with the bayonet or additional 'hand-made' killing tools.

Billy was demobilised and eventually returned to Accrington in the autumn of 1919. The town was a very different place to the one he had left nearly five years before. Black drawn curtains hung across front windows, they had done so for a long time, Accrington - couldn't and wouldn't - forget. In the arms of his sisters who were so pleased to see him home he cried like a baby for his younger brother and his cousin.

Despite losing a massive proportion of their strength the 'Accrington Pals' went onwards. Many men from outside the area continued to reinforce the battalion who fought like lions particularly at Beaulieu Farm in 1918 when they were almost completely wiped out.

The final comments regarding this story go to Rob, he asks you to try and imagine the civilian soldiers in their trenches dressed in their normal work attire. Sheffield lads in their steel-workers overalls, Barnsley men wearing their miner's helmets and the Accrington lads in their foundry workers boiler suits, ambiguous tones of reality. None of those young men had ever fired a shot in anger before they were literally butchered having spent so much time away from their normal work routines. The guys went on to form massive comradeships over a relatively long period of time within their short lives. Their friendships were destroyed within just a few hours, for Accrington in less than an hour.

John Wixted was entitled to the British War Medal and Victory Medal. We are the very proud custodians of his Victory Medal, the whereabouts of the other medal are unknown. A small piece of metal with an attached ribbon that will always belong to John brought upon the story of his family – and himself. God bless you John, wherever you may be, your loving memory and that of your family is here for eternity.

OVER SO SOON

WHEN Britain declared war on August 4th 1914, it didn't come as so much of a shock to ordinary people. The Kaiser and Germany needed to be taught a lesson as far as many were concerned.

Back in those days the main form of communication regarding everyday events came from newspapers. National publications were read mainly by those in London with few working-class people having access to their limited circulation. An ordinary person if he did get his hands on a national may have done so just once a week on a Sunday. The penny evening papers that were dotted around in different towns and cities offered the working man access to the news. Local items of interest came first followed by issues of national importance, then it was left to bar room banter.

Despite the lack of communications technology, no internet, no TV, no radio, the British people were as curious about world events as they are today. Topical discussion was much greater between individuals, ordinary everyday folk were reasonably well-informed one way or another.

The general consensus was the war would be over by Christmas 1914. Opinions started to shift when casualty reports and photos of the dead and missing started to increase rapidly in virtually all of the newspapers. The war wouldn't be over so soon after all.

For the soldier of the time, a pre-war regular and member of the original British Expeditionary Force, a territorial, a volunteer or a conscript, the individual focus would be upon survival and getting through his own war. Many succeeded, some were even glad to make it back from the front shouldering the burden of disability due to wounds received, others weren't so lucky.

The focus of this chapter falls upon a handful of men who served within various periods of the war, in different theatres of conflict, however, they all have one thing in common. Our featured subjects literally did find that for them it was 'over so soon'. Their hopes, fears and anticipations were cruelly dashed. The consequences that befell upon their loved ones were almost equally and profoundly severe, omitting just one aspect – death.

From tragedy and grief the healing of wounds is often assisted by time itself, as we shall see this can often be the case, but not in every circumstance. On a positive note Rob and I can only hope to bring along a shared sense of empathy and in more than one instance provide routes to suggest respectful solutions.

Stanley Hall
Died at Home
March 23rd 1916
Aged 21.

STANLEY Edward Hall provides us with a truly fascinating story and one that has just about everything. His enigma continues to live on and on and will do so until a certain conclusion to his life and death can be met. In the recent past efforts have been made to bring about such a conclusion, Rob and I are not satisfied, the story of this young man is far from over.

This tale revolves around the small Cumberland town of Millom, now in the county of Cumbria, a few miles from Barrow-in-Furness. We have an account of unbridled tragedy tinged with the moral stances of the day that border upon corruptive manipulation. We tell a story that affected a whole family.

Stan was the youngest of six children to his parents John and Eliza, five survived through infancy, tragically one departed at some point before he was born. His parents were extremely poor, Stan's father John worked in and around the mines throughout his own lifetime. Originally from Coniston in the picturesque Lake District, John would find himself under and above ground. He toiled in the coal mines of Lancashire and then the iron ore mines of west Cumberland. A dirty, filthy, low-paid and at the time unregulated occupation that yielded poor wages and was fraught with danger. Eliza, like many of her generation was there to provide his children and to look after the entire family. Profoundly, she had to witness the death of five out of six of her brood and see the one surviving of her flock depart far away to Canada.

Things couldn't have started better for John and Eliza with a Christmas Day wedding in 1880 for the Lake District couple in their new home village of Millom. John had regular employment at the iron ore mine and they had secured the tenancy upon a small cottage at 32 Newton Street within the village. It was time for the newly-weds to start a family.

Over the following ten years the couple had five children, Harry, Lily, William, John and another who died in infancy. Life was far from bliss, John, for what I conclude were health reasons had to down-grade his employment to labourer, his weekly wage suffered considerably as a result. With six mouths to feed from the pay packet of a mine labourer we can only imagine what life was really like. No benefits system existed at the time to help support the struggling family.

The Halls were forced to move home more than once, for reasons undefined but not very difficult to work out. By the time Stan was born at 1 Victoria Street, Millom, in February 1895, the family had already been displaced three times and another move was yet to come.

At least the older children were to become bread-winners, to support the struggling labourer. Harry gained employment on the steam engines with the local council and Lily managed to get some shop work. John junior would follow his father to the mines. Luck was something this family never really experienced.

In the April of 1909, young John died unexpectedly when he was just twenty years old. Buried in an unmarked grave at the local church he became the first of four 'grown-up' children to die within the Hall family. Less than three years later at the age of just twenty-six, Lily also passed away. Tragedy haunted and followed the Halls as they had lost two principal money earners from within the family unit.

Young Stan had impressed his tutors at school. Despite the fact that he had only received a basic and rudimentary education he managed to secure respectable employment, he became an assistant librarian at Millom Library. Whilst there Stan furthered his knowledge, met many local people and developed social skills that would set him aside. The teenager had done well for himself and his mother was proud of him.

Life was still difficult for Stan, he watched his family struggle to overcome the rigours of daily life brought upon by poverty, he did his best to help, but he wanted more. Perhaps he may have been inspired by his readings at the library as he craved adventure. In those days the easiest route to travel far and wide was to join the army or the navy. Stan plumped for the relatively local infantry battalion of the King's Own Royal Lancaster Regiment. He boarded a train to Lancaster and signed on with the 1st Battalion, being allocated the service number 10983, it was the early autumn of 1913 - Stan was 18-years old.

He wasn't to know of course that war would be declared less than a year after he joined an army that clearly saw his potential and leadership qualities. He was promoted to Lance-Corporal whilst still a teenager proving himself as a soldier. Eliza's son was a young man given a rank of responsibility for others, for those often older than himself.

When war was declared the regular 1st Battalion of the Royal Lancaster's were stationed in Dover and immediately mobilised. Those on the reserve list were recalled bringing the battalion up to its full strength of 1,000 men of all ranks very quickly. After moving around through Norfolk and north London for almost three weeks, the officers and men finally found themselves at Southampton Docks. Whilst there they made ready to board the 'SS Saturnia' bound for Boulogne. The time was 09.00am, the date, Saturday August 22nd 1914.

Stan's voyage across the English Channel to northern France was a long one, lasting over twelve hours on the lumbering crowded troopship. The men actually arrived at Boulogne not long before midnight but had to remain on the ship until disembarkation began around the bustling port at 06.00am. Sunday morning of August 23rd marked the beginning of Stan's war, which would literally be over for him within days.

After spending the remainder of the day at a rest camp, the men were sent back to Boulogne before being instructed to make a long trek towards the front. The journey would include exhausting route marches along the way. Their compatriots of the British Expeditionary Force who were completely outnumbered by the advancing Germans fought a well organised but desperate retreat. Experienced regular British soldiers were pulling away from Mons and being pushed back towards Le Cateau. The Royal Lancaster's would eventually arrive to support their stricken countrymen.

The march was long and the weather stiflingly hot, in full kit this tested the endurance of the regular soldiers. Stan marched towards Le Cateau via Bertry and Ligny on August 24th. The following day he and his comrades came under fire for the very first time when the German artillery opened up on the Royal Lancaster's as they made it to Viesly. From there they advanced onwards to Bethencourt and then Caudry, before reaching Harcourt. The Lancaster's eventually arrived suffering from exhaustion on the outskirts of Le Cateau at 05.00am on Wednesday August 26th.

Orders were given for the battalion to make its way along the Cattenieres Road and proceed down a slope to cross the Warnelle Brook and take up positions upon the higher ground, they achieved and complied with their instructions by 06.00am. Despite their relatively good strategic position, the Royal Lancaster's in their very first action of the war were ordered to go upon the offensive and consequently suffered terribly. Around a quarter of the battalion's strength found itself heavily engaged, totally outnumbered and was decimated. The remaining fighting units fought desperately through the day and night.

Stan was in the thick of the action and found himself involved in street fighting as his battalion was forced back into the town of Cambrai. Brutal combat that ensued spread literally from building to building in the dark and gloomy dusk of Thursday August 27th. The Germans were pouring reinforcements into the town and it wasn't long before a further two companies of the Royal Lancaster's were overwhelmed. Some fought to the death, others with their backs against the wall had no option but to surrender. Stan raised his arms and threw down his Lee Enfield .303 rifle, for him it was 'over so soon'. Very quickly he had to mentally prepare himself for captivity as a prisoner of war.

The first actions his captors took was to remove his overcoat and take his money, they were never returned. Stan was then taken by motor wagon to Halle and then by train into Germany. The journey was gruelling and lasted an incredible thirty-seven hours. All prisoners were actually transported in carriages, not cattle trucks, they reported their guards behaved well towards them and issued them with bread. Water was difficult to obtain and the captives found themselves ravaged by thirst.

Whenever and wherever the train stopped the civilian population spat upon the prisoners, it would be a sign of things to come. Unfortunately, the Germans didn't treat the British prisoners particularly well. The fact that Stan was eventually released as part of a prisoner-exchange in February 1916 gives us a unique insight into the conditions he endured, he went on to provide a detailed account of events when debriefed.

There is no doubt whatsoever that Stan's demise and suffering was as a direct result of the way he was handled by the German captors. His physical condition deteriorated dramatically and ultimately led to his premature death. The following accounts of his time as a prisoner came from Stan himself, the full report makes harrowing reading.

Stan arrived at Sennelager, Germany, late in the day of August 28th 1914. He was to spend most of the rest of his life interned at the POW camp within the town, housed in a stable. He had to share his accommodation with around 120 other men, they were allocated just two stoves with very little fuel. The men shared six wash bowls between them, along with a couple of horse troughs and two taps. Soap could be bought after a few weeks. An adjoining outbuilding allowed each man to take a bath once every six to eight weeks. Sanitary arrangements were primitive with open trench latrines, the stench was unbearable. A straw mattress and two blankets were issued to each man.

The general living conditions were bad enough, however, it was the food or lack of it that presented huge problems for Stan and his fellow prisoners. All the men had to undertake duties within working parties, short shifts operated from 06.00 to 11.00 and long shifts from 06.00 to 15.00. The men had to walk six miles each way to work through swamps and toiled in heavy agricultural forced labour without pay. An allocated staple diet for the men who carried out such rigours left much to be desired.

Coffee was served very early in the morning. At some point in the afternoon a bowl of watery-soup was dished-up. In the evening, one slice of bread per man with a piece of sausage or pickled fish provided supper. On occasions food packages were received from Britain but were often in poor condition.

Clothing issues were awful, the individual prisoner was allowed to keep his own clothes and had just two shirts and one pair of trousers provided by the Germans. In the winter time, life was particularly harsh. Many previously fit and healthy young regular soldiers succumbed to serious illnesses or worse. Stan was no exception when he developed a painful condition known as phthisis, a wasting disease associated with pulmonary tuberculosis.

Two huts had been set apart to act as a hospital for the sick. Not surprisingly there were not enough beds. Anyone who could walk was not admitted regardless of how poorly they actually were. Stan was in a bad way, he was losing his flesh and spent two weeks in the hospital. He was given an extra food ration to build his strength, one extra ounce of bread per day! It was something of a miracle that he survived. Shortly afterwards he was ordered back to work.

The British prisoners were notably harassed worse than their French counterparts. If any camp rules were broken the culprit would be made to stand in the blazing sun without water, or tied to a tree for long periods. If the perpetrator of an offence could not be discovered all the British captives would be made to stand for hours, this did not happen to the French inmates. Some British prisoners were ordered to work on munitions and adamantly refused. Punishments for offences of this type were severe and led to deprivation of their already meagre food rations and imprisonment in dark and wet rat infested cells. Irish and British prisoners were segregated at all times.

After enduring the harshness of this daily life, Stan found himself redeployed to heavy labouring duties unloading wagons, he was hardly in a fit state to do so. To make matters worse after an initial ration of coffee was issued at 05.30, no solid food was given to the prisoners until the evening time. Stan was growing weaker and weaker, in a desperate attempt to gain access to better food he managed to get himself attached to a working party of prisoners at Dortmund. His condition worsened and eventually he was seen by a doctor at the factory. It was by then September 1915, Stan was to live for another six months.

He was sent to Rennbahn Camp No.2 where he was examined by a Russian doctor, himself a prisoner of war who instructed the Germans that Stan was not fit to work. Undeterred his captors made him return to work after just three days, within a day Stan had collapsed. At that point the order was given by a German doctor to send him to hospital.

Stan was forwarded to a hospital at Munster Lazaret via a two-hour train journey. For five long months the young soldier from Millom endured a miserable existence. Within a few weeks of arrival he was diagnosed with pleurisy and became bed-ridden. This condition causes an inflammation of the lining around the lungs and came less than a year after the horrors he had suffered with phthisis. Stan was in a bad way and the food ration was no better than he had received at Sennelager camp. He had only one hospital suit and two sets of underwear, his bed sheets were changed just once in six months. No nursing and very little medicine was available for Stan or the sick Russian prisoners with whom he shared his dorm. The Russians were treated even worse than he was.

As Stan fell in and out of consciousness the Germans realised there wasn't much hope for him and arranged a prisoner exchange with the British. It was February 1916 and at last Stan was going home, he had hope and belief that he would once again see his family. Make no mistake about it, the Germans were cunning, cruel and barbaric, they had absolutely no desire to see Stan make a recovery. It has to be said they wanted the exchange to happen as soon as possible, as they knew he would struggle to survive no matter how favourable the circumstances.

Stan was debriefed on February 10th 1916. He arrived back in England dressed in the remnants of his own ragged clothes. After the examination or more than likely an interrogation he was deemed to be honest and intelligent. Remarkably and I have to say shockingly he was not sent to a military hospital in England. If Stan had been an officer he would have been chauffeur driven to such an establishment.

Back in Millom his parents eagerly awaited his return. With his brother William serving in the Merchant Navy and the eldest Harry also away, there was plenty of space to accommodate their desperately ill youngest son. Eliza Hall still relied upon the pittance of a wage earned by her ageing husband, John. Eventually their sick boy arrived home, he hadn't long turned twenty-one years old and had suffered terribly. The British authorities and those with influence neglected this tragic set of circumstances, Stan was very badly let down.

Eliza did everything she could for her precious son, the services of a doctor were completely out of the question as she simply could not afford such a necessity. All that she could give was her love and cradle Stan on those long dark cold winter days. His mother washed him, stroked his brow and kept him warm and safe. As winter started to fade so did the resilience of the young man. The devastating effects of the phthisis and pleurisy together with the damp and cold of the Cumberland air took their toll. Stan quietly slipped away and died in his mum's arms on the evening of Thursday March 23rd 1916.

Could more have been done for Stan? Without a shadow of a doubt that is one of the easiest questions I have ever posed to myself. Now it is time for me to 'let-rip' at the cosseted systems of the time and for once Rob doesn't want to hold me back. Let me start with the senior officers of the 4th. Infantry Division to which the 1st Royal Lancaster's were attached. The men were led by none other than Thomas D'Oyly Snow of whom I have previously described as a 'Donkey'. Snow's conduct cannot directly be attributed to Stan's capture or can it? How can a regular army battalion be literally carved to pieces in a day? Especially when they had taken advantage of the high ground in the initial stages. Uncoordinated and rash idiotic command decisions led to the Royal Lancaster's being thrown in at the deep-end and subsequently virtually wiped out.

Le Cateau was not a success for the British, however some marshmallow chewing 'metropolitan historians' have tried to claim that it was, in reality it was a disaster! Having fought a desperate and courageous thirty-odd mile retreat from Mons across the Belgian border in stifling heat, the British regulars were falling back to this little town. Stan and the fresh reinforcements from the Royal Lancaster Regiment were in a good strategic position. Other regular battalion's such as the 2nd Lancashire Fusiliers had also been rushed forward in support. It was becoming very obvious to the retreating British they were considerably being outmanoeuvred and outnumbered by the Germans. It has to be said at this point that regular and reservist British soldiers outclassed the Germans and inflicted heavy casualties upon them. Sheer weight of numbers alone helped the Germans push the British back. Had the forces been of similar fighting strength the British would have easily defeated their enemy.

The inevitable retreat would have to continue, history shows that it did as the British headed for the banks of the River Marne. Many lives were tossed away as Snow had endorsed and supported his commander, General Smith-Dorrien who had conceitedly told his men to 'stand and fight' for Le Cateau. Snow's field ambulances, engineers and artillery had not caught up with his reinforcements. Instead of covering the retreat of other British battalions from their position on the high ground, the Royal Lancaster's were forced to engage with a fully-equipped and highly motivated German force. Those who weren't killed such as Stan had little option but to surrender.

In any terms the order to 'stand and fight' without adequate logistical support against overwhelming odds was suicidal. The Lancashire Fusiliers also in action for the first time in the war were literally butchered. Fine regular soldiers snuffed-out simply because of the lunacy of a couple of 'Donkey Generals'.

Military welfare was also the responsibility of officers especially when processing exchanged prisoners of war. Some 'Rupert' mid-ranking officer decided that Stan didn't warrant specialist care despite his desperate condition. Even the Germans who treated Stan worse than an animal did more for him in that respect. A former prisoner of war was an embarrassment to the brass of the army unless they could see that he would be fit to resume active duty, impossible in Stan's case.

So what of the people of Millom? The local newspaper of the day reported Stan's death and proclaimed that much sympathy was given to his family. This report came as no surprise, for Stan had once been the local librarian and of course had already lost three of his siblings. I am pretty sure that some of the locals rallied around and tried to help Eliza in her struggle to keep Stan alive. The same cannot be said of the local church and its representatives.

Throughout time and well into the twentieth century the local parish church held enormous influence over the people who lived within its boundaries. There was no NHS in World War One and very few opportunities of financial social welfare existed. If you attended your local church regularly and of course contributed just as often to the post-service collection, this would be noted by the parish priest, curate or even the verger. Mental notes would be made of the 'good and godly'. In times of desperate need it would be the local minister who could provide 'Christian charity'- especially to the regular members of his flock, who always financially contributed to the collections.

Eliza had already suffered the pain of burying three of her children in unmarked paupers' graves within the churchyard. Almost every day for many years, she would have had to walk past the church where all of her children had been baptised. I sincerely doubt the Hall family were regular attendees of church services and had not been able to contribute financially to the collection box.

The services of a doctor especially on a regular basis would have been expensive. Certainly the vast majority of families in the village would have required an element of 'Christian charity' to provide such a service, I need not elaborate any further! Stan's funeral took place over a week after his death, contrary to some claims. This time period would have allowed Eliza and John to 'arrange' his pauper's funeral and they had to ask for pennies here and there to help pay for a basic coffin. The military seem to have been at a distance, there is no mention of them, whereas, had Stan been killed in action things would have been very different.

So came the day of the funeral. Stan was laid to rest in an unmarked grave somewhere within the churchyard, yes somewhere, parish records do not indicate the exact location. Rob tries to offer an explanation by informing me that individual parish churches often didn't keep such records. In truth no representative from the church of Holy Trinity bothered to make a record, this was not unusual. Stanley Edward Hall and his family were poor, the service was done and dusted very quickly.

For 94-years Stan lay somewhere in the churchyard as a forgotten 'unknown warrior' until the serving minister of the time decided to honour his memory as recently as 2010. The church in collaboration with the Commonwealth War Graves Commission, saw to it that an official headstone was placed within the cemetery and that a service of dedication to Stan was well attended.

Very gracious and I am sure well intended, but in our opinions, very misplaced. The official CWGC headstone was positioned at a 'selected' location within the cemetery. A headstone is I have to say a grave marker, I don't really think there is any other way of describing such an item, Rob totally agrees. This particular headstone bearing Stan's military details is NOT in the place he was buried simply because nobody knows where the actual original grave is.

In an attempt to justify the completely inappropriate placing of this headstone an inscription is carved along the top of the memorial it reads: 'BURIED ELSEWHERE IN THIS CEMETERY'. Holy Trinity, Millom, now has the perfect excuse of what it deems as rectification, aided and abetted by the Commonwealth War Graves Commission. I am not sure what the Hall family would have thought about this, after all most of them lie at rest themselves in unmarked paupers' graves within the churchyard.

Stan's lonely grave positioned randomly within his local churchyard, his original medals sit on top of the headstone.

In the summer of 2017 Rob visited the 'grave' of Stan, he also managed to obtain an old copy of the churchyard plans. He describes an area now slightly outside of the original plots as to where he thinks Stan is actually buried. There is also a wide open and slightly uneven patch of ground where the paupers' graves may actually have settled.

Our suggestion for a satisfactory conclusion will fall upon deaf ears. The CWGC who we have discovered sometimes get things mixed-up have positioned the headstone in the wrong place. An absurd inscription upon the memorial only serves to make the whole scenario worse in our view. We would like to see a plaque unveiled either within an area outside the church or even inside upon a wall. The plaque should honour Stanley Edward Hall and state that he is buried in the churchyard. As for the headstone it shouldn't have been commissioned to stand on ground that does not represent where his final resting place lies. Stan's 1914-15 Star, British War Medal and Victory Medal are with us and pictured as you will see on the illustration that accompanies this story, polished and cased, upon his headstone.

Edwin Hyde
Killed in Action
Gallipoli, June 4th 1915
Aged 45.

NOWADAYS, when we think of Turkey sometimes we imagine the experiences of beautiful sun kissed beaches, coves and Efes beer. Not forgetting dodgy designer labels upon cheap clothing hawked in and around endless bazaars and street markets. We consider the cheerfulness of a friendly host of people who sometimes may hassle or haggle for your trade. Turkish folk are proud, friendly, obliging and respectful, especially when it comes to their own sense of national pride.

The Gallipoli peninsula represents only a very small slice of Turkey. Sometimes the very mention of the word Gallipoli can often stir the mind. For it was there on just a tiny part of Turkish soil that a horrific bloodbath occurred over a period of eight months or so. Gallipoli will forever be associated with death and incomprehensible suffering. Unfortunately and yet again, ruthlessly arrogant and incompetent military command cost the lives of so many who served there.

When Eddie Hyde, a middle-aged bricklayer from the eastern fringe of Manchester arrived at Gallipoli his military service lasted barely two days. He left behind a wife and three children. Eddie remains to this day a long way from home, he lies at rest forever somewhere in Gallipoli, Turkey. Nobody knows exactly where as he has no known grave.

Just like his father Tommy and older brother Billy, Eddie became a skilled tradesman. Upon leaving school he followed in the footsteps of his dad and sibling and after completing an apprenticeship he became a bricklayer. Eddie was a seasoned professional, bricklaying was all he ever knew as far as work was concerned.

Born in the year of 1869 in his namesake town of Hyde, Eddie moved around the district, initially with his parents and then later in life when he was married. The second half of the nineteenth century and early part of the twentieth century provided many opportunities of work for bricklayers in his region. Cotton mills dominated, row upon row of quickly assembled terraced housing to accommodate the workers of that industry sprung up in their tens of thousands all across the area. There was always plenty of work for the brickies.

As the Edwardian era moved along Eddie could expect to earn around £2- £3 per week plus one or two incentive bonuses. In the winter months his earnings would fall as productivity became reduced due to adverse weather conditions. Nevertheless, a bricklayer would be expected to pick up slightly above the average wage. A couple of pounds or more per week was good money for a rugged man who spent his entire working life in the outdoors.

Eddie was pushing thirty when he finally decided to tie the knot and get married. I have no doubt that he had enjoyed a jolly period of bachelorhood life. Brickies were and still are a tough bunch of men, they like a drink and a gamble now and again, not to mention certain other pleasures in life. The Edwardian bricklayers always found a watering hole after work and there were certainly plenty of them. Beer was cheap, much less expensive in comparison to today's prices and the boys lapped it up.

Elizabeth Jane Sherlock, a fisherman's daughter originally from Fleetwood but at the time living on the Wirral, married Eddie at St. Michael's Church, Ashton-under-Lyne on Sunday January 2nd 1898. Over the years the family moved around the area presumably in situ to where Eddie could find regular work. The bricklayer and his bride went on to have no less than six children. To my surprise they consistently lived in housing at the cheaper end of the completely rental dependent housing market.

Perhaps Eddie and Elizabeth were conscious of his drop in pay during the winter months? Did they really choose to live within dwellings that in reality would be sub-standard even by the expectations of the day? Surely Eddie could have afforded to improve his living standards on the overall salary of a bricklayer? I don't want to speculate as to the reasons why or why not. A disturbing set of facts remain that I consider relevant. Three of the six children died in infancy in abject squalor, their deaths no doubt brought upon by their appalling and disease ridden living conditions.

As time moved on the burly bricklayer would have slowed down a little. His joints started to ache as he descended into middle-age. Younger, much fitter men came along and on occasions took over the work Eddie once managed with ease. Still, he plodded on for the sake of his family. When war broke out Eddie was already in his mid-forties and the conflict shouldn't have and needn't really have concerned him.

I suppose I can speculate here upon the reasons why he volunteered to join up. There was no requirement whatsoever for him to do so. He was a married man and of considerably older age than virtually every other volunteer civilian recruit. The law exempted him if he so wished at that time from serving with the military.

Despite his age Eddie presented a formidable figure of a man with a strong physique borne by his vast experience of rugged outdoor labour. This would have been immediately noticed by the army recruiting team as we will discover. So what really did motivate this man into placing himself into a position where he would have been more than aware that his life could be at risk? After all he had a wife and three children who were dependent upon him.

In my opinion this middle-aged man was tired and fed up with his life as a bricklayer. He would have known all too well that demand for his services could reduce considerably in a time of war. Eddie had experienced nothing else but laying bricks. The real prospect of periods of unemployment would have disturbed him. I am also of the opinion that he was dissatisfied with his life. Undoubtedly, Eddie saw many of his younger workmates dash off to sign up. Maybe over a drink or two in his local pub he thought seriously about joining up and boasted openly about enlisting in front of his pals. As the winter of 1914 approached work began to dry up. Eddie made his way to the recruitment centre in Ashton and was eagerly snapped up as a strong and fit man with experience of life. Allocated the service number of 6140, a number originally dispensed in May of 1898, he was posted the regular 1st Battalion of the Lancashire Fusiliers. Rob agrees with me here that such a man of experience would have been more than able to hold his own within a regular army battalion. The younger 'sweats' would not have bothered him at all.

Some in-depth research has been required to establish that Eddie was not a pre-war regular soldier as his service number suggests. His movements between 1898, the year of his marriage and 1914 are consistent with his work as a bricklayer. Furthermore, he fathered children at regular interval dates not corresponding to the battalion's mainly garrisoned duties predominantly in India. He couldn't have spent enough time upon the reserve list either. The service number was reallocated as was common, it had possibly been used sixteen years earlier and originally issued to someone else.

Training would have tested Eddie seriously, he was part of a local reinforcement contingent required to support the men who had been transferred from their Indian garrison to fight in the Mediterranean theatre. The battalion had originally arrived at Gallipoli on the opening day of the landings, April 25th 1915 at 'W Beach'. Famously, they were eventually awarded six Victoria Crosses for the heroics they performed that day when they suffered around 700 casualties. Over two-thirds of their strength was lost in overcoming the fiercely and vastly outnumbered heroic Turkish resistance fortified by formidable barbed wire defences.

The damp and soggy building sites of Oldham, Ashton and Dukinfield represented a far distance in every respect from where Eddie was heading. He set sail with the reinforcements on or around May 22nd 1915. The route would have taken him towards the sunshine with stops at Gibraltar, Malta and the Greek island of Lemnos.

A blazing sun beat down upon the Lancashire Fusiliers reinforcements as they disembarked on the beaches at the southern end of the peninsula on Wednesday June 2nd 1915. A major assault was well in place and for Eddie a horrific baptism of fire awaited him. The stench of rotting flesh and swarms of flies as well as a constant thirst distracted him greatly. Attired in

The Lancashire Fusiliers just before reaching Gallipoli in 1915.

full kit the heat was stifling, the ageing brickie must have wondered why on earth he had volunteered for such an ordeal.

Meanwhile from the comfort and safety of his office in London, the First Lord of the Admiralty was pondering a perilous situation for which he was largely responsible for. The situation by then at Gallipoli was pretty serious. Upon his almost relentless insistence the campaign that was his conception started with a failed naval assault. It began in the February of that year at the straights of the Dardanelles running along the Gallipoli peninsula. The Turks were well prepared for the land invasion that followed and commanded superbly by a General of their German allies, Otto Liman Von Sanders. This campaign also made the name of a young 33-year Lieutenant-Colonel by the name of Mustafa Kemal, later known as 'Ataturk'. He became the father of modern Turkey after completely reforming the country he led from 1923 following the demise of the old Turkish Ottoman Empire.

The First Lord of the Admiralty, a highly ambitious 40-year old man with a chequered past and from a privileged background had always fancied himself as a military strategist. Personally, I have always seriously condemned the whole notion of the Gallipoli campaign from its conception to its disastrous conclusion. Rob holds the opposite opinion and believes it was poor localised ground command that led ultimately to a catastrophic defeat. So, my friend supports the initiative of the strategist, who I will condemn for his misguided strategic ambition. The First Lord of the Admiralty at that time and the strategist was Winston Churchill.

Rob does have a valid point, the commanders in the field made decisions that left a lot to be desired. The Secretary of State for War, Lord Kitchener, oversaw their appointments. Kitchener was as bold as he was arrogant. He chose a bumbling 62-year old 'Puppet General', Sir. Ian Hamilton to take overall command of the operation. Kitchener was also instrumental in sending yet another buffoon to load upon Hamilton. Freddie Stopford was a port and brandy swilling 'Donkey General'. The old fool actually fell asleep in his cabin on the command ship during operations. Snoring his head off he was anchored safely offshore as his men stormed the beaches to be cut to pieces in hails of enemy bullets. Then of course we have to mention Aylmer Hunter-Weston who took a lashing from me in the previous chapter. 'Hunter-Bunter' was the worst 'Donkey General' of all time in my opinion. He oversaw the slaughter of his own men on several occasions at Gallipoli with tactics that could have been better master-minded by a schoolboy.

Of course none of the men in charge at the very high echelons of military power mattered that much to Eddie. He was more concerned about staying alive. His immediate superiors, a section commander [Corporal] and a platoon Sergeant would have been twenty or so years younger than himself, they could have been his sons. He looked to them for guidance and support. Suddenly the big and strong brickie knew he was vulnerable as he lumbered in the heat, struggling to keep up with his comrades.

On June 4th, at noon, a ridiculous time to attack, on the orders of the moronic 'Hunter-Bunter' and less than forty-eight hours after his arrival, Eddie's war started. It was all over very soon afterwards, perhaps in a matter of minutes. The sun was blazing down, as it would be in Turkey at that time of the day. 'Hunter-Bunter' had sent the men of the 1st Lancashire Fusiliers including Eddie into one side of a flanking action close to the village of Krithia. This objective had been attacked twice before without success. Now, I can only imagine what actually happened. Eddie striving forward up an incline was hit, more than likely by rifle fire from the heavily defended Turkish positions. He would have felt an instantaneous sharp pain and slumped to his knees and was probably shot again and again. As the blood drained from the huge punctured bullet exit wounds across his body he would have quickly lost consciousness. Maybe, there was just one last thought of his wife and children back home as he drew upon his last breath.

Back at Admiralty House, Churchill was more than likely puffing away on a cigar and no doubt enjoying another glass of brandy. He couldn't understand why the British with their dominion and colonial allies were not pounding the 'racially inferior' Turks to oblivion. Kitchener shared his sentiments, both men had expressed their total contempt for the Ottoman Turks on several occasions. These men of great power and influence had always believed the British were overwhelmingly superior in the field of battle. The Turks were seen by people like Churchill and Kitchener as uneducated savages, almost to the point of being sub-human. Churchill was also noted as referring to Indians as a 'beastly race of people'. Despite his comments Indian soldiers fought bravely alongside the British at Gallipoli suffering over 6,000 casualties. Almost 400,000 men of various nationalities became casualties at Gallipoli and of those over 130,000 lost their lives. I have absolutely no reservations about publishing the actual casualty figures below, Rob totally supports this. Incidentally, although he regretted his role in the whole campaign, Churchill never apologised, neither did Kitchener. Whatever anyone has to say or think the Gallipoli campaign was a huge tragedy, an avoidable mistake. Please take your time when reading the casualty figures.

	Died	Wounded	Total Casualties
Great Britain and Ireland	21,255	73,485	94,740
Australia	8,709	28,150	36,859
New Zealand	2,779	7,991	10,870
India	1,358	4,779	6,137
Newfoundland	49	142	191
France	10,000	27,000	37,000
Totals	44,150	97,397	141,547

	Died	Wounded	Total Casualties
Ottoman Turkish Casualties – Defending their Homeland	86,692	164,617	251,309

	Total Died	Total Wounded	Total Casualties
The Total Human Cost – Both Sides	130,842	262,014	392,856

To Winston Churchill and Herbert Kitchener the figures above represented just numbers.

Eddie's trio of medals are now with us. I have to admit to using conjectural claims based upon the fact that I could really only discover circumstantial information relating to his life. At times I found the job of building up a profile of his character pretty upsetting. In the hope of getting it right I thought very carefully about what I have had to say.

I have spoken with Rob about the matter and with his blessing I am now going to portray Eddie and his family in a completely different context. For the first time within this publication I am deliberately going to place a hypothetical scenario of total fiction in front of you. Read on, I think Eddie deserves this.

Time has moved on rapidly, Eddie Hyde is now living in the present with his wife Elizabeth and their three children. Eddie junior is aged fourteen, Katie, eight and we have five-year-old Victor. The family live in a modest house in Royton, near Oldham and Eddie has been saving hard for the annual holiday. This year they are off to Turkey and the sunshine resort of Marmaris.

Summer finally arrives, Eddie excitedly books the taxi for the trip to nearby Manchester Airport to begin the first-leg of the holiday journey. Liz is flapping around checking she has enough sun cream in her case, whilst young Ed is only concerned with his Samsung Galaxy. Katie is crying because she is scared of flying on a plane. Youngster Vic, well, he has just spilled a yoghurt all over the settee as the taxi 'beeps' its horn in the street outside.

The airport bar is crowded but Eddie still eventually manages to get served. It costs a small fortune for his pint of Becks, a large white wine for Liz and three cokes for the kids who are constantly driving their mum crazy. Eddie is told off in no uncertain terms as he heads back to the bar for another pint of Becks… It's a long way to Dalaman Airport, for Eddie his holiday has already started.

Katie is sick on the transfer coach from Dalaman to Marmaris. A combination of heat, tiredness and nerves have unsettled the little girl. The mood soon changes as the family check into their little two-star hotel on the outskirts of the resort. It has its own pool and great news for Eddie its own bar, a fact not unnoticed by young Ed. Liz always insists on unpacking anyway, so father and son head for a couple of Efes lagers, only one for Ed insists Liz. The sun begins to fall quickly as Eddie and Liz sit upon their balcony watching it sneak behind a line of palm trees on a hilly ravine in the distance, the younger kids are tired and soon fall asleep. Teenager Ed is hovering around the pool bar area paying attention to a tall fifteen-year-old girl from Birmingham. He seems to think she is gazing in his direction.

The days pass quickly and finally the time arrives to visit the bustling local market. Eddie buys enough socks and boxer shorts to last him for years whilst young Ed sneers at the fake designer labels. Liz loves the jewellery but Eddie can't afford it, or so he says. The family later head for the marina passing as they go a marvellous statue. Katie enquires to her parents as to who the monument represents. Eddie is quick to tell her that it is a statue of Mustafa Kemal Ataturk. As they sit on a neighbouring wall he tells his family the story of Kemal's bravery long ago at Gallipoli and how he came to rule and reform modern Turkey. Liz isn't listening, she is more concerned with her sun tan being just as she wants it. Ed meanwhile looks out across the marina at the gullet boats whilst Katie cries as her ice-cream melts. Young Victor though is all ears, he listens fascinated by his fathers' story.

Once again the sun begins to set in a cloudless sky. As promised Eddie takes the family out for one last time on their Turkish holiday. It is their final night in Marmaris so it is off to the 'Happy Hunter-Bunter Bar' for juicy steaks. Liz says what's good for him is good for her. Ed agrees and orders a mega-steak, Katie and Vic are happy with the chicken nuggets. The night ends with laughter and karaoke with the Turkish Lira banknotes going a long way. Katie once again notices the image of Mustafa Kemal on the currency and remarks to her dad that he must have been a very important man. Eddie smiles and nods in agreement.

The stark contrasts of fiction and reality can be very cold. For in actual fact there was of course no Turkish holiday. No bars, no steaks, no ice-creams, no markets or beaches. No fears of flying, no Efes beer or fake designer labels. Reality was a telegram that arrived at the little house in Royton on a summers' day. Elizabeth was shaking as she opened the envelope, her head dropped to her bosom as the tears flooded down her cheeks. Eddie had been reported as missing in action and presumed dead. Little Katie tugged at her soiled apron as Victor looked on and asked when his daddy was coming home.

Both Rob and I, with a tear in my eye, leave the final words to Mustafa Kemal Ataturk. His sentiments are inscribed forever on a memorial at Gallipoli. This warrior who was considered as an inferior human being by the likes of Churchill and Kitchener was not afraid to speak for all of those who perished at Gallipoli. His words are dedicated to Eddie and the other 130,841 men who never made it back home.

'Those heroes that shed their blood and lost their lives… You are now lying in the soil of a friendly country. Therefore rest in peace. There is no difference between the Johnnies and the Mehmets to us where they lie side by side here in this country of ours… You, the mothers who sent their sons from faraway countries, wipe away your tears; your sons are now lying in our bosom and are in peace. After having lost their lives on this land they have become our sons as well'.

ATATURK

Robert Bamber

Killed in Action
France, June 16th 1915
Aged 27.

LIKE all of our subjects within this chapter Robert was awarded the 1914-
15 Star, the British War Medal and the Victory Medal, all of which are now
in our custodianship. There are however other connections between Bob
Bamber, Rob and myself.

Private Robert Bamber was a volunteer soldier, an ordinary man from
the famous seaside resort of Blackpool, a place I know very well as I had the
privilege of residing there for three years. It was whilst living in the town
that I discovered Bob and his medals. I organised a dedicated memorial
ceremony at his local church to commemorate the centenary of his death
in June 2015. The service, just like Bob's life, didn't go to plan. None-the-
less here we have a story that will touch your heart and ensure that Bob's
sacrifice will never be forgotten.

**Charles pays his respects holding the medals of Robert Bamber at the war memorial
in Blackpool on which he is named. This picture was taken on the centenary of
Robert's death in 2015.**

It all started for Bob in the summer of 1888 when he was born in the upstairs front bedroom of the family home at number 28 Hawes Side Lane, South Shore. At that time Blackpool was a rapidly expanding pleasure resort. Two of the existing three piers, the north and central were open for business at that time. The third pier Victoria (south) opened amidst a fanfare when Bob was just four-years old. Blackpool Tower was yet to arrive, Bob was a mere infant when construction started on the famous landmark in 1891 to be completed three years later.

The southern side of Blackpool was relatively free of tourism, a fun park that later went on to become the 'Pleasure Beach' originally opened in 1896. A fantastic electric tramway that connected Blackpool to Fleetwood began operating in 1885 and like everything else expanded southwards as the years went by. Bob's father Eddie helped to build the tramway employed as a labourer by Blackpool Corporation. It was an exciting time for the family, their home town was expanding into the country's leading tourist centre. For the 'Sandgrownuns' – natives of Blackpool itself - as the all Bamber's were, the influx of many people with different accents would have been regarded as somewhat exotic.

Life was tough for the family, very tough. Bob was one of eleven children. Two of his siblings had died as youngsters, the remaining nine along with their parents all lived together. Indeed the rapid expansion of the family meant they had to move house, not too far as it happened to a larger dwelling across the street. The entire family moved just a few hundred yards to number 55 Hawes Side Lane. All eleven of them had the 'luxury' of living in a three bed-roomed house as opposed to the tiny two-up two-down they had vacated.

Five of Robert's siblings, his elder brother and four of his sisters, worked in domestic service within Blackpool. Their pittance wages all ensured the family could survive. The Bamber's must have been incredibly close with all of them living under one roof. Bob himself followed in his father's footsteps and gained regular full-time employment with the local authority. He started out as a labourer and then progressed to an engine driver earning him a few extra shillings a week. His job meant that he worked and mixed very frequently with 'navvies', these were men who had crossed the sea from Ireland. The Irishmen worked as construction labourers on the Blackpool tramways and expanding road and rail networks leading to the popular resort. This very fact alone had a huge bearing upon Bob's later military service.

Bob was a strong and fit man, slightly above average height for the day standing at just under 5'8" tall. His workmates from the Emerald Isle were also sturdy, physical men primarily due to the very nature of their hard work. After finishing a week's work in the early December days of 1914, Bob having probably discussed the possibility of joining up with his Irish pals decided to enlist. On Monday December 7th 1914, he signed on in Blackpool and handed in his notice to his employer alongside some of the lads he worked with. Bob Bamber enlisted as number 3462 into a territorial battalion and a famous one at that. He joined the 8th (Irish Reserve) Battalion of the Kings Liverpool Regiment. There is no doubt in my mind that he wanted to serve with his Irish pals with whom he worked, joked, drank and eventually died with.

The Territorial Force was the forerunner of the Territorial Army (1920) and was established in 1908. Thousands of men enlisted pre-war with many more doing so after war had been declared. The very word 'territorial' meant these army reservists were principally responsible for defending the homeland of the United Kingdom. When war broke out the newly enlisted men signed an agreement to fight overseas if necessary. After the regular army had suffered huge losses in 1914 and 1915, it was the territorial, dominion and colonial soldiers who came to the fore of operations. Later the men of the volunteer battalions joined them to make up the numbers of fighting men on the Western Front.

Bob, was of course a territorial, albeit like so many more a totally inexperienced one. Nevertheless, these men were rushed to the front as in accordance with the terms they had signed. In my opinion on many occasions their deployment wasn't truly considered due to the mixture of experienced reservists, who became non-commissioned officers and raw recruits. The NCO's had to take too much pressure that created a worrying unbalance.

By February of 1915, Bob was with the Liverpool Irish completing his training at Sevenoaks in Kent. He was well aware that he would be posted to the front and this duly happened. The 8th Liverpool Irish arrived as a complete unit in Boulogne on the northern coast of France on Monday May 3rd 1915. Just over six weeks later, Bob's war was over as he disappeared forever.

Bob's short time serving his country was by and large exciting and filled with banter. He first saw action at Festubert, sixty miles to the south of Boulogne. The Scouse and Irish lads were well known for their sense of humour and wayward antics. A great deal of camaraderie would have prevailed. Bob's journey to the front was via St. Omer with its taverns full of beer from local brewers and then on to Bethune, a town famous for its brothel. British soldiers would que up in their hundreds to be serviced by just three local prostitutes. The price of pleasure amounted to over a week's pay for an infantry private, it was a price many paid. A fair few of the lads also paid a very painful higher price as sexually transmitted diseases always caused problems throughout the war.

Only a fortnight after landing in France, Bob was involved in heavy fighting. He survived unscathed from Festubert, many others didn't. This was a notoriously controversial time of the war. British artillery shells were so ineffective they may as well have been firing donuts at the Germans. The scandal eventually broke but it was too late for many. Without adequate artillery bombardment, especially before an assault, the advancing infantry obviously met stiffer opposition and as a result suffered far heavier casualties. The huge problem of the lack of efficient firepower was very prevalent at Aubers Ridge on May 9th 1915, with the 'Donkeys' in charge choosing not to acknowledge the fact. There is an argument they were unaware of the problem. I don't go with that at all, neither does Rob.

Having tasted his first time in action a period of rest followed for Bob. It wasn't too long before the Liverpool Irish would be called upon again to take part in an offensive around the nearby town of Givenchy. Bob was in the thick of it, at that time of the war the army had yet to be equipped with steel Brodie helmets and wore caps. Despite the losses of the original regulars of the British Expeditionary Force, protection wasn't top of the agenda. Listening to the French certainly was as they demanded more frontline British participation.

During this period the British were very much the junior partners alongside their French allies in the mighty struggle against very well organised German forces. The French dominated in numbers and in influence and pressured the British to go upon the offensive. Certain British commanders, notably Douglas Haig let their own objectives override common sense. This trait was shared by many Generals throughout the whole of the war and is one that I am very quick to acknowledge and pounce upon.

Bob Bamber took part in particularly heavy fighting advancing with the Liverpool Irish across the northern slopes around Givenchy. This action took place on the particularly humid and sticky day of June 15th 1915. The overall offensive included the participation of their comrades from the 51st Highland Division, alongside a large force of Canadian and Indian soldiers. Rob believes rivalry was deliberately encouraged between the differing units. If that were the case it backfired, for confusion and chaos reigned. The terrain was also far from ideal and once again the artillery put on a pathetic show, as they fired ineffective and often 'dud' shells at the most powerful German position on the line.

Bob and his comrades advanced through long wet grass that had grown wildly out of control after the rains of the late spring time. We can only imagine how difficult it was for this inexperienced soldier wading through the foliage in full battle kit. The territorial non-commissioned officers, those with pre-war reserve experience, led Bob and his chums into battle. Rob tells me they would have treated their men with great consideration, given their experience and the lack of such with the newly recruited boys. Bob would have followed them to the end of the earth, as it so proved.

The strong and fit lad from Blackpool was in his prime. At 27-years old he had everything to live for. Of course he would have sensed fear and desperation, indeed he went through the whole of the first day of the two-day battle. A formidable German force was waiting for the 'hotched-potched' mix of advancing Canadian, Scots, Irish, Indian and English troops. We cannot and must never doubt the bravery of these rookie soldiers who due to reckless command often found themselves advancing in differing directions. With great courage they took the objective, some say they were allowed to take it, only for the canny Germans to counter-attack and drive them back forth to where they had come from.

Bob was caught straight in the focus of the counter-attack. Nobody saw him go down or witnessed his demise in the tangled long grasses. The date was Wednesday June 16th 1915, the men who made it back were roll-called. Bob wasn't amongst those upon the list and subsequently was officially reported as 'missing'. After some consideration on more than one occasion it was finally accepted that Bob had been killed on that day. This acceptance for official purposes was finally delivered less than two weeks later. To this day Bob has no grave, he is still 'missing'.

The family back home in Blackpool were devastated by the news, they had not received any letters from Bob for some time. Their great concerns were finally put to rest by a telegram that was personally delivered to the porch of 55 Hawes Side Lane, Blackpool, in July of 1915. Outside the sun was shining as the sea gently lapped the beaches. People strode along the piers in their straw boaters and fancy hats. Blackpool Tower dominated a skyline and the promenade was bustling with tourists on a fine summers' day. Bob would never again see those sights or experience the sounds and hustles and bustles of his hometown, they had been lost to him forever in an overgrown, damp and sticky field, somewhere in France.

As the centenary of Bob's death approached I visited a local church in Blackpool. Outside stands a small monument bearing the names of the parish lads who were killed during the Great War. Bob's name is on the stone dedication in addition to being listed upon the Le Touret Memorial in France. I spoke to the vicar who was very agreeable with regard to holding a service to commemorate Bob on the 100th anniversary of his death. No surviving family members could be traced so it was understood the service would be held for the local community to attend.

I also liaised with the local press who were very accommodating. A reporter provided a very nice and respectful article in the newspaper that goes all around Blackpool and the Fylde coast, a photograph of me holding Bob's medals accompanied the article. Everything was in print and on show over a week before the service was actually held. Having arranged similar events on several occasions and with the publicity behind it, I was confident that a reasonable amount of people would attend this special service of dedication. I was also informed the article had been well read online.

Two Standard Bearers from a Veterans Association attended the service alongside their organisation's leader and another group member. A bugler, himself a former serviceman was also in attendance. Of course I was there and was joined by just one local member of the public. Henceforth, including the vicar only eight people in total were actually within the almost completely empty church. Just like the others around me I felt a huge sense of disappointment for Bob, thankfully, the entire service went ahead with two speeches to follow.

Finally, when the last post echoed around the deserted church I held tightly on to Bob's medals. As the tune played I thought about his life and times and how much he had been quite literally forgotten, it was such a shame. There has to be a very special mention made here for the bugler who travelled from Northampton to perform the last post. This man commuted a distance of 350-miles to and from Blackpool and endured a four-hour journey each way by road. Bobby Crick was the man, what a great effort he made for his petrol money only. Blackpool, for everything it has to offer, couldn't provide a bugler or indeed an audience for Bob Bamber.

This is not the end of Bob's story. Determined to see a positive outcome regarding his legacy, Rob visited the seaside resort in the summer of 2017 where Bob Bamber is named on a third memorial. The magnificent Blackpool War Memorial in the shape of a giant finger stands proudly by the north pier. Rob took along Bob's medals and made a private pilgrimage on a warm and balmy evening. Whilst there he came across a homeless veteran who had been living rough on the streets of the seaside town. Rob shared Bob's story with the former soldier who was down on his luck. With great enthusiasm the man was delighted and encouraged by Bob's undying legacy. He left with enough money from Rob to get his supper.

Next time you visit Blackpool spare just a thought for Bob Bamber. When you ride a tram or a roller-coaster, drink a cold beer or stroll along the pier, think of him. For a fleeting moment of your time give this young man who has been lost forever just a few seconds of consideration. Bob is not and never will be forgotten.

Alfred Turner
Died
English Channel, January 1st 1915
Aged 20.

AT the very beginning of this chapter I made a reference to the war being over by Christmas 1914. To many people the war would be over so soon. Alfie Turner, a young man from the outer fringes of west London may have shared that view. He was amongst the crew of 'HMS Formidable' that escorted many of the troop ships across the English Channel shortly after war had been declared in August. He witnessed a Britannic show of strength that everyone hoped would bring a swift end to the war.

Alfred James Turner lived and grew up in the tiny hamlet of Charlton not to be confused with the south London suburb of the same name some miles away. His village lay very close to Shepperton, now world famous for its huge film studios and neighbouring Sunbury, where he was actually born. Both of his parents Alfred James senior and Alice were also from the local area. His father worked as a general labourer probably on the nearby canal network and his mother prior to their marriage had been a domestic servant.

According to official Royal Marine Light Infantry records Alfie was born on September 2nd 1893, well that is what he told them when he enlisted. Like many others of his generation he had lied about his age when signing upon the dotted line. Had that date been correct then he would have been born out of wedlock. His parents actually married at the church of St. Mary in Sunbury on October 14th 1893. Just like many of their contemporaries who lived in the later Victorian era his mum and dad were not as pure as the driven snow. Alice was three months pregnant when she walked down the aisle. Young Alfie, according to records of the time that included church transcripts, was born in April 1894, he was baptised at the same church a month later.

Today, Shepperton and Sunbury are pretty exclusive suburbs in which to reside. Both areas are well sought after for a high standard of residential living by those who can afford it. Before the Great War despite being just fifteen miles from central London, Shepperton was surrounded by rural farmland. Alfie grew up in a large family and became the oldest of eight children, together with an elderly grandmother they all squeezed under one roof into a tiny cottage within the hamlet.

The pace of life was pretty slow, although Alfie's father had to work very hard to feed such a large brood. Upon leaving school young Alfie found work as a farm labourer whilst his younger brother Fred, just a year his junior, became a gardener. Three incomes then came into the little house at 40 Holly Cottages, Charlton. The sedate and rather monotonous routines of life weren't enough for Alfie, he needed excitement with adventure and didn't have to wait long to taste both.

On Thursday January 4th 1912, Alfie aged just 17 enlisted into the Chatham Brigade of the Royal Marine Light Infantry. He could enjoy the best of both worlds. Effectively he became an infantryman similar to an army soldier, with the added bonus of the potential of sailing the seven seas. Tradition is important and that would have been very much impressed upon him from the start of his service. The Royal Marines were officially formed in 1775 being able to trace their roots back as far as 1664, they were exceptionally proud of their fighting history, just as they are today. In times gone by the Royal Marine Light Infantry was effectively one of two large sections, the other being the Royal Marine Artillery. The infantry men were known as the 'Red Marines' and the artillery men as the 'Blue Marines'. Blues and Reds reformed as one in 1923 to establish the Royal Marines as we know them today. Alfie was obviously a 'Red'.

His training was rigorous and tough, he put on weight and developed a great body strength. One of Alfie's main duties was to act as part of a ship's security force, a sort of maritime policeman. A ship's crew could consist of anything from a couple of hundred men to over a thousand depending upon the size of the vessel. Alfie would have also been trained for armed combat. As it came to transpire thousands of Royal Marines would go on to fight as part of the British forces in the trenches of France and Belgium, they were feared for their courage, strength and tenacity.

Upon the outbreak of war Alfie was a seasoned professional and posted to serve upon one of the Channel Fleet's larger vessels, 'HMS Formidable'. By 1914 although far from being obsolete, it was over-shadowed by the larger 'Dreadnought' class. Still the 'Formidable' was very well armed and armoured and presented a huge threat to any potential enemy invaders or hostile craft in the English Channel. The ship had a total crew complement of 780 and weighed in at over 15,000 tons. Alfie and his warship were based at Portland, Dorset, on the south coast of England.

The young man enjoyed his many routine crossings over the English Channel as his ship escorted the troop carriers brimming with soldiers across the open sea. Alfie felt safe and secure on such a huge floating war machine. He would have witnessed the combined might of the Royal Navy and the British Army as they made their way to France. On August 25th banter and rivalries were exchanged aboard the 'Formidable' as it transported the Portsmouth Marine Battalion to Ostend, these men were off to secure the Belgian port and surrounding areas. No doubt Alfie, one the 'Chatham Marines' would have relished and enjoyed 'policing' men of the rival 'Portsmouth Marines'.

Many of us are well aware of the threat of invasion that Nazi Germany caused to Britain back in 1940. This happens to be a slice of history that has been very well documented and portrayed. What is less well known is that Britain took very seriously a threat of invasion from Imperial Germany in 1914. Politicians and military leaders considered and feared a potential occupation by the enemy as a genuine possibility.

With that in mind 'HMS Formidable' was duly transferred to Sheerness along with other large vessels to protect the homeland against any possible invasion threat. Alfie would have been aware of that and put on full readiness for action. It transpired, as it did later in 1940 that no such invasion took place. As Christmas 1914 came and passed it became clear the war would not be over so soon. Britain was safe and well patrolled by the mighty Royal Navy.

The crew of the 'Formidable' probably got a short spell of Christmas home leave from Sheerness. Those of whom had family around the southern region of England expected a break from operations. I suspect Alfie did get his leave and if so returned to the little cottage one final time to spend Christmas with his family. He reassured them all he was safe and well protected aboard his great ship, he wasn't too far wrong. Actual naval fatalities during the war amounted to around 5% of those who served in all of the forces. The safest and most survivable service to be a part of during the First World War was the Royal Navy.

It was back to routines as the 'Formidable' was incorporated into the 5th Battle Group Fleet redeployed to Portland in order to extend its range across the English Channel from all approaches. A new commander had taken over the whole of the Channel defence fleets. His name, Vice-Admiral Sir Lewis Bayly, a 57-year old career sailor with over forty years of experience. Young Alfie would have known very little about him or the decision he would take that some would agree cost the young Royal Marine his life.

On board the 'Formidable' life wasn't too bad. Rations were pretty good and the threat of invasion was over. The ship was designated to venture out into the open sea back to Portland. Before returning to port she was ordered to engage upon gunnery exercise with the rest of the 5th Battle Group Fleet to the south of Lyme Bay. This particular area is around twenty-five miles from what was their Portland base.

Alfie would have been far more familiar with the ship's Captain than the Rear-Admiral. The 'Formidable' was skippered by 40-year Arthur Noel Loxley. This man was a highly respected naval officer and was accompanied almost everywhere by his fox-terrier, Bruce, who also acted as the ship's mascot. Alfie like most of the crew would have found Bruce's antics amusing. It was a nice human touch from Loxley to allow the little dog to roam the ship with him. In a small way it boosted the morale of the men under his command.

The Battle Group Fleet that consisted of nine large vessels left Sheerness on Wednesday December 30th 1914. Alfie knew that any celebrations for a new year would have to be put upon hold due to their forthcoming manoeuvres. Crucially, they were escorted by no fewer than six Destroyers and two Light Cruisers as they headed for the straights of Dover. No German maritime force would dare attack such a flotilla. Safety was well within their own hands and the responsibility of the senior naval officers in charge.

Weather conditions were worsening, a wind had started to pick up and visibility became restricted. A decision was then made that would change the course of British naval history. As the impregnable and awesome group passed Dover the main escort of six Destroyers was instructed to retire to nearby Folkestone. In effect the Battle Group Fleet was releasing its protection, compromised only by the two Light Cruisers. It was considered that no threat was apparent due to the deteriorating weather conditions.

A decision was also made to allow the group to steam ahead towards the Devon coast and carry out their operational duties as planned.

The English Channel is not very deep but it proved an easy place to hide for a deadly U-Boat. In the middle of this busy shipping lane the U-24 German submarine lurked menacingly like a shark hunting for prey and it was heading in the direction of Portland. Even though there had been reports of enemy submarine activity, Vice-Admiral Bayly considered potential attack by a U-Boat impossible, given the conditions. After all not a single British warship had ever before been sunk by one of these stealthy craft. The weakened Battle Group Fleet being virtually unescorted, sailed on.

Alfie awoke on the final day of 1914 to a clouded vision of the Isle of Wight in the distance to the north. It was cold and blustery as the waves slightly rocked the ship. He was glad to get back down below and was looking forward to the forthcoming gunnery practice. Nearby, in the morning mist and cloud Rudolf Schneider commanding the U-24 had spotted the enormous Battleships in the distance behind him. He knew their course would be in the direction of Portland. Rudi was a wily and skilful U-Boat commander. He became one of Germany's best and received both the Iron Cross awards, first and second class. The 32-year old fox of the deep knew he had to get to Portland first as the larger ships were faster with the potential to catch and ram him. He also knew that he could bag the greatest prize to date for a U-Boat of the Imperial German Navy.

Alfie was thrilled at the sight of his ship letting off her guns to ring in the New Year. The Battle Group Fleet placed itself in the southern section of Lyme Bay. This was far enough away from the towns of Devon and Dorset but close enough to get back into Portland if necessary. The ships had been ordered on a night patrol lacking sufficient escort support. Maybe Vice-Admiral Bayly was keeping them 'on their toes' after all according to him there was no threat. Schneider and his crew of thirty-four working in split shifts had stalked the British Battleships throughout the day and into the night. By now Rudi had gained enough confidence given the lack of escort attached to his prey to sneak-up upon them.

The exhausted U-Boat crew armed with six torpedoes waited patiently for Rudi's instructions. It was pitch-dark when Schneider opened fire upon 'HMS Queen', his torpedo missed but wasn't spotted by the ship's crew. Undeterred the U-24 pressed on and like a collie dog rounding up a sheep they closed in upon the ship holding up the rear of the group, the mighty, 'HMS Formidable'.

Rudolf Schneider the commander of U-24, the German U-Boat that sank HMS Formidable. Alfie Turner was one of 547 souls who went down with the ship'.

Alfie would probably have been awoken sharply when the first torpedo struck at 02.20am as it damaged and flooded the engine room. All aboard the 'Formidable' immediately became aware of a serious problem, maybe they had hit a mine? Could one of the boilers have exploded? Alfie and the whole of the ship's crew were immediately ordered to do whatever they could to alert the rest of the fleet. All hands had to assist in any measures to rectify the ship as it slightly started to list. Captain Loxley on the Bridge with Bruce knew that he had to make for Portland, some twenty or so miles away. With his ship damaged in the engine room it would be a struggle, it was all hands on deck as no order was given to abandon ship at that time. Rob informs me that Loxley would have done his upmost to save his ship and by keeping the crew on board in that process he was also considering their safety.

The Royal Marines were highly disciplined, Alfie wouldn't have panicked and was ordered to prevent others from doing so. With the wind howling and the sea getting rougher, the darkness created a bigger problem as the crew struggled to negotiate their plight.

Rudi Schneider was not satisfied although he knew he had damaged the huge British Battleship. Still he couldn't claim the prize of being the very first U-Boat Captain to sink a Royal Navy war vessel. He became prompted by his skill and determination and that of his crew who were aware they would have to quickly resurface to recharge the U-Boat batteries. Schneider decided to go in for the kill. The lumbering U-boat got across the Port side of the stricken 'Formidable' and fired a second torpedo at 03.05am. This time the missile hit the boiler room, the big ship was by then in grave danger.

The rising seas didn't help. Alfie knew that his chances of survival were slim as the 'Formidable' started to take in huge amounts of water and complete chaos prevailed. Captain Loxley had no alternative but to order the ship to be abandoned. Lifeboat barges were released, one immediately capsized in the freezing rough sea crushing the men inside. She finally went down at 04.45am.

I can't determine exactly how young Alfie met his end. His death was almost certainly caused by drowning or exposure. Over 200 men survived, mainly due to the rescue efforts of one of the remaining two Light Cruiser escorts, 'HMS Topaze'. Aware by then of the U-Boat she couldn't show her lights and the rescue took place in total darkness. Captain Loxley and Bruce remained on the Bridge until the very end. The little fox-terrier's body was later washed-up upon a beach. Alfie was never found, he was one of 547 men and boys who became the first ever British warship victims of a German U-Boat.

Lessons were learned. Vice-Admiral Bayly was criticised for pulling out the principal escort ships. It is highly unlikely Schneider would have attacked had the six faster Destroyers been around. Bayly was cleared and later became responsible for commanding the naval defences from the Western approaches in the Atlantic and Irish Sea. He was later credited for his part in the destruction of many U-Boats during the remainder of the war.

As for Rudi Schneider and the U-24, they had differing fortunes. The submarine survived the war and surrendered in 1918. Rudi was redeployed to take command of the larger U-87, whilst serving with her he met a very similar fate to young Alfie. On October 13th 1917 Schneider had surfaced his U-Boat. As he stood observing upon the conning tower he was washed overboard by a huge wave. Members of his crew retrieved their stricken commander from the sea but it was too late. Schneider had died from exposure or drowning, just like Alfie. His body was committed to the sea just as Alfie's was, albeit in differing circumstances. The U-87 went on to be rammed and sunk off Ireland on Christmas Day 1917. Around 17,000 German men served upon U-boats during the First World War, over 5,000 were killed, almost all of them drowning, a huge ratio. It was a dangerous and very stressful undertaking to serve within the underwater killing machines. Once they were hit there was virtually no chance of escape.

Alfie has become part of a tragic historical statistic. The former farm labourer from a simple ordinary family has been lost forever. His parents and siblings by and large kept themselves to themselves. Alfie's quest for adventure and to escape the monotony of day to day life in the fields came about. He came, he saw, he went, he did not return. God bless him.

Despite first serving in 1914, Alfie was entitled to the 1914-15 Star and not the 1914 Star as he did not actually serve in that year on foreign soil in battle. He was also awarded the British War Medal and Victory Medal, all posthumously. We have just his Victory Medal in our possession and custodianship. It remains to this day and for all time to come a lasting legacy of his sacrifice.

William Slater
Died
North Sea, September 2nd 1914
Aged 18.

Our final story of this chapter is tinged with tragedy. On a positive note we use this opportunity to highlight little known facts with regard to the war. These facts being the bravery, courage and fearless endeavour of ordinary British fishermen. You may be surprised to learn these men contributed a vital role to the war effort and in so many instances paid the ultimate price in doing so.

William John Slater was born in the Blundeston area of Lowestoft, Suffolk early in 1896. He was the second son of Ambrose and Gertrude nee. Miller. His father was a fisherman and also a Skipper in charge of a fishing vessel. The couple had eight sons in total born between 1894 and 1911. Gertie and Ambrose had married on Boxing Day 1892 with their own parents' permissions as they were both just under the age of majority or official adulthood status. A person had to be twenty-one years old to be recognised as an adult at that time in Britain.

Lowestoft was a bustling and thriving fishing port and represented as it still does today the most easterly dwelling settlement within the UK. The town could trace its origins to fishing right back to the middle ages. As Billy Slater entered his teens Lowestoft was booming with a well-constructed harbour and adjoining railway network. The huge catches of herring could therefore be distributed across the country. Herring a low cost fish was smoked to make kippers, a favourite of the working classes. My granny who was born before the First World War would often treat me to kippers. Nowadays, with so many global foods available off the shelf and via takeaways, the good old kipper has faded away into an almost remote culinary wilderness.

The young lad followed in his father's footsteps and upon leaving school he became a fisherman. Despite his youth he was readily accepted. A couple of his brothers also joined the herring hunters, other siblings weren't so fortunate. Billy had two brothers called Simon. The first one was born in 1903, tragically he died as a baby. In tribute his parents named their next son born some four years later after the little boy they had lost. Another son, Alec suffered the same fate as the first Simon. Born in 1911, he too was only a baby when he died in 1912.

Life for Billy could be harsh. The Lowestoft fleet would often be out at sea for twelve or so hours at a time or more. Conditions would vary depending upon the weather. The Trawlers and Drifters, so called differently because of their style of nets were tough vessels that had been built to last. Nevertheless, tragedies did occur. Fishermen would literally risk their lives on some occasions to bring back a decent catch. Unlike many other traditional working class industries that paid out earnings weekly the fishermen had to wait to be paid. These rugged men waited for long periods to collect their pay. In the modern world many people moan about being paid monthly.

Edwardian fishermen would be cashed-up at the end of the fishing season, this period varied and depended upon location. Billy like his colleagues would be given a share of the net profits over the season. Herring were perishable, at times not all of their catches were sold for profit. With that in mind it was important to catch as many of the fish as possible. Millions upon millions of herrings were snared in the North Sea, year upon year. The hard-working fishermen of the day couldn't determine how many of the silver fish would actually 'pay out'.

When Billy was out at sea as a teenage fisherman he was totally unaware of an event that would change the course of history for the men and boys of his trade. In 1910, four years before the outbreak of war the Admiralty had decided to form a special Trawler Section. Fishing vessels would be incorporated into the Royal Naval Reserve. Intelligence had warned the powerful men in London that explosive mines could be laid around the coast of Britain to destroy all forms of shipping in the event of a war. Germany certainly had the means and the capabilities to create minefields around the British coastline, especially along the eastern coastal routes.

It was decided that if any such war would be declared then initially around 100 fishing boats would be hired by the Admiralty. Their crews to be recruited into a Royal Naval Reserve Trawler Section. These rugged boats and crews would specialise in minesweeping, destroying and disposing of any threat posed by the mines. This recruitment initiative was well placed as time would tell when war was in fact declared, additionally it was certainly carefully planned.

As war approached Billy and his family were more concerned with their ever increasing workloads. In 1913 the 770-strong vessels of the Lowestoft fishing fleet were responsible for catching countless numbers of herring, in tonnage it was in six figures. The vast majority of the fish by then went for export to countries that included Germany and Russia. Over half of the town's fishing fleet were made up of Scottish boats. The Scots dominated the herring fishing industry. Young Billy would have been very familiar with their distinct accents and no-nonsense customs. For the young fisherman life was going very well. War was to bring about a dramatic and ultimately very abrupt tragic end to Billy's life in a way he would have hardly expected as 1913 drew to a close.

Soon after war was declared the Drifter that Billy worked upon, Lowestoft registered LT1121 'Eyrie', officially became known as Admiralty number 121 'H.M Eyrie'. This fishing boat was allocated the role of a minesweeper, like so many others of its class. The requisition of the boat and transfer to service was as I will explain swift to say the least. Billy was hastily drafted into the Royal Naval Reserve taking the service number of 888DA. He would remain upon the boat as a deck hand. Effectively the small crew of eleven men from Lowestoft became a maritime bomb disposal unit. This became a huge transitional and highly dangerous vocation and a duty to King and country.

There was hardly any time to adjust, the 'Eyrie' was transferred to minesweeping duty on Tuesday September 1st 1914. At dawn the following morning she was hastily ordered to commence duty. Prior to all of this frenetic official activity Billy had been involved in a dramatic rescue operation over a week earlier in the North Sea.

On Saturday August 22nd the fishing boat was still operating as a commercial vessel. Off the coast on the previous day two Danish steamers had come into contact with German mines. The 'SS Maryland' was sunk. The 'Chr Broberg' attempted a rescue but had to wait until the following dawn before making a serious attempt. She too struck a mine that killed the ship's engineer. The 'Eyrie' brought the stricken Danish crew back into Lowestoft. Billy was amongst others, a hero. With the taste of adventure upon his lips, a daring escapade completed, what more was to come for the young fisherman?

Just three days later two German mine-laying ships and their escorts entered the North Sea. One of those vessels the 'Nautilus' headed for the Humber with a cargo of 200 contact mines. She proceeded to disperse the mines in rough seas along a course from Flamborough Head to Outer-Dowling thirty or so miles off the Norfolk coast. Commencing at 23.00hrs the 'Nautilus' was unmolested and set back on a course for home at 01.50hrs on Wednesday August 26th 1914, her mission successfully completed.

Now Rob and I bring forward our individual opinions with regard to Billy's tragic final days. Always seeking to point the finger I am a little reluctant to do so here. There is no real evidence of blame as to how he actually met his end. However, I will state the timing of the requisition and subsequent first operational mission were incredibly close. The 'Eyrie' was skippered by a probationary Captain, a 48-year old Lowestoft man, Thomas Scarll. He too was a fisherman drafted swiftly into the Royal Naval Reserve. Perhaps given the time scales a more experienced man should have been placed in the role, but Scarll knew the crew.

Rob is of the opinion the men simply had to go as soon as possible to acclimatise to their new role. Mines were a serious threat to all shipping, they had to be cleared. No fishing season would be afore them in any case. So, hypothetically Rob had he been in the position to send them he would have done so. I would have held back and concentrated more upon theoretical tactics in the first instance. All of this conjectural opinion beggars the real question as to what actually happened to Billy?

As the sun rose on Wednesday September 2nd 1914, the Drifter 'Eyrie' accompanied by two Trawlers were already at sea. A course had been set northwards to embark upon their minesweeping mission, their destination, the Humber. The fishing boats were escorted by the gun and torpedo boat 'Speedy' to protect them against hostile enemy craft. For Billy this would have represented sheer excitement and a voyage into familiar territory along with a sense of fear of the unknown.

The small flotilla had made good speed and entered the Outer-Dowling Shoal off the Norfolk coast close to Cromer shortly after nine in the morning. The group still had a long way to go. This particular area represented the extreme southerly mine dispersal point from the 'Nautilus' just a few days earlier. Rob and I now seek to combine the facts of what actually did happen together with opinions as to why. The 18-year old Billy Slater and his comrades aboard the 'Eyrie' where certainly in the wrong place at the wrong time.

We have discovered the fishing boat was actually snagged by a contact mine. This event suggests to us the explosive device was actually caught upon retrieving wires and pulled towards the hull of the ship. We are not sure whether Billy and the other crew members would have noticed such a sinister situation. If the men had been aware of the mine perhaps they frantically tried to take evasive action. Minesweeping was generally done with wires spread across an area between two vessels. Rob offers a possible theory which I think stands up pretty well regarding the circumstances surrounding the ultimate destruction of the 'Eyrie'.

Perhaps two of the flotilla were out in front extending their wires to sweep with the 'Eyrie' being one of those? She was making her first real operational attempt under the supervision of the group commander. The gun boat could move in to destroy any mines brought to the surface. Rob also suggests that 'Eyrie' may have been attempting to retrieve the mine in order for it to be examined by the authorities. I find that suggestion a rather unlikely scenario. If there is any truth in it then I can only say that such an inexperienced crew should never have been placed into such a situation.

At 09.20am disaster struck, it was the end for Billy and five of his colleagues, including the Skipper, Thomas Scarll. The mine detonated and virtually blew the 'Eyrie' in half, she went down in less than three minutes with all of the crew tossed into the sea. Frantically and bravely despite the obvious threat of other mines in the immediate vicinity, 'Speedy' and the two Trawlers moved in close to attempt a rescue. Incredibly five men were pulled out of the water. Billy couldn't be located and tragically he drowned. Could he have seen his potential rescuers as he struggled amongst the waves? We will never know.

Back in Lowestoft the news arrived back. Billy's father Ambrose was completely devastated. He too was a Skipper and would himself be eventually recruited in that role to command his fishing boat for minesweeping duties. Ambrose Slater survived the war racked with guilt that he wasn't able to save his son, he became a broken man. Less than four years after the end of the war he died in Lowestoft aged just 50. Billy's mother passed away in 1936 at the age of 63. Both parents therefore were not around to experience another ironic and cruel twist of fate that happened during the Second World War.

On July 9th 1942 off the coast of Harwich the HM Boom Defence Vessel 'Tunisian' hit a mine and sank very quickly. Amongst the crew who drowned that day was Billy's younger brother Percy, he was 42-years old at the time of his death.

The Slater family having suffered the loss of two of their eight boys in infancy also infamously lost another two boys to the sea in both world wars. Of the four remaining brothers, three of them spent some parts of their lives as seafarers. Somewhere, maybe in Suffolk their descendants may remain. We have the 1914-15 Star, British War Medal and Victory Medal awarded posthumously to Billy, they stand proud and neat in their own case. Alongside the trio is the 1914-15 Star awarded to his father Ambrose. A vintage folding double photograph display frame accompanies the medals. On one side you can see an old and faded photo of Billy sat between two ladies. On the other you see Ambrose, cap on head, pipe in mouth, rowing a boat. Pictures of happy times that were eventually cruelly and unexpectedly extinguished by war.

The Drifter, Eyrie, this fishing boat was destroyed by a German mine, Billy Slater is one of the boys pictured on the starboard side.

THEY CAME FROM AFAR

THE First World War was fought across a number of operational theatres in different parts of the world. By far the largest of these blood soaked arenas was the Western Front, stretching across north-eastern France and Belgium. Other notable and heavy engagements took place in the Middle East, particularly in Mesopotamia, now territory of modern day Iraq. Egypt, Palestine, Gallipoli, East Africa, Italy and Greece also provided war zones that produced immense human suffering on a scale as never seen before.

In 1914 Great Britain with her mighty Empire and Dominions still rated as a global super-power. Britain had the world's largest navy fully equipped to patrol its territories across the seven seas. The dramatic rise of Germany a country federated by a number of small states just over forty years previously was profound. Old empires who became our enemies such as the Austro-Hungarian and Ottoman dynasties were also hugely powerful in manpower resources. France exercised huge colonial power with the capability to mobilise citizens from its territories very swiftly. Russia with its expansive might was yet to see its great revolution. Developing rapidly across the Atlantic the mighty United States was upon the threshold of what was to become a world dominance in more ways than one.

The British soon realised after declaring war on Germany the struggle for supremacy would be huge. With an army in 1914 consisting of under 733,000 men across the globe, mobilisation would be difficult. Only a relatively small percentage could be hurried and readied to cross the Channel to assist the Belgians and the French whose lands had been unceremoniously invaded by the Germans. Vastly outnumbered, the British recruited heavily and quickly. Over the whole course of the war an astonishing 8.7-million men saw some kind of service to the King and the Motherland, the majority being from the British Isles. From England over four million were recruited, Scotland provided over half a million, a further quarter of million more came from Wales and 134,000 from Ireland.

Almost 2.5-million men came from afar, from the Empire and Dominions. A staggering 1.5-million of these servicemen, all of whom were volunteers came from the Indian sub-continent. Another million set sail from Canada, Australia, New Zealand, Tasmania, South Africa, Newfoundland and the West Indies. The incredibly admirable and moving loyalty of all of these men was often paid for in blood. Their sacrifices ensured a victory that otherwise may not have been achieved. We can never underestimate their bravery and devotion, these men will always stand equal in death to anyone – as they should have done so in life. This chapter is dedicated to them all. Five men represent them, with an amazing diversity of backgrounds that makes their stories very special indeed.

Many of the men who served travelled across the world and had previously emigrated from the British Isles, they had made successes of their lives, opened businesses and started families. Their prosperity thousands of miles from Britain was truly deserved and well earned. These ex-pats didn't have to put their lives on the line for the Empire, they chose to fight for our cause.

Almost thirty years after the end of the Great War, India became an independent nation. Partition created East and West Pakistan, with Bangladesh coming later from East Pakistan. Ceylon became Sri Lanka. The divisions came largely about because of religious differences, it was and still is a huge cause of controversy to this day. Back in 1914, India was one, Hindu, Sikh and Muslim all came together as volunteers to fight far from their homes for the British Empire.

Many a 'Donkey' General and other senior officers considered the men who came to fight for a common cause as 'Damned Colonials'. Their contempt was often taken very lightly sometimes with defiance and humour particularly by the Australians. The attitudes of the so-called colonials would sometimes infuriate the cigar puffing, port swilling, red-tabbed British General Staff Officers. Their opinions changed after the Aussies altered the whole course of the war in 1918 with their heroic and almost fanatical bravery at Amiens. We start this chapter with another example of fearsome and amazing courage as we highlight our first man and his brave comrades in arms.

Ajab Khan

Killed in Action
France, Dec. 19th 1914
Age Unknown.

BANNI is a village close to Mianwali in the north-western Punjab region that is nowadays a part of Pakistan. It was once home to a young man who came from a simple and non-complicated background. This man's story is incredible. He was totally unremarkable in many ways yet his legacy opens up a tale of glory, honour, loyalty and once again utter stupidity on the part of a 'Donkey General'.

We have in our possession the single Victory Medal awarded to Ajab Khan. The whereabouts of his other two medals, the 1914 Star and British War Medal are unknown. This single medal is all that remains of the life and times of Ajab. Personal histories from that part of the world are notoriously hard to research. With Ajab we have a fascinating story.

According to some sources many names have meanings. Ajab with its Arabic and Muslim origins is said to relate to a person who is jovial and loves to talk. Creativity and the ability to try out many new things with ambition are other attributes attached to the name. Maybe we can paint a minds-eye picture here of Ajab Khan.

Ajab lived near the river Indus, he explored lands of open desert close to his home and watched camels transport goods across the sandy plains. His family worked on parts of the fertile land dotted around the village. Life was all about being self-sufficient. The British Indian Army recruited many young men from the Punjab. Ambitious and forward thinking Ajab joined up for excitement and the opportunity to travel. He enlisted into the 59th Scinde Rifles (Frontier Force) as an ordinary infantryman with the rank of Sepoy, the British equivalent of a Private.

The Scinde Rifles by 1914 were made up of eight companies, not too far short of 2,000 men, they were a mixture of Pathans, Punjabi Muslims, Sikhs and Dogras. As part of the Jullundur Brigade they were integrated with the garrisoned 1st Battalion of the Manchester Regiment. Regular British soldiers from Lancashire and also the 47th Sikhs. So, the force itself was very multi-cultural with Muslims, Sikhs, Hindus and Christians all being a part of the same brigade. These men fought and died together on the Western Front in 1914 and later in other theatres of war.

After war was declared Ajab and the rest of the Jullundur Brigade were required to embark for the Western Front in Europe. The brigade became an integral part of the 3rd (Lahore) Division. Ajab was amongst the very first soldiers from the Indian sub-continent to arrive in Europe during the war. A long journey began with an arduous sea voyage for Ajab. He left his homeland for the very last time on Saturday August 29th 1914. It would take almost a full calendar month to arrive in France.

The weather was pleasant and probably not too different from that of the Punjab, Ajab disembarked at Marseille in the south of France exactly four weeks later on Saturday September 26th 1914. Local residents came out in force to see the Indian soldiers for the very first time. The general public were kind, friendly, cheerful and polite. The war raging to the north seemed a long way off for Ajab at that particular time.

Uniforms of ordinary Indian soldiers of the time were not particularly suited to harsher climates. This became apparent as the journey north towards the front grew colder, the soldiers were passive and didn't complain, they were obedient to their officers. The men who led them in companies and platoons were a mixture of British and

A soldier of the 59th Scinde Rifles. Ajab Khan served with this famous frontier force before being killed in action serving in France in 1914.

Indians, from different faiths and backgrounds. At that time an Indian had to serve for at least ten years before he could become an officer with the rank of Jemadar, the British equivalent of Lieutenant. The Indian officers themselves could only hold three ranks. Subadar held the same status as a Captain and Subadar-Major that of a Major, no advanced ranks thereafter were made available to them. Ajab and his ordinary comrades were very loyal to their officers be they British or Indian. At this point I have relied upon Rob with his vast experience as a former servicemen himself to give his qualified opinion as to how it worked the other way around.

Rob tells me the British officers at subaltern and field level commanding colonial soldiers were far more loyal and understanding of their men and would always lead by example. He also makes a point of them being much more down to earth and straight-forward. Likewise their Indian counterparts took upon the same attitudes. The successes of the huge British Indian Army were in a large part attributed to the quality of the command where it mattered.

Ajab was placed into a baptism of fire upon his arrival in Belgium with his comrades. The men from the Punjab were hurled into battle at Ypres on October 24th 1914 just one day after their arrival. Together with their Indian comrades they made a huge impression, it only took one week for the first Indian soldier to receive the highest award for valour, the Victoria Cross. Khudadad Khan, a Muslim, was awarded the honour. He was at the time a 26-year old Sepoy from the Chakwal area of the Punjab, now a part of Pakistan serving with the 129th Baluchis. Khudadad, despite being wounded was the last man of his machine-gun section alive to continue engaging the Germans in a fierce and prolonged fire-fight. His statue now stands at the entrance of the Pakistan Army Museum in Rawalpindi. Ajab Khan himself fought in the same vicinity and in the same battle.

Despite the ongoing hardships suffered by Ajab, especially with his lack of equipment as winter set in, he was allowed just like his Muslim comrades time to pray at as many intervals as possible demanded by his faith. This wasn't always practical in times of battle and was accepted by Ajab. He stuck to his tasks as a soldier and was again involved in heavy fighting around Neuve-Chappelle. Back in France his final ordeal would arrive, by that time he had become a seasoned professional soldier.

I can't help thinking to myself what went through Ajab's mind as the dark nights set in against the constant threat of instant death or serious injury. Freezing rain, filth, mud and fog descended as the end of 1914 set in upon the wretched Western Front. He must of experienced thoughts of his family thousands of miles away back home and of his former village life. The smells, noises and sights of oxen, camels, mules and carts. He would have remembered fondly the taste of his mum's cooking. Trips to the well to draw water or a walk across open land without a sound to be heard reminded him of a tranquil life.

Exactly one week before Christmas Day and with no end to the war in sight as some had optimistically predicated only a few months earlier, the men of Ajab's unit lay in wait for orders. Their officers on the ground were concerned and had every right to be so. Having examined war diaries of the period it is clear that criticism was being levelled at the orders that were set upon them. The diary entries could have warranted a breach of discipline and placed the authors into a tricky situation. Reading between the lines it is not too difficult to decipher what would decide Ajab's fate and that of many of his comrades.

Introducing here and now another 'Donkey', Lieutenant-General Henry Watkis of the British Indian Army. This wretched buffoon ordered a hideous assault against complicated and fortified German trench systems around Givenchy. Officers had gone to plead with him to be given time to perform reconnaissance in order to direct their men correctly, they complained the orders handed down by the wine swilling pompous General were - 'contrary to principals and everything taught'.

Their final requests were brushed aside, the night was drawing to a close as they motored to the General's HQ in a final attempt to ask for common sense to prevail. Watkis who had probably slugged down several glasses of vintage claret was undeterred. Like many others of his generation who wielded power his thirst extended beyond fine wines, he wanted to wallow in glory. The men would do as he said, it was as simple as that.

Chaos ensued, the Indians left their billets at Beuvry a few hours later in the pitch darkness drenched by pouring rain. There were no provisions of food or blankets, this was insanity ordered by a maverick 'Donkey' who safely lay snoring in his comfortable bed, billeted in a chateau miles behind the lines. The German trenches at this stage of the war lacked the composition of those that were well constructed some time later. A dreadful situation was compounded by consistent freezing rain that had further damaged the terrain. As a result the attackers who included other units from the Highland Light Infantry and the Gurkhas slipped and fell into pools of mud. In the darkness and crowded trenches confusion reigned. Poor visibility and heightened tension led to men bayoneting their own comrades by mistake

The Scinde Rifles fought with tremendous courage over a prolonged period of time. Ajab Khan was very much in the thick of the fighting and was spurred on by his officers. Although this could be described as a relatively small action of the war it represented in our opinions one of the bravest assaults that any force mounted throughout the entire conflict.

As previously stated the bond between the officers and men of the 59th Scinde Rifles was unbreakable. The Punjabis went on, Sikhs and Muslims alongside their officers, British and Indian. At the end of the day thirty-three Sepoys [Private Soldiers] perished, alongside three Lance-Naiks

[Lance-Corporals], two Naiks [Corporals] and two Havildars [Sergeants]. Six officers also laid down their lives, three British and three Indian.

Lieutenant William Bruce, a 24-year old Scotsman from Edinburgh led his Indian platoon to capture a German trench, the fearless Punjabis held out for hours. Bruce, despite being wounded in the neck refused to leave his men and declined treatment. Wounded again he eventually bled to death. His faithful men would not leave behind the lifeless body of their officer. The Punjabis refused to retreat and stood firm fighting until the last man had fallen, they all died beside him. For this action, William Bruce was awarded the Victoria Cross.

Elsewhere, Captain Harry Lee - Mentioned in Despatches - for his bravery, was butchered when overwhelmed trying to fight his way through a communication trench. Lieutenant John Atkinson a reconnaissance expert who had been denied the opportunity to prepare for the attack also went down fatally wounded.

The most senior ranking officer that day in the field was Subadar-Major [Major] Muhammad Khan awarded the – Indian Distinguished Conduct Medal – for gallantry. He led totally by example. The fearless Major perished alongside his subaltern, Jemadar [Lieutenant] Maghar Singh. Both of these officers, a Muslim and a Sikh, were severely wounded and lay out in the open after they had attempted to storm a German trench lashed by pouring rain. The two brave Indian officers died in agony, they couldn't be rescued. Subadar-Major Khan had over twenty years of military experience, Jemadar Singh well over ten years of similar service. Another highly experienced officer, Jemadar Zaman Ali also a gallant recipient of the Indian Distinguished Conduct Medal fell dying close by. Men of great military distinction and experience were lost. General Watkis meanwhile was sticking pins into maps plotting his next move just like a child playing upon a board game.

All of the forty-six men who died that day, December 19th 1914 of the 59th Scinde Rifles were not recovered from the battlefield. None of them, including Ajab have a final resting place, they are all lost but certainly now not forgotten. I asked a Muslim friend of mine to take Ajab's Victory Medal to his local mosque in Lancashire. The Imam and worshippers were very gracious in saying prayers for Ajab and his comrades who time had totally forgotten.

Ajab and his chums are all commemorated on the Neuve-Chappelle Indian Memorial located not far from where they made their ultimate sacrifice. Their names are dispersed around the monument. This memorial contains the names of over 4,700 Indian Army officers and men who made the ultimate sacrifice and whose bodies were never found.

In a final and lasting tribute to Ajab Khan and his comrades both Rob and I now dedicate a 'Roll of Honour' to the men of the 59th Scinde Rifles who perished that day. We believe this is the first time all of their names have been listed together in documented form.

Roll of Honour

3562	Sepoy	ADAM KHAN.
3445	Sepoy	AJAB KHAN.
4625	Sepoy	ASAL DIN.
	Lieutenant	JOHN ATKINSON.
3169	Lance-Naik	BELA SINGH.
	Lieutenant	WILLIAM BRUCE. *VC. (Victoria Cross)*
3873	Sepoy	BUTA SINGH.
3822	Sepoy	DHERU KHAN.
3841	Sepoy	HARNAM SINGH.
4850	Sepoy	HASAN KHAN.
4473	Sepoy	HAZARA SINGH.
3322	Sepoy	IMAM DIN.
166	Sepoy	JAMAL KHAN.
4801	Sepoy	JAN MUHAMMAD.
3846	Sepoy	JAWALA SINGH.
36425	Sepoy	JUMMA KHAN.
4936	Sepoy	KANAT GUL.
163	Sepoy	KARIM DAD.
3863	Sepoy	KATHA SINGH.
4792	Sepoy	KATOR KHAN.
3443	Sepoy	KESAR SINGH.
3623	Sepoy	KHAN GUL.
3537	Sepoy	KHUDA BAKHSH.

44	Sepoy	LAL KHAN.
4067	Lance-Naik	LAL KHAN.
	Captain	HARRY LEE. *M.I.D.* (*Mentioned in Despatches*)
	Jemadar	MAGHAR SINGH.
42	Sepoy	MAHTAB KHAN.
4285	Sepoy	MAKHAN KHAN.
3510	Sepoy	MARWAT KHAN.
4929	Sepoy	MIR DAD.
3927	Naik	MOTA KHAN.
178	Sepoy	MUHAMMED AKBAR KHAN.
4738	Lance-Naik	MUHAMMED HUSSAIN.
	Subadar-Major	MUHAMMED KHAN. *IDSM.* (*Indian Distinguished Service Medal*)
3621	Sepoy	MURTAZA
381	Naik	NAWAS ALI.
4916	Sepoy	NIAZ ALI.
3350	Havildar	PAIO DIN.
4578	Sepoy	PHULA JAN.
3800	Sepoy	RAHIM DAD.
4839	Sepoy	RUKHMAM DIN.
102	Sepoy	SAWAR KHAN.
3815	Havildar	SHER BAZ.
4948	Sepoy	SHER ZAMAN.
	Jemadar	ZAMAN ALI. *IDSM.* (*Indian Distinguished Service Medal*)

James Golden
Killed in Action
France, April 5th 1918
Aged 25.

THERE are many quaint little villages dotted around northern France. One such place of tranquillity will always hold a special place in my heart. Back in 2016 I had a very special reason to visit. My journey took me off the beaten track to a little Commonwealth War Graves Commission section of graves that are hidden behind the main village communal cemetery. Just fifty-eight grave headstones commemorating fallen soldiers from the Great War are dotted around the rear of a small church. No fewer than forty-nine of the plots are the final resting places of Australian soldiers, the majority of those having served with the Australian Field Artillery.

This fascinating tale of a young man who had achieved so much within his short life is also warmly wrapped within my personal ambition to share with you a story. It has to be said this is a story of maybe what should or could have been.

We begin in the picturesque former hamlet of Hayfield, an area within the town of Glossop standing in the Peak District of Derbyshire in England. It was there on Wednesday July 6th 1892 that a boy named James Neville Golden was born. He became the first of three children born to a successful local chemist, Alfred, who originally hailed from Rye in Sussex and his dressmaker wife and well-known local girl Emily, nee. Statham.

Young Jim's father, Alf, ran a pharmacy right upon the town's main road achieving his lifetime ambition. It hadn't always been easy for the chemist who between his studies served as a footman servant within a large house in London's exclusive Chelsea district. Ambition drove Alf and although still in his twenties he had opened his first shop. The entrepreneurial spirit shown by his father would inspire Jim to become a self-made man himself. Just like his dad he would also achieve a lifetime ambition. Jim had the world at his feet at a time of not having reached the age of twenty-five.

Glossop is less than twenty or so miles from Manchester. As the twentieth century dawned, Alf, Emily and schoolboy Jim moved to larger premises with living accommodation just to the south side of the city. Business was brisk at the pharmacy standing on the main Stockport Road between the highly populated districts of Ardwick and Levenshulme. The popular chemist would remain at the new shop for a further thirty years until his death.

Inevitably the family extended, another son, Cuthbert, was born above the shop on October 21st 1903. A daughter, Celia, followed, born on April 18th 1906. Cuthbert and Celia both survived into their nineties and lived all of their lives' within their local area. The siblings both passed away in Stockport during the same year of 1998, Celia having never married.

Charles beside the grave of James Golden at Frechencourt in France.

Jim showed little desire in joining or later possibly succeeding his father as a chemist in the family business. He had taken an interest in horticulture whilst at school. This surprised his family as they lived in a built-up sub-urbanised area of Manchester. Very little greenery or localised opportunities for building a steady career as a gardener were readily available. For that reason alone Jim decided to pack his bags and head south. His destination was Cheshunt in Middlesex a place where a steady job was on offer for him. He was ambitious and knew what he wanted.

In his later teens Jim worked as a nursery assistant cultivating plants and flowers under the supervision of a horticultural foreman, Frank Martin. Jim's new life meant that he also became a lodger of the widower. Frank was to become his mentor and encouraged him to fulfil his ambitions further. Jim listened and certainly took his advice.

Whilst still just about in his teenage years the plucky 19-year old bought a third-class travel passage ticket from the Australian Steam Shipping Company Ltd. He boarded the vessel 'SS Ajana' at the port of Avonmouth near Bristol on Wednesday June 19th 1912, his destination, the port of Fremantle, Western Australia. His ambition, to seek his fortune and a new life.

In life nothing great ever comes easy for ordinary working-class people. This certainly applied to Jim when he first set foot on Australian soil. He had to find work, the red hot summer was approaching down-under and he needed to earn money. The twenty-year-old had to start somewhere. It was a long journey south from Fremantle to Carbarup Siding north of

Albany. For nearly three years Jim toiled as an agricultural labourer and saved what he could for a deposit to help him achieve a dream.

Thousands of miles away in Europe and in the Dardenelles war was raging. Australian soldiers were tasting their first action at Gallipoli and the casualty rates were soaring. The campaign in faraway Turkey was big news. Some of Jim's former workmates had gone off to fight and had not returned. As the Australian summer of 1915/16 approached Jim had made up his mind about his future. Compelled by patriotism to his home country and a sense of duty to his adoptive one he too decided to join up. By that time he had made his way northwards through Western Australia and settled into a new role in the small city of Swan just a few miles east of Perth. Jim was enjoying his life as an orchardist cultivating fruit in the district of Guildford. The young man had big plans. Yes, of course he wanted to go off and do his duty but he also desired something to return to, something special of his. Jim had his own aspirations. He wanted land and his very own orchards and was determined to get both.

His employer was impressed with his drive and ambition and in the later part of 1915 agreed to sell Jim an incredible forty-three acres of land at a bargain price. The ambitious young entrepreneur would still have to persuade a bank to loan him the majority of the money to complete the purchase. He required over £600 – around £25,000 Sterling at today's value. The ambitious chirpy 'ex-pat' made overtures to the Commonwealth Bank of Australia and was accepted for a mortgage. The loan was agreed despite the bank being aware of his forthcoming service as he set up an account in Maribyrnong near Melbourne. This location was on the other side of the country where he was to undertake his military training. Perhaps the manager of the bank was impressed by Jim's patriotism, drive and ambition. The young man was still just 23-years old with his lifetime in front of him.

On the bright sunny morning of Wednesday December 15th 1915, James Neville Golden went along to the Australian Imperial Force Recruitment station in Perth. Jim was of average height for the period standing at just over 5'6" (1.68m) tall. He was in reasonable shape physically having worked on the land but wasn't particular a well-built man, in fact he was rather thin weighing in at under average. His eyesight was good, hazel eyes, light brown hair, fit for service but perhaps he was considered just a little too small to serve as an infantryman at that time. He was allocated the service number 22513. Jim was deployed to 40 Depot A.I.F Artillery Reinforcements and to the 23rd (Howitzer) Brigade a part of the 3rd Australian Division. The young recruit had no military experience at all and was allocated the rank of Private in the first instance.

Jim would spend his last Christmas in Australia. Hastily he set forward other plans for his expected return from war and with some guile he put everything into place after he had signed up. He knew he would struggle to pay off his mortgage for the orchards he had carefully set-up having to rely on the basic pay of a low ranking artilleryman.

Jovial Jim had no plans to marry and couldn't manage his orchards whilst carrying out his military service. He only had one option as he had signed on for the duration of the war. The ambitious orchardist could afford to pay the interest on the mortgage if the orchards were producing marketable revenue. He decided to allow the former owner a Mr. A.E. Ammetts to claim all further profits from sales if his employees kept the orchard in production. In the event of his death the mortgage couldn't be paid so the land would be seized by the bank. Ammetts had already been paid for the land and would continue to reap the profits – he couldn't lose.

The orchardist was canny, he had obviously considered the fact that he may be killed and in his will he bequeathed all his assets to his father, including the orchards. His dad was himself a man of means. Perhaps Jim thought he would pay the mortgage off if he were to be killed. If he returned safely then the rest of his life was planned around his beloved orchards, his own thriving business to walk straight into.

Over at camp near Melbourne, Jim was allocated driving duties whilst he was completing his training. Once that was over he was given the rank of Gunner, no higher or lower than a basic Private. He would become an integral part of a six-man gun team on a Howitzer. Jim was trained and familiarised with every duty required including quick fire methods. Although not in command of the weapon he would be expected to perform any role upon the gun, especially in the instance of crew casualties.

Jim left Australia for the final time on May 20th 1916 departing from Melbourne. It took almost two months to reach Plymouth on the south coast of England by sea via several stop-over points. After a short period of rest Jim and his comrades were sent to Larkhill. Their gunnery skills would be honed on nearby Salisbury Plain in readiness for their combat duties. Over in France the Australians had distinguished themselves during the Battle of the Somme, suffering 24,000 casualties alone around the village of Pozieres.

The blood-soaked battle of the Somme was over and nothing of any significance had been achieved. Douglas Haig had thrown hundreds of thousands of men into a catastrophic confrontation that had seen so many of them perish. More folly was to come in 1917.

In readiness Jim and the reinforcement Australian Brigade left Southampton on the final day of that infamous year, December 31st 1916. Less than a week later the men were officially attached to their Division in the field. It was a relatively quiet period so acclimatisation to military procedure was good for Jim after his long period of training. Although lacking battle experience he would have been very well prepared for what was to come.

Under pressure from the French and in particular Robert Nivelle, Haig agreed to launch a major British offensive around Arras in France. This campaign will forever go down in history as producing the worst daily casualty figures for the British of all time. Although not as numerous in complete periodic total as those suffered in other battles this daily ratio was horrendous. It also profoundly demonstrated the inept, calamitous and often reckless command of 'Donkey Generals' such as Edmund Allenby. The Australians played a vital part in the later part of the offensive after tens of thousands of lives had been callously lost.

Jim had by that time been absorbed into the 11th Field Artillery Brigade a part of the 4th Australian Division, he was a member of the six field gun equipped 111 (Howitzer) Battery, each gun had a six man team. It was a small military unit, the men were incredibly close and formed a bond similar to that of brothers and totally depended upon each other for their survival. Men of the mobile Howitzer Batteries were under constant threat, from bombardment, air attack and dreaded infantry ambushes. When they were over-run there was little option but to fight to the death.

The orchardist got his first baptism of fire on June 1st 1917 when a stray bullet caused a gun-shot wound to his right arm. He was removed from the battle zone and treated by the 1st New Zealand Field Ambulance. Deemed as sufficiently fit to re-join his unit just over a week later he was back in action around mid-June.

After yet another blood bath at Arras something even worse was being planned by the General Staff aided and abetted by others. Having failed to learn lessons from the Somme or Arras or make any serious dents to the consolidated German defensive Hindenburg Line, Haig was at it again. This time his huge offensive around Ypres got stuck in seas of mud. The attempts to gain higher ground particularly around Passchendaele were murderous. Huge casualty figures saw men butchered, drowned in mud, gassed and mown down like swathes of corn by machine-guns. I would describe the whole offensive as a crime akin to the deliberate creation of a human abattoir.

Jim was indeed there in Belgium at the very beginnings of the Third Battle of Ypres and he paid a high price. His gun section was hit by German gas shells less than a week into the campaign on August 5th 1917. Not only did he suffer from gas poisoning he also received a serious head wound and injuries to his back. He was rushed to the 37th Casualty Clearing Station at Godewaersvelde who transferred him immediately to a Field Hospital. His condition was so serious that he had to be evacuated back to England arriving at the Edmonton Military Hospital on August 9th 1917.

After some excellent respite care Jim recovered sufficiently to be transferred to an Auxiliary Hospital at Dartford some five weeks later. Eventually he was returned to Depot at Weymouth on September 26th to be monitored. Jim had suffered a very nasty experience and almost lost his life, his back injury problem prevailed and he was hospitalised again on November 4th.

During his weeks in hospital and throughout his recovery period he must have longed to return to Australia and his orchards, Rob doesn't agree with me on this point. Despite his ordeal in Rob's opinion Jim would have wanted to re-join his unit fighting on the Western Front. He didn't want to let his 'brothers' of 111 Battery down and Rob maintains he insisted upon being reconciled with his chums. In the end, if this is so, he got his wish and was duly despatched back to his section. After arriving back in France on January 9th 1918 and under the supervision of his Medical Officer he was allowed back to join his gun team a week later.

With Russia by then out of the war the Germans now with huge reinforcements transferred from the Eastern Front became determined to end the war for good. Enormous numbers of American soldiers who had joined the war on the side of the British and French would soon be properly mobilised. On March 21st 1918 the Germans launched a massive offensive, they had to overcome what was left of the British Expeditionary Force. Haig a commander who didn't understand the word 'consolidation' had overseen the slaughter of the majority of his regular, territorial and volunteer soldiers. Yes, some of these men were left to fight another day, although many more of them would be required to die for the cause. Eventually they were reinforced by the British 5th Army made up of large numbers of conscripted men who had previously been turned down for military service.

Haig now pushed in men aged in their forties and early fifties, some with poor eyesight and others with minor physical disabilities. Those who couldn't read or write and men with learning difficulties also went to the front. Despite a lack of experience and other handicaps they fought with tremendous unswerving loyalty and courage under General Gough. At times they succeeded in holding up masses of German Stormtroopers. Eventually and inevitably they were pushed back across the former Somme battlefields westward towards the strategic German objective target of Amiens. The French were also taking a thrashing and falling back.

In one last determined push to take Amiens in early April 1918 the Germans attacked with 93,000 men – waiting for them were the Australians. The battle hardened Aussies knew what was expected of them. Heavily outnumbered in some areas such as Villers-Bretonneux by six-to-one they were more than willing to accept the challenge. With tremendous zeal, bravery, courage and sheer physical effort they halted the German advance and as a consequence changed the final course of the war. Their tremendous efforts inevitably resulted in huge casualties.

Their own commanders decided initially upon methods of consolidation. Having to fight against overwhelming odds they made a series of minor tactical withdrawals before standing firm to smash the German advance. These very tactics Haig never appreciated or approved of until it was far too late for so many.

Jim's role at this turning point of the war was to cost him his life. At dawn on April 5th 1918 the German infantry swarmed like ants upon the Australians holding positions to the east of Amiens. Jim and his Howitzer crew covered the strategic withdrawal of the Australian infantry back to the railhead close to Frechencourt. Firing rapidly at four rounds per minute the gunners knew they could be over-run at any time. Under the supervision of Captain Archibald Martin, 111 Battery too was ordered to withdraw its guns covered by one of the remaining Howitzers to protect the retreat.

Jim Golden alongside his gun crew mates manned the last gun and covered the final withdrawal without question. Captain Martin remained with his men as inevitably they became surrounded by hundreds of attacking German Stormtroopers. There was no mercy given to the Aussies, the Germans were not taking prisoners in their push to take Amiens.

The end when it came was brutal. Captain Martin and the small team including Jim found themselves very quickly overwhelmed. Some mercifully received bullets, death was probably swift - others would have taken the bayonet as the attackers preserved their ammunition.

A couple of days later the Germans began to fall back, the gun crew lying dead next to their Howitzer were recovered by advancing Australian infantry soldiers. Jim and his comrades who had all died together as brothers in arms were taken by motor transport to a nearby cemetery. A small section of plots had been given over for burials to the Australians. In an emotional service the chaplain attached to the Brigade, the Reverend G. E. Shaw oversaw the final act of dignity as they were buried together in separate graves.

I can't help wondering what happened to Jim's orchards back in Guildford, Swan, Australia. His father didn't pay off the mortgage. Maybe Mr. Ammetts bought them back from the bank? Or did the bank re-mortgage them to someone else? I hope they didn't fall into decay or dereliction.

Jim's medals – the British War Medal and Victory Medal – arrived at his father's pharmacy shop on Stockport Road in Manchester on October 27th 1922 and remained with the family for some time afterwards. His parents cherished them until they passed away in the 1930's. The medals are now proudly in our custodianship and will remain so in order to preserve the memory of James Neville Golden.

My mind sometimes wanders back to the day when I drove westward from the former Somme battlefields along the D929 road. I turned towards the village of Querrieu, once the headquarters of the Australians before reaching Frechencourt. The village was so still and quiet as I parked up alongside a sign that directed me to the Frechencourt Communal Cemetery Extension, well hidden from the road.

It didn't take me very long to discover Jim's headstone. I pondered for a while before placing my arm around it. I thought of what could and should have been for a young man who went to achieve his dream in a far off land, a land he loved so much, a land for whom he served and died for.

Rob wishes to make a final and very poignant statement regarding Jim's last stand beside his gun alongside the other five men of the team and the officer Captain Martin. The men knew they had little chance of survival as they covered the retreat against incredibly overwhelming odds. As they were eventually surrounded they refused to abandon their Howitzer gun. This weapon represented their 'colours'. In a final act of respect the Germans acknowledging that fact did not capture the weapon and left the men to be recovered for burial.

Alex Butt
Killed in Action
France, October 8th 1918
Aged 24.

OUR admiration for the roles that stretcher bearers played during the Great War is huge. These brave men, many of whom chose not to bear arms and take the lives of fellow human beings undertook enormous personal risks to save others, as were unarmed heroes.

One such young man was Alexander John Francis Butt who hailed from what was Cape Province, now Eastern Cape in South Africa. His presence on the Western Front was short lived. The sacrifice he made being a terrible tragedy of war at a time when the conflict itself was almost over. Personal and family records from South Africa are notoriously hard to find. Nonetheless, I have built up a good and practical researched profile of the life and times of Alex. We hope this story and our tribute to him will provide fascinating reading.

The Union of South Africa as it was at the time was a British Dominion. Populated mainly by indigenous black African people from different tribal backgrounds and white colonial settlers of European origin. Boers who took their heritage from the Netherlands and the British made up the larger part of this minority. People of German heritage also added to the demographic diversity of what was and still is a multi-racial nation.

Alex was of German ethnicity. His father Franz Julius Freidrich Butt was the son of a white settler. Franz's own father had once joined the British German Legion. This organisation made up of men of Germanic stock was recruited by the British to fight in the Crimean War (1853-56). As it transpired these men played a very small role within that war. For those of you surprised at the very existence of a British German Legion at that time it can be noted that Queen Victoria's husband Prince Albert was himself born in Bavaria. The un-federated Germanic states of the period were very much upon co-operative terms with the British.

Alex's grandfather like many others from the former GBL moved to the Cape in South Africa to start a new life. A large percentage of the ex-Legionnaires relocated to King William's Town. This settlement had been established a few decades earlier by British missionaries and colonialists who wrestled the area from the Xhosa tribe. Nelson Mandela was a descendant of this famous tribe. The town quickly became known as King,

Alex was born within its borders in 1894.

By the time of Alex's birth his hometown had become a desirable and affluent place to live. The majority of its white population were middle-class businessmen and professionals. King had a public library, a town hall, five banks, four newspaper offices and rows of elegant shops selling largely imported goods. The rail link to the port of East London had considerably increased business opportunities for traders in the region. Alex's father Franz was himself a trader, he imported goods from afar to sell on a wholesale basis to the shops and business around the town. For the local black population life wasn't as prosperous. These people lived in run-down suburbs around the edges of the town and were often employed in menial occupations by their white neighbours. The black indigenous workers were poorly paid and often badly treated.

As a youngster in 1901 Alex and his family like the rest of the population of King were affected by an outbreak of bubonic plague. Fortunately seven-year old Alex escaped danger like the rest of his family as the Butt's lived on the town's affluent outskirts. It had been the central area of the town that suffered the worst of the plague's effects, so badly that it had to be evacuated. When the threat of the plague was over the white population had already expanded the town away from its original centre. Uneasy and nervous about returning they began to move in black tenants and rent their former properties without investing money into refurbishments. In reality they became slum landlords and created more division and resentment within the local community. Acceptance of one's place in King would have been far more agreeable as it was a Garrison town for many years until 1913. Once the home of the Cape Mounted Riflemen and moreover the Armed and Mounted Police, the prosecution of law and order wouldn't have been a problem at all.

Like many of his young contemporaries including his brother Augustine the young Alex was well educated and enjoyed good schooling. Unfortunately the same couldn't be said for the coloured and black populous. Many of their youngsters had no schooling at all and through no fault of their own became illiterate. The class and colour divide was very prominent and accepted as normal by virtually all of the townsfolk of King, times of course changed as the years went by. Alex was from a comfortable background with very little to trouble him.

Upon leaving school both Alex and his brother followed in their father's footsteps to become traders. Franz Butt was a respected well-heeled businessman who had traded in commodities all his working life. He taught them well, Augustine went on to set up his own business in Bethlehem, Orange Free State. Both brothers had much to look forward to as South Africa as a whole had much to offer in terms of importing and exporting. Before the opening of the Suez Canal the nation's ports became major trading stop-over points on the way to the Far East. European traders were always eager to buy and sell in their droves.

At the outbreak of war South Africa retained major divisions within many communities, amongst these were ones of European origin. Just over a decade earlier the Boers and British had fought bitter wars against each other for supremacy. Old rivalries and hatred were still abound. The indigenous black tribal peoples too had issues of their own, sometimes with each other and often with the white population. Despite being very much in the minority the whites enjoyed much higher standards of living.

Despite their differences South Africa joined Great Britain as a fierce fighting ally. Leader Louis Botha and his military guru Jan Smuts were keen to foster relations further with Britain regardless of some objections from the Boer population. South Africa despite its size had a population of around just 6.5 million at the time, considerably smaller than that of Great Britain. Their war casualties eventually amounted to over 18,000, with around 6,600 becoming fatalities.

Significantly the South African government would not allow black or coloured people to join their armies and fight alongside their white countrymen. Tribal leaders offered their own warriors who would no doubt at all have made excellent fighting soldiers, these gestures were ignored and treated with contempt. As it transpired the South African Native Labour Corps represented the black and coloured people in the war. These men worked as labourers at ports close to the battlefields and were treated with very little if at all any respect. On more than one occasion some of them were shot and killed by white soldiers when they rebelled against unfair conditions or enforced imprisonment for breaking strict rules. These shootings were in effect summary and illegal executions that were disgracefully hushed-up. Acts of murder in war time were often never brought to justice.

Alex in his mind held a desire to taste adventure. Realising that he had a bright future and career ahead of him he wanted to join the war effort, he was determined to return after victory was assured and prosper as a trader. Quite possibly for this reason and more than likely on the advice of his father he decided to join the South African Army in a non-combatant role. Alex would also probably have held some principals being well educated and having been a regular attendee and conformer of the Roman Catholic Church.

I bring in Rob here. Having lived and worked for a period of time in South Africa he endorses as a witness himself the deeply held Christian religious beliefs of white South Africans. He also tells me of the hypocrisy of some of those said people who for generations have passively encouraged social and class divisions. There are good and bad people in all communities. One principal aim of this publication is to highlight what war and division can create for ordinary people. It can't be denied that Alex Butt was himself an ordinary man whose own opinions forged upon his upbringing we will never know. He paid the ultimate price for a cause in which he believed in, a better world. We cannot or must not detract from that.

Alex joined the South African Medical Corps in early 1917, he was 22-years old. In March of that same year he embarked from Cape Town on the converted transport vessel 'HMS Durham Castle' and set sail for England. The year previously a purpose built hospital for South African forces had been erected on a twelve-acre site at Richmond Park in London. The hospital itself held 600-beds and over the period of the war received 9,500 patients. Over 2,000 operations were performed there including one upon the famous South African Army mascot, 'Jackie' the monkey. The unfortunate animal had to have a leg amputated as a result of a wound caused by a German shell.

Alex arrived for duty at the hospital on April 27th 1917. He was duly despatched duties as an orderly and would have assisted nursing staff in all kinds of situations. At that period the South Africans had just taken a mauling over in France at the battle of Arras. Their commander was largely responsible for that. In my documentary film - 'Murder on the Hill' (2010) - I squarely blame General Allenby and round upon him as a cold-blooded and calculated murderer.

The white South African soldiers were despised by Allenby, who had fought against the Boers some years before in South Africa. His reckless 'experiments' against German machine-guns using South African infantrymen as 'guinea-pigs' were nothing short of appalling. Even Douglas Haig, a cold-hearted butcher himself, was shocked and dismayed at his bloody-mindedness. What many soaking wet 'metropolitan historians' fail to acknowledge when they proclaim Allenby as a great wartime General, is that he was 'sacked' by Haig. Allenby was actually removed from the Western Front theatre of war because of his brutal prosecution in battle at Arras. This butcher was a 'Donkey' moreover a 'Murderous Donkey'. Young Alex's first experiences at the hospital in London would have involved assisting victims of Allenby's disgusting folly.

After spending well over a year at the hospital Alex became accustomed in how to perform basic medical procedures for treatments on a battlefield. In one sense he became a very well trained and highly skilled medical operative. Over in France the Germans were being pushed further and further back. Despite their struggle they fought on with stubborn and brave resistance against what had become a mighty allied force facing them.

The South Africans by September 1918 had moved into the 66th (2nd West Lancashire) Division after spending the previous two years with the highly acclaimed 9th (Scottish) Division. Like the Scots, famed for their courage, they had often been used to fight in some of the more difficult engagements of the war and had suffered for that.

A man with practical experience to offer such as Alex would have been invaluable. The 24-year old volunteered for duty in France as a stretcher bearer, a brave and dangerous undertaking but one of huge importance. Not only would he have required physical strength he also had to work alongside another man. Alex would be ready, willing and able to literally

Alex Butt was serving as a stretcher bearer when he was killed in an enemy air attack in October 1918.

go out into 'no-man's land' to rescue the desperately wounded dying infantrymen. Both stretcher bearers had no weapon to protect them. Their tasks were to save and rescue in the most dangerous conditions imaginable.

On October 8th 1918, the British and South Africans were taking part in the Second Battle of Cambrai forcing the Germans eastward. One objective to be taken was the village of Serain to the south of the French town, this was achieved by nightfall. Some German soldiers holding on desperately held serious grudges against South African soldiers. This was borne by the fact their countrymen had backed the Boers against the British some years before. The Germans also couldn't understand why some South Africans of German descent – such as Alex – would want to fight against them. Rob has managed to obtain some incredibly detailed South African records that confirm how Alex Butt was actually killed whilst in action.

Many soldiers respected the work of the stretcher bearers. Mutual admiration had been demonstrated on countless occasions throughout the war. The bearers from both sides had often rescued enemy soldiers and taken them to safety. On this particular day and threatened with their positions being over-run, the Germans facing South Africans coming towards them showed no mercy. Alex was one of four stretcher bearers – two crews – deliberately bombed in a ruthless German air strike. Six South African infantry soldiers also perished. Alex had been at the front for just three weeks. The end of the war was forthcoming but the Germans didn't see it that way.

Back in the town of King life moved on. Franz Butt continued to trade his commodities for many years to come. Times indeed have changed. The population of King William's Town is now more than two-thirds black and coloured, many of whom are of Xhosa tribal descent. It has been suggested the town is to be renamed because of its colonial connections, after all it was named after King William IV. I wonder what Alex would make of that. His full medals entitlement of the British War Medal and Victory Medal are with us. Like all South African medals from the period they have bi-lingual inscriptions, in English and Dutch. Sadly, some of the medals awarded to South Africans are frequently copied to be sold on for profit.

Alexander Butt now lies at rest with the comrades who died beside him on that fateful day all those years ago. He is buried within the Prospect Hill Cemetery at Gouy in northern France. We hope he died for us all to realise that no matter where we come form, or who we are, his sacrifice has helped to make the world a better place.

Wilfred French
Killed in Action
France, Sept. 30th 1918
Aged 34.

THIS is a truly fascinating story and takes us upon a journey across the Atlantic and back again. Rob, very fortunately managed to obtain a pair of medals, the British War Medal and the Victory Medal as well as a Death Plaque and Canadian Memorial Cross to a remarkable man who perished in France. Our interpretation of his life and times are shared with you right here, we are sure you will enjoy the experience of reading them.

Life started for Wilfred Reginald French on Wednesday September 24th 1884. He was one of seven surviving children who made it to adulthood out of ten born to his parents Samuel and Annie. Wilf entered the world in the small Cotswolds town of Northleach in Gloucestershire. The family moved several times around the county as his father was a well-respected

I join with my grateful people
in sending you this memorial
of a brave life given for others
in the Great War.

George R.J.

The medals and death plaque posthumously awarded to Wilf French, the Canadian Memorial Cross is on the left of the picture.

policeman holding the rank of sergeant. For many years he was continuously posted from station to station around Gloucestershire, eventually settling in Monmouthshire before retiring to Swansea.

There is no doubt that Sam French made a lasting impression upon his children. Wilf's father would have ensured that discipline, order and respect were prominent in his home life as well as vocationally. Smartness was the order of the day in the French household. The keenness of this orderly upbringing was to be the making of Wilf as he embarked upon what would be a wonderful life's adventure whilst still in his teens.

Wilf's good manners and attention to detail landed him a very respectable position in a large country house as a domestic servant. He was only 15-years old when he started his working life as a footman at the splendid Langton House in Dorset. From this point in his life he would be known and referred to by his Christian name of Wilfred, to both his fellow servants and masters alike.

Sometimes in life we are fortunate enough to get a real break and a chance to better ourselves, Wilf's break came when he was still just about in his teens. At some stage his vocational skills came to the attention of a wealthy American businessman, a banker by the name of Edward Wassermann. With financial interests in Britain and Europe the merchant banker of German-Jewish origin travelled regularly to England and the continent.

At the age of nineteen Wilf was personally 'head-hunted' by Mr. Wassermann who needed a valet, a personal assistant to tend to his basic everyday requirements. The man-servant would attend to his masters' needs at home and as he travelled to and fro across the United States and Europe. This was a life changing opportunity for the young footman and he didn't hesitate to accept the wealthy banker's offer. On Wednesday May 4 1904, Wilf embarked upon the aptly named 'SS Kaiser Wilhelm II' at Southampton alongside his new master. Their destination, New York and Mr. Wassermann's grand house in Manhattan.

As a domiciled resident Wilf successfully applied with the assistance of his employer for official residential status and became a United States citizen. He was by then a part of the American dream and held in high esteem by his master who relied upon him for a long period of time. Wilf served the wealthy banker for almost ten years before his early death at the age of fifty-four in 1914.

The relationship between Edward Wassermann and Wilf would have been held upon much more than just an ordinary boss/employee platform.

Rob, who grimaces a little when he tells me about his own personal short-term experiences as a valet, helped me to build up a picture of perhaps what that relationship was actually like.

Wilf would have been well attired himself and was responsible for making sure his master certainly was. He attended to his benefactor's everyday needs in precise detail. Ironing and pressing his masters' clothes, helping him dress for all formal occasions and ensuring that all of his possessions were neatly packed represented the more routine aspects of the job for Wilf. There was more to being a valet than what was generally understood.

We both agree that Wilf could have been privy to many of Wassermann's more intimate and personal matters or indeed secrets. Edward trusted Wilf impeccably and certainly would have confided in him regarding issues that concerned him. The two men from opposite ends of a well-defined social spectrum relied upon each other. This is defined by the length of service given by Wilf to his master. Had it not been for Edward's rather untimely death their special relationship surely would have continued.

There is documented evidence that Wilf travelled across the Atlantic back to England to accompany his master on business trips. The young valet experienced some of the 'high life' himself. He certainly would have been accommodated in very close proximity to his boss in luxurious hotels or perhaps on the odd occasion, a country house. In the U.S, Wilf also travelled and enjoyed the perks of good food, hospitality and respect as he stood by the money making businessman.

Mr Wassermann became ill in the autumn of 1913 and was confined to his home as his health deteriorated. Wilf tended dutifully and diligently to his master through his failing health and subsequent premature death. Both Rob and I agree that Edward Wassermann's demise caused Wilf terrible anxiety and deep sorrow, when it eventually and inevitably happened, Wilf moved on.

The faithful valet took upon another position in New York at a smaller yet still grand residence close to Central Park on 46 West 66th Street. He had already started to court another servant, a maid by the name of Sarah Wilson McDonald, known as Sallie, who had herself emigrated from Scotland a few years before. The two were married in 1915 in New York and together both worked at the same household in domestic service.

After the death of his former master Wilf struggled to adapt to the chores of his everyday duties, he yearned to travel as he had once done and craved adventure. The monotony and added responsibility of being a husband weren't satisfying or matching Wilf's ambitions. I would have liked to have been a fly on the wall when he was discussing with his wife the prospect of joining the army to serve in the war. At that stage the United States had not yet declared war on Germany, however on April 6th 1917 it did just that. As a U.S citizen he could have been considered for military service with his adoptive country. He wouldn't have been prioritised as he was not American-born and furthermore he was more familiar with British customs and cultural familiarities. The solution for Wilf was simple, his decision would ultimately cost him his life. I am convinced Sallie didn't approve, however, her husband had made up his mind and nothing was going to stop him.

Canada is a wonderful nation and a proud member of the Commonwealth. Achieving a form of autonomy in 1867 the country remained a British Dominion until 1931 when she declared independence fully following the Statute of Westminster. The Canada Act, sometimes referred to as the Constitution Act of 1982, allowed Canada to become wholly independent from Britain whilst retaining the British monarch, Elizabeth II, as the nation's queen. At the time of the Great War British-Canadian relations were very close. Many Britons had settled in Canada and the bonds between the two nations were immense.

On a bright New York summers' day in July of 1917 Wilf packed his bags to make the 500-mile railroad journey via Buffalo to Toronto in Canada. As he kissed his wife goodbye it would prove to be their last tender moment. It was indeed the final occasion on which they would hold each other or talk face-to-face ever again. Wilf was 32-years old, his wife three years older. The married couple had no children together and the likelihood of that changing should he return was remote. Their duties as domestic servants and Sallie's age would cast doubts over them ever raising a family.

The journey overland saw Wilf take in some of the most picturesque scenery that America has to offer. He was aware that at some point in his near future he would be returning to England, the land of his birth. From there he knew not what to expect, perhaps that was all part of the excitement of joining-up. Reaching Toronto after an arduous journey lasting over fourteen hours he was ready to attest into the Canadian Overseas Expeditionary Force. The fact that he was of British birth would qualify him for selection, he knew that, but would he pass the requirements set before him?

Wilf had no previous military experience, he was reasonably fit of just below average height and weight, intelligent, polite and unassuming.

It would take some training to lick him into shape as an infantryman, especially as his eyesight wasn't at all perfect. He did however have one special skill, that of being a highly experienced valet. All officers required a 'batman' a military term for a valet or personal servant and Wilf fitted the bill perfectly. Both Rob and I have no direct evidence to clarify that Wilf actually took upon such a role, however we believe he did so. After studying his movements from the point of enlistment there were delays in his progress to the actual front line. This suggests that he was attending to an officer as a valet in the wake of completing his basic military training.

Wilf was despatched to the 2nd Canadian Reserve Battalion having actually enlisted on July 14th 1917 and was subsequently allocated the service number of 2304438. It would be a few months later before he embarked from Canada aboard the 'SS Scotian' on November 20th eventually arriving in England on December 7th 1917. The following week he was billeted at the Sandling Military Camp in Kent where a couple of months later he would still remain before transferring to the 8th Canadian Reserve Battalion.

After undergoing routine training he was finally attached to a Canadian fighting battalion the famous 54th. The men of this battalion had already distinguished themselves upon the Western Front in both France and Belgium. By April of 1918 Wilf had arrived in France and was duly acknowledged and taken on strength. It would be another four months later in August of 1918 when the valet with 60% acceptably good eye-sight was eventually sent to his unit. As previously stated we assume he would have accompanied an officer as a 'batman'.

There had been a blot on Wilf's character prior to his front line posting and he was punished in accordance with military discipline routines of the time. On July 6th 1917, Wilf had gone absent without leave from his billet without a pass between the hours of 21.30 and 22.30 in the evening. Perhaps he had sneaked off for a secret rendezvous? He was consequently convicted of the offence nine days later and sentenced to number one field punishment, very harsh in my opinion given the nature of the offence.

This form of punishment meant that Wilf was tied by handcuffs or fetters to a fixed object, possibly a gun-carriage, or alternatively he could have been strapped to a fence-post. The punishment would be metered out for around two hours per day for a few days. It was designed to humiliate the offender in the presence of his comrades. Maybe the Wilfred of days gone by was indeed embarrassed by this considering his background, or perhaps he had a little bit of a naughty side to him and wasn't really bothered at all?

By the end of September 1918 things were certainly getting heated in France for the Germans who stubbornly and doggedly fought on against overwhelming odds. Out-manned and out-gunned by a huge allied force opposing them comprising of men from the United States, Great Britain, Canada, Australia and France amongst others, they refused to give up the fight. Facing them of course were the Canadians under the superb command of General Arthur Currie. The rugged men from a far-away continent were setting new standards of efficiency and ingenuity. Like their cousins, the Australians, they learned how to become tough and very uncompromising with the enemy. Throughout the war the Canadians had suffered at the hands of the Germans, now they could smell victory.

I have made and will continue to make numerous references to those who are in my own opinion 'Donkey Generals'. Now, for once, I am actually praising a General. Canadian-born Arthur Currie was by 1918, a young, energetic, intelligent and inspiring leader of his nations' land forces. The 42-year old had actually risen all the way through the military ranks from the lowly position of Militia Gunner to General. He had previously been a teacher and an insurance salesman and understood his men as they understood him. Currie was also a great strategist and wasn't afraid to confront his contemporaries of very high similar rank. These particular men were mostly British 'brass-hats' and the odd 'Donkey' or two all of whom came from privileged backgrounds.

Just days after his 34th birthday, on September 27th 1918 and having been at the front for less than six weeks, Wilf was thrust into the thick of the action around the village of Bourlon in northern France. Close by the notorious killing ground of Bourlon Wood where the Germans held slightly higher ground as a vantage point – as they often did – had to be taken. The Canadians swept the Germans aside in the village and through the wood before moving with great skill across the Canal du Nord.

Wilf witnessed the newly dug canal that was at the time completely empty of water being flooded at certain points by the Germans. The enemy were attempting to create defensive chaos against blood-thirsty and vengeful attackers determined to destroy them in their midst.

With great speed and precision Canadian Engineers constructed wooden bridges to cross the swampy, water-logged and flooded canal banks. The infantry then pressed on relentlessly towards Cambrai with fierce determination and without mercy, their efforts as always were essential in the pathway to victory.

On the fourth day of operations, September 30th 1918, zero-hour came and went as the Canadians continued their relentless advance. After three hours of moving forward Wilf was struck fatally by enemy fire and went down dying in the swampy ground alongside his brave comrades. Inside his tunic pocket his pay-book and will were recovered along with some very minor personal effects. Wilf's body was removed from the battlefield and buried with dignity close to where he fell at the Cantimpre Canadian Cemetery close to the village of Sailly. The very name of the little settlement rang similar to that of his wife Sallie who was waiting for him to return from war back at their home in New York.

This is a tale of a man who for much of his life enjoyed himself and travelled extensively in the company of gentlemen. We are certain he witnessed things or events that many of his generation wouldn't have. The tragedy of it all is that his spirit of adventure would ultimately be his downfall, for he needn't have gone to fight. His widow Sallie never remarried, she briefly moved across to Manhattan to continue her service as a maid. For most of the rest of her life she lived and worked in the sunshine state of California. Sallie resided in the pretty surroundings of Santa Barbara right up until her death in 1961 at the age of 79.

I am left wondering if Wilf ever remembered Sallie's objections to him leaving her all those years ago. Wilf's medals, plaque and memorial cross have always been kept together. The cross itself was awarded by the Canadian government to their service personnel who had paid the ultimate price and was sent either to the mother or the wife. As Wilf's mother had passed away in 1899 it would have been Sallie who obtained the cross and we assume the plaque and medals also.

All of these artefacts made their way back across the Atlantic to the land of Wilf's birth. At some point and probably in the final testament of Sallie's will they passed to one of Wilf's siblings or another relative back in the early 1960's.

Like many other medals they have passed out of their respective family custodianship and we now find ourselves as the current caretakers. Rob's find opened the door to tell the story of Wilf's life. Ultimately, we can be grateful for the fact that he will be remembered for the person he was and for the service he gave both in his life as a valet and as a soldier. What a story indeed, Wilfred Reginald French, born in England, a citizen of the United States of America and a warrior of Canada.

Joe Knowles
Killed in Action
France, Aug. 25th 1918
Aged 33.

THIS story takes us to the other side of the world and to New Zealand from where a man left his home and business to fight and perish in a foreign field. Driven by a sense of duty his conscience got the better of him. Perhaps a loyalty to the land of his birth may have contributed to the decision he made, or maybe it was peer pressure or family ties that influenced his thinking.

We begin in the former West Riding of Yorkshire, England, with the focus being upon a very large family. Thomas and Mary Ann Knowles had no fewer than twelve children, eight boys and four girls. Their baby-making activities were spread over a period of three decades, their eldest, Septimus being born in 1867, the youngest Charlie, came along in 1888.

This couple married very young, Tom being just 19-years old at the time with his bride having just entered her twenties. The pair married in Tom's home town of Keighley and going completely against the standards of the day both managed to live to ripe old ages. Mary made it to the age of eighty, her husband was seventy-eight when he kicked the bucket. Astonishingly, Tom had spent half a century working in textile mills across the western part of the county, gruelling work to say the least.

Our subject within this story is their tenth child Joseph, born on October 29th 1884, in Bramley on the outskirts of Leeds. As previously stated the family had moved around various parts of western Yorkshire, eventually they settled and lived for many years in nearby Bradford. The parents had to consistently seek larger accommodation to house their offspring. Gaining employment was never an issue for father Tom. His experience of the weaving trade set him in good stead, textile mills sprawled across the area offering many job opportunities.

After two spells in Leeds and another in Bradford and with the family shrinking as the children left home the remainder of the Knowles brood finally settled in Halifax. Young Joe was particularly close to the siblings who were born within just a few years of him, they included his immediate older brother Thomas and younger brothers Fred and Charlie. Joe also formed a vocational relationship with his sibling Fred as they both became boot repairers. The two lads soon established a reputation for the standards of their work. In the West Riding many working-class men of the day couldn't afford to buy new boots when they became worn. A good repair would suffice, Joe and Fred obliged and kept themselves out of the daily drudgery of the textile mills or local coal mines.

By 1911 and entering his later twenties Joe had saved up enough money to escape the dreary and mundane routines of industrial Yorkshire. The skills he had developed by repairing boots extended to the capability of actually making them. At that particular time those who had the opportunity and a specialist skill or trade made the decision to emigrate to pastures new. Some chose Canada, others South Africa or the United States. Joe decided upon New Zealand and a journey that would take him across oceans with a distance of over 11,500 miles to cover. It was a bold move for a young man who had been born and raised within a large family unit. Nothing was guaranteed for Joe, he had to go out and make it on his own and it didn't take him long to achieve his ambitions.

Joe settled within a suburb of the nation's capital Wellington in the district of Ngaio, so named after a native tree of New Zealand. It was a far cry from the dirty, grimy streets of the towns and cities of Yorkshire. The small closely-knit district nestled underneath the slopes of Mount Kaukau, an original Maori settlement and home to the squawking Kaka parrot. The Yorkshire lad set up his own boot-making business and shop on the main road through the town and soon became well known to the local inhabitants.

Life would have been pretty serene and pleasant for Joe with the clean and fresh mountain-side air gently drifting across his neighbourhood. As months turned to years he became well settled within the small and parochial community. Virtually everyone residing there would have known each other. The closest he came to war was by reading the newspapers or receiving letters from home, mail that could take months to arrive. It was one such letter from his parents that altered his way of thinking and attitude to the war in general.

Joe hadn't seen his elder brother Thomas for many years. His sibling had gone off to join the army way back in 1904. As children growing-up the two had been close, with Joe looking up to Thomas as his protector. The news that came from home in 1915 was grim, Thomas had been killed in Belgium, or so it would seem.

I can't be certain how much information regarding Thomas' death was actually relayed via the letter to Joe. Thomas Knowles had been reported as 'missing' on May 5th 1915, six days later his body was discovered. Official records do not chart his death as being killed in action, they merely state

Joe Knowles became a successful boot shop owner in New Zealand after leaving his native Yorkshire.

that he died on May 11th. I can only assume that he was hastily buried and that his grave was later destroyed by enemy artillery fire. This assumption is based upon the fact that his name is listed on the Menin Gate Memorial to the missing in Ieper [Ypres], Belgium. Further investigations by Rob revealed that Thomas had been caught up in a gas attack. This being the case it would have been one of the very first instances of chemical warfare in military history.

Curiously, the decision to inform the parents of his death was taken over two weeks after his body was found, suggesting some kind of inquiry was carried out. What Joe's mum and dad were told and what they passed on we will never know. There must have been some lingering doubt as to the tragic fate of Joe's beloved brother.

This was the year that New Zealand forces had been initially engaged in the war within the Dardenelles theatre at Gallipoli. Young men from the town had joined-up and not returned, a fact that didn't go unnoticed by the locals. As the war went on more lads from the area set sail for France and Belgium and didn't return.

Rob has no doubt that as the war progressed Joe Knowles would have come under increasing peer pressure to take the oath himself, after all he was a British born subject. Some of his boot-shop customers had sons, husbands, brothers and friends who had gone off to fight. We also take into consideration here the haunting and enduring sadness that Joe would have felt regarding the death of his elder brother Thomas. It is likely the comments of locals and the emotional feelings he held for his departed sibling influenced his own decision. Joe eventually made the short journey to an army recruitment station in nearby Wellington soon afterwards.

The date was Tuesday July 17th 1917 when Joe attested and was accepted as medically fit to serve. He was allocated the service number of 63621 and went on to serve with 'F- Company' of the 1st Battalion Otago Regiment within the New Zealand Army. After a relatively short period of training he left his adopted land in the November of 1917. It was a long arduous sea journey to England and a very different one to which he had experienced going the opposite way some six years earlier.

Joe undertook more training after his arrival in England in the first three months of 1918. He just happened to be one of only a few men of his unit who were actually born in Britain. Upon his return to the land of his birth there would have been a desire for him to see his family before he was posted to France. Rob now brings to light the attitudes of the New Zealand officers with regard to the general well-being and welfare of the men who served under them.

Based upon his own experiences Rob is almost certain that special dispensation with regard to a seventy-two hour leave pass would have been granted to Joe. This gesture allowed him to return to the West Riding in Yorkshire to visit his family. The uniform of the Otago boys was similar to that of British soldiers except for alternative badge markings and essentially completely different headwear. Distinctively, the cap worn by Joe was similar to that of the American 'dough-boy' soldiers. His officers were proud of him wearing the uniform of New Zealand in his homeland and also understood there was a likelihood it could be the last time he would ever see his family. There wouldn't have been many, if any complaints from his New Zealand born comrades who had already said their own final farewells.

Joe wouldn't have had much time to stay with his family members, after all the London to Leeds return journey with a couple of line transfers by rail took up much of his actual leave duration period. When he arrived back 'home' in the smoggy industrial winter time he would have been seen as a local celebrity. He probably lapped up all of the attention in his exotic uniform.

Joe eventually set foot in France just one day before the huge German Spring Offensive took off on March 21st 1918. Still, he wasn't rushed immediately to the front. It would be another two weeks before he was sent into reserve with his battalion, further weeks went by before he actually saw any real action.

By the late summer of 1918 the New Zealanders were involved in some very desperate and heavy fighting in northern France. It has been said by some cod-liver oil swallowing 'metropolitan historians' they were more placid and disciplined than their Australian counterparts. If they were indeed different in those respects they proved to be equally as brave as any of the allied soldiers fighting a desperate German rear guard.

On the bright sunny morning of Sunday August 25th 1918, Joe met his death in a little field. The New Zealanders had helped to sweep back the Germans across the former Somme battlefields around Beaumont-Hamel, Thiepval and Ovillers. With courage and fierce determination the Kiwis pressed on relentlessly eastward towards Bapaume and the important strategic centre of Cambrai.

Joseph died beside many of his Otago Regiment comrades. His body was recovered and became one of the first to be placed within the very small military cemetery close to where he fell. He now rests forever at peace on the outskirts of the tiny hamlet of L'Homme Mort. The enterprising Yorkshireman and adopted son of New Zealand was 33-years old when he was killed. Joe Knowles had travelled a total distance of over 23,000 miles to New Zealand and back again to fight for the cause of freedom. This very ordinary man who had everything to live for never married nor had children. The shrieking sounds of the Kaka parrot still echo upon a cool mountain breeze and across the neighbourhood where he once made shoes and boots for the locals.

Joe's lasting legacy is just one Victory Medal bearing the engraving of his name along the rim, it is safely in our custodianship and like all of the others will one day be exhibited. Sometimes when I lace up my own boots I think of Joe at rest in the little Commonwealth War Graves Commission cemetery in France. In my minds-eye I see his cheery smile as he greeted his customers so long ago at the little boot shop in Ngaio,

BEYOND THE CALL OF DUTY

EXPECTATIONS that fell upon the ordinary soldier, be him a regular or volunteer were pretty straight-forward. To serve the sovereign and the nation and be prepared to die for both sounds pretty serious, it was. The men who took up arms really didn't think too much about death, for they were young and immortal or so they thought.

This chapter contains the life stories of five outstanding soldiers four of whom were highly decorated for their courageous bravery. Of the five men, two had been pre-war regular soldiers, the remaining three were civilian volunteers. These ordinary every day young men wouldn't have warranted a second glance walking down the street in peace time.

Perhaps their own feelings of immortality drove them to achieve remarkable deeds. An inner sense of purpose may have contributed to their actions at the time. What is for certain is that their acts of heroism and gallantry in the face of danger were acknowledged by awards of specially created medals. Rob and I hold these medals within our custodianship, for us this represents a great honour, they are truly magnificent. The stories behind them are historically very significant as these guys demonstrated what it really did take to actually win gallantry awards.

Just like all of the subjects within this book these men paid the ultimate price and lost their lives. Three of the men had been very much alive when they were decorated with their respective medals. Their survival having carried out such acts of bravery in undoubtedly life threatening situations only added to their individual senses of immortality. Sadly and tragically they never grew old and didn't live to tell of their acts of bravery. It is now left to Rob and myself albeit the irrelevant passage of time to share with you their wonderful legacies.

Alan Smith
Killed in Action
France, March 28th 1918
Aged 23.
Awarded the DISTINGUISHED CONDUCT MEDAL in 1917

WE have in our custodianship a beautifully court-mounted Distinguished Conduct Medal awarded to a young man who served in the 7th Battalion of the West Yorkshire Regiment, also known as the Leeds Rifles. The medal first brought Rob and I together and will always remain as a totally inspirational artefact to us both. This particular DCM was bestowed upon Alan Smith, an artist in civilian life from Wakefield in West Yorkshire.

The Distinguished Conduct Medal represents an extremely high level of honour, it was awarded to ordinary ranks of the British Army and Commonwealth or Dominion non-commissioned officers for gallantry in the field. All DCM's are held in significance as only one place behind the coveted Victoria Cross making them the second highest award for gallantry for those who qualified. These very special medals were introduced by Queen Victoria and instituted on December 4th 1854, they continued to be awarded until 1993. In the period of a history of 139-years a relatively small number of around 29,800 were dispatched, the majority of approximately 25,000 DCM's were awarded during the course of the First World War. Each Distinguished Conduct Medal carries with it a written citation, a description in brief of the actual action of the recipient that led to the award being bestowed.

It has to be said the fighting citation that accompanies Alan Smith's DCM is one of the most incredible of those ever written. There were at the time of his award a number of people who had been convinced that his astonishing act of gallantry merited an even higher award. If that had been the case then Alan surely would have been decorated with the Victoria Cross. Rob and I will let you make up your own mind about that particular viewpoint.

From here on I will refer to Alan as Smithy, as Rob and I do when we converse about him. Smithy came from a modest background, he was a gentle character, a talented and creative artist. This young man quite literally proved that he had an alter-ego, one that demonstrated beyond doubt that he was an exemplary soldier and leader of men. It was also widely acknowledged by everyone who actually knew Smithy that he was a very cheerful and friendly young man. We sometimes chat about how such a tender and sensitive human being as he was became a fearless and determined warrior. One of Smithy's contemporaries and old school chums put it on record that Alan Smith was of -'a nature quite foreign to warfare'- war affects people in different ways as this story will no doubt prove.

Life started for Smithy on a warm summers' day. He was born at the family home in Wakefield on July 14th 1894. Smithy was the only son of brewery cashier Henry Smith, a local man and his Somerset born wife, Mary. He was one of three children to the couple who survived into adulthood, one other perished. Smithy had two female siblings, Marion, two years his senior and Dorothy eleven years his junior.

The family resided on Stanley Road in the city. Henry an astute financial accountant wanted the very best for his children and knew of the vital importance of them gaining a decent education. His two elder offspring, Marion and Alan were given the opportunity of advancing in life. Marion became a life-long career school teacher, eventually reaching the position of headmistress. Smithy's elder sister remained a spinster throughout her long life. As for Smithy himself, he attended the Wakefield Grammar School before eventually embarking upon a short career as an artistic colour work designer. He was directly involved in the actual design and production of a number of promotional posters. Many copies of these works of art appeared in every town and city in the land, at railway stations, attached to shop gable ends, the outer walls of football stadiums, upon lamp-posts and bill-boards.

Printing was a major industry in the city of Leeds only a few miles from Wakefield. It was there that Smithy found employment in the artistic department of the esteemed printing firm of Chorley and Pickersgill. His position was formal and he would have addressed his colleagues in such a manner, wearing a collar and tie. Smithy was soon gaining awards for his work as a colour poster designer. He was at the forefront of his profession and certainly became a modern man of his time with his initiative, creativity and forward thinking. Smithy had plenty to look forward to, then war broke out.

The talented artist enlisted soon after war was declared and he did so in Leeds, more than likely on his way home from work. He became one of over 700 former pupils of Wakefield Grammar School to join the war effort as a front-line soldier. At the time the Leeds volunteer force [Leeds Rifles] that became the 7th and 8th battalions of the West Yorkshire Regiment when the Territorial Force was formed in 1908, were struggling to cope with the numbers of volunteers. So much so they split into four separate units the 1st and 2nd [7th Battalion] and the 1st and 2nd [8th Battalion]. The battalions retained their original famous identity of the Leeds Rifles who were originally formed in 1859. I have ascertained that Smithy initially joined the 1st/7th before eventually transferring to the 2nd/7th whilst on active service in France. Perhaps one of the reasons Smithy enlisted into the Leeds Rifles was the fact they had always been sponsored by the local Tetley Brewery. Smithy's father was a brewery cashier, maybe he was employed by the Tetley organisation.

With no previous military service to his name Smithy was literally a raw recruit. In accordance with the terms of signing on with the Territorial Force he was required to serve for the duration of the war and be ready and able to be deployed overseas. Smithy didn't have long to wait, after spending some time in preparation at York he was then sent to Lincolnshire. Departing from the training camp at Gainsborough he eventually arrived with the original detachment of the 1st/7th at Boulogne in France on the morning of April 16th 1915. Just over three weeks after his arrival in France, Smithy tasted action for the first time at the battle of Aubers Ridge on May 9th 1915. His war career as a soldier really did take off as he proved himself to be very capable and versatile. The young artist had intelligence, organisational skills and an ability to control men and situations, attributes that were all recognised. Smithy rose to the rank of Sergeant by the time he was just 22-years old. By that time he was a seasoned veteran and had taken part in some of the most horrific battles of the war, particularly on the first day of the Somme offensive in 1916 around Thiepval and later at Arras in 1917.

At some point around the first half of 1917 his experience was utilised when he was transferred to the 2nd/7th who had arrived in France just a few months beforehand. Smithy became second-in-command of a platoon under an officer. In real terms he was the lynch-pin of the platoon, overseeing newly deployed volunteer soldiers. Even his officer, a young subaltern would have depended upon him greatly.

By the November of 1917, the British had suffered appalling casualties at the Third Battle of Ypres [Passchendaele] in Belgium. Douglas Haig under mounting pressure was persuaded by the 'Tally-Ho Donkey General' Julian Byng to launch a massive offensive on the strategic German stronghold of Cambrai across the border in France. Haig never really needed an excuse to prove or redeem himself and went along with yet another expedition of callous slaughter.

It was around the area of Cambrai that Smithy really came to the fore. After a huge initial attack on November 20th 1917 supported enormously by the Tank Corps with over 400 machines the British found themselves seriously counter-attacked. Haig eager to 'pass the buck' back to the eternal optimist Byng ordered the 'Donkey' to rectify the situation around Bourlon Wood. The British were up against the most heavily fortified German position in France and once again paid a very heavy price.

At dawn on November 27th the Leeds Rifles headed to stop a German counter advance around the northern sector of the wood. Close by the 2nd Guards Brigade consisting of the 1st Coldstream Guards, 3rd Grenadiers and 2nd Irish Guards were sent into a suicidal mission. This was overseen by the cognac swilling, swashbuckling 'Donkey General' Byng. The Guardsmen were cut to pieces by murderous German machine-gun fire from all directions. Their so-called supporting Tanks didn't initially accompany them. When they did arrive they raced too far in front, the attack was a shambles, completely disorganised and utterly reckless. Hundreds of fine Guardsmen many of whom had served for years were massacred. Once again another 'Donkey' had blood upon his hands.

Smithy's determination just a few hundred yards away would see him decorated with the Distinguished Conduct Medal. The incredible citation is detailed in exact form as follows:

'For conspicuous gallantry and devotion to duty in going out with his Lewis gun to engage machine guns in a wood. When rushed from a flank he remained behind his officer, and helped to cover the retirement, firing from behind tree's at point blank range. Later he was one of a party of ten who, under the same officer, charged with the bayonet and dispersed a large body of the enemy.'

Both Rob and I think the words speak for themselves, this was a truly outstanding act of bravery from the young man and his comrades. Rob has actually managed to obtain a genuine Lewis gun from the First World War, it gives us a fascinating insight as to what Smithy had to do to handle such a weapon. Although this gun is portable it still requires a certain amount of strength and great skill to handle effectively. When we take into consideration the actual fighting conditions that Smithy was involved in, as described in the citation, then his feat really was remarkable.

The terrain was scarred, uneven, wet, boggy and dangerous under foot. Weather conditions were cold and damp and there wasn't much natural

The shattered remains of Bourlon Wood, France in 1917. Alan Smith was awarded the Distinguished Conduct Medal for his outstanding gallantry at this horrific location.

light, yet Smithy scared the s*** out of a large number of Germans who made a run for it. The stresses of being pushed back and surrounded also would have had a great deal of danger attached but Smithy lived to fight another day.

Our fearless artist from Wakefield had been involved in many horrendous situations that included life threatening incidents such as mustard gas attacks. When the end came for him it was sudden and unexpected. Smithy lost his life on Thursday March 28th 1918 as he stood in a trench close to Rattendy Farm near the village of Bucquoy in northern France. The Germans were sweeping back the British towards the former Somme battlefields during their great offensive that had started a week before. It was a stray German shell launched by a far-away artillery piece that exploded close to where Smithy stood, he was killed in an instant.

Hastily his comrades managed to get his body across several miles of battle scarred terrain to get behind their own lines near the former northern sector of the Somme battlefield. Smithy was buried in the Gommecourt British Cemetery No.2 at Hebuterne, where he now rests forever at peace.

The announcement of the award of Smithy's Distinguished Conduct Medal was as the norm published in the London Gazette. This would have been a proud moment for his family to see their son's achievement recorded in such a prestigious publication. There was however a tragic irony attached to that very announcement. It was published for all to see on the very day that Smithy was actually killed.

Both Rob and I are united in our belief that Smithy's story will not end at the beautiful Commonwealth War Graves Commission cemetery in a serene and peaceful piece of a foreign land. We are extremely honoured to hold his Distinguished Conduct Medal in our custodianship. Both of us are determined to see that Smithy's legacy and great gallantry will continue to be appreciated by a wider audience.

Being no stranger to controversy and certainly not afraid to say things from the heart I am now going to heavily criticise certain people. Their passive attitudes towards this great young hero leave a lot to be desired and will not deter us. It is fair to state that Smithy's DCM award was separate to that of his other medal entitlements, the 1914-15 Star, the British War Medal and the Victory Medal. He would also have been entitled to a Death Plaque and a scroll. At some point the remainder of his entitlements have been split from his DCM. More than likely a greedy medals dealer from the past has been responsible for that, trying to maximise profit by splitting the DCM from its group.

Like all of the medals we hold in custodianship they were released from the possession of their respective families. Some simply due to the fact the last member of the family line had passed away and others because the descendants of the recipients needed to sell them to pay basic bills. Disturbingly and now more often relatives sell them because they have no interest at all in the deeds of their ancestors. Rob made a very concerted effort to track down descendants of Smithy, eventually he succeeded and traced one of them by making direct contact. Unfortunately and rather sadly this relative showed no enthusiasm or interest.

Travelling to the local library in Wakefield, Rob found it difficult to source any material information or photographs of Smithy, the local hero. Despite the efforts of members of the library staff it became apparent that this man's deeds of great gallantry have faded into the murky mists of passing time. It is possible that Smithy himself was an extremely modest young man and shunned the limelight. If that had been the case it may explain why information remains so sparse today regarding his deeds.

Rob did manage to get a small amount of interest from a local historical society but that very soon fizzled out. Further attempts to contact local councillors came to nothing. No surprise there as many of us are very much aware the majority of politicians are only ever interested in procuring themselves. Obviously Smithy's legacy could do nothing for any of these people. No, it's not over. Smithy's DCM has been exhibited in educational environments, I have told his story many times and we will continue to do so.

One day we hope to especially share this story with the people of Wakefield and not be denied the opportunity to do so by selfish pot-bellied local officials. Obnoxious sherry swilling politically correct do-gooders don't have to come and listen to the story of one of their city's greatest ever heroes.

Sharples P. Driver
Killed in Action
France, May 3rd 1917
Aged 21.
Awarded the MILITARY MEDAL and BAR in 1916

With a name such as Sharples Parkinson Driver it would be easy to assume that I am referring to a public school boy or even a senior army officer. On the contrary, Sharpy as we will get to know him was very much an ordinary man. Having said that you will see as this story unfolds just how extraordinary he really was.

Sharpy was a fearless young man who was decorated TWICE with the Military Medal for acts of bravery in the field. His medals were both granted for his actions upon the Somme battlefields in 1916. What makes his story all the more remarkable is the fact that he had not reached the age of twenty-one at the time of both medal awards.

The Military Medal was instituted by King George V on March 25th 1916. This bravery award was granted to non-commissioned officers and ordinary soldiers, the MM ranked one place below the Distinguished Conduct Medal in terms of prestige. Therefore, the Military Medal was the third highest level of award for gallantry behind the VC and DCM. Approximately 115,000 were awarded to British and Dominion soldiers during the First World War.

The actual Military Medal and Bar awarded to Sharples Parkinson Driver for Bravery in the Field. He was awarded this honour twice for actions on the Somme in 1916, before he was 21-years old.

At the time of its original issue the MM was subjected to some criticism from regular soldiers. Many of these men suggested that it was only instituted in order to reduce the number of higher level Distinguished Conduct Medal awards. I have to state clearly the award of a Military Medal should ever be understated, only an exceptionally brave warrior would receive one. Both Rob and I agree that a third tier bravery medal was necessary and we share the sentiment that recipients had to earn the right to receive one. The acknowledgement of the Military Medal was published in the 'London Gazette' normally around eight to twelve weeks or so after the action for which it was earned. Paper citations were issued in some instances to the recipients only, many of these didn't last the test of time and only a few remain. Their losses due mainly to wear and tear unfortunately makes the actual actions that led to Military Medal awards notoriously difficult to research.

Sharpy was one of only 5,700 men to receive the Military Medal twice. The second award was marked by a bar across the ribbon as you will see via the actual picture of his medal and bar accompanying this story. There can be no doubt whatsoever this brave young man was a hero. He had no previous military experience before the war making his achievements all the more sensational.

We have to start off by explaining how Sharpy got his name. He was in fact named after his mother's brother Sharples, he also was given his mum's maiden name of Parkinson as his middle name. His father was a plain and ordinary farmer named Thomas Driver whom he obviously took his surname from, henceforth we have Sharples Parkinson Driver. If that sounds a little bit complicated then I suppose it is, there was nothing quite straight-forward regarding the brief life of Sharpy, who basically liked to do his own thing.

Our man was born at the 11-acre Stanhill Road Farm in a little town with a name almost as peculiar as his. He hailed from Oswaldtwistle in Lancashire, around three miles or so from Blackburn. His parents Tom and Isabella had taken over the farm upon the death of her father. Tom Driver had worked as a carter and Bella in the cotton mill when they first met. The happy couple were married on March 14th 1885 at their local church. Five of their six children, all males survived into adulthood. Sharpy had three elder brothers and a younger one, he was the only one of the five to be killed whilst serving in the First World War.

Life would have been interesting on the farm with six males and just one female in residence. The provision of food wouldn't have been as much as a problem as it was for others at the time. All the Driver lads were fit and strong, with three elder brothers Sharpy was down the pecking order. He would have learned about life very quickly and been one of the last to get a shared bath. The older boys picked the best of the meal portions if he didn't make to the table quickly. Eldest brother John was ten years his senior and would very much have been in charge in the absence of his father.

The farm wasn't big enough to accommodate and secure full-time regular employment for all of the sons. Sharpy joined one of his elder siblings by finding work in the local coal mines, it was either that or the cotton mill. At the outbreak of war he was still too young to officially sign on for overseas service. His work in the pit was essential, however, it was dangerous, dirty and extremely unpleasant as well as relatively poorly paid. Like so many of his contemporaries he wanted to taste the action and seek adventure.

Only a couple of miles to the north-east of Oswaldtwistle, known as 'Ossie' to the locals is the town of Accrington. By 1915 the famous

'Accrington Pals' recruited from all over the area had been deployed overseas yet recruitment in and around the town continued. It may surprise you to learn that a number of Scottish regimental recruiting teams often toured the working-class regions of England. The Scots recruiting fellows were very successful in attracting young Englishmen to join their ranks whether or not they had any Scottish heritage.

We cannot find any Scots descent for Sharpy, he was a Lancashire man through and through. After suffering from some horrendous losses at the Battle of Loos in 1915 one particular battalion from north of the border became desperate to regain their strength. The 6th Battalion King's Own Scottish Borderers indeed had a busy war, they were decimated more than once. KOSB recruitment teams were keen to offer places for young fit men to join their ranks as replacements be they from Lancashire or any other part of Britain.

Sharpy signed-on with the 6th KOSB after having a discussion with one of their recruiters as he walked through Accrington. Rob and I have asked the question why he decided to join a Scots battalion and not one of the local formations. It has been suggested by Rob that Sharpy fancied himself as a tough young man and the Scottish recruiting Sergeant would have assured him of that. The Scotsman would also have informed the recruit of how notoriously physical Scottish regiments were and promised him plenty of action.

Sharpy the young pit worker with the unusually posh sounding name was different and proved that by enlisting into a battalion that nobody would have expected him to do. This made him stand out as strong willed with self-determination and the ambition to go against the grain. The King's Own Scottish Borderers wore 'trews' [trousers] only the pipers and bandsmen were kilted, so any English recruit didn't have to worry about wearing the kilt.

Sharpy was off to adventures new, the rugged miner and farmers' son was only 19-years old, his sense of immortality would be exceptionally demonstrated within a year. It has always been generally accepted although not by some 'metropolitan historians' that Scots line regiments were often used as 'shock troops'. History does record they were almost always sent into the most dangerous attacking situations. Many seasoned German infantrymen respected the Scots greatly and feared them tremendously.

The 6th KOSB with Private Sharples Parkinson Driver in their ranks were very heavily involved in the actions of the Battle of the Somme in 1916 from an early stage. Like something out of an all action movie, the men of the battalion alongside the 12th Royal Scots stormed across a huge open gap of land stretching 500-yards near Montauban on July 3rd 1916. Their destination, slightly to the east, Bernafay Wood.

I cannot imagine what went through the minds of the German defenders as they saw 2,000 flying Scotsmen and their English recruits charging straight at them with huge bayonets glinting in the sunlight. A lot of stomach problems would have immediately descended upon them. The KOSB's and Royal Scots overwhelmed the enemy and captured the wood. Sharpy was right at the front of the assault that amazingly cost his battalion only six casualties. This tells us the Germans fled in fear and panic, the ones that took on the Scots battalions paid a heavy price. Sharpy we believe was awarded his first Military Medal for this action and must have helped to terrify the defenders into submission.

It wasn't an easy time for him and his comrades in the days that followed. The German infantry were too fearful to attempt to retake the wood. It was left to heavy German bombardments with high explosives to smash the wood and weaken the resolve of Sharpy and his pals. This wasn't achieved although the 6th KOSB's went on to receive over 300 casualties from the shelling.

Sharpy was again involved in heavy fighting around Longueval on July 17th 1916, this resulted in another decimation for the 6th KOSB's following their destruction at Loos in 1915. A day later his battalion or what was left of it was once again blasted by German shells. The brave KOSB's had suffered a 90 per cent casualty rate in just over two weeks, Sharpy had received a massive baptism of fire.

Having walked around these areas in recent years I have to say that it is almost impossible to believe what really happened there. The whole vicinity across the rolling Caterpillar Valley is strangely quiet and peaceful. A devastating casualty rate suffered by the 6th King's Own Scottish Borderers didn't deter them, the battalion was bolstered by more reinforcements and soon on the offensive again.

High Wood on the Somme is an eerie place. It was the scene of vast slaughter and around 8,000 bodies still remain lost within it. This is an area that is not open to the public. I admit that I have sneaked in there and twice recorded film documentary work amidst its dark shadows. The atmosphere in High Wood is chilling, it was there in October 1916 that Sharpy once again witnessed devastation that was beyond belief.

On October 18th 1916 the 6th KOSB had to move forward in the rain to take up a front line position at Eaucourt-L'Abbaye. To get to that destination they had to fight through a section of the notorious High Wood. Their own war diary entries recall the journey as being full of horrors, death and a fate more diabolical than could ever be imagined. We believe this is where Sharpy was awarded the Military Medal for the second time. It is hard to contemplate what he actually did and witnessed.

Many soldiers who had won the Military Medal once, never mind twice, would have been earmarked for immediate promotion after accomplishing their awards. In Sharpy's case Rob thinks his officers regarded him as too much of a valuable asset as a tough natural born soldier. His speciality was demonstrating extreme bravery, to dilute that by affording him levels of responsibility could have reduced his better fighting qualities. Of course there is also the possibility that he did not want to gain promotion and take charge of others.

Sharpy was well aware of the recognition of his awards and lived to receive them. He wore the medal ribbon with a small rosette attached to symbolise that he had won the Military Medal twice. The fearless young volunteer had been just 20-years old when he received both awards and was a man who had seen the brutality of warfare at first hand. It wasn't the end for Sharpy, he became involved with the reinforcements of his battalion in another very nasty engagement in May of 1917.

The Battle of Arras has been understated by a number of soppy cranberry juice sipping 'metropolitan historians'. It was a horrific area that came to resemble a slaughterhouse. Haig's decision to launch the campaign was yet another example of his disregard for human life. It was here on the final day of the offensive, May 3rd 1917, Sharples Parkinson Driver the young coal miner from Lancashire, a double gallantry winner was lost forever. He perished alongside 6,000 other British, Canadian and Australian soldiers.

Certain images that portray the actions of this final day around the Scarpe in northern France speak a thousand words. Bitter close-quarter hand-to-hand savage fighting saw the men of civilised nations, claw, rip and batter each other to death. Sharpy, lost on the battlefield became a statistic, one of the worst I have had to describe in this publication. Of the 6,000 killed that day, 5,000 are unaccounted for and have no grave, a shocking and disgusting figure. Haig and his whisky slugging cronies continued to persevere with highly controversial offensively cavalier tactics. Later that year they were collectively responsible for hundreds of thousands of deaths at Ypres, Passchendaele and Cambrai.

There are no images or photos of Sharpy. No newspaper seems to have reported his incredible feats of bravery. He is correctly commemorated on the Arras Memorial in France to the missing and he also features on his local war memorial. When Sharpy left Oswaldtwistle for war it was a little town of just over 14,000 inhabitants. Today around 11,600 people live there. Sharpy is a local hero and it would appear that nobody from the small Lancashire town is aware of his deeds. He was quite literally forgotten, until now.

Finally and not surprisingly his other two medals the British War Medal and Victory Medal are not with his Military Medal and bar. We obtained his bravery awards from the Isle of Wight, almost 300 miles away from Oswaldtwistle. Sharpy indeed throws a lot of different aspects into the fabric of his own story, a story that we really do hope will live on as an inspiration to future generations.

Roland Casemore
Killed in Action
France, Mar. 21st 1918
Aged 26.
Awarded the MILITARY MEDAL in 1916

ROLAND Sidney Casemore has proven to be another fascinating subject we have been privileged to investigate. His bravery for an action on the Somme in 1916 was recognised, he also went on to achieve attainment of the rank of Company Sergeant-Major, a warrant officer Class 2 in the British Army. Crucially he has also demonstrated to us how difficult it is to obtain true and accurate research, for his story has taken some forensic analysis to put together.

This long deceased warrior also introduces us to the present day as direct communications with a distant, albeit, indirect family line relative have been achieved. With the extra information we have gained we can put together an often troublesome tale that affected his widow throughout her long life.

The importance of accurate research is crucial. In the modern age many online services containing official records are readily and easily accessible. How to interpret the information is a skill in itself as certain documentation can often be misleading, mistakes can result in false testimonies, the scourge of any historian. We can never claim to be 100%

accurate on absolutely everything nor can any historian no matter who they are. Roland in particular tested my researching skills. I am confident despite the difficulties encountered that here we have an accurate portrayal of the life of a brave soldier who deserves nothing less.

Roly was born in Bromley, Kent, in the very early part of 1892. His father Henry, originally from Norwood in Surrey married Emily Allen in 1878 at a local church in Bromley. The Casemore's went on to have seven children in total, all of whom survived into adulthood. Henry spent his entire working life as a French polisher, he must have been very good at his job as he retained it for five decades. The family lived in at least four dwellings within Bromley where all of their children were born between the years of 1879 and 1895.

Of their four sons, at least two became soldiers. Eldest lad, Henry junior known by his middle name of Stewart, served for two years from 1900 to 1902 in the Kent Artillery, until classed as unfit for further service. He later became a coachman and specialist with horses based upon that experience. Roly went on to become a career soldier, enlisting around his seventeenth birthday at the very end of January or early February 1909. Ernie, another brother became a full-time fireman, whilst youngest Billy worked as shop assistant. I can find no military history at all for him. The three sisters worked in retail or domestic service.

Roly enlisted into the 1st Battalion West Yorkshire Regiment, at the time garrisoned at Colchester in Essex, sixty-five miles away from his home. We can't be certain as to why he actually chose to join this particular regiment who obviously held their traditions enshrined in the northern county. Perhaps he had seen them marching on a parade somewhere and was suitably impressed? Maybe he had joined alongside a close pal who originally hailed from Yorkshire? We will never be able to clarify as to the actual reason why.

What is for certain is that Roly became a very competent and highly respected non-commissioned officer. He had already accumulated nearly six years of military service when the First World War began. At the outbreak of hostilities he was an experienced Lance-Corporal with sufficient knowledge for him to be considered for the training duties of new recruits. That very consideration maybe explains why he wasn't on the original draft with his battalion that landed in St. Nazaire in France on September 10th 1914. Roly was back in England helping to supervise the training of new volunteers who would inevitably be required to bolster the battalion who most certainly were expecting war casualties.

The next detachment of his battalion arrived in France on January 27th 1915. Roly was with this draft and had either already been promoted or was about to receive his second stripe to become a full Corporal. The 1st West Yorkshire's would spend their entire war upon the Western Front in France and Belgium. After examining the battalion war diaries it is fairly clear these regulars were mainly held in reserve. The Yorkshiremen were classed as quality troops and could be relied upon to bolster or effectively consolidate certain situations. Nevertheless, as we shall see Roly was involved directly in some bloody engagements. The battalion only became very heavily involved in continuous serious actions from the date of the German Spring Offensive, March 21st 1918. Co-incidentally it was the day that Roly was killed in action.

One of the most feared weapons that was actually banned by the Geneva Convention after the war was the flamethrower, first used by the Germans at Hooge, near Ypres in Belgium at the end of July 1915. Roly had spent his first part of the war billeted at Houplines just a mile over the French border before he arrived with the battalion at Wippenhoek, east of Ypres on May 31st 1915. Two months later he really did encounter his baptism of fire when his battalion attacked at Hooge on July 30th, they were swiftly counter-attacked by the horrendously frightening German flamethrowers. This weapon damaged morale more than it caused actual burns casualties. I certainly know which direction I would head in if confronted by a flamethrower!

It would be the following summer before the battalion found themselves in vicious fighting again, this time upon the Somme where they were actively involved from mid to late September of 1916 at the battles of Flers-Courcelette, Morval and Le Transloy. There are no actual records that survive to recall which action Roly was involved in that led to the award of his Military Medal. Using a process of elimination by studying the movements of the battalion and descriptions of battle situations, we are suggesting that Roly was decorated for an act of bravery that occurred on Monday September 18th 1916.

At 05.50 in the early morning mist Roly and the battalion with other divisional units attacked a huge German strong point known at the Quadrilateral. After initially being forced back to their original starting point the men reorganised and eventually achieved an incredible feat. Roly by then a Sergeant was in the thick of it and led by example.

The battalion stormed forward in a ferocious attack and captured 100 enemy prisoners and some of their weaponry. There was a heavy price to pay with 153 casualties sustained by the 1st West Yorkshire's, including several officers killed, two of them company commanders. Sergeant Roland Casemore was in the aftermath very quickly promoted to Company Sergeant Major, effectively a promotion in the field.

Newly promoted and decorated for his bravery Roly was given leave back to England where he was reunited with a sweetheart from his home town, Nellie Longhurst, the daughter of a chimney-sweep. Nellie worked as a domestic servant for a wealthy merchant and agent at a large house in Catford, around three or so miles away from Bromley. Interestingly, Rob suggests that considering Roly's experiences and his belief that he would survive the war it came as no surprise that he proposed marriage to Nellie. He wanted her to feel secure, particularly considering his rank and position, he could have provided for her and assured the girl two years his senior of that. The couple were married in the local parish church in Bromley on Sunday December 3rd 1916. Being a regular soldier and a Sergeant-Major it was likely that he was attired in his number one service dress and actually wearing his Military Medal, the medal I am looking at right now as I write this. From an account of our contact who claims to have seen a photograph of the newly married couple, the event appeared to have been a grand occasion.

Nellie came from a family of chimney-sweeps, her father and two elder brothers and even her mother had practised the vocation. It is reasonable to assume that her father John who was a master-chimney sweep wouldn't have dressed up in his work attire, chimney-sweeps were common guests at weddings to bring luck. John Longhurst we think would have been dressed in his best suit to give his daughter away. Her elder brother William, a sweep himself probably made the 'lucky' appearance.

Roly returned to his battalion a happily married man with plenty to look forward to, he was back in France in 1917. Once again in action in March of that year he was actively involved in trench raids against the infamous strategic positon of Hill 70, famously taken by the Canadian Corps later that year. Roly also saw heavy action at Cambrai in November 1917. His final stand was back in the northern Somme region in March 1918 when German storm-troopers massed for a huge offensive in an attempt to end the war for good.

Roly's battalion did not expect the huge bombardment they would face early on the morning of March 21st as they manned their trenches at Morchies. Operation Michael, the huge German Spring Offensive began with shells hurtling in massive numbers towards the men. Assisted by Austrian gun batteries the Germans were incredibly ruthless as their bombardment started at 05.00. High explosive and in particularly a large number of gas shells were launched on to the British positions. Roly was killed as the shells rained down, Rob suggests it is more likely that it wasn't a high explosive shell that took his life and thinks it was a gas shell that was responsible.

The reason for this is that Roly's body was recovered from the battlefield and buried, had he taken a direct hit from an explosive shell his body would have been shredded. It is very sad to even contemplate that if indeed it was a gas shell that finished off the brave warrant officer he would have met a very gruesome end. These chemical weapons caused incredible suffering and in many instances death for the ones upon the receiving end wasn't instantaneous. The horrific reality of this is that Roly probably suffered terribly.

A hideous chart describing German Gas Shells, one particular type of these horrendous chemical weapons took the life of Roland Casemore.

Back home in Bromley, Nellie would have kept up a correspondence with her husband. When she actually did receive the telegram informing her of Roly's death I certainly believe the actual circumstances of it would not have been described to her by the officer who sent back the tragic news. The death of her young husband had a dramatic effect upon Nellie who would never talk about him as she progressed through her own life. One year later in the summer of 1919 Nellie married another Bromley man, John Pankhurst, who was considerably older than herself. They had a son, John junior. Perhaps because of the age difference of around thirty years between them it didn't come as a surprise when the marriage ended in divorce.

Sadly, Nellie had to see custody of her young son pass to John Pankhurst after the divorce as was common at the time. She once again found happiness with another Bromley chap, Alfred Frisby, who was almost six years her junior. The couple had a daughter and were eventually married in 1951 in Bromley, they were together for over forty years before Alfred passed away in 1973.

Nellie died in 1978 at the age of 88, sixty years after the loss of her beloved Roly. She had been widowed twice, divorced and although she never spoke of Roly we are sure he was never far from her thoughts. Our acknowledgements here go to Carol Etherington, Nellie's granddaughter for some of the information supplied regarding her grandmother's life.

Company Sergeant-Major Roland Sidney Casemore MM lies eternally at rest within the Queant Road Cemetery in Buissy, France, close to where he fell at the age of 26. Here we hold his Military Medal with pride in wonderful custodianship. Not surprisingly it has been split from the rest of his entitlements that include the 1914-15 Star, the British War Medal and Victory Medal.

William Mallin
Killed in Action
France, Sept. 1st 1918
Aged 38.
Awarded the DISTINGUISHED CONDUCT MEDAL
and the MILITARY MEDAL in 1917

THERE are fifty chronicles of soldiers who died as a result of the First World War in this book. Willie Mallin is the most highly decorated of them all. Incredibly he was awarded both the Distinguished Conduct Medal and the Military Medal within two months of each other in 1917. The gallantry and bravery of this man was rarely seen, for dual awards like his were relatively few and far between.

Willie was an Irishman, born in Dublin in the summer of 1880. I cannot understate the contribution throughout history of the 'Fighting Irish'. The British Empire wouldn't have existed but for the huge part that Irish soldiers played, before and during Willie's time. As the colonies were conquered the British relied upon enormous numbers of Irish soldiers who signed-on for life. The men from Ireland made up around a third of the entire strength of Britain's military force as it conquered and garrisoned huge swathes of the world.

SERGEANT W. MALLIN, D.C.M., M.M.
Killed in Action.

An old and grainy photo, but one of greatness. Willie Mallin wearing both his Distinguished Conduct Medal and Military Medal upon his tunic.

Even the Duke of Wellington sometimes begrudgingly admired the Irish soldiers for their tenacity and fighting abilities. Wellington was an Irishman himself, although he would never accept that despite the fact he had been born in Dublin. The great iconic figure in history knew how vitally important it was to recruit from Ireland.

This is not the place to refer to Irish political history and its complexities but I have to say that for men like Willie it could be awkward to serve the Crown. After the Easter Rising in 1916 and with many Irish soldiers losing their lives fighting for Britain and her Empire, feelings amongst Irish people were not surprisingly strained. At that time huge reforms were still in their respective processes. Irish soldiers with fair reasoning expected that Britain would acknowledge their contributions and that once hostilities had ceased Ireland's issues would be resolved. It didn't quite work out the way they may have expected. Willie was just one of six Mallin brothers serving with the colours during the war.

Although Willie was undoubtedly an Irishman, he actually saw very little of the land of his birth. His parents like so many hundreds of thousands of others emigrated to the north-west of England via the port of Liverpool in search of better lives. His father, Patrick was a native of Dublin, his mother Mary Ann (Polly) nee. Mullen, was originally from County Wicklow. The couple had been married in Dublin in 1879, within a year Willie was born, followed by another son, Patrick, in 1882 who was also born in Dublin. Young Patrick was known by a version of his middle name of John, referred to as Jack. This was not uncommon for a son who shared the same first name as his father.

Later that same year the Mallin family eventually settled in Wigan, Lancashire, a famous pit town and home of heavy industries with plenty of work available for all. Pat and Polly were blessed with seven more children. Mary, Gerry, John, Richard, James, Peter and Rose-Ann all arrived between 1884 and 1894.

It is difficult to begin to imagine what life was like for the Mallin clan, all squeezed into a tiny terraced house in Wigan. This town has a very distinctive accent of its own, Wiganers have their own twang. Although Willie was barely an infant when he arrived in the Lancashire pit town he would have interestingly have spoken in two tongue dialects. Growing up in the town with his contemporaries he would have developed the Wiganer tone without any doubt at all. However, within the confines of his own home and when speaking especially to his father his dialect would change to the same strains as his dad, to an Irish accent. Willie also probably did the same in the company of other Irish relatives or even friends later in life.

Responsibility was never far away from Willie, being the eldest child. He was barely 14-years old when his father died just after the birth of his little sister Rose-Ann. He had to take over the role of his dad and ensure that discipline was maintained within the household. This went on until some of his siblings and indeed himself were old enough to make their own way in their respective lives. Willie was a tough young man and would have dealt squarely with the prejudices that were metered out to families of

Irish stock or descent in Lancashire at that time. Within a few years after the death of Pat Mallin, the siblings began to go their separate ways easing the pressure on their mother, Polly. Willie Mallin didn't fancy working in the coal mines of Wigan and so he moved on.

Using some pretty deft techniques of research and piecing everything together relating to Willie's movements throughout his life, I am very confident regarding my portrayal of the facts after he left home. The young man enlisted into the Lancashire Fusiliers aged 17 in the early part of December 1897 and became a regular soldier. His service number allocated was 5870. Army life didn't quite suit Willie and as a result he 'claimed out' of service or in other words bought his discharge, this was agreeable if the reason was valid. Unfortunately we cannot confirm the actual reason. However such an exit meant the door was always left open for a recall or re-enlistment, although he wouldn't have been held on the reserve to claim gratuities. After all, Willie had completed basic training and drill, he had also accumulated military experience and a file of his service was always at hand should he wish to join again.

At this point Rob and I have a difference of opinions. My explanation as outlined above correctly describes the fact that Willie was 'claimed out' of military service. I have stated that I believe this was of his own will, Rob does not agree. He is of the opinion that Willie was 'claimed out' possibly by his mother in order not to receive a posting to South Africa and the Boer War. Although estranged from his family Willie was still the eldest of a number of children. No matter where he was, served or worked he would still be expected to financially support them in the absence of their father. Polly couldn't afford to potentially lose her son in a conflict. Willie didn't return home to his mother. Rob tells me that it is rare for men to 'go home' after they have served in the forces for whatever length of time. He moved to the Manchester suburb of Gorton, a grimy, tough and heavily industrialised area and initially found work in a local cotton mill and had to start all over again.

When Willie moved in as a paying boarder at the turn of the twentieth century into the cramped two-up, two-down, terraced house in east Manchester the circumstances were a little bizarre. The tenant of the little house was a certain Matthew Sylvester an ageing iron foundry labourer. At 50-years old his job would have tested him physically to say the least. Matthew had been married for only a few years, tying the knot in 1896 to his wife Alice, thirteen years his junior, both originally hailed from the Stoke area of Staffordshire.

Living with them was their 18-year old son, John, also an iron foundry labourer born in Beeston, Nottinghamshire in 1882. This date suggests he had been born out of wedlock, at a time when Matthew would have been 31-years old and Alice herself just 18. This doesn't quite seem to add up, why would the parents get married fourteen years after the birth of their only child? Both Matthew and Alice knew each other from their own district of birth. For them to move over to Nottinghamshire as an unmarried couple and then have a child before moving to Manchester and get married years later seems highly unlikely.

None-the-less according to official records they were a married couple and had a son. I am tempted to speculate as to what I believe really happened, however, I would be unable to back up my own theory. Interestingly, some years later on the 1911 census Alice is recorded as having no children born to her. I believe John was her step-son, Matthew being his biological father. Another boarder made up this dysfunctional household, 43-year old John Grice, originally from Derby and working as a factory furnace man. The two male boarders and John, the son, all shared the tiny back bedroom. Alice was the only one of the five, none of whom were natives of Manchester who didn't actually go out to work. Her hands were full taking care of four grown males, all of whom were bringing revenue into the household.

Willie as a boarder would have been well tended for by Alice who cooked all of his meals, washed and pressed his clothes amongst other domestic duties. In return he handed over a portion of his weekly wage. It is also very probable that he sent a few pennies each week back to his mother over in Wigan.

Alice almost became a surrogate mother to Willie, she was seventeen years his senior. As time progressed she would eventually become much more to him. She had already been subjected to cruel gossip about her pre-matrimonial status, a reason why Rob thinks she eventually got married. If as the records suggest her long co-habitation with Matthew did actually take place then she 'lived in sin' or 'over the brush' for many years. The gossip mongers in such a tight-knit community were given a further opportunity to lambast this woman with Willie also becoming a focal point of their cruel attentions.

There can be no doubt that Alice and Willie grew more than just fond of each other. On December 7th 1906, Matthew Sylvester worn out and tired after years of heavy labour passed away at the age of 57. A little over five months later his 44-year old widow Alice and 27-year old Willie were married at the register office in Warrington on May 17th 1907. Cruel fishwife type gossiping locals were in their element. Willie more than likely punched his way out of trouble more than once and it wasn't long before the newlyweds left Manchester for good. The whereabouts at this time of step-son John are unknown.

It is very fair to assume the reason as to why they married must have been because of a genuine love for each other. Willie was a strapping young eligible bachelor and certainly a worldly street-wise individual. Alice, middle-aged, wouldn't have been able to give him children. There is no question as to the familiarity between them and the way that Alice had taken care of him. The couple would have been absolutely 'hung out to dry' by the gossips. Willie being from an Irish catholic family and his bride a woman who had previously 'lived in sin' were verbally slaughtered by their contemporary working-class critics. For Alice and Willie, love conquered all.

What is for certain is that Willie and Alice then went on to enjoy the best years of their lives together. The happily married couple moved eastwards to Warrington and into their own little house at 27 Plumpton Street, a distance of thirteen miles and a short train journey away from his family in Wigan. Willie found steady, reliable and fairly well-paid employment at the factory of Monks, Hall and Co. Ltd. This company specialised in steel tube workings and was well established. Willie and Alice had no children to support and were able to afford to spend money that others couldn't in addition to having quality time together.

At the outbreak of war Willie had worked alongside his colleagues for several years. No doubt he had told them of his days in the army, some of the younger men were very keen to join-up and did so. Willie wasn't far behind them, I am sure that he sat down and convinced his wife who was by then in her fifties that he would get through anything and would return a hero. She couldn't stop him, on September 4th 1914, exactly one month after Britain had declared war upon Germany, Willie made his way to the local recruitment office to sign up.

Considering his previous military experience and the file of information to go with it he was readily accepted despite being in his mid-thirties back into his old regiment, the Lancashire Fusiliers. Willie was reallocated his original service number. The Fusiliers despatched Willie to the 4th Reserve Battalion, a unit that remained in the UK for the duration of the war. This battalion was specifically used for training. Despite his previous experience Willie was a good few years older than most of the new recruits. It was decided that he would benefit from being attached to a regular training battalion where conditions were tougher and the regimes harder. He held the lowest rank of private soldier during his six months with the battalion at Barrow-in-Furness and was subjected to all of the disciplines just the same as young men almost half his age.

Surely Willie held influence and this was recognised, his life experience and general demeanour gave him some advantages. He wanted to go to war and fight and he also wished to be posted to a regiment that was close to his home. I am certain that he persuaded the powers that be to allow him to join a regiment that had its base depot in Warrington, ideal for when he would get leave. He was successful and transferred to the South Lancashire Regiment (Prince of Wales's Own Volunteers) on March 6th 1915 and was reallocated the service number of 17628. Arriving at the depot in Warrington he was able to spend some time with his wife, a very short time later on March 16th 1915, Willie was in France.

Private Mallin was with the 2nd Battalion of the South Lancashire Regiment, one of the busiest regular army infantry units who fought through the war in its entirety. My grandfather served as a sergeant for years in this regiment, losing his life in the Second World War due to medical complications. Ironically at the time of his death he had been the same age as Willie. I know how proud the grandad I never met was to have served with the Prince of Wales's Volunteers, I'm sure Willie felt the same.

Willie himself had a very busy war and as we will discover he crucially developed very important skills. He was involved all along the Western Front from 1915 at the first attack on Bellewaarde and the actions at Hooge. In 1916 he was in action at the defence of Vimy Ridge in May and then proceeded to fight in the infamous Battle of the Somme encountering action at the Battle of Morval and subsequently the capture of Geudecourt.

The battle hardened steel tube worker enjoyed a period of two weeks home leave in January 1917 and was informed that he was to be promoted to the rank of Lance Corporal. At that time Willie was 36-years old, he had demonstrated that he could be relied upon to undertake a very important and dangerous duty and also be responsible for others doing the same. L/Cpl. Mallin was attached to the battalion headquarters just behind the front lines. He was designated to deliver messages to officers commanding companies directly in the face of the enemy when other communications broke down as they often did. Willie was in constant danger, he had to negotiate his way across difficult terrain continuously at the mercy of enemy snipers. These marksmen were detailed to specifically take out the 'runners' in order to disrupt the logistical performance of the enemy. In addition to dodging the snipers, Willie faced the prospect of being hit at any time by ferocious machine-gun fire or high explosive shells.

In 1917 Willie was in the thick of it as the battalion helped to push the Germans back to the Hindenburg Line, then came the blood-soaked battle of Arras. This battle produced the worst daily British casualties of all time during the duration it was fought in appalling weather conditions. Willie's skills and his organisation and mentoring of others was fully recognised and as the battle raged his responsibilities were expanded. On April 18th 1917 in the field he was promoted to Corporal and given command of the section of battalion HQ orderlies. These men had to deliver hundreds of messages after all other communications had completely broken down in the sleet, hailstone and mud of Arras. The terrain was badly cut up and the Germans were raining down merciless firepower upon the beleaguered British battalions, many of them Scots.

Corporal Mallin was a trusted and valuable leader of the HQ despatch team and well known by all the officers. He led totally by example and knew that he had to inspire the young orderlies as they diced with death on a daily basis, they looked upon him as a father figure. It was here at Arras that Willie was to achieve the award of the Distinguished Conduct Medal – second only to the Victoria Cross – just look at the citation as to why detailed below:

'For conspicuous gallantry and devotion to duty. When in charge of battalion HQ orderlies on several occasions he accompanied them through heavy shellfire to give them confidence. He has on all occasions shown himself absolutely fearless and tireless and can be depended upon to carry any message anywhere'.

After the slaughter of Arras the late summer gave way to the hideous Third Battle of Ypres and the assault upon Passchendaele in Belgium. The battle began on July 31st 1917, just over a week later Corporal Mallin was at it again. This time he was decorated with the Military Medal for bravery in the field. A week later he was promoted to Sergeant and held huge influence at battalion HQ. He was respected, admired and certainly revered by the young orderlies who not only took his advice and guidance but trusted him with their lives. Perhaps Willie thought of them as the sons he never had or remembered the times as a teenager when he had to take charge of his young family when his own father died.

Another spot of leave was on the horizon in the late January and early February of 1918. Willie returned home to his wife a hero. He had been through some of the worst battles of the war to date and survived them all. Surely there couldn't be much longer to go and he had proved to all that he knew exactly what it took to be a specialist soldier. He was confident that he would see out the war and I am certain he reassured Alice of that. Whilst half way through his leave he sent out a letter to the authorities requesting the delivery of both his DCM and MM awards. The administrators responded very quickly and sent them out before his return to barracks at Oxford prior to his re-posting to France.

We are so pleased to have an actual photo of him wearing both these prestigious awards upon his tunic. In the picture you can see that Willie is trying his best not to beam a smile across the camera as was frowned upon at the time. He was formally presented with both awards at the barracks. His photo also appeared in the local newspapers. Certainly these were proud times for his wife Alice, his mother Polly and five of his brothers whom were also serving in the army at the time.

Back in action in France in 1918 Willie was on the Somme again before heading north towards what was to become the Battle of the Lys and the eventual push into Flanders. The all-action hero was taking the war in his stride as it was approaching a conclusion. Surely the highly decorated soldier would return home for good, to his home, the security of his employment and the love of his wife and family. It wasn't to be, with just over two months of the bitter conflict to go Willie found himself in the wrong place at the wrong time.

I have driven across the Belgian border from France on the motorway many times. The little town of Nieuwkerke always sticks in my mind because its name rings so differently from French towns and villages dotted around just across the border. Nieuwkerke was once known as Neuve Eglise, rather more French sounding. It was in this vicinity that Willie lost his life, it's a quiet place today, even on the motorway.

After pushing hard along the Lys the 2nd South Lancashire's were poised to cross the border and help to take Neuve Eglise. Battalion headquarters was slightly behind the lines and just about on the French side of the border. After relaying through the night with carrying parties the battalion readied itself for attack, the date was Sunday September 1st 1918. The Lancashire men were confident, even though the Germans were putting up resistance almost everywhere they were being pushed back, it would seem as though victory could be in sight.

With preparations in order and in support of the Inniskilling Fusiliers the men were poised. A senior officer was detailed to make a routine visit to battalion HQ to confer with the Adjutant, Captain J.R. Beall MC and to also speak with a man he knew well, Sergeant Mallin, whose preparations for his tasks to come would have been well in order. The Major arrived before two o'clock in the afternoon and very shortly afterwards whilst speaking to the Adjutant and Willie Mallin who was in the company of two orderlies, disaster struck.

It would appear all of the men were standing just outside the HQ entrance when suddenly a shell exploded only two yards to the right of the group. Willie was at the closest point of impact, he was killed probably instantly, although his body remained largely intact. The Adjutant and three others were wounded as recorded on the war diary transcript, the Major escaped without a scratch.

Willie's luck had ran out, he wouldn't have believed that he could possibly lose his life so randomly after everything he had been through and achieved. His loss affected all of his comrades very deeply. The longest serving orderly who served under him was compelled to write to his wife Alice. This man was in the burial party at the funeral, he described his sergeant as - 'a pal' – Willie wouldn't have minded that at all. A week later the Major an officer who had served before the war wrote emotionally to Alice. It is clear from reading his words the untimely death of his sergeant affected him personally, he had trusted Willie for a long period of time.

Writing this story has also had an effect upon me and certainly has more than touched my heart. There is an enduring feeling inside me that I have really got to know Willie Mallin even though he died so long ago. I suppose this was reinforced when I read the list of personal items that were recovered from his body, it just seems so close. The items were; ID disc, photos, pipe, wallet, pocket shrine (religious), 9ct gold ring, 9ct gold ring broken with one stone, purse, diary, metal mirror, glass mirror, DCM and MM ribbons, badge, two razors and a shaving brush.

Willie's final resting place is only a couple of miles across the Belgian border from the place of where he met his death in France. He lies today and forever more at peace in the tiny Westoutre Churchyard extension cemetery. With great respect the town of Wigan also remembers him upon their cenotaph, he is also commemorated in Warrington and very importantly upon Ireland's memorial records.

Back at home in Warrington, Alice was by the time of her husband's death 55-years old. She grew old gracefully and alone in the little house she had once shared with her hubby and lived throughout the struggles of the 1920's and 1930's. So many times as she sat all alone huddled around the fireplace she must have thought of the days when her beloved Willie walked through the front door, with a beaming smile upon his face. Alice would have always cherished the moment when he returned back on leave in January of 1918 keeping the promise that he would be a hero. Through sheer bad fortune he was unable to keep his final promise of returning home for good. Alice Mallin died peacefully at the little house at 27 Plumpton Street, Warrington in October 1940, aged 77.

I know this story has also had an impact upon Rob who purchased the Distinguished Conduct Medal and Military Medal awarded to William Mallin all those years ago. He acquired them from an auction in the south of England, many miles from their spiritual home. Now they are safe and Willie's story has been told – the memory of this great and wonderful man lives on.

George Graham
Killed in Action
Belgium, Nov. 7th 1917
Aged 30.
Recommended for the award of MENTIONED IN DESPATCHES in 1917

THE final subject within this chapter didn't receive any award for his final act of bravery. Our man was recommended for a decoration by the officer commanding the Siege Battery in which he served. George Graham's name was put forward to be 'Mentioned in Despatches'.

This form of acknowledgement of a brave or honourable deed did not constitute the award of an actual medal. The senior commanders in the field in particularly Sir Douglas Haig would write despatches detailing prolonged actions to the War Office. Names of certain individuals recommended by officers in the field would be mentioned in those despatches. Any individual referred to would receive a certificate and be entitled to wear an oak leaf emblem upon the ribbon of their Victory Medal, they would also have their name published in the 'London Gazette'. The MID recognition is accepted as the fourth highest level of award for a brave deed ranking directly beneath the Military Medal or Military Cross, there was no limit on how many times a man could receive this distinction.

It has often been noted that men who were killed in certain heroic circumstances and were initially recommended to posthumously receive the coveted Victoria Cross, actually saw their deeds downgraded to 'Mentioned in Despatches'. We have the evidence that George was recommended to be mentioned, however it would appear that no record appears to determine he was. We will let you decide if you think he should have been, you may come to the conclusion he deserved much higher recognition.

George Graham was a Geordie, he was born in the Newcastle district of Elswick in 1887 and like his siblings lived and grew up there. His parents George senior and Hannah Birkett originally came from rural Cumberland. George senior spent almost his entire working life on the railways, Hannah prior to her wedding in 1875 had worked in domestic service before becoming a full-time mother to seven surviving children of eight. The Graham's moved to Elswick in 1876 shortly after the birth of the eldest daughter who sadly died in infancy. Seven more children followed, all born and raised in Elswick. Esther, Robert, Dorothy, Hannah, George, John and Ethel all lived with their parents. The family moved around the district a few times as they expanded. George senior was a railway guard on the goods trains, a hard working career man who wanted the very best for his family.

The importance of receiving a good education and doing well at school was impressed upon his children, some of whom went further past initial school leaving age. We have a superb original photograph of his young son George with all of his class mates and teacher as a seven-year old at the local school, St. Martin's. Young George stayed on a little longer at school and upon leaving gained respectable employment as an accountants' clerk. His younger brother John Willie became a law clerk and his sister Ethel also stayed on at school. Another sister worked for many years as a retail assistant. In the Newcastle of the period most working-class people had to get their hands dirty, especially the men, either down the pit, in the factories or the shipyards.

Within their neighbourhood the respectable Graham family were pillars of the local community and well known to all. It came as no surprise that George would meet his sweetheart in his own parish. Florence Nightingale Kitching, had been orphaned as a child and was adopted by the Hall family who resided in Elswick. George Richard Hall was a railway porter who probably knew young George Graham's father through their employment. He and his wife Ann had lost three of their four children, with only one daughter surviving. The Hall family were very poor and lived in squalid, harsh conditions in just two rooms of a tiny house that was shared with other extended members of the family. This shabby dwelling had no running water or other utilities.

Times were hard, six adults living in two rooms is almost unthinkable, Florence was grateful, after all she had been adopted by the poor family and was loved and cherished. Her pitiful wages as a domestic servant helped to maintain the awkward family unit, it was a means to an end. George Graham the respectable well-dressed clerk was her knight in shining armour, she was a pretty girl and we have a photo of her to prove that. There can be no doubt as to why George was attracted to her.

When war broke out in August 1914 many young men from Tyneside who worked in the traditional industries enlisted and peer pressure played a part. George was insulated from that by working in a small office environment. His employer would have been keen to hold on to his trusted clerk, no doubt making overtures to him as to his capabilities for progression. George had done well at school, he had managed to secure employment that was reasonably well-paid, comfortable and held prospects. His father probably reasserted these points, why should George volunteer to go off to war? He had a lot to lose.

The young clerk intensified his relationship with Florence, who herself was yearning for a better life, they eventually married in January of 1916. At around this time conscription was being introduced for single men over the age of 18 to go and fight for their country. George's father had passed away before he had married Florence, his siblings were also making their own ways in life. I believe that George and Florence the newly-weds moved to live with his ageing mother and elder sister Dorothy at 51 Hartington Street in Elswick. Florence almost immediately fell pregnant, everything was looking up for the young married couple.

Later that year conscription was expanded to encompass married men. George Graham was a healthy 28-year old man. I am convinced he was conscripted as his subsequent postings had no localised familiarity about them at all, had he volunteered there would have been a high probability they may have done. Taking into account my previous comments and the fact that he was a newly married man, expectant father and certainly a career minded individual with a lot going for him, then it all points to his conscription. His service number shows he was a relatively later entrant.

Florence and George were delighted by the arrival of their little baby daughter Vera who entered the world at their home on Saturday September

18th 1916. Their lives now seemed to be complete, but it wouldn't be much longer before George would have to oblige and honour his call for duty, baby or no baby, he simply had to go to war. I can say with confidence that Florence and George kept themselves pretty private within their community. George's employment would have surely kept him on a straight and sober path. It would not be in his interests to go boozing in the street corner pubs with shipyard labourers, miners and foundry workers. Florence I believe was a homemaker, her previous experience as a domestic servant would have made this very likely. Nevertheless, it is highly probable that George received some abuse and was on more than one occasion handed a white feather in the streets of Elswick. Many mothers, wives and sisters had lost their beloved sons, husbands and brothers, George knew he had to go.

As 1916 gave way to 1917 George became an integral member of the newly formed 375th Siege Battery of the Royal Garrison Artillery. This particular unit had been formed at Prees Heath Camp in Shropshire, many miles from his home in Newcastle-Upon-Tyne. The battery officially came into being on February 12th 1917 with many of its members being conscripts like George. A siege battery was heavily armoured and relied upon around 180 men and half a dozen or so officers. The unit also accommodated over 100 horses with ten four-horse wagons and three two-horse carts in order to become fully operational.

George spent a number of months at the base training camp in Shropshire before he finally left England on August 18th 1917. The Third battle of Ypres was already underway in Belgium and the 375th found themselves pitched well truly into the thick of it. Weather conditions worsened as the eventual struggle to take the village of Passchendaele came to a conclusion when the Canadians eventually succeeded on November 6th 1917. Just a day later with the Germans still clinging on around the salient the 375th Battery positioned just to the north of Ypres were being heavily shelled by a ferocious bombardment.

Horses were panicking and crazed with sheer terror they became very hard to control. The conditions of both terrain and weather as well as poor visibility and extreme exposure to shellfire rendered the situation as very serious. One of George's comrades Driver F. Neale lost control of his limber when one of the horses bolted, the others terrified and screaming with fear were also out of control.

George Graham, a man who realised the suffering of the horses was unbearable also understood the whole situation was extremely dangerous. The German gunners realising they were causing total chaos amongst the

British battery were now taking further aim. George reached the stricken animals and took hold of their bridles, he then began to calm them in an effort to bring about a sense of orderly control. Older and more battle hardened and experienced servicemen would more than likely have let the horses run free or be blown to pieces as they took cover. George did what he thought was right, he believed he could save the animals and stabilise the overall situation. The Germans then threw a direct hit upon the horses and limbers, all the animals were killed along with Driver Neale and George. Another casualty was the Battery Sergeant-Major who also perished, perhaps he had been going to the aid of George and the horses.

The officer commanding the 375th was incredibly impressed by the heroic act of bravery demonstrated by George Graham. In an emotional letter that is right in front of me at this moment in time he wrote the following words addressed to Florence.

Somewhere in Belgium
10th November 1917
Dear Mrs. Graham,

I feel I must write on behalf of myself and the battery with regard to the sad loss of your husband, Driver George Graham, on November 7th. On this day Driver Graham was engaged on bringing forward gun limbers to their positions near our front line.

The enemy were shelling our whole area which was particular heavy on the day in question. The horses were very hard to control because of the noise, when a limber driven by Driver F. Neale bolted and would have caused serious damage and possible loss of life. Your husband who saw the situation at once ran forward and took the horses bridles and began calming them. At that precise moment the limber received a direct hit which instantly killed both men and the horses.

Driver Graham, without hesitation and thought for his own safety went forward in an unselfish act which showed the character and steadfast determination of the man. If it is any consolation he would not have felt any pain and would have died instantly.

For this heroic act, I shall be recommending the award of a Mention in Despatches and may I once again on behalf of myself and the men of the battery offer our sincere condolences.

In the aftermath of Third Ypres and Passchendaele, Douglas Haig did not mention George Graham in his despatches to the War Office. The Geordie accountants' clerk was not recognised for his individual act of heroism in any form. The fact that his deeds went unrewarded comes as no surprise to me at all.

Rob is unsure as to whether the officer commanding did the right thing by writing the letter to Florence and suggests it could have compelled her grief, especially as George was not recognised as he should have been. I have to say the officer in my opinion was attempting in his own way to express what a brave man her husband really was, but I agree that I don't think Florence would have appreciated that. George had nothing to prove to her or their infant daughter, I cannot begin to imagine the scale of the mental anguish she suffered.

George's story also offers us the opportunity to express the shocking treatment and appalling casualties that horses, mules and donkeys had to cope with during the First World War. A staggering eight million of them perished. Many of the animals were plucked from the fields of their respective countries and literally plunged into hell. It may shock you when I reveal that after the war as the men were being demobilised and repatriated, that took some time, many thousands more of these animals were simply abandoned and left to die. If they couldn't find enough food on the scarred former battlefields then they would starve to death. In many instances the animals were rounded up, slaughtered and eaten, sometimes their prime meat went to the local population, the rest was fed to the pigs. Total shame for this has to be heaped upon the British cigar-puffing bureaucrats in the War Office at that time.

The legacy of George's sacrifice and the suffering endured by his wife are further illustrated by the way this whole story was conceived. George's two medals, the British War Medal and the Victory Medal didn't come just as one lot. A number of his personal possessions had been stored for many years inside an old Ogden's Redbreast Flake tobacco tin, they were all neatly wrapped in an old piece of newspaper. These items give us a further insight into the closeness of George and Florence, the items in the tin were as follows: RA cap badge, official-tag ID disc, RA stick badge, cloth badge bearing a picture of Jesus Christ accompanied by the words 'Apostleship of Prayer', button stick with service number engraved, two medals, two medal ribbons, original medal boxes of issue, RA sweetheart brooch and a double-sided picture locket with a photo of George on one side and Florence on the other. These items were purchased directly by

The artefacts of George Graham including the locket picture of his beloved wife Florence.

Rob in 2018 from a house clearance. The tin had been kept locked away for many years.

Looking at the pictures inside the locket you can see that George was indeed a smartly dressed professional young man. His wife with her large attractive eyes meant everything to him. Florence kept the sweetheart brooch that she undoubtedly would have worn whilst George was away on service in Belgium. The artefacts graphically tell their own story of a tragedy and are a poignant reminder that there are no victors in war.

Florence Nightingale Graham and her daughter Vera continued to live in the house at Hartington Street in Newcastle. There is no question that Florence would have received offers to remarry as many war widows did. She refused them all and struggled to bring up her daughter who had no recollection at all of her father. Florence was not alone, she continued to live with her elderly mother-in-law, Hannah and older sister-in-law, spinster, Dorothy. Hannah Graham eventually passed away in 1939 at the ripe old age of 86. Florence had devoted her life to looking after her and was dealt another blow. Her daughter Vera who had followed in her father's footsteps to work in an office environment returned home to console her mother Florence. The short-hand typist who had lost her father as a baby and now her grandmother was by Florence's side when she died at the house aged just 52 early in 1943. Her mother had endured a very hard life from the start, from being orphaned, to living in poverty and then losing her beloved husband, it all took its toll upon her.

The final stinging sentiments concerning the non-award to George go to Rob. He now attacks the senior High Command with regard to their attitudes towards the heroism shown by George. It is usually myself who rips into Douglas Haig and his former gang of 'Donkey Generals'. This time Rob who has lost sleep thinking about George's unfair treatment wants to make his view-point very clear. He believes Haig should have mentioned George in despatches but didn't do so because he regarded him as a fool for trying to save horses, he would also have been probably aware that George was a conscript. Haig's attitude towards conscripted men bordered upon him viewing them as 'shirkers'. Haig, the former cavalry officer knew horses very well, he cared nothing for them for they were simply machines to him. Rob points out that had George's deeds have taken place today he would have been awarded a humane medal for gallantry. Words inscribed upon George's headstone where he rests in Belgium quite simply read – 'Until the Dawn Breaks'. The dawn broke many more times for Florence Nightingale Graham with her husband no longer by her side.

ROUGH JUSTICE

ATTITUDES towards the men who served during the First World War ranged from passive expectations to great levels of respect. The soldiers themselves came from all backgrounds, from every village, town, city and shire, no two were the same. Their own personal feelings and emotions with regard to the war spread across a broad protracted spectrum. Some individuals had no hope, faith or belief in the cause, others embraced the war with great enthusiasm and excitement.

For some the probability of the next day being their last was a constant worry. A surprising number of individuals shunned strict military discipline, they lived for the moment and broke the rules wherever and whenever they chose to do so. Others were rotten to the core, some even enjoyed the 'legalised murder' that could be committed upon enemy soldiers. Thieves, con-artists and other criminal elements found their way around the military systems and tore up the rule book.

The character of any individual is moulded more often by their own life experiences. In this chapter we will look at five men who one way or another didn't receive a certain form of justice, be it official or moral. These guys each lived through their personal individual war. Survival was paramount to them, sadly, none of them manged to live or grow old.

It is easy to form stereotypical opinions or judgements upon those who served in the Great War. After all when we visit a war memorial we see rows of names carved along the sides in neat lines, they all look much the same. As we shall discover in this chapter not all of those men who went off to fight delivered what was expected of them. All five of the guys featured here made the ultimate sacrifice and we will always be indebted to them, no matter how naughty they may have been.

Thomas Hoy

Killed in Action
Belgium, Oct. 31st 1914
Aged 37.

IT is difficult to know exactly where to start with our fiend Tommy Hoy. I wish that I had been given the opportunity to meet him. We could have enjoyed a lot of banter over a few pints, although I would probably have had a very bad hang-over the day after. Every time I think about Tommy he brings a smile to my face, you will see why as this story unfolds.

Thomas Hoy was an out and out rascal throughout his life. He came from the Lancashire town of Darwen. I discovered his story after obtaining his absolute and complete medals set entitlement. The 1914 Star with Bar, British War Medal, Victory Medal, all with ribbons, Death Plaque and Scroll with its container as well as the original transmittal letter and medal boxes of issue. Someone, somewhere had made an effort to preserve Tommy's legacy by keeping this whole lot together.

His parents had left their respective native lands as teenagers. Thomas Hoy senior was an Irishman who married Scots-born Sarah Clark in Darwen in 1860. The couple spent the rest of their lives in the Lancashire town, all of their seven children who survived into adulthood including the youngest, Tommy, were born in Darwen. Thomas, the father was engaged for his entire working life employed in a local paper mill, until his death in 1896 before he had reached the age of fifty. His wife despite having several children also had to go out to work in a local cotton mill.

Tommy was born in 1877, there was a big age gap between him and his older brothers. James was sixteen years his senior, Michael, fourteen, Andrew ten and John six years older than him, he also had two elder sisters. It is fair to assume that Tommy was literally at the bottom of the pecking order in a large and poor working-class family. He was probably overlooked as a child and this may explain why he developed his personal characteristics. The life and times of this man took many turns. He was clearly an unsettled soul and moved around the town frequently throughout his life. Following his father to the paper mill he had by then left the family home. Restless and frustrated Tommy went to reside with his older brother Andrew and his wife when he was just thirteen years old.

A few years later whilst working as a colour-mixer Tommy was living with his sister Elizabeth, her husband John, their two children and two lodgers at another address. He had also spent some time living with his widowed mother. Tommy was well known in the town of Darwen that had at the time a larger population than it has today of around 40,000 people. He was still a teenager when he caused an absolute scandal within his community in 1896. The Hoy family were Catholics, Tommy didn't really bother about his church's tradition and got 18-year old local girl Elizabeth Noel pregnant. She was a close neighbour of his mother. Elizabeth and Tommy were married at St. Joseph's church in the town on May 16th 1896. Their son, John Charles Hoy arrived less than three months later on August 4th 1896. The couple initially went to live with Elizabeth's father. This was around the period of when Tommy's own father had passed away. There was a lot going-on in the life of the 19-year old rogue at that particular time.

The marriage didn't last, Tommy left his wife to go and live with his sister and brother-in-law. He was also getting disillusioned with the mundane routine of working in the paper mill and decided he wanted adventure. At the turn of the twentieth century and shaving a couple of years off his age he joined the local Militia, the forerunner of the Territorial Force as a part-time soldier. What he failed to declare was that he was a married man with a child. In 1902 he signed on full-time and joined the 2nd Battalion of the Loyal North Lancashire Regiment based in Preston. By this time the military authorities had received a plea from his wife asking for some of his pay to be deducted to support her and their child. The fact that he was married was endorsed by his brother who was forced to reply to a letter from a senior officer to confirm that. Private Thomas Hoy had three-pence a day forfeited from his army pay and had to admit his matrimonial situation.

Tommy was an impish little character standing at just 5'2 tall, he became an awkward and outrageous soldier. His full disciplinary conduct record still exists, it's the worst one I have ever witnessed with numerous charges and subsequent punishments. Tommy was a serial drunkard, he couldn't help himself. The charges against him started just a month into his four year full-time service period and continued right until the end of it. Within a month of becoming a regular soldier he was absent from a military tattoo and was found staggering around drunk outside the barracks at 11.00am.

Tommy was then caught a couple of times being absent without any reason from duty, looking slovenly and in possession of an untidy kit. When at Shorncliffe he was discovered lurking suspiciously in the hospital grounds contrary to the strict rules. His first five offences received punishments confining him to barracks. Things got an awful lot worse when Tommy was posted to Gibraltar, his drinking became out of control and he faced numerous charges for drunken behaviour at various times of the day. Tommy was found to be heavily intoxicated whilst on stand-by guard duty. He was later convicted of causing disturbances in the barrack room whilst drunk on more than one occasion. The boozy little soldier had also been charged with having a dirty kit and swearing at a Lance-Corporal!

A year later Tommy was serving in South Africa. Whilst stationed in Pretoria he was found to be the worse for wear after drinking excess alcohol when on a parade ahead of night duties. Further disgraceful drunken behaviour and causing trouble in the barrack room followed and soon afterwards he was embarrassingly charged with soiling his bed! Tommy's numerous punishments included many periods of being confined to barracks, a number of fines that he really couldn't afford and periods of hard-labour.

Despite all of the offences Tommy committed he wasn't dishonourably discharged or court-martialled. Rob offers an explanation for this based upon his own experiences. He suggests that Tommy being such a small man was easily picked upon and the officers felt a little bit sorry for him. Rob also believes that Tommy had been a good soldier in relation to the military expectations placed upon him that included musketry and field-craft. The authorities could have ditched him at any time, they didn't. Rob is convinced Tommy found barrack room life difficult and his officers had been aware of that.

The pay of an ordinary infantryman of the period wasn't especially great. It would have been lower than that of what he had received whilst working in the paper mill at Darwen. Access to alcohol depended upon availability to get out of the barracks. Also let's take into account the postings of Gibraltar and Pretoria. In the early twentieth century there were brothels and one or two drinking establishments in both venues, gaining access to them required permission. In my opinion Tommy had developed another more crude way of obtaining alcohol. Considering some of the states that he got himself into, my suggestive comments that follow may not come across as just mere guess work.

Tommy had an Irish father who had left the emerald isle in the mid-nineteenth century in the aftermath of the potato famine, he escaped that with some of his relatives. The Hoy way of things in Ireland prior to the famine probably revolved around the growing and cultivating of po-tatoes. Almost the entire population of Ireland ate them on a daily basis.

Was Tommy Hoy partial to the 'moonshine' alcohol that blighted his military service before he was tragically killed in action in 1914?

The wily growers had also learned how to develop very quickly and easily another derivative by-product from the potato. Poitin, pronounced 'poteen' was illegally produced 'moonshine' made from potatoes, incredibly it was around 95% proof. Only a couple of mouthfuls would render the consumer extremely intoxicated.

I have no direct evidence that Tommy was involved in the production of 'poteen', However, I suspect he was and that others, including one or two non-commissioned officers knew about it. The NCO's would have been supplied with the potent spirit by Tommy in a mutually agreeable arrangement. What I do know is that Tommy somehow managed to get himself into the kitchens as a company cook. Access to potatoes was readily there for him, I'm sure he took advantage of that!

Tommy left his regular stint as a soldier and remained on the first-class reserve for a further eight years. He returned to the paper mill in Darwen and attended regular summer camps as was required by reservists, only just scraping through the physical tests as the years went by. Tragedy struck in late 1905, his estranged wife Elizabeth died aged just 27, leaving behind her and Tommy's son who was himself just a mere boy. The youngster continued to live with his grandfather as Tommy's chaotic and rollercoaster ride through life sped on.

The intrepid hell-raiser carried on living between addresses in Darwen, with relatives, once again including his mother. He then pops-up at another address on his own for a brief period in 1911. At around this time he had lost his identity certificate for his reserve service and wasn't paid on stand-by until it was replaced. By February of 1914 Tommy's whole time on the reserve had expired and he was taken off the list, his military career as it would seem was over.

It is reasonable to suggest that Tommy didn't know the First World War was looming on the horizon when he decided to re-join as a full-time soldier in June of 1914. The Loyal North Lancashire Regiment accepted his application despite him being in his late thirties and considerably older than many of those wishing to join-up. Tommy's record was there for all to see, his overall conduct marked as 'fair' from his previous twelve years of military service with regular and reserve experience. There would have been one or two words advising him on how to conduct himself, he had matured, possessed the required knowledge and I am pretty sure it could be seen that he was fearless.

Tommy was posted to the 1st Battalion and reallocated his original service number of 6723 but for some reason he didn't make the original draft on August 13th 1914. Just over two weeks later he was posted and arrived in France on September 3rd 1914. He was involved in action at Priez before being engaged in a horrendously costly battle at Cerny-en-Laonnois. The 1st Battalion Loyal North Lancashire Memorial stands upon the sight of this blood-bath that took place on September 14th 1914. This was overseen by the then commander of the Corps in the field, Douglas Haig.

October 31st 1914 used to be known as 'Ypres Day'. Veterans and relatives of those who were killed in the first desperate defence of the Belgian town wore blue cornflowers on their left lapels upon each anniversary after the war. In a similar way as to what we do now with the poppy on Remembrance Sunday this used to be very common, until the veterans started to leave us in large numbers in the late 1960's. It was on that symbolic day that Tommy Hoy lost his life. The previous day the 1st Loyals had been detailed to cover the strategic withdrawal of the 2nd Battalion West Surrey Regiment at Zandvoorde. Haig's blundering public-school educated staff officers were confused and repositioned the Lancashire men into the path of the withdrawal causing a bottle-neck. The eventual tactic was therefore slowed and casualties mounted, at some point on the morning of October 31st 1914, Tommy went missing.

Given his appalling service record it would be tempting to suggest he absconded… he didn't at all. Tommy faced his fate as brave as any man could possibly do. It wasn't until the following year that his death was actually confirmed. In a tragic irony Tommy would remain lost as he had done so during the course of much of his life. He had never settled and lived wherever he laid his hat. Even in death uncertainty followed him.

Somehow, maybe by the grace of God, Tommy was eventually found, more than likely in a hastily dug grave. His remains were later officially interred sometime between the summer of 1916 and the early part of 1919. He was buried within the fourth plot at the Bedford House Commonwealth War Commission Cemetery just south of Ypres. At last Tommy, for the first time ever was at peace and remains so to this day.

His son John prospered and lived all his life in Darwen becoming a master upholsterer and also served as an air-raid warden during the Second World War. John obviously treasured his father's full medals entitlement that slipped out of his possession following his death in 1966. The collection is now with us.

When asked hypothetically who you could or would have met if you had been around at a certain time you may reply - Winston Churchill… Nelson Mandela… Princess Diana or even Bob Marley! If you asked me the same question I would have to say that Tommy Hoy would be my choice. One day I will visit his grave and pay my respects to the little man who may have demonstrated many weaknesses and faults. The same wee man had the heart of a lion and gave his life for a better world, a world that never really gave much to him. Tommy broke the rules many times, tragically he was killed as a result of unjust military command decisions that were not governed by rules.

Thomas Dunlavey

Died of Wounds
Home, Nov. 2nd 1915
Aged 27.
Served under the alias of his older brother James Dunlavey (aka-Dunlavy)

WHEN Rob purchased a 1914-15 Star trio in late 2017 at a price substantially below the real market value he was not aware of the truly incredible story behind the medals. The significance of that very acquisition in this instance is profound, I really do mean that. Medals that come at discounted rates usually do so for a reason, especially if the basic research behind them doesn't appear to make sense or add up. Collectors get uneasy if they can't stitch together the facts, suspicions are formed and the medals are left to drift around the open market, passing from custodian to custodian.

In this instance the stitching has been done with awe and absolute fascination. Helped by a series of co-incidences alongside some very intense research, here we have something that will have you on the edge of your seat. Secrets buried long ago are revealed for the very first time. In a somewhat tragic way we tell the story of a young man who has NEVER been acknowledged for his ultimate sacrifice… until now. This was no fault of anyone, he was and still is entirely to blame for this, yet we have to honour him no matter how many years have passed. Hopefully his legacy can begin here and continue.

With a name such as Dunlavey, often also referred to as Dunlavy there has to be a huge Irish connection, there is indeed. Tom's parents were both the children of Irish immigrants who arrived in Yorkshire to escape the potato famine and had settled in Bradford. James Dunlavey followed in his father Michael's footsteps and spent his entire working life in the building trade as a mason's labourer. He married Annie Callaghan in 1880, they moved in together with her widowed mother and went on to have a staggering number of thirteen children. Tragically eight of their offspring died, just five surviving from the total. Thomas was born at 15 Low Street, Bradford in October 1888.

Life was incredibly harsh for the Dunlavey family. Despite losing eight children Annie still had to go out to work in the mills to make ends meet. Of the surviving children, three daughters also worked in the textile mills. Eldest son James went along the line of the family tradition and like his father and grandfather he became a mason's labourer. That left Tom, the youngest living son who would eventually turn out to be a complete and utter scoundrel.

I have to say it must have been particularly difficult for young Tom as he was growing up. He witnessed the deaths of several of his siblings and experienced the grief of his parents that came with that. Being from a Catholic family and considering the circumstances described Tom would have seen the priest call at the home many times. He probably couldn't understand why his family had suffered so much. Also, being the youngest he may have felt slightly alienated and decided as he got older that he would choose his own destiny no matter what. He was four inches above the average height size for the period. I'm more than sure that he could and would deal with anything he considered as a threat towards him.

Tom Dunlavey had something to hide as a young man. There are records of a chap with his name spelled slightly differently having served a prison sentence in 1907, I don't believe this was Tom. I do believe he had been in trouble with the local police and magistrates for what could be termed as minor offences, probably involving some form of violence. Had this been the case he would have acquired a criminal record and more damaging in a tight-knit community, a reputation. I am convinced he was a handful of trouble. Local employers would have been wary of him, finding regular work may have been difficult for Tom.

The strapping young man couldn't even find employment as a labourer with his elder brother and father, so he made a decision, one that would have devastating effects upon his own future. He decided to join the very prestigious and glorious Scots Guards, but he had a problem, a criminal past and an unsavoury reputation to boot. The solution was cunning, deceitful and in some respects took courage upon his part. He succeeded with a plot to map ahead the future of his life, after all he had experienced nothing but misfortune.

On July 22nd 1910, Tom was at the recruitment centre in nearby Leeds. He would have known that by joining the Scots Guards his life would inevitably move on from the West Riding of Yorkshire. The crafty young man could become anonymous to those who once knew of him and start all over again. Somehow, Tom managed to obtain an employers' reference, he had been working as a carter for a coal merchant, citing the reason he left was because trade was slack. Tom knew the initial 'T' could easily be mistaken for the initial 'J'.

With incredible nerve he attested into the 1st Battalion of the Scots Guards as James Dunleavy, effectively taking the identity of his elder brother and was allocated the service number 7677. He didn't however use his brother's date of birth, he decided to use his own, maybe that kept the deception to a level of lower proportion. As for the Scots Guards, they took him at face value, his physique and height were all important to them. Just what had they let themselves in for?

From Yorkshire he was despatched to Caterham Barracks four days after signing-on. Within three months he had committed his first offence, it wasn't looked upon lightly by the Scots Guards. Just like all of the other Guards regiments they enforced strict and uncompromising discipline. Tom was caught breaking out of the barracks and sentenced to twenty-eight days detention. This was the first of a huge number of misdemeanours and chaotic offences committed by the maverick young Yorkshireman.

Further absences occurred at Caterham, he was charged with wilfully smashing a gas-light in his cell whilst detained. Tom was frustrated with barrack life and was relieved when he was posted to the bright lights of London and Chelsea Barracks. He was arrested by the Military Police for being found drunk and disorderly staggering down the Chelsea Road. At Christmas time he decided to have his own celebration and went missing on the night of December 26th returning back to barracks at 04.45 the following morning in a 'state'. Three further offences of making very inappropriate remarks to non-commissioned officers were also on file for good measure, add to those two more of being improperly dressed.

Early in 1911 Tom and the battalion were sent to Egypt, destination Cairo, with its compliment of brothels, gambling dens and drinking establishments. The daring and mischievous Guardsman was in his element and wasted no time in visiting local prostitutes. Most of the two year posting for Tom was spent in the military hospital. It started with scabies, along with tonsillitis and laryngitis and then more than one instance of gonorrhoea and other medical conditions involving 'discharge'. I will have to leave it up to you to work out exactly what Tom had been up to. The list of his ailments saw him admitted to hospital on eight separate occasions, sometimes for a number of days at a time.

Tom's medical problems were so bad that he was sent back to London before the posting was completed, he spent further periods of time in hospitals at Netley and Rochester. Just for good measure Tom's erratic behaviour continued whilst at Purbright camp, he quit his section and was seen entering the 'White Hart' public house. This came after two more offences of being absent from a tattoo and missing on parade. Another charge of drunkenness went on his record before he was found absent once more sleeping on a bench in Parliament Square.

His active service finally came to an end shortly afterwards in July 1913 at Chelsea Barracks. I don't think the non-commissioned officers were shedding any tears as he left to remain upon the reserve list for a further nine years. At this point in his life I think Tom took the easy option and returned to Bradford. I believe he spent his time getting by as best he could once again living with his family. A year later war was declared and Tom knew he would be recalled from the reserve list. Inevitably, he was, but not in the manner he expected.

Having served under his brother's name this was his secret, he had to cover his tracks regarding notifications of a recall to the colours. Tom was well aware of his brother's keenness to enlist. The 'real' James Dunlavey did just that, signing on with the localised 2nd Battalion Yorkshire Regiment (The Green Howards). As for the Scots Guards, Tom's old battalion the 1st were off very quickly to France in August 1914, Tom couldn't possibly have joined them. The 2nd Battalion Scots Guards followed in October. A specially created 3rd (Reserve) Battalion of Scots Guards was created in the same month at Chelsea Barracks. Tom or should I say 'James' was there to join them and reallocated one of the reserve battalion's specially created service numbers of 11845. Henceforth, there were two men by the name of James Dunlavey, from the same address and with the same parents serving in the First World War, but of course one of them wasn't the real deal.

Tom was posted to France as a reinforcement from the reserve battalion and immediately sent back to the 1st Scots Guards, he would have been recognised instantly by the non-commissioned officers. Despite his past Tom was a tough guy and certainly would have been suited to the rigours of combat. As for his deception... well as long as he didn't get killed then nobody would be the wiser!

His parents James senior and Annie having lost eight children had their two remaining sons fighting on the Western Front in France. Tragedy struck a cruel blow when notification came to them that James, the real James, their eldest son had been killed. He lost his life on June 5th 1915. James was never found and is commemorated on the Le Touret Memorial. I am pretty certain that Tom was informed by his parents of the death of his older brother. The Guardsman would have been more overcome with the loss of his sibling rather than thinking about any complications thereon. Tom had been at Festubert not far from where James perished at around the same time. Nevertheless, things were now getting more complicated for him.

In the early autumn of 1915 Tom found himself fighting desperately with the Guards Division and his battalion at Loos. It was there that he was badly wounded and subsequently evacuated form the battlefield. Tom's injuries meant that he was sent back to England for further treatment. I am certain he made it back to the little house in Bradford to complete his recovery. Things took a turn for the worse and infections set in, the brave pretentious Guardsman saw his life slipping away before him. I can't imagine his mother's anguish as she lost her tenth child of thirteen. Just before it happened I believe Tom made a confession on his death bed to his parents.

I have good grounds to think that Tom told his mum and dad about the deception, they would have known at that moment in time what the Scots Guards were never to find out. This is apparent when you see the family headstone it's not difficult to work out the truth from there. As it transpired the Scots Guards and the Imperial War Graves Commission of the time did acknowledge the death of 11845 Guardsman James Dunleavy (Tom). Both accepted the fact he was commemorated upon the family plot and had died of wounds received. The actual James Dunlavey inscribed on the headstone is the real one who is also on the Le Touret Memorial. The Commonwealth War Graves Commission as it is now and the Scots Guards have never recognised Guardsman Thomas Dunleavy, simply because to them he

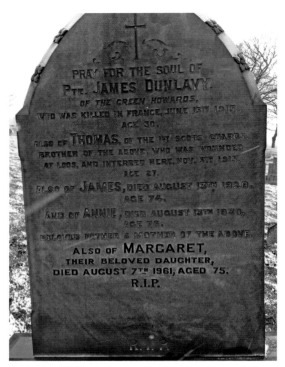

If you read the story of Tom Dunleavy this gravestone image answers more than a few questions.

never existed. Furthermore, Tom is actually buried in the family grave and not in an official war grave, how could he have been? As already stated he did not exist and still doesn't to the authorities responsible.

On a cold and snowy day late in 2017 Rob picked his way around the cemetery in Bradford looking for the grave of the man whose medals he had acquired, a Scots Guardsman named James Dunlavey. Eventually, he came across the headstone with the information upon it not seemingly making any sense at all.

Tom Dunlavey lost his fight for life on November 2nd 1915, not long after his 27th birthday, three days later he was the first of four family members to be buried in the plot. No military recognition for his deeds at all were made. Now over one hundred years later he rests in peace still having not been honoured properly for his sacrifice.

After a tough and difficult life in which he worked very hard, lost ten of his children and both his sons within months of each other the old man James Dunlavey died on August 13th 1928, aged 74. The direct family bloodline had gone despite thirteen children being born to him and his wife. He was laid to rest beside his son Tom. Exactly two years later, on the same date, August 13th, Annie who had suffered so much grief died, she too lies in the family plot. The final person to rest alongside them is Tom's sister Maggie who passed away in 1961.

This simply cannot be the end of the story for Tom and his family. Both Rob and I are united in our ambition to see that Thomas Dunlavey is properly commemorated for laying down his life for his country, no matter what the circumstances surrounding his military service had been. What happened regarding his 'bluff' is irrelevant now as the passage of time continues to ignore this remarkable and somewhat disturbing story of real life.

We hope the Scots Guards Association or another creditable body will share our sentiments. One day in the near future some form of organised service of dedication may take place to truly commemorate Thomas Dunlavey.

There are two sets of medals to James Dunlavey, one set is all true and correct… the other isn't. The custodianship of the set wrongly named is with us. In a final twist the Medal Index Card issued to the wrongly named medals states the 1914-15 Star was 'forfeited'. This was later crossed out and the medal was obviously issued. Could the initial forfeit have been suggested because the authorities were suspicious? Or could it have been stated because of yet another blatant act of bad behaviour by the so-called recipient?

Thomas Black
Killed in Action
France, Sept. 6th 1916
Aged 36.

THE third of our subjects in this chapter just as the two previous characters is also named Thomas. This particular man was a burly Scotsman by the name of Tommy Black. He was born and grew up in abject poverty and deprivation. An only child, with no siblings, at the time of his death the closest living relative to him was named as a cousin.

Tommy was born out of wedlock to a young woman who had to cope with everything that life threw at her. In the closely knit Presbyterian Victorian community of Linlithgow, twenty miles west of Edinburgh, she would have been lampooned for being a single mother. Esther Black had to take in other people's washing to make ends meet in order to feed her baby son. The 23-year old washerwoman was also forced to recruit a lodger, there weren't many who would oblige to help to pay the rent. Incredibly, a very elderly lady who herself was working in a paper mill came to the rescue. The 79-year old Isabella Steel who must have been literally worn out became a boarder at the run-down and damp dwelling in the centre of town. Taunts and sneers from the locals as Tommy was growing up only served to toughen his resolve. Soon the tormentors would stop for he developed into a very large young man for the period, standing at over six-foot tall. Perhaps as a warning sign to those who wanted to provoke him, he deliberately had a tattoo of a horse's head emblazoned upon his right forearm. The old lady died and it is not quite clear as to what became of his mother Esther. She passed away at a relatively young age as her son approached adulthood.

Tommy Black was brought-up by his single-parent mother Esther who toiled as a washer-woman to feed and clothe him.

Tommy decided to join the army, he had nothing left in Linlithgow, a historic little centre of elegance famed for its church and picturesque loch. The palace overlooking the town had been the birthplace of Mary Queen of Scots and James V. Local lad Tommy made the relatively short journey to Edinburgh and enlisted into the Royal Scots, the oldest infantry regiment in the British Army, founded in 1633, the famous 1st of foot. The young man was placed within the first one of three especially newly-formed Volunteer Service Companies. These units had been created for service in South Africa and the Boer War. Tommy set sail in February 1900 for the Cape aboard the 'SS Gascon'. He was alongside the company commander, Captain R.W. Campbell, a couple of subaltern officers and 111 other men.

His service in South Africa was fraught with danger. Tommy frequently took part in raiding expeditions, scouting patrols and mobile column work. In recognition of his efforts he was awarded the Queens South Africa Medal. Rob acquired that very medal alongside his Victory Medal and Death Plaque acknowledging his action and death in the First World War. The strapping Scotsman served for a total of ten years. After his South African adventures with the 1st VSC he became a member of the regular 1st Battalion Royal Scots before he was discharged to return to civilian life. The veteran soldier could only find menial work as a general labourer, no doubt his strength would have made him a very reliable and hard grafter.

Shortly after the outbreak of the war in August 1914, Tommy once again travelled to Edinburgh to re-enlist into the Royal Scots. The recruitment officer didn't hesitate in his acceptance of the regiment's former muscle bound giant, despite the fact he was by then in his mid-thirties as he joined the 12th (Service) Battalion. In preparation for operations in France the battalion was sent to Bordon military camp in Hampshire. Initially things seemed to be going well for Tommy, on February 6th 1915 and whilst still at the base he was prompted to Lance-Corporal.

The burly soldier had plenty of experience and knowledge of matters relating to virtually every aspect of military life, however, he had never been placed in a position of responsibility for others before. I am not quite certain how he handled his promotion. Did it go to his head? Or could he simply not cope with certain aspects of dealing with a junior command role in charge of men he knew well? Three days after receiving the promotion it was unceremoniously stripped from him. For apparent acts of misconduct he was relieved of his stripe and demoted back to the lowest rank of Private soldier. I can comfortably speculate the 'busting' hurt his pride and that inwardly he was seething.

Tommy was on the original draft with the battalion and arrived in France on May 11th 1915. It wasn't long before he was in action alongside his comrades. Less than three months later he had what can only be described as a miracle escape when he was injured by a gun-shot wound to the head. In those days the steel Brodie helmet had still not been issued. It can only be suggested the injury was superficial, nevertheless it must have shaken him up and possibly contributed towards his further downfall.

Whilst out of the front line on February 26th 1916, he reacted to a situation he would have understood in the immediate aftermath was totally unacceptable for a serving soldier. Tommy physically assaulted an officer by striking him. I wouldn't have liked to have been on the receiving end of a thump from the big man. This utterly reckless act from a highly experienced pre-war regular who in mitigation must have been provoked was very foolish. Tommy was arrested with the likelihood that it would have taken more than the usual compliment of men to detain him. He was charged, imprisoned and had to await trial for a week. Military law at the time dictated the death penalty could have been considered. This must have crossed his mind many times as he paced around the confinement of his cell.

As it transpired the trial did convict him and imposed an inevitably harsh sentence. His previous good conduct over a number of years and his record as a serving soldier were taken into account. The officers presiding over the trial also had to consider that he had previously received a head wound whilst fighting in action. Nevertheless, they set an example to humiliate the beefy troublemaker in order to teach him a lesson.

On March 5th 1916 he was sentenced to 56-days No.1 Field Punishment. This meant he was strapped to a gun-carriage for two hours at a time, twice a day in full view of all his comrades and others from various passing regiments. The weather wasn't particularly great over those two months. To make matters worse this form of punishment was often administered where the convicted man was placed against the gun-carriage in the firing line of the enemy. Barbaric is the very word that springs to my mind. Tommy was crestfallen, tied up and put on show as a criminal. Rob speculates he would have thought of his life in general and how things had unfolded as the rain soaked him to the skin. He probably asked himself what he was fighting for and why? His chums had wives, families, girlfriends, mothers and fathers waiting for them back home whilst Tommy literally had nobody but a cousin anticipating his safe return. That said, he realised his momentary outburst of such magnitude would inevitably carry severe punishment, it was a mistake he would not repeat.

The illegitimate son of a washerwoman was no less a man than anyone else. Perhaps steeled by the experience of the field punishment he would prove in no uncertain terms that he could withstand anything. The humiliation I believe turned to determination, his military service had represented the only real successful aspects of his life. He wasn't a young man and knew better than to punch a privileged junior officer. Some of his mates may have been wary of him and themselves could have been on the receiving end of his temper. When it came to officers it was a completely different scenario.

The end for Tommy came upon a day of normal front line routines on September 6th 1916. As the battalion was being relieved by the South Africans the Scotsman just happened to be in the wrong place at the wrong time. As a member of 'C- Company' 12th Royal Scots – who will be mentioned later in this book – he was one of a section of the last remaining platoon to withdraw to make way for the relief contingent. Just after 1.30pm a high explosive shell landed in his trench at Gouy-Servins. The big man was killed outright alongside eleven of his pals, three more later died of their wounds and fourteen were wounded. Tommy's large frame was torn apart, there was nothing left of him. He has no grave and is commemorated upon the Arras Memorial in France. The burly Scotsman disappeared into history, until now.

Both Rob and I believe that Tommy has left behind a legacy for us to express how fortunate we are to be living in today's world. By reading this relatively short testimony of his life it is obvious that Tommy had lived and suffered in extreme poverty as a young boy. At that time there was absolutely no form of financial welfare or social services granted to people like his poor mother. The only charity she could have hoped for was from the church, denied due to the fact she was a single parent with a child born out of wedlock. It took a very old lady to come along and help, a kindly soul who went out to work to provide assistance. Human, not state or divine intervention prevailed to a degree.

The effects of his childhood undoubtedly shaped Tommy as a person. He couldn't handle responsibility for others despite the fact an opportunity to do so had been given to him. This went on to cause mental health problems after he was rejected and humiliated by the removal of his stripe. Tommy reacted defensively fully aware of his physical attributes. We also both agree that he suffered from depression, anxiety and incredible loneliness. Army life in some ways compensated for that, but not entirely. There was a four year gap before his second stint of service from 1910 to 1914. This is when the isolation of Tommy would have once again have had a bearing upon his character.

Extremely rudimentary forms of state welfare were introduced around 1912. These provisions did not extend to the granting of medical assistance and were mainly put in place to relieve very basically the unemployed. Tommy would never have been able to see a doctor, a counsellor or even visit a contact centre, the NHS was many years away. It is easy for people to comment that Edwardians 'just got on with it and didn't complain'. I have heard these kind of views from soppy 'metropolitan historians' who prosper after having been born and raised within their comfortable middle-class bubbles. The truth is that even today many of our vulnerable members of society are completely ignored as Tommy was. Unacceptable and disgraceful treatment of the homeless, the mentally ill and the elderly still goes on.

Tommy Black gave his life for this country. He has been formally commemorated in perpetuity and equality to all those who fell during the war. Yet, there is something about him that stands out, the words written here come from the heart. I feel the opinions Rob and I have shared with you regarding his legacy somehow come along with his blessing.

The subject of the First World War has been removed from some school history curriculums. Perhaps some of the 'egg-headed' academics who are responsible for that should read this very story, the story of Tommy Black.

Thomas Clayton
Died of Wounds
France, May 4th 1917
Aged 18.

YET another Thomas, continuing the theme merely by co-incidence I must state. Rob will have to calm me down before I get to the end of this particular story. The upset and anger regarding the treatment of the boy of whom I write about has boiled over. My finger of blame is once again going to be pointed. I will not hold back my utter contempt for certain authorities and individuals despite the passing of time. This roguish lad was bullied into his grave. So now we can fully intend to try and bring some justice and righteousness back for him and his family,

Tom Clayton was born in the Kirkdale district of Liverpool in 1898. He was the second and youngest son to James and Susan. His father worked in a maritime support role at the docks in Liverpool. He had progressed from a marine engine driver to a pump engineer. James Clayton was a native of my home town, Bolton. His wife Susan Fynn, Tom's mother, was a Scots lady who originally came from Glasgow. Susan and James married at St. Anthony's RC Church on Scotland Road, Liverpool on August 23rd 1893. The bride was 19-years old, her husband somewhat older at 33-years old.

The newly married couple were blessed with five children, one of whom died in infancy. Their four surviving offspring, two boys and two girls all grew up together in a family unit. Tom had an elder brother, Charles born in 1895 and two younger sisters. Elizabeth was born in 1901 and Susan arrived in the world in 1905. The family resided in a five roomed terraced house on Walton Road, close to Stanley Park. Life was pretty straight-forward although they did take in a lodger to help pay the bills. Michael McEvoy a Liverpool dock labourer and friend of James paid his way to financially assist the Clayton's.

Upon leaving school the two sons soon found employment, Charles became a draper and Tom found himself an apprenticeship opportunity to become a plumber. When war broke out in 1914, the elder brother was just about old enough to serve overseas. Tom, certainly wasn't and should not have even been considered for military service. The intrepid and ambitious apprentice plumber wanted to get in on the action, however, he was just 16-years old. As young men from all over Liverpool flocked to the recruitment centres he decided to have a go. Tom knew that he had a reasonable chance of being accepted because of his physique.

The young Clayton lad was a good three inches above the average height for a male of the time. He stood at five foot nine inches tall, was fit and healthy and looked older than his years. Declaring himself to be 19 years and 200 days old he deliberately lied to the recruiting officer, he got away with it and was accepted. The date was September 1st 1914. There was a two-week gap until his posting to Seaforth Barracks, during that period he would have found it difficult to explain to his parents what he had done. James and Susan I am certain reacted unfavourably to their youngest son's enlistment. His mum and dad could in effect have prevented him from serving by informing the authorities. Had that been the case both they and Tom could have found themselves all in trouble with local magistrates. I am also sure that Tom persuaded his parents to give him their blessing, after all he would have to join up at some point.

From the outset it became obvious that a lot of work was required to mould Tom into a soldier. As time went on things got more and more difficult for the youngster. Army life was nothing at all what he had expected it to be. A whole series of problems started to occur and re-occur. Tom could not adjust to the rigours of discipline, reading between the lines of his documented service records I believe his issues were further compounded by bullying. I have to say that in my opinion Tom literally signed his life away when he enlisted. He certainly endured a thoroughly miserable existence as a soldier.

Whilst stationed at Seaforth Barracks it was decided to attach Tom to the 14th Battalion Kings Liverpool Regiment, a third line service battalion. The men were sent to the south of England in readiness for their posting to France and were set to sail to Boulogne on September 4th 1915. Tom missed the deployment as he was hospitalised in Aldershot the day before they left. He spent six days confined to his bed after contracting gonorrhoea, his first experience with the opposite sex had been with a prostitute. This sort of behaviour was not discouraged by the military, although they weren't too pleased at some of the consequences that affected tens of thousands of soldiers.

Having missed the boat to France upon discharge from hospital he was transferred to Prees Heath training camp in Shropshire. His problems really started at the sprawling base, regimented discipline was the order of the day. All of his pals had gone to France and Tom found himself isolated. Word spread amongst the non-commissioned officers responsible for his induction and training that he had missed the draft. Some of those very men would have regarded him as a 'shirker'. The bullying then started,

Tom was taller, leaner and younger than his tormentors who revelled in 'character building' to shape the men under them.

Young Tom Clayton grew totally disillusioned and in a relatively short space of time was found absent from parade on more than one occasion, absent from a guard mounting and asleep in bed at reveille. He was also caught breaking out of barracks. The boy was dealt with very severely and suffered a number of humiliating field punishments. Older men who had committed similar offences had been fined or confined to barracks, with the odd field punishment metered out. Tom was singled out, he probably tried to write home to tell his parents of his treatment and suffering. Any letters with such comments would have been destroyed or heavily censored before they got to the post-box. The non-commissioned training officers would be told of his disharmony and go on to make things worse for him.

At this point the finger of blame starts here. Let's start with the camp Adjutant - an administrative officer - responsible for the logistical elements regarding matters of discipline. From information gathered by him from non-commissioned officers relating to Tom's conduct it would have been obvious the young plumber had serious problems. A decision could have been made to transfer the boy or discharge him on the grounds that he wasn't capable of becoming an infantry soldier. In my opinion the Adjutant looked at Tom's physical outlook, his size and youth and dismissed any notion of him being transferred.

Awful continuous misery continued for Tom. Finally he was embarked and sent to France on March 24th 1916. Having already been pressed into an extensive period of training things just got worse for the boy. Tom was not being deployed to the front line for action. It had been decided that he required even more training and toughening up. He was immediately sent to the hell of the Etaples training depot in France and the notorious 'bull-ring'. Systematic bullying and violence towards the youngster continued, those who sent him there knew that would happen.

The base depot at Etaples was notorious. Officers presided over non-commissioned officers who wore yellow arm-bands, they became known as 'canaries' and were responsible for enforcing strict discipline. This notorious camp was just south of the northern French coast and was flanked by sand dunes and a river estuary. Men were forced to march at the double for hours over the dunes. Many of the 'canaries' were soldiers who had been considered too old to fight at the front. These particular men were experienced NCO's who in the most part were sadistic, brutal and cruel. Becoming almost a law unto themselves they would kick, beat, chastise,

The infamous Etaples training camp in France, also known as the 'bull-ring'. This is where Tom Clayton suffered systematic bullying.

bully and punish any man who defied them. The brutes were encouraged by their dysfunctional champagne swilling officers. This group of privileged non-combatant former public schoolboys would spend most of their time across the river relaxing at Le Touquet.

Some punishments were summary and not recorded, such as a severe beating behind a barrack block or a victim being tied to a post in blazing sunshine without water for hours. Tom would have especially been singled out, I can't imagine what he went through. To illustrate how bad and repressive conditions were at Etaples I need to mention a couple of serious incidents that occurred there.

In 1916 an Australian soldier had the water cut off whilst he was taking a shower. When he complained he was dragged naked by the 'canaries' towards the punishment block. Others intervened and released him from the grip of his captors. Four were identified, three Australians and a New Zealander, they were all court-martialled and received the death penalty. The Australians had their sentences commuted because their commanders would not allow the sentence of death to be enforced upon their countrymen. Tragically, the New Zealander wasn't as fortunate. Douglas Haig himself signed his death warrant, simply because he could, the ruthless cold-hearted butcher of the Somme ensured the poor Kiwi was executed.

In 1917 there was a serious mutiny at Etaples and took it some time to bring under control. The men were sick and tired of the harsh regime and the brutality attached to it, blood was shed. Haig pontificated that unruly elements from a different social class were to blame for the uprising. What could you really expect from this butcher, sympathy? Haig was a monster who lacked any form of empathy with ordinary working-class men, he culled them without the slightest degree of remorse.

After enduring three weeks at Etaples, Tom was duly despatched to a battalion. He couldn't return to the 14th who were by then engaged in Salonika, Greece. By mid-April he was assigned to the 12th Battalion Kings Liverpool Regiment. He would have been absorbed as a reinforcement soldier and inducted with some familiarisation as it was a battalion from his city. The 12th were heavily engaged in 1916. Tom was more than likely involved within the famous action at Hill 62, the Battle of Mount Sorrell in June of that year.

The battalion was very busy during the Battle of the Somme that year. They were engaged in action at Delville Wood, Guillemont, Flers-Coucelette, Morval and Le Transloy. Almost immediately after his involvement in all of those bloody battles young Tom found himself in trouble once more. On October 21st 1916 he was 'convicted' of the very minor offence of 'inattention on parade'. In most instances this kind of incident would have been dealt with swiftly. A sergeant could have offered a punch in the ribs and a bawling, or a restriction of privileges. The penalty metered out to Tom was once again extremely harsh. He received ten days field punishment. This tells me the bullying and victimisation had continued to haunt Tom as he fought his way through the hell of the Somme.

Looking at Tom's records and examining the circumstances of his movements I can see no evidence of him ever being granted home leave. Tom never had the opportunity to tell his parents what his life was really like. Censored mail put a stop to that. The Catholic boy who had grown up in a loving family and regularly attended church could only hope the war would come to an end in order to release him from his woes.

Tom's war did come to an end rather abruptly as his nineteenth birthday approached. Whilst in action on May 3rd 1917 - his mother's birthday – he was mortally wounded. The battalion were in action as a part of an offensive strategy forcing the Germans back to the Hindenburg Line. Positioned just to the east of the former Somme battlefields they were in constant danger of counter-attacks and gas shells. Yellow gas attack warning lights lit up the sky and alerted the Germans to the battalion's position. The enemy then proceeded to bombard the Liverpool men with high explosive shells. Tom was hit and severely wounded, he died in excruciating pain less than twenty-four hours later.

I have spoken very frankly with Rob regarding Tom's treatment and welfare. He is of the opinion that Tom had an 'attitude' that very much went against him. He informs me those who had the responsibility of enforcing the King's regulations and military law did so in different ways. Some went strictly by the rule books, others used discretion, but he does acknowledge the bullying. Rob explains this went on well into the 1970's and beyond. As a young soldier himself in the 70's he had experienced his share of it. Unfortunately, Rob is also of the opinion that bullying is still apparent within the armed forces.

Thomas James Clayton became another sad statistic of war. I really don't think any of his officers or those in immediate command of him really gave a damn about the boy. Back at home in Liverpool his parents were none the wiser as to the treatment he had received. Anxiously they waited for news of his safety and that of their other son, Charles, who had been serving with the Royal Field Artillery in France. Susan and James Clayton received two telegrams. The first in 1917 to inform them of the death of their youngest son Tom. Less than a year later the second telegram arrived at Walton Road. Their elder son was missing in France. He was later confirmed to have been killed in action, his body was not recovered and today he is commemorated on the Arras Memorial. Charles Henry Clayton's death meant his parents had lost both of their sons.

James Clayton never got over the distress of the double tragedy, he died three years later aged 61, in 1921. Susan lived until the ripe-old age of 85 before she too passed away in Liverpool in 1959. The whereabouts of Tom's British War Medal and Victory Medal are unknown, these represented his full medals entitlement. Rob has very carefully polished the death plaque that stayed with his mother until her final days, it is now with us.

Tom's remaining entitlement is acknowledged by just the bronze plaque that marks his death. He now rests eternally at peace, a peace that only came to him in tragic circumstances after much suffering. The boy was originally buried in the churchyard at Fins in northern France. His remains were later reinterred within the Fins New British Cemetery where no harm can come to him anymore.

James Smith

Shot at Dawn
Belgium, Sept. 5th 1917
Aged 26.

THE story of Jimmy Smith that includes one of the most appalling conclusions in British military history has been told many times. Newspapers, TV documentaries and even a stage play have all provided their own portrayals of his tragic biography. Total accuracy of their versions of events surrounding his life are cursory. To date there are inaccuracies and added elements of drama that continue to revolve around his life and times. Nobody has been able to demonstrate properly the real truth, for the simple reason that all of the information has never been at hand, it is now.

Jimmy had a difficult start in life. He was born in the Great Lever district of Bolton in Lancashire in 1891. Unfortunately his parents split when he was a tiny baby. Jim's father, who I don't really think is worth mentioning continued to live in close proximity to his son as he pursued his womanising ways. His mother Eliza eventually found happiness with a local man, John Culshaw and the pair were married. Due to the stigma of the time young baby James was described and known as Eliza's nephew, he grew up believing his mother was his aunt. John and Eliza went on to have six children, James' half-siblings of whom he was told were his 'cousins'. He wasn't fully accepted and was often sent to stay with his maternal grandmother.

Nasty and vindictive playground taunts affected young Jimmy, he retained the surname Smith as the gossiping parents of the children he attended school with let it be known he was a 'bastard child'. He grew up with five 'sisters' and a 'brother' and was always out of place at home in the crowded two-up, two-down terraced house. At the earliest opportunity he was off, it would be a military career for him. In February of 1910 at 18-years old he made his way to the Wellington Barracks in nearby Bury and enlisted into the 1st Battalion of the Lancashire Fusiliers. Private James Smith was allocated the service number of 2022.

The battalion, the regiment and his comrades became his family. He was soon posted to India taking up garrison duties with his battalion. At the outbreak of war in 1914 he was stationed in Karachi. The battalion was to be recalled for active service, they left India and arrived back in England on January 2nd 1915 before moving to Nuneaton in readiness for deployment.

When orders were officially processed it would be destination Gallipoli for Jimmy. The battalion first landed in Egypt on March 16th 1915, just over a month later they were immortalised for their heroics during one of the greatest ever actions in British military history. The 1st Battalion Lancashire Fusiliers stormed 'W Beach' at Cape Helles on the Gallipoli peninsula on the morning of April 25th 1915. History will forever celebrate the brave deeds of this battalion that were awarded six Victoria crosses to two officers and four other ranks on that particular day, an all-time record. Jimmy was on the beach where the six VC's were earned before breakfast.

The experienced regular soldier fought his way through the entire disastrous Gallipoli campaign. He saw sights of unimaginable human suffering through battle actions and disease whilst enduring extremely harsh day-to-day general conditions. Jim was eventually evacuated with the remainder of his battalion in January 1916 and made it back to Egypt. Soon afterwards the battalion set sail for France, landing at Marseille in March of 1916. Jimmy's next destination would take him to the hell of the Battle of the Somme.

Our young soldier was involved right from the start. On July 1st 1916, the blackest day in British military history when we suffered just under 60,000 casualties with almost 20,000 perishing, he was in the thick of it. The Lancashire lads had been detailed to attack and capture the village of Beaumont-Hamel. Not everything went to plan, they suffered horrendous casualties. The German snipers even shot the wounded as they lay screaming in agony. Jimmy witnessed it all and was lucky to escape with his life. Meanwhile General Rawlinson, Haig's puppet in command was four miles behind the lines, Haig was nowhere to be seen.

Just a few short weeks later life would change beyond all comprehension for Jimmy on the Somme. A German shell exploded and sent a huge mound of earth into the air and created a crater 'in no-man's land'. Jimmy was thrown into the hole by the blast and was literally buried alive. Frantically he had to dig his way out wading through the dismembered limbs and body parts of his pals. He made it but was badly wounded with a huge gaping hole in his upper back, he was also terribly shocked and traumatised.

His condition was deemed as so bad that he had to be repatriated back to Lancashire and sent to a hospital in Bolton to recover. Jimmy, never, ever, fully recovered from his ordeal. He couldn't forget the sight of his chums wailing desperately, buried alive with their arms and legs blown off, he was a broken man. Upon his discharge from hospital he went to stay with his mother. Jimmy couldn't face being recalled. The military police finally caught up with him hiding in a cupboard under the stairs shivering with fear. He was unceremoniously and immediately sent back to the front.

Jimmy found himself transferred twice, taken out of his original battalion. He went on to serve with the 15th Battalion Lancashire Fusiliers, the 1st Salford Pals, who had suffered appalling casualties on the first day of the Battle of the Somme at Thiepval Ridge. The disturbed regular soldier found himself serving alongside volunteers. He rebelled against the commands of non-commissioned officers and lost his long service stripes. Jim found life increasingly difficult at the front and tried to obtain help from the field medical services but was turned away as his requests were unauthorised.

His service ended with the 17th Battalion Kings Liverpool Regiment, the '1st Liverpool Pals' - this city pals battalion was the very first of all the pals' formations that served in the Great War. The men were predominantly from Liverpool with reinforcements drafted from elsewhere to replace casualties, they were fiercely proud of their short history and to a degree somewhat parochial in their outlook. Once again Jimmy found it difficult taking instructions from volunteer NCO's who had singled him out. He continued to disobey them and demonstrate contempt. Disorientated and confused he was found wandering around an area not associated with his military instructions. When challenged he claimed to be seeking medical help. This was not believed and he was charged with 'desertion' a second charge related to disobeying a direct order from a sergeant was also filed. This however, wasn't the first time he had faced the prospect of a field court martial, Jimmy had already been tried twice before.

Convicted at both previous trials he had been sentenced to No.1 Field Punishment for thirty days on each occasion. The full sentences were never carried out as he was released to join his battalion in action. Now, for the third time Jimmy was on trial again, this time is was very serious, 'desertion' was punishable by death.

Presiding at the hearing were three officers. Jimmy Smith should have been represented by a 'prisoner's friend'- an officer who basically would have been acting as his defence counsel. None of the officers holding court had any legal experience and Jimmy was not represented, he was alone. This was in effect a 'kangaroo-court' and in my opinion for the reasons just outlined – illegal. Jimmy pleaded guilty to the charge of disobedience and not guilty to desertion.

The pre-war regular battle hardened soldier was convicted on both counts and sentenced to death by firing squad. In his condemned cell at

Poperinge he showed no apparent fear or remorse. Jimmy had commented to his guards on several occasions of his professionalism as a regular soldier. He was more concerned about keeping his kit in good order than the fate that was to confront him. The brave young man did not fear death and certainly was not a coward. Inevitably, the day came and the execution would be carried out, albeit, as it transpired, in horrific circumstances.

A section of men from a platoon in which he had served were returning from a night patrol and ordered to a barn to clean their rifles, these men would make up the firing squad. Jimmy was led out of his cell just after 05.35 on the morning of Wednesday September 5th 1917. The 26-year old had never had the opportunity to marry or have children. Jimmy Smith who had experienced a disadvantaged life in so many ways was strapped to an execution chair shortly afterwards. The men of the firing squad were horrified and initially refused to carry out the gruesome task. Lieutenant Collins, the officer supervising backed up by his sergeant threatened to have them all court-martialled if they refused to do their duty.

At 05.50 the firing squad aimed, fired and did their best to deliberately miss the target pinned on to his chest. One bullet caught him on the shoulder, the execution chair toppled over leaving Jimmy writhing in agony upon the ground. Collins then had the responsibility to 'finish-off' the job. He approached Jimmy and drew his Webley revolver. It was his duty at that moment in time to fire a bullet through Jimmy's heart. Collins was facing a brave regular soldier who had been wounded in battle. Jimmy was in a desperate state, Collins shaking with the fear of this daunting task couldn't pull the trigger.

He turned and ordered the man on the end of the firing squad to complete the deadly deed, handing him the Webley. Private Richard Blundell knew Jimmy Smith. In recent times some newspapers and their 'blood-thirsty' journalists have stated that Richard was Jimmy's best friend to sensationalise his tragic story. This claim is nonsense and the reporters who have stated it should be thoroughly ashamed of themselves.

Richard, a Liverpool dock worker in civilian life saw the suffering that Jimmy was enduring. Mercifully the big man ended the agony. The whole contingent of the firing squad was immediately given home leave, it was all over but not for Richard Blundell. Many years later as a very old man he went to visit Jimmy's grave at Kemmel Chateau military cemetery in Belgium. Richard stayed for hours at the graveside and had to be assisted from the cemetery. The old man lived to the grand old age of 97. I was told by his daughter that he was calling out Jimmy's name upon his death bed, seventy years after he had been forced to end the life of his comrade. Douglas Haig who signed Jimmy's death warrant in my opinion committed a war crime and moreover a crime against humanity. Haig and the subaltern Collins also condemned Richard Blundell to a long life time of remorse and post-traumatic stress disorder.

Successive governments refused to pardon the 306 British soldiers executed during the First World War for offences other than murder or mutiny. It took almost ninety years before the then Secretary of State for Defence, Des Browne, finally signed the official pardon document, sanctioned by section 359 of the Armed Forces Act 2006. I have a copy of Jimmy's pardon document it reads as follows:

> *This document records that*
> *Pte J Smith of the 17th Battalion,*
> *The King's (Liverpool) Regiment*
> *Who was executed for desertion on*
> *5 September 1917 is pardoned under*
> *Section 359 of the Armed forces Act 2006*
> *The pardon stands as recognition that he was*
> *One of many victims of the First World War*
> *And that execution was not a fate he deserved*
>
> *Des Browne*
> *Secretary of State for Defence*

For many families who received identical pardons naming their unfortunate relations who had suffered the same fate as Jimmy, the document brought closure. In the case of James Smith this pardon didn't go far enough, for another form of justice still had to be brought about for him. In his home town of Bolton he had been left out of the book that commemorates the war dead of the borough, the official 'roll of honour'. That very situation had to be rectified.

In 2008 I started a campaign to have Jimmy officially recognised by the inclusion of his name upon the 'roll of honour' of his home town. Supported by the then serving local Member of Parliament for the constituency in which Jimmy once lived, the campaign gathered pace. Brian Iddon the MP brought upon a parliamentary debate that was televised with direct regard to Jimmy Smith. Bolton Council duly obliged and the young man was finally honoured and recognised in the town where he was born and raised.

The headstone marking the grave of Jimmy Smith. The young regular soldier was executed by a firing squad made up of his own comrades in 1917 after suffering from mental illness.

On Saturday June 27ᵗʰ 2009, Jimmy's name was finally added to the 'roll of honour' over ninety years after he had perished. A civic reception attended by the Mayor and many local dignitaries followed to respectfully honour Jimmy. Finally, in an emotional service upon the steps of the magnificent town hall, the flag was lowered from its summit and presented to me, a moment I will cherish forever. Richard Blundell's 84-year old daughter Jean was in attendance, shaking with emotion, she was apologising for her father's tragic role all those years ago. Jean was rightfully assured that no apology whatsoever was required and comforted in the knowledge that her father ended Jimmy's suffering.

Determined not to let Jimmy's death be in vain I embarked upon many fundraising activities in the years that followed and cited his story as an example. This enabled me to deliver hundreds of thousands of pounds to military charities to pay for the treatment of PTSD for surviving veterans in today's world. Jimmy's inspiration has also allowed me to successfully campaign on a number of occasions to have forgotten soldiers placed upon war memorials. His ongoing legacy has proved to be positive and helped to relieve the suffering of others.

After the war Jimmy's gratuity pension to his relatives was cancelled because he had been executed for desertion. His mother Eliza successfully campaigned against that decision via the popular magazine of the day, 'John Bull'. With the help of the publication's editor the pressure paid off and the pension was re-instated. Eliza only received half the amount, Jimmy's father who hadn't seen his son for years claimed the other half.

The same conclusion was not fulfilled regarding the award of Jimmy's service medals. His entitlement included the 1914-15 Star, the British War Medal and the Victory Medal. All three of his medals were forfeited for desertion. Despite his pardon the Ministry of Defence have refused to issue them and have cited that no more First World War Medals can be issued or re-issued for any reason whatsoever.

In complete and utter defiance of this absurd decision both Rob and I have replica medals to Jimmy Smith and I wear one set mounted on my right breast on each Remembrance Sunday. Rob has not made any comments regarding this tragic tale, he respectfully believes the words all belong to me. James Smith was my paternal grandmother's uncle, he is therefore my distant relative.

There is no distance between Jimmy and me, since I was five-years old when I very first learned of his tragic fate, he has been my inspiration - he is in my heart, he is my soul and he is my blood.

WE LED, THEY FOLLOWED

NATURAL leaders of men are few and far between. There are those born to lead and others who had to learn. My comments regarding officers have thus far been somewhat uncomplimentary, although not entirely so. Of course I realise and understand the prosecution of any war could not be fulfilled without the direction of officers, it's just that some were far worse than others.

This chapter deals with five officers who led totally by example. It is safe to comment their men would have followed them to the end of the earth, in some instances they did just that. The genuine duty of care and the diligence in which they held their responsibilities shines through for all of the five subjects we bring to the fore.

Rob whose huge military experience plays a vital part in the construction of all of our stories himself served as a senior non-commissioned officer over many years. He met hundreds of officers during his service and is more than qualified to comment, as he does in every piece. His explanation of the principal role of a good officer is confined to just one word that really does say it all, that word being 'leadership'.

The casualty rate amongst British officers, especially the lower ranking ones was high. Many of them were extremely young, innocent and I have to say due to their backgrounds in some respects somewhat naive. At the outbreak of war almost every officer, with very few exceptions had received a good standard of public school education. Many of them came from privileged families and started their lives with certain advantages of wealth and security encompassing them. As the war raged on and the officer casualties mounted, men who came from middle-class backgrounds, professionals in civilian life were commissioned as officers. The progression of the conflict led to more working-class men rising from the ranks to also become officers. Many of these rough and ready soldiers discovered their commissions would be held on a temporary basis for the duration of the war.

I have to state the First World War was the greatest leveller of social class in modern British history. Many of the rich and fortunate realised this, some of whom had been officers themselves. The slaughter of the conflict is often described as wasteful and futile. One aspect that did arise from it was the realisation by many, certainly not all, that all men are equal. Our officers described here we are pretty sure subscribed to that ideology, for they really did get to know their men as their men got to know them.

Leycester P. Storr
Killed in Action
France, Mar. 29th 1918
Aged 38.
Awarded the DISTINGUISHED SERVICE ORDER in 1917
MENTIONED IN DESPATCHES in 1918

Major Leycester P. Storr an officer who always led from the front. He was awarded the Distinguished Service Order in 1917.

MAJOR Leycester Penrhyn Storr was a distinguished, gallant, brave and highly decorated officer who led totally by example. It is a privilege to be able to write this transcript of his life. Leycester came from an advantaged background, was privately educated and like many of his brother officers never had any money problems. He was certainly a man of his time and very forward thinking, enterprising Leycester became an entrepreneur and without a shadow of a doubt a fine leader of men.

His father was the rector at the church in the picture

postcard village of Great Horkesley, three miles to the north of Colchester in Essex. Leycester was born on October 19th 1879 at the rectory, his elder sister had also been born there a year earlier. The siblings were cared for as they grew up by a nursemaid, more commonly referred to as a nanny. John Storr the rector had married Amy Theodosia Leycester, a lady from a wealthy family in Cheshire. Her own family had commercial interests extended from their heritage in the United States. The two exchanged vows at St. Georges Church, Hanover Square, London early in 1877. Leycester's Christian name derives from his mother's surname. The young boy being the only son of a rector was expected to conform to religious and moral values. I am convinced these attributes strengthened his integrity and shaped his personality as a fair, just and kind human being.

There is no recorded information regarding his schooling as he entered his teens, however, I am of the opinion it was financed by his mother's family, I believe he was further educated in Cheshire. Upon leaving his studies he joined the newly created 22nd Company (Cheshire) of the 2nd Battalion Imperial Yeomanry. This unit along with other similar formations was especially created as a mounted infantry force to serve in the Boer War in South Africa. Leycester joined at the very beginning of the 22nd Company Imperial Yeomanry's establishment in 1900 and was soon sent off to South Africa. The young man started right at the bottom of the ranks as just an ordinary Trooper, it wasn't long before he was promoted to Lance-Corporal in the field. Just over a year later he was commissioned as an officer transferring to the 18th Battalion Imperial Yeomanry as a Lieutenant.

This kind of rapid elevation and indeed bypassing ranks is unusual. The fact that Leycester hadn't been commissioned before undertaking active service considering his background and education also requires an explanation. I think it is very likely my assumptions are correct regarding these issues. The Yeomanry was formed quickly for rapid mobilisation and deployment to South Africa, the Boers had been gaining the upper hand the year before [1899] and had to be dealt with. This required utilising fast moving mobile mounted infantry. There simply wasn't enough time to put Leycester through an Officer Training Corps. If he wanted to serve with the Cheshire Yeomanry he would have to prove himself in the field of battle and start at the bottom, he did just that. His experiences of serving in the ranks would stand him in good stead as he established an empathy with ordinary soldiers that other officers simply couldn't achieve.

Leycester served his time in South Africa and was awarded the Queen's South Africa Medal for his efforts. He left the military retaining an officer reserve recall should he be required to serve again in the event of a war. His mother's family contacts in America had various business interests that he became involved with. Trips across the Atlantic followed to New York, Leycester was putting himself about as a prospective entrepreneur.

Eventually life became very interesting for the former dashing officer. He acquired Lime and Cocoa plantations on the island of Dominica in the Caribbean and employed a local workforce to cultivate his crops, actively becoming involved himself. Leycester also purchased a residence on the island and became a well-known local character. On April 30th 1907 at the age of twenty-seven he married a titled lady, Elizabeth Lucy Eily Blake, the daughter of Erroll Augustus Blake, 4th Baron Wallscourt and Lady Jane Herriot Stanhope. He tied the knot in a ceremony surrounded by pomp and glamour on the Isle of Wight where his Galway born noble bride resided.

Their first child Norah was born a year later on Dominica in the capital Roseau. The family retained their roots in England purchasing a country residence in Ware, Hertfordshire, also staying frequently upon the Isle of Wight on his father-in-law's estate. One of their other daughters was born on the little island off the south coast and another daughter was born at the rectory in Essex. Leycester brought a man-servant back and forth with him from Dominica complementing the family staff, they also had a housekeeper and nanny at their matrimonial home in Hertfordshire.

When war broke out in 1914 Leycester was recalled from the pool of officers held in reserve. He was reallocated his former rank of Lieutenant and posted to the Kings Liverpool Regiment, joining the 12th Battalion. By the time the battalion had landed at Boulogne in France in July 1915 Leycester had already been promoted to Captain. This position gave him command of a company within the battalion, around 250 men. Captain Storr led his men into action many times during the Battle of the Somme in 1916. He was also heavily involved in the fighting at the Third Battle of Ypres in 1917 around the Menin Road Ridge, Polygon Wood and Passchendaele. Around this time he had been promoted again to the field rank of Major and effectively became second-in-command of the whole battalion of 1000 men. Shortly afterwards he was seconded temporarily to the 7th Battalion Kings Own Yorkshire Light Infantry when their commanding officer took leave. Leycester the former low ranking trooper took on the responsibility of taking complete command of the battalion. Eventually, he returned back to the Liverpool Regiment to resume his original position of IC2, second-in-command.

During his time at war his business affairs in Dominica continued under the supervision of his wife and loyal staff upon the sun-kissed island way off in the Caribbean. Leycester had been involved in many dangerous actions upon the Western Front for over two years with the added responsibility of command. He could with his newly bestowed rank of Major have been considered for a post on the General Staff and kept out of further danger. After all, he had so much to live for, another baby girl had been born to him in 1917 having been conceived when he was on leave. Leycester had such a bright future ahead of him and a wonderful family to return home to. The prospect of a transfer out of the line was unthinkable to him, he would stay in the thick of all actions to come alongside his junior officers, NCO's and ordinary ranks, all of whom respected and trusted him.

Rob explains here that Leycester's close bond with his men after having been in so many major confrontations of battle was unbreakable. He goes on to say the responsibilities that were extended to him via his promotions would have made his devotion and sense of loyalty to his men even stronger. Rob also believes Leycester would have been a calming influence as well as being looked upon as a role model by all those who served under him.

The points Rob make can only be endorsed by what happened on November 20th 1917. Leycester's actions on that day at Cambrai would result in him being awarded the Distinguished Service Order. A gallantry medal bestowed upon officers ranking just one place below the Victoria Cross. He was on that day in command of the whole battalion. The citation for the DSO really does say it all, it describes the Major's superb bravery in a co-ordinated infantry and tank attack. Read the words of the citation below, all of which confirm Rob's earlier comments.

'For conspicuous gallantry and devotion to duty. When in command of the battalion, on both company commanders of the leading companies becoming casualties, he personally led the men under heavy fire to the capture of the first objective. Having reorganised the battalion, he led it on to the second objective which was successfully taken. By his coolness, courage and ability he set a splendid example to all ranks and the success of the operations was due to his good leadership and initiative during a critical period.'

Major Leycester Penrhyn Storr, DSO was presented with his prestigious decoration on January 31st 1918 as he was about to enter his fourth year of service upon the Western Front. Germany was far from defeated and determined to make one huge final push to encircle and capitulate the

British Army, It started on March 21st 1918. German 'storm-troopers' in huge numbers thrust across the British lines from the east of the former Somme battlefields and drove on relentlessly. Leycester and his men fought desperate holding actions at St. Quentin, on the Somme crossings and at Rosieres, before finding themselves overwhelmed in a wood close to Pozieres.

The gallant Major fought desperately until the end alongside his men as the Liverpool lads were driven out of the wood. He stood his ground and was seriously wounded, the evacuation of the area had to continue. Leycester urged his men to retreat to safety and leave him behind, he died shortly afterwards. In the bombardments that followed his body was lost for all time, consequently he has no known grave. The enterprising businessman left behind a wife, five children, a host of loyal staff all of whom he thought so well of and the men under his command. Leycester is commemorated upon the Pozieres Memorial in France.

Back in England his wife Lady Elizabeth was devastated. She had always known that her husband would risk his all for his men and her worst fears were now confirmed upon the news of his death. It especially would have hit her very hard in the knowledge that she would never have a grave to visit. Lady Elizabeth never remarried, she lived for almost another half-century, her wealth and comfortable lifestyle could never compensate for the loss of her husband. She was 86-years old when she passed away on January 9th 1966. In Roseau on Dominica, Leycester is also remembered upon their war memorial. He is one of thirteen officers from Dominica named upon the monument, alongside eleven ordinary ranking soldiers from the British West Indies Regiment, all casualties of the First World War.

In one final twist to this story Rob and I are united in our belief that Leycester was considered and overlooked for the highest of all awards for gallantry, the Victoria Cross. His selfless actions as he met his death appear to have been acknowledged by the fact that he was 'Mentioned in Despatches' after he had been killed in action. It is widely accepted that any such posthumous honour was often seen as a 'down-grade' from the award of the Victoria Cross. Bars, or second awards to the Distinguished Service Order were very rarely awarded posthumously as was the Military Cross. It would have been possible to bestow the Victoria Cross in any such instance. We believe the consideration was made initially to Leycester but had been withdrawn for any one of a number of reasons.

Leycester Storr could have gone on to be a grandfather and possibly great-grandfather, had he lived, there is no doubt that his descendants still live in this country. We hope that one day they read this account of his life and be proud of their ancestor. Leycester was well loved and respected by all of those who had the honour of knowing him. He came from the ranks, knew exactly what it took to be a soldier and refused to leave his men in their darkest hour, for that alone he paid the ultimate price.

The exact whereabouts of Leycester's Distinguished Service Order decoration are unknown. His British War Medal, Victory Medal and Death Plaque are also in the possession of someone. Unusually, for such a distinguished officer his 1914-15 Star was split from the rest of the group. That very medal, representing Leycester's legacy is now with us.

Alan E.P. Joseph
Died of Wounds
France, May 10th 1917
Aged 21.

SECOND-Lieutenant Alan Edward Palfrey Joseph lived a short life. He is just one of so many young junior officers who perished in the Great War. His story is pretty remarkable with many twists and turns, tinged with tragedy and grief especially suffered by his father who had been an eminent surgeon and doctor. There was nothing the medical man could have done to save his eldest son and that very fact haunted him until the end of his days.

Young Alan was one of ten children born to his parents, nine of whom survived into adulthood. Although he came from a very advantageous background he was level headed and fully understood the concerns and issues of the men who served under him. Alan initially served in the ranks as an ordinary soldier before being commissioned into his local regiment. He had started his working life as an apprentice engineer and became familiar with working-class culture and traditions. His way of life crossed the social divides of the time, he was conscientious, consistent and loyal - those attributes did not however prevent him from courting with controversy.

Alan was born on June 23rd 1895 in Nuneaton, Warwickshire. His father Alan senior was a very highly qualified doctor and surgeon who held his own practice. Born in Colombo, Ceylon where he first studied medicine he moved on to university in Edinburgh to complete his medical training. Alan senior also worked in the General Hospital in Nuneaton after moving from Loughborough. In addition to those well paid duties he was also the medical superintendent of a specialist sanatorium at Bramcote. This institution treated people with tuberculosis, a disease that was rife at the time.

Dr Alan Joseph married Lucy Palfrey in July of 1891. His wife was the daughter of a farmer from Somerset who had moved to Bradfield in Berkshire to run a 260-acre farm. Lucy was a clever lady, qualifying as a teacher at the age of just fourteen. The pair were married in Bradfield and initially went to live on the rambling farm. Their first born, a daughter, Alurine Muriel Palfrey Joseph was born in the farmhouse. All of their children used both the surnames of their parents, Palfrey-Joseph. The young family later moved to a large house in Nuneaton where the doctor set up his practice that he went on to hold for over forty years and became a pillar of the community. Alan junior and the remainder of his siblings were born in the Warwickshire market town.

The Joseph children all experienced a very regimented and strict upbringing. Alan was after all the son of a respected doctor and former school teacher and was educated at the prestigiously disciplined King Edward VI Grammar School in Nuneaton. He was allowed to choose his own career path and probably against the grain decided to embark upon an apprenticeship in engineering. The intelligent young man joined the L.N.W. Railway at their new station works in Nuneaton and wasn't afraid of hard work or getting his hands dirty. When war broke out Alan saw many of his colleagues volunteer to join-up, early in 1915 he followed suit, persuaded by a recruiting officer with a specialist agenda.

The Royal Fusiliers (City of London Regiment) raised forty-seven battalions for service in the First World War. Some of these battalions were bespoke as the recruitment officer's hand-picked men from certain walks of life. The Royal Fusiliers were famed for their sportsmen battalions and also public schools battalions. Four of the schools battalions were formed by the Public Schools and University Men's Force at Epsom in September 1914. Selective recruitment continued across London, the home-counties and the southern edge of the midlands. In February 1915 the public schools recruitment teams had been active in Warwick and Rugby.

On February 8th 1915, 19-year old Alan signed on with the 19th Battalion Royal Fusiliers (2nd Public Schools Battalion). He had the family and educational background that met their requirements. The recruitment officer would have informed Alan that most of the men joining would one day be considered for commissions to become officers. His soldiering began soon afterwards at the bottom of the ranks.

After spending some time at Clipstone camp near Mansfield in Nottinghamshire Alan received his final training and firing practice at Salisbury Plain in readiness for deployment to France. He sailed with the battalion as they left England in November 1915. The men were deployed and concentrated around Morbecque not far from the Belgian border behind the lines. This particular battalion was eventually disbanded just five months later with many of the men going on to be commissioned as officers.

Both Rob and I agree the men of this battalion and two of the other public schools battalions were more or less familiarised with day-to-day life in and around the front. The duration of existence of these battalions was during a period of no major actions, they were to come just later. We both suggest that although Alan and his comrades in arms would have probably been involved in routine patrol work and fatigues they didn't see any serious action. Preparations were in progress to turn as many of them into officers in readiness for the campaigns to come.

As the battalion broke up those selected for commissions were given two options for whom they would like to serve with as officers. Officer Cadet Alan, still only 20-years old made his first choice the Royal Flying Corps, harbouring ambitions of becoming a pilot. His second option was with his local infantry, the Warwickshire's. The powers that be decided to post him to the regiment, he took up the most junior of officer roles as a Second-Lieutenant. Alan was initially attached to the 3rd (Reserve) Battalion Royal Warwickshire Regiment a domiciled UK based training unit stationed upon the Isle of Wight. At some point he was seconded and sent to the front, he wasn't there for very long.

Just over a week before the Christmas of 1916, on December 17th, Alan was wounded whilst serving in France. He had received a gun-shot wound to the arm and was repatriated home. Looking at his records it would appear that he did spend Christmas of that year at home in Nuneaton before having to report back to depot on the Isle of Wight. What happened a few weeks later was truly remarkable. General headquarters and the Adjutant Generals office were still unsure of his exact whereabouts and an official directive to have him arrested was issued. The transcript of the notice is below, obviously referring to his gun-shot wound.

'20.2.17 – Place 2ⁿᵈ Lieutenant A.E. Joseph Royal Warwickshire Regiment in arrest on charge of self-wounding and send him under escort via Folkestone to Boulogne with orders to escort to hand him over to Embarkation Officer, Boulogne AAA. Uncertain in this department whether 2ⁿᵈ Lieutenant Joseph has joined Third Battalion in Isle of Wight or whether still at home, Rocklands, Church Lane, Nuneaton, but take action as circumstances require AAA. Telegraph name of escort and date of departure giving six days prior notice in that G.H.Q may be apprised.'

The authorities were clearly accusing Alan of self-inflicting his injuries, a very serious charge and one that would have taken some prior consideration before being decided upon. What actually happened as a direct result of this action is a mystery, so Rob and I will try to explain what conclusions we have come to. We know for certain that Alan was not court-martialled. He was redeployed and sent back into the line. I believe Alan was arrested and taken back over to France to answer the charge at some form of preliminary hearing. The officers presiding were satisfied with his explanation of events and dismissed the charge. A question remains as to why the charge was levelled in the first place? The incident would have been reported by a suspicious 'third-party'. Certain authorities weren't sure of Alan's whereabouts that increased those suspicions.

I am also of the opinion that given Alan's strict upbringing in his home life and taking into consideration his educational background he would have been a character who followed the rules. The fact that he was selected from the ranks to become an officer also demonstrates that he knew how to obey orders. He was regarded as one who could also issue orders and hold responsibility. I further suggest that Alan would not bring about such a potential disgrace that could and would have affected his family's reputation. The charge of self-wounding doesn't stack up to me, I don't believe he committed that act.

Rob gives a more practical explanation based upon his military experience and I have to say it does make sense. Officers used Webley service revolvers drawn from holsters attached to Sam Browne belts. If Alan had drawn quickly with his right hand to discharge his rounds it is possible he accidently injured himself to the left arm when firing. Webley's were not 'water pistols', Alan who had been used to handling a .303 Lee Enfield rifle with two hands was inexperienced with a pistol, especially in a battle situation. It is Rob's opinion the likelihood of an accidental injury occurred. He shares my sentiments regarding Alan's integrity and does not believe this young officer self-inflicted the gun-shot wound.

Alan was later transferred to the 14th Battalion Royal Warwickshire Regiment, the famous '1st Birmingham Pals'. He would have commanded a platoon of up to forty men from the city, many of them having joined up together. A number of the Birmingham lads were skilled engineers themselves. It was the apprentice who would go on to lead them into battle right from the front, with his men following behind. The average life expectancy for a British infantry Second-Lieutenant in the First World War was six weeks. Alan knew that, he watched as others of the same rank perished in front of his eyes. He wasn't afraid to accept greater responsibility as a temporary Lieutenant as his brother officers fell dying beside him. Under no circumstances would I question his courage or loyalty to those who followed him, he knew the risks and took them. In complete contrast the average life expectancy of certain senior British officers on the General Staff was living to a ripe old age, they received enormous gratuities after the war and in many cases a title. These oafs sent young men like Alan into battle knowing full well many of them would be maimed or killed.

The young subaltern found himself sent off to Festubert in France with his battalion to prepare for the forthcoming Battle of Arras, a much understated disastrous campaign. I have previously commented that daily losses around Arras during the course of the battle were the worst in British military history. Add to that atrocious weather conditions and shambolic command from the top and you can only imagine what Alan had to face. He was involved in the actions at Vimy Ridge where he was wounded in both thighs. The young officer was evacuated to a casualty clearing station. In conditions resembling a butchers' market stall he was hastily operated upon before being ordered for immediate transfer to a military hospital.

Alan endured a rickety journey north and was admitted to the No.9 British Red Cross Hospital at Calais. His journey was an uncomfortable one and it had been noted that he was in considerable pain. Alan's injuries were not thought to be life threatening however the surgeon medical officer was concerned about an infection in his upper right thigh. As it transpired more shrapnel debris had to be removed from Alan's leg after another operation and he appeared to be making an improvement. The situation then rapidly deteriorated. In official correspondence the surgeon expresses that he wrote on more than one occasion to Alan's doctor father. The medical officer relayed the seriousness of Alan's condition informing the civilian doctor that his son had developed a general septicaemia, acute blood poisoning. Alan's father was to later claim he hadn't been informed of the critical condition his son had been in and expressed dissatisfaction at his treatment.

Alan died of complications arising from the blood poisoning on May 10th 1917. Had he been in a general hospital in England with much greater standards of equipment and hygiene he would probably have survived, his father knew that. Considering the circumstances I believe the medical officer and all the nursing and Royal Army Medical Corps staff did everything they could for Alan. Conditions were horrendous in France, the hospitals lacked vital resources and were extremely over-stretched. Surgeons worked tirelessly covered in blood performing all kinds of emergency on-the-spot operations, death was routine.

There was a good deal of correspondence made between Alan's father and the people who had been responsible for his son's welfare. Dr Joseph would simply not accept Alan's death could not have been prevented. The Duchess of Sutherland who directed certain logistics at the hospital wrote frankly to the doctor. She assured him that everything that could have been done for his son, was so. Exchanges continued with the medical officer until 1919, it was clear the remorse felt by Dr Joseph was profound and furthermore that he understood how his son had actually died in the most unfortunate of circumstances. At the end of the day no blame could be attached to anyone regarding the demise and death of Second-Lieutenant Alan Edward Palfrey Joseph.

It is difficult to conclude this story. I have to say I would completely exonerate the Royal Army Medical Corps surgeon, his staff and the Red Cross nurses for any implied negligence. These people worked in exceptionally difficult conditions under tremendous and continuous stresses. Despite his extensive medical knowledge and experience Dr Joseph couldn't possibly fully understand the environment where his son had died. Rob completely agrees with this but sympathises greatly with the civilian doctor, who in reality could have done nothing to alleviate his son's suffering. Alan wasn't given any special treatment above and beyond others who were

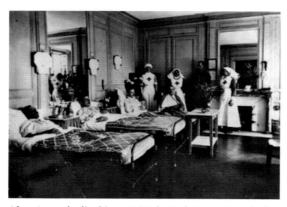

Alan Joseph died in a British Red Cross Hospital in France.

suffering at the Red Cross hospital in France. Officers of a more senior rank did on occasions receive privately funded ambulances provided by their families to get them to hospitals in England. Class and money sometimes made all the difference.

Young Alan's potential was never fulfilled, he was extremely unfortunate and even in his own mind he wouldn't have believed his life would end shortly after his arrival at the hospital. This story is so tragic albeit just for that very reason, Alan had a vision of safety and hope that so cruelly never materialised. Back at his home in Nuneaton his family simply couldn't believe that he had slipped away from them. Perhaps the words written on the bottom of his headstone at the Calais Southern Military Cemetery really do sum up this tragedy:

'*We will not think of him as dead, but living forever in our love enshrined*'

Alan's 1914-15 Star, British War Medal and Victory Medal are all now safely with us.

William Urquhart
Killed in Action
Belgium, July 7th 1917
Aged 31.

IT is difficult to contemplate how to begin this account of the life of Billy Urquhart. The story of his time on earth and the mysteries he left behind that have out-foxed historians for over a century are amazing. After a number of lengthy discussions with Rob one of his comments attempts to sum up Billy. Rob smiled as he stated that people like him were invented for the purpose of producing gripping drama. Billy Urquhart

A smiling Billy Urquhart, the officer and the gentleman who always seemed to be one step ahead, until his luck ran out.

wasn't a fictional creation, he was very much a real character. This man was an Edwardian 'dare-devil' who appears to have bluffed his way along to achieve the ultimate goal of becoming an officer and a gentleman.

William Thomas Urquhart was born in Aidin [Aydin], Turkey, on September 30th 1885. He was the youngest son and child of the enterprising Andrew Urquhart and his wife Jean. Andrew was employed by a large American liquorice manufacturing company as an area manager at the Meander Valley plant in nearby Smyrna. The sweet delicacy was exported via the port of Scala Nova, known today as Kusadasi, now a tourist resort frequented by many Britons. I have sat around the harbour there in modern times watching the cruise ships come and go. In 1887 with their family complemented by several children the Urquhart's settled in Edinburgh within the fashionable Portobello district by the sea.

Once everything was organised Andrew was off again to set up his own liquorice processing plant in southern Russia. He was away for many years making his fortune, sending enough money back home to see that his family were well provided for. The children all received a private education. Billy the youngest lad grew up barely knowing his father alongside his three elder sisters and two older brothers. As this story unfolds it may become apparent the youngest member of the family felt that he had a lot to prove. I believe he became disillusioned when his elder brothers left home. His sisters lived a life of leisure as Billy became bored with his role as an apprentice chartered accountant upon leaving college.

The ambitious young man wanted to follow in the footsteps of his father and become a respected gentleman with means. He also had a lot to live up to when attempting to emulate in any way the achievements of his eldest brother. Leslie Urquhart followed his father to Russia and became a mining magnate and oil baron, even by the standards of the day he became extremely wealthy, a multi-millionaire.

Billy's life suddenly went into overdrive. He went on to claim that he had taken part in the Anglo-Boer War [1899-1902] and had enlisted at the start of the conflict. The would-be all action hero also stated that he was awarded both the Queen's South Africa Medal and the King's South Africa Medal serving with the Imperial Light Horse. It doesn't take a genius to work out that he had fabricated all of those claims. If what he was saying is true he would have been fourteen years old at the start of the conflict and sixteen as it finished. The entitlement to both medals meant that he would have been in action with a mounted infantry unit at the age of fourteen. I do not believe he was. He is listed on the 1901 census as living at home with his mother and sisters and being employed in the role I have previously stated. Co-incidentally, there was one member of the Imperial Light Horse who served for six months in the conflict, his name was John Urquhart. Billy's elder brother was called John.

The fantasies continued with Billy boasting that he had served as a Lieutenant in the ILH and had fought in the Swaziland Campaign of 1906? The award of the Swaziland medal was apparently bestowed upon him, yes a Swaziland Medal? Both Rob and I are still scratching our heads trying to work out those claims. It is probable that Billy had gained some form of military experience - that he grossly exaggerated - and his claims would stand him in good stead as he progressed with his ambitions in later life. This story really does get even more intriguing and as you will see there was a method in Billy's madness. Our man was definitely very well-known in Edinburgh for a number of years whilst in his twenties. He was a renowned talented rugby player and captain who was known as 'Togo'. Somehow he managed to fit in all of the foreign military adventures alongside his sporting achievements, really?

The daring young chancer went on to turn up in Australia, there are no outbound passenger lists to say how he got there - he ended up in Brisbane. Billy informed his family he was doing well trading as a sugar refiner. It really did appear the swashbuckling entrepreneurial traits of his father and eldest brother had continued down the family line. Perhaps Billy was out there making a fortune as a respectable businessman? The truth never seemed to follow Billy around as he was to stop bragging to be a sugar refiner when war broke out.

It was claimed that Billy enlisted into the Australian 5th Light Horse at the outbreak of war in August 1914, a claim he probably made himself. In reality he hastily enlisted on December 15th 1914 at Brisbane in not surprisingly somewhat bizarre circumstances. Never before have I seen attestation papers so incomplete with gaps everywhere. The information he provided was sparse and not exactly accurate. Enigmatic Billy decided to slightly alter his identity based upon his rather well-to-do family residence in Edinburgh. He took upon the mantle of a Scots gentleman and extended his name to suit. Billy attested as William Thomson Bruce Urquhart and for good measure added five years upon his real age. There was as we shall discover a shady motive behind the extended age claim. The enterprising rascal also described his occupation as that of a humble clerk. In a final declaration of respectability he listed his father as next of kin, being none other than 'Major' Andrew Urquhart.

Rob and I have discussed this unusual set of circumstances, both of us aware that Billy was being economical with the truth. We also know he re-attested properly, with different details once he had arrived in Egypt with the Australian Light Horse in February of 1915. Rob believes that Billy wanted to create some form of hasty confusion to disguise his motives. He had to make it to Sydney, some 570-miles away to catch the embarkation ship that would leave just four days later. There wasn't time to really perform thorough checks and once Billy was preparing for the campaign at Gallipoli he would be just one of many thousands of men.

Determined to succeed Billy found himself in the presence of a junior officer, a Lieutenant as he completed his attestation in Egypt. He retained his extended Scots name and the claim that he was 34-years old, he was in fact 29-years old. It is noticeable and I think rather funny as we see that Billy appeared to be going slightly grey-haired, did he add a little bit of grey to make him look older? His occupation changed dramatically on the papers, he was no longer a clerk, sugar refiner was not mentioned either. To all intents and purposes he described himself as a career soldier with thirteen-and-a-half continual years of service recording this in an unconventional style. Billy maintained that he had been a former officer and also a senior warrant officer but somehow the unit formations don't make sense on the forms. He also added the five years on to his age to 'substantiate' that he had served in the Boer War. We have to remember here that Billy was a distinguished Rugby club captain in Edinburgh, playing regularly, so where did the service record come from?

His father was untraceable in southern Russia, Billy once again named him as his next of kin, this time referring to him as Lieutenant-Colonel Andrew Urquhart. To the young officer supervising the attestation Billy appeared to be the son of a distinguished former battalion commander. The Lieutenant may have raised his eyebrows, for in front of him was a man who claimed to have also once been a Lieutenant in a Light Horse Squadron. Billy was duly accepted, the former 'officer' being allocated the lowest rank of Trooper, completing an almost unbelievable chain of events. The likelihood of his father being a retired Lieutenant-Colonel or the immediate lower rank of Major as Billy had claimed is remote, I will go further and say untrue. For a start he had been working in a liquorice manufacturing industry plant in Turkey. Andrew Urquhart had worked hard to become a manager whilst he was still in his twenties. In his thirties he had started his own concern in Russia. I really don't think anyone could combine such a career in far-away locations with the role of high level distinguished military responsibility attached. However, Billy's proclamation of being the son of a senior officer would in his mind help to propel him on – and eventually, it did!

The 5th Light Horse a mobile mounted infantry set-up were not initially considered suitable for service in Gallipoli due to the unfavourable terrain. However, as the losses and casualties mounted they were eventually deployed from Egypt to the battle front, arriving in mid-May 1915. At last Billy, the tall, elegant, former back-row Rugby captain had a chance to prove to everyone what he was really made of and he didn't disappoint. Attached to 'A-Squadron' he distinguished himself as a messenger, running across dangerous ground under fire to deliver essential instructions and orders. He was acknowledged and rewarded for his demonstrations of bravery and valuable service by being 'Mentioned in Despatches' by Major-General Legge. Billy received special praise in Divisional Order No.156 alongside three other men of the 5th Light Horse, one being an officer, for… 'Acts of Conspicuous Gallantry or valuable service during the period of May 19th 1915 – June 30th 1915. He was noted as having carried messages in the firing line under heavy fire and also tended wounded men.

The words 'Conspicuous Gallantry' are associated with the award of the Distinguished Conduct Medal, the second highest gallantry medal bestowed upon non-commissioned officers and ordinary soldiers, ranking just below the Victoria Cross. I have read the despatch a copy of which was sent to Billy's father and carefully examined various other documents relating to Billy's service. Both Rob and I have also made searches of many other sources that could confirm Billy was awarded the Distinguished Conduct Medal. None of the searches relay this, moreover, others have done so and have come to the same conclusion. There is no doubt that Billy was 'Mentioned in Despatches', a feat that equates to the fourth highest level of award for bravery. The DCM? I don't believe that Billy was bestowed with the award of the Distinguished Conduct Medal. Undeterred and I hope, but doubt, that he was right and I am wrong, Billy claimed to have been decorated with the DCM. He added the ribbon on to his medals bar that contained his ribbons for the previous awards of, the Queens South Africa Medal? The King's South Africa Medal? And of course the Swaziland Medal? Make up your own mind here?

In August of 1915 Billy finally achieved his dream, he was made a temporary Second-Lieutenant in the field, at last he had been commissioned - he became an officer and a gentleman. His guile, bravery, ability and no doubt charisma had all contributed to his elevation, not forgetting his background also! The 5th Light Horse however didn't require his services further, something that both Rob and I really can't understand, but can speculate upon. Second-Lieutenant William Thomson Bruce Urquhart was almost immediately transferred to a British infantry unit, the 9th Battalion Nottinghamshire and Derbyshire Regiment (The Sherwood Foresters).

Billy continued to serve in Gallipoli and was hospitalised in Egypt due to sickness in September 1915, after discharge he then spent a period of leave at a convalescent camp before returning to Gallipoli in the autumn. He was injured in November and repatriated home to England. Billy would later claim that he had been wounded a total of no less than four times in Gallipoli, twice seriously, no surprise again that we can't confirm the number of apparent injuries he suffered. However, Billy must have been pretty badly hurt in Gallipoli as he didn't serve at the front at all during 1916, only returning to his battalion in March 1917. During the course of his absence he appears to have a married a lady who became Mrs. Ann Urquhart in Staffordshire. The newly-weds set up home at 'The Bungalow' in the village of Weeping Cross.

Returning to the front Billy saw action at the Battle of Arras in France in 1917 and quickly became popular with his men and brother officers. Everyone held him in great esteem as much for his cheerfulness as well as his courage and of course he had such distinguished military experience. In readiness for the Third Battle of Ypres and the assault upon Passchendaele Billy found himself attached to the 1st Battalion Sherwood Foresters. Once again he quickly distinguished himself, gaining a temporary promotion to Lieutenant. There is no doubt whatsoever that Billy was a competent and very capable officer, so much so that there was no hesitation in granting him further responsibility. He was asked to deputise as a company commander in effect granting him the role of temporary Captain, only an officer of great ability and trust would be required to undertake such a task.

It was whilst leading his men that Billy was killed on July 6th 1917, close to Ypres. The tributes paid by two of his fellow officers, including the Captain he deputised for must be read. Also, we want you to take note of the grainy photo of Billy that accompanies this story. Just look at him, grinning like a 'Cheshire Cat' and then really do make up your own mind about him and everything written here. The tributes start with Captain R.F. Moore, his words regarding Billy are below:

'I have always held great respect for Lieut. Urquhart, as he has seen a great deal of service, not only in this war but others. I cannot speak too highly of his great bravery, as I cannot say more than the decorations say for themselves. During the last few weeks he has been in command of my company during my absence and has very much impressed the men by his cheerful disposition and courage. It was very evident to me that the whole of my company will miss him greatly.'

Second-Lieutenant A. Millward added his own personal tribute to Billy:

'Poor old Billy was a splendid type of soldier… the best of pals… I am sure he gave up that which is dearest to us all – his life, willingly for the cause of right'.

Billy Urquhart left a total of almost £87 in the British old currency, a modest amount that was awarded in probate a few months after his death to his widow Ann back at home in Staffordshire. Over 200-miles away a tribute in the form of a roll of honour appeared in the Newcastle Journal, it read:

'Killed in action July 6ᵗʰ, William Thomas Bruce Urquhart, beloved husband of Nancie Urquhart (nee. Emmerson) Water Villa, Newbiggin-by-sea, son of Andrew Urquhart Esq. of Baku, Russia and Mrs. Urquhart, Edinburgh, nephew of the late Sir Thomas Urquhart.

So were Ann and Nancie Urquhart the same woman? Did they have two houses over two hundred miles apart? Or did Billy have two wives? I can find no official record of a marriage between Billy and Ann or Nancie - that may not entirely surprise you. What of being the nephew of Sir Thomas Urquhart? Well, that particular gentleman died in the mid-seventeenth century apparently of a laughing fit.

Billy lies at eternal rest in the Vlamertinghe New Military Cemetery close to Ypres in Belgium. The gravestone does not carry the post-nominal letters of DCM after his name as would be normal if he had been awarded the honour. His name is also carved magnificently on the tombstone of his family grave plot at Portobello Cemetery in Edinburgh. Both his mother and father are also named on the headstone. Billy is correctly named as a Lieutenant on the stone, there is no inscription of his father naming him as a Major or Lieutenant- Colonel. The letters DCM are proudly carved post nominally after Billy's name on the monument, is this correct? Does it really matter?

What is for certain is that Billy was entitled to the 1914-15 Star, his sister Annie took delivery of that medal unusually late in 1922. He was also awarded the British War Medal and the Victory Medal. Rob purchased his Victory Medal in 2018, the whereabouts of the others and the 'DCM' remain unknown as the final mystery.

William Golder

Killed in Action
France, Oct. 5th 1918
Aged 21.

Despite his youth and boyish looks, Willie Golder was a fearless and brave young officer who served with distinction.

SOME people raise their eyebrows when I mention that Blyth in Northumberland is actually one of my favourite places. The good folk of this relatively small town of around 37,000 inhabitants are warm and friendly. This story to a degree revolves around the port town where our subject Willie Golder was born and raised. I still have my 'Blyth Spartans' green beanie hat that honours the local football team that I bought for £1 from a charity shop in the town centre. Blyth does have another significance for me personally as well, for I was able to exhibit Willie's British War Medal and Victory Medal in the town on two separate occasions in 2015. The locals actually did take an interest that was refreshing as I went on to tell many of them the story of Willie's life.

Blyth can trace its history to as far back as 1138. Once a thriving and bustling port the traditional industries that grew there included ship building and coal mining, it was also an important centre for the salt trade and the railway industry. As the port expanded especially during the Victorian period the urgent requirement of building new homes was very much upon the agenda. It was against this backdrop that Willie was raised, for his father William senior became a very well-known local builder. The family as a whole enjoyed the trappings of wealth that came with the particular vocation of house building.

William Golder senior was a self-made man. He was born in the town and saw little of his own father who was away at sea as a maritime sailor. The enterprising Golder lad went on to build many houses in Blyth and settled down into marriage when he tied the knot with Violet Lee in 1875. They had two children together, the eldest a daughter, Annie, was born in 1879, followed three years later by their son George. A terrible tragedy hit the family hard in 1888 when Violet was struck down by illness. She passed away at just 33-years old leaving behind her devastated husband and two small children.

A year later William senior married a Scots-born woman, Annie Patterson who hailed from Lanarkshire. The lady was some fifteen years younger than her husband and took on both his children as her own, before giving birth to three girls and a boy. Margaret was born in 1891, quickly followed in successive years by Hannah and Violet, young Willie arrived on November 6th 1896 and was the youngest of all the brood. The enterprising builder with money and resources to spare built a nine-roomed house for his family and was able to retire as a man of means. His two elder children had left home to get married by the time that youngest boy Willie started his schooling that would very significantly shape his short life.

Money can buy a decent education and William Golder knew that. He sent Willie to the prestigious North Eastern County School some 70-miles away in Barnard Castle, County Durham. The youngster became a resident boarder there and enjoyed such pursuits as boxing, wrestling and fencing as well as the traditional sport of Rugby. This private institution purposely encouraged a regime that was designed to not only educate the young charges but also to toughen them up with vigorous physical exercise. The school became the first in Britain to open its own swimming pool in 1896. Willie then spent a short time at Durham University and was seconded to their own Officer Training Corps at Armstrong College in Newcastle, only 14-miles south of his home. The keen young sportsman had been earmarked for a commission into the Durham Light Infantry. He passed his courses and despite being only 18-years old became a Second-Lieutenant. His distinguished military career would end in tragedy just five weeks before the end of the First World War in 1918.

At this point I have to say that young Willie had for the larger part of his short life been enveloped in male dominated environments, from his schooling to formal officer training. With the emphasis placed upon learning and physical well-being he would have been a conscientious and strong young man who was able to undertake many challenges. It is interesting to look at his photo that accompanies this story. He appears rather child-like, very much like a boy, however, the image is slightly misleading. Willie became an extremely capable officer who accepted and undertook great responsibility at a very young age, endorsed by the very men who served under him.

It wasn't until July 13th 1916 that Willie arrived on the Western Front. He had impressed his superiors within the 15th Battalion Durham Light Infantry and had been promoted to Lieutenant before he arrived at the front, he was still just 19-years old. I have to say that my admiration for young Willie gets greater as this story moves along. After several weeks of further specialist training he was given a huge responsibility when he was attached to the 64th Trench Mortar Battery as the commander. This highly mobile specialist bombing unit constantly faced danger even from their own equipment. The men of the battery, some of them twice Willie's age were tough, hardened characters and very physically able. Combat missions saw them venture out in relatively small numbers, they had little protection and were always upon the offensive. The teenage officer had to oversee the dangers, organise the logistics and write the letters home to the families of the casualties.

In 1917 Willie Golder was transferred to the 13th Battalion Durham Light Infantry and fought as a platoon commander at the Third Battle of Ypres. He was involved in some particularly nasty engagements along the Menin Road, an area I know very well. In October of that year his battalion was posted to Italy. The Italians at the time were allies of the British and had been humbled by the Austrians assisted by the Germans at Caporetto. Northern Italy was in danger of being over-run. The Durham men were far superior to their Austrian counterparts in terms of battle skills and experience and had little trouble dealing with them. Less than a year later Willie was back on the Western Front in France to take part in the final push against a resolute and determined German opposition in the autumn of 1918. Although on the back-foot they were relentlessly clinging on and fighting desperately. The experienced Durham men would require all of the qualities of leadership from their officers in the field. Officers like Willie would lead by example and provide inspirational endeavour to push for the final victory.

At around one o'clock on the morning of Saturday October 5th 1918, Willie's battalion with a total strength of 34 officers and 720 men assembled in their positions at Prospect Hill close to the village of Beaurevoir in northern France. The men had to wait in the cool, damp and darkened early morning for five hours before commencing with their assault. Willie would have spent most of his time before the attack reassuring his men, talking with non-commissioned officers and preparing himself for what was to come. To the left of the Durham men the 11th Battalion Sherwood Foresters held the ground and to the right the 9th Battalion West Yorkshire Regiment made up the three-pronged attacking force. The battalions were to go in together, they had fought on numerous occasions side by side previously and were confident they would succeed in a co-ordinated action. British artillery had already pounded the defending German lines.

Within minutes the commanding officer of the 13th Battalion Durham Light Infantry, Lieutenant-Colonel Denzil Clarke DSO, MC, was badly wounded. Captain Lennie Greenwood DSO, MC, his second-in-command took over the responsibility of leading the central thrust of the attack. Greenwood was once described as one of the best officers of the war by his General, by his side was Lieutenant Willie Golder leading his men. The Durham lads were heavily shelled and machine-gunned as they made rapid progress across the dim terrain. Greenwood had gone too far, too fast, the Yorkshiremen and the Sherwood Foresters on their left and right flanks were way behind. The Durham men were caught like rats in a barrel by deadly enfilade German machine-gun fire from all sides. Willie was one of the first officers to go down, he was hit by ferocious fire and killed almost instantly.

Captain Greenwood knew he had to withdraw and reluctantly the Durham soldiers retreated to a position not far from their starting point. The battalion losses were heavy with over 200 casualties, including almost half of their officers, 10 wounded and 5 killed, around 50 other ranks also lost their lives. Was Greenwood reckless? Was he to blame for the position he led his men into that ultimately cost Willie his life? To a degree I believe he was, Rob does not agree at all with me. He points out that had the two flanking battalions been as efficient as the Durham battalion the situation would have been totally different. Greenwood lost his life less than a week later. After being elevated to Acting Lieutenant-Colonel at the staggeringly young age of just twenty-five he was gassed in an assault. Refusing medical treatment and insisting on continuing with his duties the stubborn commander succumbed to bronchial problems that ultimately killed him.

Willie Golder had no reservations whatsoever in following Greenwood. I am convinced that he knew he was in mortal danger when the position became obvious. The 21-year old fought on right at the front of the assault until he was cut down. In the aftermath of the disaster the men who had been at the side of the young Lieutenant paid remarkable tributes to him. The battalion Adjutant wrote:

'Coming through the various dressing stations, his own men… forgot their pain and suffering when telling me how splendid he was… He was a dear friend of mine and was greatly loved by officers and men'.

One of the ordinary soldiers of his platoon, Private Stamp, wrote to Willie's mother in Blyth a simple dedication:

'You had a very brave son, something to be proud of'.

Back in the small port town Annie Golder had lost her only son. Both she and her retired husband were devastated, no more would he come bounding through their front door with his laddish looks and energetic demeanour. The comfortable lifestyle the Golder's enjoyed did not compensate for their tragic loss. Willie had known nothing else but the military and had made his parents proud, then he was gone, suddenly gone forever, try to imagine how that would feel if you were his mum or dad.

Looking through the roll of honour attached to the former Armstrong College where Willie had completed his officer training I noted some very interesting points. The roll describes Willie has having been given the responsibility of Temporary Captain. Considering that Captain Greenwood had been granted command of the battalion, Willie could have taken over his original company of men. I think he more than likely did just that, a massive undertaking for a twenty-one year old. Also, the roll notes that Willie had been 'Mentioned in Despatches' twice for his bravery in battle. The De Ruvigny's roll of honour - that I find somewhat unreliable at the best of times – also mentions one such acknowledgement, however they date it incorrectly as to before he even arrived at the front. I can find no official records of the MID's so therefore I cannot confirm them. Rob believes the college had the correct information but can't substantiate it either.

Nowadays, you can sit on one of the tranquil benches that face the docking area for ships that unload their cargo at Blyth. Vessels arrive from Scandinavia to deliver their loads of paper and pulp that are turned into newspapers in England and Scotland. The pubs and cafes in town are also busy and the little shopping centre and adjoining market provide the bargains. Nobody knew of Willie Golder when I was there, he had faded like so many others into history. Every time I visit Blyth I know that I walk in the footsteps that Willie once walked, the same applies as I walk down the Menin Road near Ypres in Belgium. Sometimes in the winter time as I pull on my Blyth Spartans beanie hat in readiness to walk my dog through the countryside, I think of the young man who gave his life all of those years ago.

Willie now rests at the age of twenty-one forever in the relatively small Beaurevoir British Cemetery in France. The inscription that is written on the bottom of his headstone is unique. To me it reflects what he was best at, the consideration of the welfare of his own men, they knew that. The inscription reads:

'We have found safety with all things undying'.

Rev. Charles Buchan

Died of Wounds
Belgium, Dec. 2nd 1917
Aged 29.

THIS chapter comes to a conclusion with the story of a very special human being, a man of great strength, a man of divinity. Charles Buchan served in two capacities, primarily he was charged with the responsibility for a platoon of men in his role as a junior ranking officer. The second role he undertook was that of being a minister on the front line. His work was vital and gave great inspiration and invariably the final dignified hope to those who knew their lives were slipping away. Charles provides this publication with something entirely different with regard to what both Rob and I believe is essentially

A photo of the Minister-Soldier Charles Buchan.

part of the history of the Great War. A certain part that is often ignored or over-looked. For everything I have said in brief so far, there is, as always, a twist in the tale.

Charles' background was traditional, he was born just outside Fraserburgh in the far corner of Aberdeenshire on Monday September 24th 1888. He became the eldest of four sons to his fisherman father William and mother Christian. The family eventually all settled together in a stone cottage close to the quayside of the little port. William was a drifter skipper and led out his crew to catch herring, everyday life revolved around routine, it was straight-forward and respectful. Nowadays, Fraserburgh despite having a population of only around 13,000 is Scotland's largest shellfish port, one of the biggest in Europe. Yes, times have changed but not to a vast extent in this niche of northern Scotland. Christian values, community spirit and good old fashioned traditions remain.

Young Charles was a thoughtful, caring and considerate adolescent, he regularly attended church and gained a place at Fraserburgh Academy before moving on to Aberdeen University in 1908 to study economics. In 1912 he graduated with a first-class honours Master of Arts Degree [MA]. Charles wasn't just a very good student he was also pro-active in various societies within the university and was noted as a very keen, competitive and fair sportsman. His religious beliefs were very important to him so he decided to seek a career with the Free Church of Scotland. Charles became a student at the U.F.C Divinity Hall in Glasgow as a probationary member upon leaving university. His social conscience led him to volunteer with the Boatmen's Mission whilst continuing his studies. He would go on to spend some time with a mission in Canada for a whole summer before volunteering to work with the YMCA at the outbreak of war in 1914.

Charles' younger brother John enlisted into his local territorial unit at the outbreak of war, he joined the 5th Battalion [1st/5th] Gordon Highlanders. Tragically John was killed in action on June 4th 1916. Rob believes this had a serious affect upon his elder brother as he will go on to explain as this story unravels. The death of his father William at home in Scotland also probably exasperated and tested his faith. Before this double tragedy Charles had felt compelled to sign up for active service himself, this was regardless of the fact that he was a probationary minister of the Free Church of Scotland. In January of 1916 he too joined a territorial battalion of the Gordon Highlanders local to his native Fraserburgh. Within weeks he was transferred to a regular battalion's specialist newly formed unit, he had obviously attracted the right kind of attention to have been selected, or did he volunteer? A man of the cloth, spreading the word of God drafted into the 2nd Battalion Gordon Highlanders 'A'- Company – Machine-Gun Section!

The young preacher started at the bottom as an ordinary soldier, serving with this newly created unit he was well briefed on how to actually fire the Vickers machine-gun. Everyone in the six to eight man team had to be able to operate the weapon, simply because if the gunner became a casualty, he would be replaced by one of the other team members. If the subsequent gunner went down the process would continue. Machine-gun crews were not taken as prisoners if captured or over-run, they were bayoneted on the spot - it was a hazardous service role. Charles Buchan would have seen at close quarters the devastating effects of what machine-guns could do to the human body. The Vickers could discharge around 450 rounds per minute, a three-second burst aimed at an enemy soldier advancing within a hundred yards would cut the man in half. To be on the end of a five-second volley would see the victim literally appear as though he had been put through a mincing machine.

When Charles arrived for active duty with the machine-gun section on the Somme in 1916 his brother had already been killed. The man of God had to live with the fact that he was very much an integral part of a highly trained mobile killing unit. His conscience would have dictated his actions to a degree, however he would not hesitate in performing his duties or he could have put other members of his team at risk. Rob is of the opinion he considered that an 'eye for an eye' in relation to the death of his brother eased his very conscience, I'm not too sure I agree with that. We do know that Charles regularly preached sermons to his comrades in the field whist he was serving with the machine-gun section.

In October of 1916 arrangements were being made to elevate Charles for a commission as an officer, this meant he would skip the ranks to take up the role. It is interesting to note that whilst undergoing assessment he was granted a certificate of what we can only describe as an ordination from the Free Church of Scotland. He officially became the Reverend Charles Buchan. After some time he was discharged from field and combat duties to complete his officer training at Purbright early in 1917. At this point we have reasonable grounds to believe that he would have been posted as a minister to a Scots battalion, that didn't happen at all, as we shall see. The Free Church of Scotland was relatively new at the time having been formed in 1900. An Evangelical Presbyterian order it held a lot of influence and was noted as holding strong theological and practical values as well as being accepted as liberal and fair. Charles went on to continue his military career as an officer in the line. Even though it is very likely he preached, comforted and inspired others he retained his status as a soldier and was expected to perform his duty – to kill the enemy.

Charles was posted to the Lancashire Fusiliers in 1917. At first joining the regular 1st battalion. Many of its original members had been killed but it still retained men from the industrial heart of the red rose county. The Lancashire men were textile workers, coal miners and railway workers, they had very little if anything in common at all with Charles Buchan, least of all his church. He was very quickly transferred to the 15th Battalion Lancashire Fusiliers prior to the Third Battle of Ypres. These men were the 1st Salford Pals, many of the original members had been wiped out on the Somme in 1916. Reinforced by men from different parts of the country they still held their Salford identity to a diluted degree, Charles quickly gained their respect.

I am not a religious man, however, I am aware of the ten-commandments as dictated by the bible. Whether or not I believe in them or the interpretations of them is irrelevant. One of the instructions interestingly is interpreted in two different forms; 'Thou shalt not kill 'or 'You shall not murder'. Is there a difference between the two? Do we have a 'murdering vicar' here? Or an officer of the crown performing his duty whether or not he takes the lives of other human beings in doing so?

It is wise to think about the social attitudes of the time. The church had much more influence than it does today in the ordinary everyday lives of the masses. A perceived threat to the very existence of what was deemed as good and Godly had to be eradicated in order to protect the will of God, so it was said by some. For officers like Charles it didn't help when concocted and ridiculous lies regarding German atrocities were circulated deliberately by senior staff officers, although Rob thinks he took no notice of them. The hypocrisy of not only the church but also of Charles' senior officers having the knowledge of the position he was placed in doesn't come across very well. But what of Charles himself, how could he live with his predicament?

I have no doubt that on many occasions he was at the side of those who needed his support as they took their final breaths, mortally wounded. It is also very likely he performed ministerial services and comforted the mentally afflicted suffering from 'shellshock' all unofficially. When he came face-to-face with administering death to others that Rob is absolutely certain happened, he just 'got on with it' and was intelligent enough to realise he had no other option. Today it is almost unthinkable to imagine a vicar on the front line, armed and charging at the enemy, shooting from the hip.

Rob and I have had many conversations regarding this story, trying to understand the man himself and whether or not his actions as a minister were very rare or almost unique. It would appear they weren't. Within minutes of researching Rob discovered another war-mongering, gun-slinging clergyman who was killed near in Ypres in 1917. Perhaps there are many more and if so they surely belong in another publication.

What can't be disputed is the fact that the Reverend Charles Buchan was a fine officer and a good leader of men. This is very well endorsed as we shall demonstrate with various testimonials. When the end came for Charles it was with great dignity, however, tainted by sheer misfortune. After being in the field of battle in difficult wintry conditions around Ypres Charles was slightly wounded. He refused medical treatment and insisted on remaining with his men until they had achieved their objective. The date was December 2nd 1917, Charles had been in action from the very early hours of the morning and all throughout the day. Finally, he agreed to go to an ambulance after having his wound dressed, it was whilst on his way to the vehicle he was hit by a shell. Charles was hastily taken by stretcher bearers to an advanced dressing station. The surgeons fought to save him in vain but he died of his wounds, the fighting vicar was 29-years old. In a sad but rather poignant irony he was not alone when he died, by his side was another man of God, the battalion Chaplain who wrote afterwards the following words to Charles' mother:

'You have lost a very noble son, and we have lost a very gallant officer. He was slightly wounded in an attack made in the early morning, but he carried on all day until his men had consolidated the position won. He came to the aid post at about 4.30pm and had his wound dressed; he then started off to walk to the ambulance together with his servant and must have been hit by a shell, for I found him about two hours later at the advanced dressing station. He fell asleep while his wounds were being dressed and did not rally. He was a true servant of God and I feel that God has called him to higher service'.

His battalion and company commanders also paid tribute with their sentiments passed on to his mother in a far corner of Scotland. Charles' Colonel wrote:

'We all feel that we have lost an officer and companion who cannot easily be replaced and whom we will always miss'.

Not easy to replace was Charles, was he replaced with another man of the cloth? Somehow I doubt it. His Captain was a little more understanding and compassionate with his words to the grieving mother, they were:

'He was first slightly wounded and refused to leave his post. Later on we prevailed on him to go to the doctor, but unfortunately he got badly wounded on the way down and died in hospital. He was one of my most trusted officers and I could rely on him to do anything; also all his men swore by him and would have followed him anywhere'.

The final tribute I am going to place here to Charles is held within the National Museum of Scotland, it was made by members of his alumni from Aberdeen University. Considering everything I have written and what Rob and I have discussed it would be easy to pass some form of judgement or opinion upon Reverend Charles Buchan, the 'fighting vicar'. The words of this final tribute therefore we consider as extremely important, they come from those of whom were some of the closest to him:

'Charles Buchan's great desire had always been to do something for the world. He loved men and found good in everyone; he knew how to be widely tolerant and sympathetic without for a moment lowering his own high standard or yielding his principals; and his perfect sincerity and earnestness won him the love and respect of men of all types and characters'.

Charles crossed the spectrum of life in more ways than one. He now lies forever at peace within the Ypres Reservoir Cemetery in Belgium. One can only speculate as to how he would have held redemption and practised had he lived. Some people say we are judged by only one entity or being, is that or was that the case with Charles? His full medals entitlement of the British War Medal, Victory Medal and Death Plaque were purchased by Rob, alongside many articles relating to his life. His brother John who perished in France was also entitled to three service medals. For some unexplained reason they never made it back to the family home in Fraserburgh. The medals were ordered to be disposed of in 1922, despite family members still residing at the address.

A WOMAN'S GRIEF

IT was Rob's idea to create this chapter. Having to process hundreds of sets of medals and then carry out the preliminary research upon their recipients always creates stories abound. So many times after having examined the information gathered a woman's grief becomes very apparent. Mothers, wives, sweethearts, sisters, nieces, grandmothers, godmothers, there were countless numbers of them left to grieve the loss of a loved one. In some instances it would be more than just a single son, husband, father, brother, nephew, grandson or godson to mourn. Male family members were literally wiped out, some just disappeared altogether.

Of all the British battle fatalities during the First World War nearly half of those still to this day have no grave. They are 'missing', their bodies having been torn to pieces, evaporated or buried beneath masses of rubble. These men have no final resting place, no everlasting peace and no dignity. Of those who do have marked graves they are far away from the green grass of home. Our boys lie still in France, Belgium, Greece, Turkey, Russia, Germany, India, Iraq, Iran, Malta, Italy, Egypt and other parts of Africa. Working-class mothers, wives and sweethearts never had the opportunities to say a final farewell as it was impossible for them to visit the graves and lay their tributes.

In the treacherous conditions of field hospitals close to the front lines, thousands of nurses, professional and voluntary toiled away as angels of mercy. Almost every day they saw their patients slowly slip away, the pain and anguish these particular women suffered was always held within. There are no winners in wars that are always created by men, yes so many men have suffered since the dawn of time because of war, as have women.

Walter King

Killed-in-Action
Belgium, May 12th 1915
Aged 25.

THERE were no fewer than eight important females in the life of Walter King. His mother, two step-mothers and five sisters. He also had three brothers, a father and a step-father. Sounds complicated, it was. Walter's life was very difficult right from the beginning. You really wouldn't think so looking at him cheerfully smiling attired in his army uniform in the picture that accompanies this story. Every credit to him, he made the most out of his life and travelled to far-away places, sadly his was a life

Despite enduring many hardships in his life, Walter always managed to keep a smile upon his face.

that was tragically cut short. I often wonder how Walter would have got on had he lived to prosper, marry and have a family.

His father Harry King was a brewery engine driver who hailed from the small medieval market town of Tewkesbury in Gloucestershire, famed for its wonderful Norman abbey. In the Victorian era the town was much the same size as it is today, but poorer with living standards at average for the period. Against this backdrop Harry married a local girl Emma Sutton, three years his senior, she was 23-years old when they tied the knot in 1861. The couple lived in a small cramped dwelling in the centre of town and had four children in just over five years, two sons and two daughters. Emma found life difficult raising the youngsters in squalid conditions having to rely upon her husband's sole income to do so. In 1889 she fell pregnant again for the fifth time and was not in the best of health. Early in 1890 another son, Walter, arrived, with four little ones already running around Emma's health deteriorated further. Within weeks she was dead, probably suffering from severe exhaustion, malnutrition and disease.

It is difficult to even begin to imagine what Emma King went through both physically and mentally during her final days. The horrific thought of having to leave her young ones behind alongside baby Walter must have been terrifying as she weakened and gradually slipped away. With no health care provision at all and no money to afford the services of a doctor Harry would have been desperately distraught when she passed away. Emma was buried in a pauper's grave, Harry couldn't even afford her a decent funeral.

Graciously the small local community rallied at Harry's desperate plight. The brewery worker had been widowed with five children all under the age of nine. No form of social security existed whatsoever other than that of charity from the church, it was not forthcoming for the beleaguered King family. A well-known member of the community William Burrows, the town's barber for decades and his wife stepped-in. Although William was nearly 70-years old and Lydia his spouse not far behind they took into their home the baby Walter. The elderly couple fed him, clothed him and cherished him, effectively for a short period becoming his step-parents. Walter's three-year old sister Ethel went to live with her grandmother Elizabeth, Harry's mother. The gutsy brewery driver took upon bringing up his other three children alongside working full-time. He moved to a house next door to his mother, a nurse, who also assisted.

Harry eventually found happiness once again when he met Elizabeth Lawler the daughter of a clerk. In a simple ceremony the two were married on June 11th 1893 in Tewkesbury. The new Mrs. King had no reservations about taking on Harry's five children including the infant Walter. Harry's elder children from his first marriage eventually went out to work to help with the household budget as four more youngsters were born into the family. We also have to remember that Walter's elder sister Eliza was very close to him and helped to take care of him as he grew up. For Walter himself he realised the pressures his family endured and had seen the struggles they underwent on a daily basis. The tough times got worse when his father passed away aged only in his late-forties, leaving behind a widow with six children all under the age of seventeen. To make matters even worse Walter's grandmother was ailing and close to death, he had seen enough and decided upon a career with the military.

At some point in October 1907 Walter joined the 2nd Battalion Gloucestershire Regiment and was allocated the service number of 8642. He was still just 17-years old at that time and would go on to serve for nearly eight years in the battalion as a professional soldier. His untimely death ended a military career that had been colourful and interesting.

Walter spent the Christmas of 1907 at home with his family. The new recruit was released from barracks along with many others as this was a period of relative inactivity. He arrived home proudly wearing his uniform eagerly anticipating the reaction of his family. Walter was aware that his grandmother who by then was in her mid-seventies would be so thrilled to see him in his military attire. Tragically he was just too late, she had died shortly before he returned. The young soldier's first 'duty' in his new uniform was to attend his granny's funeral the day after Christmas on December 26th 1907. This lad had lost his birth mother, father and grandmother, death was more than a common occurrence for so many families in the days of pre-NHS Britain. The services of a medical doctor were beyond the financial reach of millions of ordinary men, women and children. British people lived in the motherland of a nation that presided over a huge colonial empire but couldn't or should I say wouldn't provide basic welfare for its own citizens.

Walter received a garrison posting to the Mediterranean island of Malta with its healthy climate, hours of sunshine and clear blue waters. It wasn't all as it appeared to be, the island was constantly plagued by sand-fly fever, many soldiers developed its flu like symptoms and quite a number perished alongside the civilian inhabitants. An exciting yet daunting deployment came along for Walter in 1912. His battalion was sent to north-east China to be stationed at Chang Wang Tao in order to protect commercial interests in Tianjin. British colonial history is well documented, soldiers were billeted and garrisoned around a huge empire across the world, postings to India and Africa were common, but China? Not at all a part of the British Empire, so why did Walter end up there?

Although Britain had no intentions of conquering the huge nation with its colossal population, it harassed and cajoled the Chinese into furthering its commercial interests alongside Japan and France. To put it bluntly if the Chinese refused to make small commercial trade concessions, by in effect ceding territory to the three powerful countries, then military action could and I think would have been used against them. Soon afterwards Germany, Belgium, Italy and Austria-Hungary also jumped on the trade bandwagon for their share of the spoils. China gave way albeit by handing over a very, very small portion of territory. The European strong-arm tactics undoubtedly represented a form of bullying. Walter and the small garrison made sure the British traders got their own way as well as actually starting trouble with the Germans, in some ways nothing changes!

The Chinese posting demonstrated to Walter the extremes of climate, in the winter time it was far colder than anywhere he had ever been. I am sure he was pleased when the battalion found that it was to be posted to Sialkat in the Punjab region of India, now a part of Pakistan.Weather conditions in northern India were more consistent and favourable, for Walter it would be another exotic adventure. The young soldier set sail from China on the 'HMT Arcadia', not long into the voyage the men were informed they were to be diverted back to England in readiness to take part in the campaign on the Western Front. Walter arrived back in Southampton on November 8th 1914 and then moved to Winchester with his battalion. A week before Christmas 1914 the Gloucestershire men had landed in France but Walter wasn't with his comrades.

Rob suggests the seasoned soldier was retained for further specialist training alongside a small number of other men from the battalion. With seven years military experience although having seen very little or no action he was very familiar with weaponry. In the early days of the First World War the British infantry line regiments had specially created machine-gun sections and small bands of men who made up bombing parties. These men had to be conditioned and trained. It is therefore very likely that Walter spent the Christmas of 1914 at home alongside his step-mother Elizabeth and his younger sisters Evelyn and Florence. His little brother Harry would have been excited at his return for he had only ever seen Walter very fleetingly. Another brother Edgar who had just entered his teens saw his soldier brother as a hero and begged of Walter to tell him tales of military life.

The training was pretty prolonged suggesting to us that Walter may have been groomed to become part of a special machine-gun section, although in the absence of his service record this can't be confirmed. He arrived in France on Tuesday April 27th 1915 and was immediately rushed to the front in the direction of Ypres across the Belgian border where intense fighting was ensuing. Amidst continuing reports of German atrocities there could be no denying they were responsible for the very first sustained attack using chemical weapons during the Second Battle of Ypres. Walter arrived to a scene of chaos, the Germans had earlier deployed chlorine gas in the region. His battalion had been pushed right up against the front line in Sanctuary Wood after fighting their way through St. Eloi.

Consistent and heavy shelling with high explosives forced the Gloucester men up towards the Menin Road and the Hooge Chateau after holding a line at Zillebeke. Behind them the ancient town of Ypres was in flames, the noise of gunfire was deafening. German infantry sweeps following huge bombardments intended to surprise the resolute British infantrymen. The action was non-stop, the Gloucester boys were so heavily shelled their trenches started to cave in. Undeterred they rallied and stormed forward with their bayonets driving off the German infantry assault, it was May 12th 1915, the bombardments continued. Without the cover of their trenches the regular highly trained west-country men fought on. Against this backdrop Walter perished, he was blown to pieces by a German high explosive shell. What remained of his mutilated body was washed into the Flanders mud by the torrential rain that followed. The boy from Tewkesbury was gone forever, he has no grave, there was absolutely nothing left of him, he was literally destroyed as a human being - that is war, not glory, war.

At their home in the little market town Elizabeth, Florence, Evelyn and the boys grew anxious. Walter hadn't sent letters for a while and there had been no official news as to his well-being. His mum became extremely anxious and over four months after Walter had been killed she was appealing in the local press for any potential sightings of him. I have to comment here and slam the ineffectual and utterly ridiculous lack of logistical competence of his battalion officers. The company commander and adjutant knew that Walter was missing and were more than aware he wasn't coming back given the severity of the action in which he died. Communications with his family weren't good enough, the compassion wasn't there. Had Walter been a decorated officer the situation would have been entirely different. When Elizabeth finally got the confirmation she was devastated. This woman had taken on Walter as three year old along with four of his siblings. The four children she had with his father were treated no differently. She had been widowed at the age of forty and had now lost her boy, step-mother or not, she was his mum.

Walter is commemorated on the Menin Gate Memorial to the missing in Ypres. This superb monument carries the inscriptions of the names of nearly 55,000 British and former Dominion and Empire servicemen. These men were lost in the defence of Ypres between 1914 and August 1917, their names represent them personally, they have no grave. Nearby, close to Passchendaele another 35,000 men are commemorated at Tyne Cot, they too have no graves. A staggering number of 90,000 human beings who literally just disappeared defending a town only about the same size as Tewkesbury where Walter came from.

Every night, yes every night at 20.00 hours a service of dedication is held for these men. The Belgian fire brigade play the last post at the end of each daily service and the venue is absolutely packed every time. Some people think the First World War is a back water of history, a visit to the Menin Gate more than proves otherwise.

Personally, I have attended a number of the services at the memorial, and yes, I have paid my own private personal respects whilst there to Walter amongst others. His mum, sisters and brothers never had that opportunity. Rob and I intend to lay a wreath bearing their names next time we visit the Menin Gate. Elizabeth King was so upset at the death of Walter that she initially failed to acknowledge the awards of his 1914-15 Star, British War Medal and Victory Medal. The Death Plaque was never accepted and officially disposed of. In 1920 the medals were facing a similar fate until the family finally agreed to receive them. All three medals now are beautifully cased and safe in our possession having been released by the family some years ago.

Walter's sisters married and had children of their own, of the four King boys only Walter served during the First World War. His mum Elizabeth died alone taking with her the cherished memory of the day her boy first walked back into their little house in Tewkesbury wearing his uniform for the very first time. The smile on Walter's face demonstrates how he conquered adversity, he was much loved, love that went along with him on his journey to heaven.

Edwin Millett
Killed-in-Action
Belgium, Oct. 4th 1917
Aged 26.

There were two females very dear to Edwin Millett, he was devoted to his young wife Emily and their little girl Elizabeth. The doting family man left them both to go to war and fight for what he believed in, the prospect of a better world. The life he left behind could hardly have been any worse for his wife and child who had to cope with absolute abject poverty that ultimately led to tragedy. Edwin's life and times and those of his small family provided a huge challenge in terms of how they were researched. Many of the basic methods I normally use were not available. A lot of facts are provided here, however, as you will see I use some conjectural theories at certain points.

I have no wish to do so to create unnecessary drama and honestly believe my selectively placed assumptions could well hold a certain degree of truth.

Edwin was born in Clerkenwell a rough and ready part of London in 1891, he eventually settled in what I personally believe was one of two neighbouring districts that were the most deprived in England. Hoxton and Shoreditch on the fringes of London's east end were extremely difficult places to live within. Social conditions there in the Victorian and Edwardian eras were appalling yet a community spirit prevailed, it had to do so or otherwise life would have been completely intolerable.

The young man hadn't had an easy life. He was the son of a bookbinder, James who worked hard to maintain his family that included nine children. Edwin was listed as out of work in 1911 when he was 20-years old, the pressures of that alone were difficult to say the least. For a man to be unemployed in 1911 was bad news, social reforms didn't really cover rudimentary benefits until the year after. To make matters worse for the family his elder brother Tommy was also out of work. The house on Margaret Street was absolutely crammed. James, his wife Mary and three adult sons, including Edwin, two of whom were unemployed all lived in four rooms. In one other room lived James Edwin Millett another son with his wife Mary and two children under two years old. This lad worked as a milkman and would eventually manage to find work for his younger brother Edwin. All sounds confusing? It was... and I find it difficult to begin to imagine what it really was like for seven adults and two small children virtually living on top of each other in poverty.

Emily Elizabeth Clark was born in Bethnal Green, in the east end of London in 1890. She was the daughter of Walter and Eliza Clark and had

a number of siblings. Her father worked in the building trade principally on road works and roofs, the family had to move around north and east London to wherever he could find work. In 1913 the Clark's were also living in Margaret Street, Edwin lived next door to Emily and the two fell in love. It wasn't long

Edwin Millett came from Hoxton, an area of London that was once one of the most deprived parts of Great Britain.

before they were married on Christmas Day 1913 at the Church of the Holy Redeemer in Exmouth Market, Clerkenwell. The newly-weds set up home in Islington but struggled to cope financially and moved to wherever they could afford. Eventually they got a place in the rather affluent sounding Chatham Avenue in Hoxton. Affluent could not be further from the truth, the dwellings were slums, disease was rife, the area was filthy and described by one journalist as -'motley, struggling, anxious and poverty stricken'.

Edwin and Emily had to get on with life, it was as simple as that. He continued to work as a milkman and was kept busy. Hoxton, alongside Shoreditch was the most crowded, dilapidated district of London. Nowadays, our life expectancy is far greater than ever. We have to cope with the three major causes of death, dementia, cancer and heart disease. In Edwardian Hoxton, cancer and heart disease killed fewer people than tuberculosis, bronchitis, pneumonia and believe it or nor diarrhoea. The infant mortality rate was horrendous and the number of children born out of wedlock was way above the national average. These unfortunate youngsters went on to make up the majority of the population in the local workhouse. Alcoholism was also very prevalent with Gin being often cheaper to buy than beer. Public houses were on every street corner and drunks were considered as funny and hilarious, unless they caused trouble or public order offences. If they persisted in unruly behaviour they would be condemned to prison, the worst offenders suffered the misfortune of being sent to the local lunatic asylum. Those unfortunate souls were incarcerated amongst the severely mentally ill. Not surprisingly they became psychological damaged themselves as they sobered up to find there was no escape from a horrific and desperately cruel environment. Upon their eventual release some of them contributed to the relatively high suicide statistics in the area.

In Hoxton with its huge population there was no mortuary. The dead had to be carted to other London boroughs and often that could take time. Corpses that were ravaged by disease often lay in tiny cockroach laden squat dwellings for days on end. Flies, maggots and all of the infectious conditions they spread especially in the heat of the summer only served to make general living conditions very dangerous. This partially explains why diarrhoea was responsible for killing more people than heart disease or cancer. The food chain was also accountable for the prolific spread of disease in Hoxton and Shoreditch. With a very large populous that had to be fed dozens of slaughterhouses mainly provided pork from pigs. There was no welfare consideration for the animals, the abattoirs were disgusting, inhumane and filthy. A number of cow sheds provided the milk required, when the cows started to suffer from malnutrition and disease they were slaughtered without mercy and their contaminated meat was put into the local food cycle. All of this occurred in the later part of the Victorian era and the early part of the twentieth century. Britain during this period presided over a huge colonial empire, once the mightiest the world had ever known whilst millions of its own citizens lived in poverty. Hoxton and Shoreditch were at the far end of the scale but there were hundreds of other districts whose populations suffered similar deprivations. In historical terms this really wasn't that long ago.

In Hoxton and Shoreditch the locals did find time for recreation. There were a number of theatres, 'flea pits' that offered bawdy and cheap entertainment. Pubs served beer very cheaply sourced from a host of local breweries. In Edwardian Hoxton women drank heavily, smoked and slept around, a number of war widows sold their bodies to make ends meet. For men it was 'anything goes' as far as socialising was concerned. Hoxton may have been dirty and poverty stricken but it was a lively place. As a treat you could buy pie, greens and potatoes for 'tuppence' [2d] from a café on the Nile Road.

After trying for a child for over a year Edwin and Emily were delighted when baby Elizabeth Emily Millett was born on July 12th 1915. The Hoxton milkman at that time wasn't required to sign-up being a married man but he would have been subjected to many comments as to why he hadn't done so. Mothers, wives and girlfriends on his rounds had lost loved ones of the same age as him and he possibly suffered a loss of income and one or two white feathers because of that. On December 10th 1915 Edwin I am sure against the wishes of his wife travelled to Finsbury Barracks and signed on with the newly formed 3rd/10th Battalion [Territorial Force] Middlesex Regiment. He was immediately placed upon the reserve list to be mobilised at their discretion. Joining the territorials meant that he received small payments during an interim period, welcome income for his struggling family. Avoiding conscription because he had already signed up he was mobilised for full training on September 18th 1916. It would be some time before he was eventually deployed to France.

The tattooed Edwin continued to get home to see his wife and baby daughter for a few months. He finally embarked at Southampton on May 31st 1917 with his battalion, they arrived in Le Havre the day afterwards. Edwin had cards and photos of his little girl and wife among the few possessions in his pockets and would write home regularly. The soldier/milkman found himself pitched into the Third Battle of Ypres and the advance towards Passchendaele in Belgium. After spending some time with his battalion within the South African Brigade he would have been involved in the attack on Polygon Wood in late September of 1917. Here, having been transferred to the 4th Division the Middlesex men fought alongside the Australians, fierce and determined soldiers with an almost fanatical hatred of the Germans.

Back in 2007, I went into Polygon Wood whilst filming one of my documentaries. It is a haunting and desolate place completely different in its appearance as to when Edwin was there, however, some creepy relics still remain. The wood in 1917 was smashed to pieces by artillery fire, stumps replaced trees and there was no cover for the attacking men. Nowadays it is lush and green with various tracks leading in different directions. Inside the wood the deserted remains of an old German command bunker remain and chillingly so do a couple of 'pill-boxes'. These are little partly submerged shelters that poked up to the surface with slits to fire machine-gun bullets through. The small fortifications caused huge casualties to the advancing British and Australian soldiers, Edwin would have come across them with feelings of trepidation and sheer terror. The sinister little shelters looked menacing to me nearly a century later in their ruined states. Edwin's involvement at Polygon Wood was the second of three 'bite and hold' tactical procedures. These manoeuvres are deemed as successes by many, especially the green welly wearing, cheese and pickle sandwich munching 'metropolitan historians'.

Edwin's next serious involvement at the front came in the third and final 'bite and hold' manoeuvre on October 4th 1917 at the Battle of Broodseinde. I refer to these actions as manoeuvres because of the very limited ground they gained on small geographical scales in relation to horrendous casualties. Yes, the Germans lost more men, the tactics were based upon attrition with the object of wearing down the enemy by causing more casualties than your own. It has been argued they weren't, oh yes they were and Haig alongside his 'flunky' General Herbert Plumer knew it. Consolidation wasn't accounted for if things were to go wrong, inevitably they did go badly wrong. The weather turned very, very nasty with torrents of rain. Not even a fool would 'bite and hold' in swamps yet our men were ordered by 'Donkey Generals' to do so. Haig would have persisted even further had the weather not put an eventual stop to the final battles around Ypres, attrition was the name of the game to him. Milkmen like Edwin, alongside postmen, bank clerks, train drivers, school teachers, coal miners and fisherman, British civilian soldiers were Haig's pawns in his grotesque master plan. Even British Prime Minister Lloyd George was appalled at Douglas Haig's detached disregard for the men of his civilian armies. It has been stated on many occasions, particularly by prosecco swilling 'metropolitan historians' that tactics around Ypres in 1917 were critical in as to how the war was eventually won. Absolute nonsense and a claim that never could or ever will be proven.

Edwin died in conditions that were quite frankly horrendous. He would have been lucky if his boots were still on his feet in the freezing rain and pools of mud that he tried to wade through. The milkman went missing and was apparently never found, although somehow I think for a short time he was. Postcards and photos along with a small hand razor and mirror were recovered from him. This suggests to me that his body was not torn to shreds by a high explosive shell. Maybe he was wounded and literally drowned in a pool of mud. He wasn't recovered from the battlefield and has no grave. Meanwhile, Haig and Plumer were far behind the lines in a chateau stood by a roaring fire awaiting their afternoon tea, with fresh milk of course. Edwin was never to deliver another pint of milk in Hoxton, he is commemorated alongside thousands on the Tyne Cot Memorial, those names representing ordinary guys whose lives were appallingly thrown away like cheap commodities. As for the 'metropolitan historians' when it trickles with rain they pop up their golf brollies and head to their Range Rovers dashing from an upmarket bistro or the local freemasons hall.

Back home in her cold, damp and decaying dwelling Emily received the news of her husband's death at the same time as their little daughter Elizabeth was gravely ill. The 27-year old widow would have stopped weeping for a short while as the poor little mite was actually admitted to a local hospital. This was done as much as to protect the others within the crowded community as to help the tiny girl who had developed measles severely. Little Elizabeth was then struck down with bronchial pneumonia and became far too weak to fight it, she died only seven weeks after her father at just two-years old.

The emotional grief that Emily suffered is almost beyond comprehension against the backdrop of grinding poverty. She was awarded a weekly pension for her husband's sacrifice in 1918 amounting to a pittance. A very small one-off token was paid in relation to help her cope with the loss of her daughter. Of course Emily was just one of hundreds of thousands of war widows, many local women had suffered the same fate. I am now going to put forward some theories of how she coped with her grief intermingled with one or two facts.

Many war widows of Emily's age, especially if they were good looking remarried. Their suitors were very often older men, some much older who considered such women as 'fair game'. The ladies married them for financial security especially if they had children. What I do know is that Emily never remarried, she lived as a poor woman until her death in 1965 when she was 75-years old. To find an opportunity of meeting a prospective new husband in Hoxton who could provide financial security was in any case, remote. The young widow had lost her husband and child and lived alone for several years, until she reached her mid-thirties. This indicates that she managed to cope with her life. By 1925 her ageing parents Walter and Eliza moved in with her, probably because they themselves became destitute as the old man would have found work very difficult to find. Or could it be they wanted to keep an eye on their daughter? Was she leading a life of loose morals? In Hoxton that would have been the easy option. After much dialogue with Rob he refuses to believe she participated in prostitution or became a shambling drunkard.

Emily remained in the squalid dwelling in Hoxton until her parents had died. By 1932 she had took up residence with her brother-in-law James in Islington. He had lost his wife Mary Ann [Polly] a couple of years earlier. Emily by then was 42-years old and James three years older. The two of them had once been next door neighbours many years before when she had originally married his younger brother Edwin. Now they could share their common grief and comfort each other, however, both Rob and I think there was a little more to it than that. Both of them shared the same surname and lived under the same roof together for well over thirty years until Emily's death in 1965. James died ten years later aged 88. Emily Elizabeth Millett nee. Clark married the boy next door, a milkman. She gave birth to his child and suffered the agony of losing them both within a couple of months of each other. Emily then lived with another boy from next door, his brother, also a milkman. The physical resemblance to her husband would have been profound and we are sure she found happiness as she grew older with James Millett whose middle name just happened to be Edwin. What a fascinating and incredible journey this has been. Edwin's British War Medal is safely in our custodianship.

Oscar Hansson
Killed in Action
France, April 9th 1917
Aged 22.

OSCAR Nathanael Hansson was born in Hull in 1894. He was the youngest of three sons to his Norwegian born mother, Marte Talette Larsdatter [Larsen]. Known as Martha she hailed from Voss, Hordaland in Norway. Born in 1860, Martha was the daughter of migrants who settled on the east coast of England in Hull. Her husband shared exactly the same name as his youngest son Oscar, he was Swedish originally from Gothenburg. Oscar senior was a career able seaman who

Oscar Hanson was the son of a Norwegian mother and Swedish father.

arrived in Hull in August 1881, on December 19th 1882 Oscar and Martha were married in the English sea port. The couple also had two daughters, tragically their eldest Eugie died of disease before she was ten years old. Her surviving siblings were the sister Inga and brothers Hans, Otto and Oscar.

The family 'anglicised' their surname firstly to Hansen and then Hanson, for practical reasons and also in part to deflect certain prejudices that were prevalent at the time. Martha's father Lars and mother Inger Jorine had like numerous others from Scandinavia dreamed of a better and more prosperous life. Many people from Norway and Sweden crossed the North Sea after sailing from Gothenburg and Hull was the first stopping point upon their journey to the United States. Unfortunately a number of them realised the passage onward would be beyond their means, they ended up settling in the east coast port where plenty of work was available. Lars Larsen a joiner didn't live long enough to achieve his dream, he died young. His daughters Martha and Marie along with their mother Inger Jorine all lived together afterwards. Marie married another European migrant, a sailor from Germany, the family continued to stay together until Martha married Oscar.

Hull's Scandinavian community were reserved, private and quiet people who spoke with a slightly clipped accent even though many of them commanded a perfect understanding of English. Cultural prejudices against them weren't very common until the outbreak of the First World War when many of them were mistaken for Germans because of the way they spoke. On occasions their very names resembled Germanic ones, Oscar's older brothers Hans and Otto would have been particularly singled out by those who didn't know them.

Oscar senior was very rarely at home as he was always away at sea, he was a stranger to his children. Young Oscar being a number of years younger than his siblings had hardly seen him. Tragically his dad died at sea when he was only in his early forties, little Oscar was just an infant. The onus then fell upon Martha who had been virtually bringing up her children alone to continue with those responsibilities. Two of Oscar's cousins moved into their home to help with the family budget, they were the sons of Martha's sister Marie and had a German father, their surname being Kramer. The Hanson and Kramer lads were all born in Hull, they would have spoken with the local dialect and certainly considered themselves as English, which indeed they were. Unfortunately the snide remarks and bullying as war was declared and then progressed always blighted them, they had to develop thick skins to cope.

As a child Oscar would have been spoiled, he was five years the junior of the next brother, eight years younger than his other brother and eleven years younger than his sister. His mother cherished him as her little boy who of course shared the same name as her husband who had died so far away from home. Oscar grew up in a loving home with two elder brothers to watch over him, a sister who mothered him and even his grandmother's wise affections came along when she too moved in with the family. Nevertheless, Oscar was raised without his father, this would have had an effect upon him throughout his short life and probably encouraged him to try harder to achieve modest ambitions. My own father lost his dad, my grandad, during the Second World War and I saw with my own eyes how hard he tried to get on throughout his life, he never retired and worked right up until he died himself.

The young Hanson boy was a diligent student at school, upon leaving he gained employment as a clerk in the offices of a local oil merchant. He was good with figures, numbers and words. Oscar, clean and sober was a handsome young man as we can see from the picture of him that accompanies this story. The local girls noticed him and he would have known that. I am pretty sure the lassies chased him all around Hull!

Oscar and his brothers were eligible to volunteer for active service when war broke out in August 1914. I do believe that Hans the oldest joined the

Royal Army Medical Corps and Otto the Royal Artillery, we know that
Oscar eventually served with the East Yorkshire Regiment. None of the
brothers appear to have volunteered to enlist in the early days of the war as
many did, Rob and I try to explain why we think this is so.

The matriarch of the family Martha tried her best to keep them together,
their individual incomes were important. The old lady, the granny of the
boys also had to be taken care of. Times were hard, the elderly woman
had to work part-time in a laundry and Martha made dresses and clothes.
Then there were the cultural issues to contend with. Rob and I have slightly
differing opinions with regard to the attitudes of the family towards the
war in general. With their Scandinavian heritage the lads grew up with an
absent father who died when they were young, I believe they were all true
Yorkshiremen. Their dad hadn't been around to introduce aspects of his
culture to them.

It is true to say Martha and their grandmother would have
complemented superficial elements of their background to the boys. I
think the efforts of the women would have been cursory and of secondary
importance. It is also fair of me to suggest the Hanson boys were not
the type of lads to go boozing, brawling and womanising with the
dock workers and labourers of Hull. The lads grew up playing football
in the cobbled back-streets with all of the other boys, they spoke with
the local accent and went to school alongside everyone else. To all they
were just like the rest in many ways. I believe their later enlistments were
eventually enforced due to the financial pressures imposed upon the
family in the absence of the father. Rob agrees to a point but suggests
another reason also. The Hanson's were slightly different, until shortly
before the war their cousin Theo Kramer the son of a German lived with
them. Strong anti-German feeling was inflamed by the shelling of the east
coast by German war ships. When the boys of Hull fell dying in France
and Belgium tensions grew. Rob thinks the family had reservations about
the lads joining up due to some of the prejudices they were facing and
partly because of their own heritage. I don't agree, although I have to say
I can recognise the stigma they faced. The National Registration Act of
1915 the forerunner of conscription saw everyone become part of a huge
database, those eligible to go to war would eventually be told to do so.

It was June 1916 when Oscar was enlisted into the 14th (Reserve)
Battalion East Yorkshire Regiment he also spent some time serving with
the 15th (Reserve). It would be several months before he was posted to

the front with the 8th Battalion East Yorkshire Regiment. Both Rob and I are of the opinion that Oscar was conscripted as he was immediately put on the reserve mid-way through 1916. He was fit and healthy and had he volunteered it would have been very likely that he could be immediately despatched to a service battalion for operational training. His brother Hans we believe was also conscripted just a few weeks later. Older and not as physically fit as Oscar he probably requested to be posted to the Royal Army Medical Corps in which he served overseas. There is some evidence to suggest that Otto the middle brother was also conscripted in 1917 into the Royal Artillery, however this is not totally conclusive. For Martha Hanson things would never be the same again. The old grandmother, her mother, died, leaving just her and shop assistant spinster daughter Inga living at the family home in Hull when the boys were away.

At this point I refer to an observation I made earlier when I described the Hanson's as slightly different. The three boys and one girl never married, Oscar obviously didn't get the chance to do so. Hans and Otto survived the war as of course did their elder sister Inga. The three surviving children of Martha all stayed with their mother and lived with her throughout their entire lives. Without doubt this was a very close tight-knit family, some may think rather odd, something we will look at again as this story moves on after our explanation of what happened to young Oscar.

The family spent their last Christmas together in 1916 or at least most of them did so. Hans may have been posted, however, I have a feeling the Hanson's were all together at that time. I am pretty sure that Martha followed Norwegian tradition with their modest festivities celebrating Christmas on December 24th as they do in Norway. Krumkaker cake would have been baked and served and candles lit for departed relatives, Oscar's dad in particular as well as for Eugie his sister who died in childhood. Sadly young Oscar would have a Christmas candle lit for him for many more years that followed this final family get-together. Oscar left in January 1917 to be posted to the 8th (Service) Battalion East Yorkshire Regiment and was deployed to the Western Front in France, tragically, I believe he was killed on his very first serious action.

After a few weeks of preparation and manoeuvers with his battalion Oscar found himself on the front-line just outside Arras in northern France. Back at his home in Hull on Easter Sunday, April 8th 1917 his mum would have prayed for him and his brothers. The day after the battlefield from north to south and east to west of Arras became blanketed in snow as temperatures dropped severely. For Oscar this would be his baptism into warfare, it was also his swan-song, for within a very short time he was gone, his body riddled with bullets from German machine-gunners. Who knows, one of those gunners could have been related to his uncle who came from Germany?

I know where Oscar fell, I have walked through the villages of Feuchy and Fampoux, only once did I visit Feuchy, just as Oscar did before he was torn apart in a hail of red hot metal. Now, as I write I cast my mind back and remember how still and silent it was there when I strolled peacefully along, how fortunate I am to live in the times I do. The officer commanding number eight platoon of 'B-company' of the 8th East Yorkshire's couldn't be sure of what initially happened to Oscar Hanson. He held back for a week before accepting the fact that the young clerk from Hull had been killed. I think I can offer an explanation as to why. The terrain was very badly scarred by heavy artillery fire and became coated in varying layers of snow. As the temperatures rose the bodies of the fallen revealed themselves, one of those bodies was of Oscar.

This truly upsets me as I can see in my mind's eye his chums trying to put together what was left of his smashed-up body so they could bury him. His pals succeeded and Oscar was taken to the nearby village of Tilloy-Les-Mofflaines that had been successfully captured. To this day he sleeps peacefully within the Tilloy British Cemetery. Oscar with his film star looks was just 22-years old. The delay in the confirmation of his death came eventually to Martha and Inga back at home in Hull. They cradled each other tightly when the telegram came, their little Oscar was gone forever, try to imagine given their closeness and family history how that moment in time was for those two women.

Hans and Otto returned home after the war stunned at the loss of their 'baby brother'. Remarkably it would appear the family made a pact together. Rob and I have talked about this and believe the loss of Oscar to them all was totally and profoundly significant as to how they planned their future. Inga, Hans, Otto and their mother Martha all lived together until the end of their days.

The family unit as it became eventually moved to a comfortable house in Howden, not far from Hull. Inga, the eldest of the siblings suffered from ill health for a number of years and lost her fight for life when she was 55-years old in 1939. Hans, Otto and their mum endured the stresses of another world war but continued to stick together. The two men went out to work every day before Hans became incapacitated and had to give up his job, he then took full-time care of his ageing mother whilst Otto continued to be the main bread winner. Martha Hanson was remarkable, she kept her family together. On her deathbed in 1951 she was comforted by her sons Hans and Otto, one son who had been absent for 34-years was perhaps also present in spirit by her side. Mrs. Hanson shed a tear for the boys that she had to leave behind, despite them being by that time in their sixties. Oscar, her baby, was at the forefront of her mind as she closed her eyes for the last time, she was 91-years old.

Hans and Otto were devastated, within a year they also passed away just weeks apart in 1952. The Hanson or should I say Hansson dynasty was over, no children followed. Oscar senior, Martha, Eugie, Inga, Hans, Otto and Oscar had all gone with no direct blood line to follow them. Rob and I are now responsible for picking up their truly deserved legacy and sharing it with you.

In 2016 Rob purchased Oscar's medal entitlement of the British War Medal and Victory Medal, he did so because he could see a story with a special and unique name. Oscar therefore has given us all this story to share, especially the prolonged grief of his mother who lived to a very, very old age and carried the burden of her loss for so many years. It is not the fault of the family that Oscar's medals came on to the 'open market'. Hans was the last of the family to pass away, eight weeks after his brother Otto. His estate that went into probate was administered by a local solicitor of the time [1952] from Howden, a man named George Miller. The solicitor and a local clergyman the Reverend Maurice Clark who was obviously close to the Hanson's became joint beneficiaries of the last will of Hans.

Included in the possessions of the will were Oscar's medals. The two pieces of metal went around the circuit of dealers for many years until Rob rescued them and I brought the story of their owner and his family to light. When we talk about light, Rob and I will light a candle together on the traditional Norwegian Christmas Day of December 24th. It will not be just Oscar we will remember and honour, it will be his entire family and especially his mother, Martha.

William Robinson

Died
France, March 22nd 1918
Aged 22.

TO grieve the loss of a loved one, especially a close relative is extremely difficult and can affect certain people for many years. Indeed there are individuals who never get over the grief, some of those unfortunate souls literally die of a broken heart. Jane Robinson was an ordinary wife and mother from a humble and traditional Scottish working-class background. Her beloved son Willie perished after being rescued from the battlefields of war torn France in 1918. He has no final resting place and the conclusions surrounding his death are far from satisfactory. Jane had to endure the agony of never being given the correct information regarding the death of her boy. For some time she believed her son had not been killed due to the confused bungling incompetence of those who should have known better.

Now, we bring you this story, I know of no other First World War historians who would be able to provide anything of similarity. It would appear that young Willie Robinson's dead body was 'lost' whilst within a medical facilitation unit. A letter from someone who actually comforted the young man as he lay dying was sent directly to his mother. Then came the confusion and afterwards the 'cover-up'. How can it be possible that a soldier's body could literally disappear without anyone seemingly knowing anything? There will be theoretical conjecture later on within this very story, read on.

Just like his mother, Willie was born in the small picturesque town of Alva that sits directly below the Ochil Hills in central Scotland about eight miles to the east of Stirling. His mum Jane was the daughter of the local blacksmith James Chalmers and his wife Isabella who practised as a nurse, they were well respected in the neighbourhood as decent hard-working folk. Willie's grandparents had already retired when his mother met Englishman William Robinson who had moved to nearby Stirling with his work as a van-man. Jane and William went on to have five children together, two girls and three boys. The entire family including Jane's elderly parents all relocated to Stirling where Willie spent most of his short life.

Upon leaving school he took up employment as a coal miner in one of the local pits. At that time this was an extremely hazardous occupation fraught with many dangers as well as being a very poorly paid vocation.

There is some evidence to suggest that Willie had received some form of minor injury to his back whilst working down the pit. In Edwardian times no compensation, social welfare benefits or sickness pay existed. Willie simply had to go to work to earn money no matter what, injured or not. When war broke out in 1914 it wasn't long before the young collier signed up for active service. He enlisted in Dunblane, six miles to the north of his residence in Stirling.

Willie joined the Army Service Corps on October 15th 1914. He was 19-years old and just below average height for the period, his weight was low, under nine stones, [51kg]. At that time it is very likely that he wasn't considered quite strong enough to be enlisted into the infantry and so he was duly despatched to the ASC. Willie was very quickly posted to Yorkshire in England to undertake reserve training duties initially with horse transport. It would be over a year before he was eventually deployed to France to undertake base depot duties as a warehouseman/clerk.

The men of the Army Service Corps in my opinion are somewhat unsung heroes. These guys were often derided and described as 'Ally Slopers Cavalry' a mocking reference to a hapless newspaper cartoon character who had been around for a while. In truth the whole of the war effort would have ground to a halt without the ASC. Their numbers were initially made up mainly of men not quite as fit as front line infantry soldiers, many of them were slightly older, yet they were trained as infantrymen as well and were responsible for their own local defences. The role of the ASC was to provide transport and supply, two huge logistical undertakings throughout the war. Duties assigned to the ASC were numerous, they transported hundreds of thousands of horses, ran and maintained motor transport, canal barges, distributed essential food rations, parcels, engineering equipment, medical supplies, tanks, ammunition and essentially post. The ASC also administered prisoners of war and were very often in the firing line as they travelled from base depots and also to the front lines and back again.

Towards the end of 1918 they were renamed the Royal Army Service Corps in recognition of their efforts. It is interesting to note here a point that Rob and I would like to make. Medals to the men of the Army Service Corps often appear on the open market, these include casualty victims. It is a sad fact they are valued by the whole of the collecting fraternity as being worth considerably less in monetary terms than those issued to men of line regiments. Their efforts and in particularly the sacrifices made by the ASC are therefore not regarded as equally important by the collectors and that is a fact. A price is put upon the legacies of these men, a lower price. It is somewhat ironic the pay of ASC men during the war was higher than that of standard infantrymen.

Willie Robinson arrived in France a week before Christmas 1915. He worked in various base-stores away from the front line. The letters he sent home would have reassured his parents that he was fine and well. In all honesty his job held certain privileges that were resented by soldiers of other branches of the Army in France and Belgium. As well has being relatively safe, base stores depot ASC men had access to all rations and it was known that on occasions they broke the rules and would sometimes help themselves. The ASC men were better paid and fed and got access to local leave destinations without any problem. Willie put on weight with the physical demands of his job that included lifting, carrying and loading. His meals would probably have been more substantial than he had ever experienced, the military life suited him. Much to his dismay his own positional circumstances changed dramatically as British losses mounted, soon it would be his turn to be thrusted into the front line to directly face the enemy.

In 1916 an official act had been passed to compulsory transfer men to where it would be deemed necessary. The following year in 1917 the British were once again on the offensive at the Third Battle of Ypres. I have made several references already to that campaign that was in my opinion 'Haig's muddy bloody abattoir'. Willie Robinson by the time of the start of that battle had turned 22-years old, he was fitter than when he had joined and it was deemed appropriate to transfer him to the infantry. This news was given to him when he returned from ten days home leave, he must have been horrified. It came as no surprise to me to learn the warehouseman didn't last long in the field of combat, as we shall see.

On September 24th 1917 as young British civilian soldiers were being butchered in their thousands around Ypres, Willie was compulsory transferred to the 8th Battalion West Riding Regiment, the Duke of Wellington's, who hailed from Yorkshire. He had spent a good deal of time during his initial training with the ASC back in 1914/15 within the white rose county, whether this had anything to do with his deployment is unknown. Despite his enforced move he was allowed to retain his ASC pay. It wouldn't have been easy for him as a former member of 'Ally Slopers Cavalry' to adapt to the surroundings of an infantry battalion. The young Scotsman would also have had to come across some critical comments from his battle hardened comrades. Research indicates that Willie was given at least a three months familiarisation period with his battalion. It is unlikely that he saw any real offensive action during that time. In January of 1918 Willie was once again given a period of leave after proving himself capable of being a competent infantry soldier.

On February 10th 1918 Willie was back in France as his battalion was about to be disbanded. He was redeployed to the 9th Battalion West Riding Regiment. The British High Command under Field Marshal Sir Douglas Haig were expecting localised and moderate scale offensives by the Germans in France. What happened a month later was far more serious, as the enemy launched a huge scale attack in an effort to end the war. Willie who I believe had never been in any serious action had to face German 'storm-troopers' as the assault began on March 21st 1918. Within twenty-four hours of the start of the clinical offensive Willie was badly wounded. He was evacuated by stretcher to the nearest Field Ambulance, number 58, one that wasn't in fact attached to his Division.

A Field Ambulance was not an emergency vehicle, it was a self-contained mobile front line medical unit. Operated by members of the Royal Army Medical Corps the unit had a normal strength of around 220 men and 10 officers led by a Lieutenant-Colonel. It was in effect normally

Willie Robinson literally disappeared from a front line medical facility.

a tented temporary small-scale hospital, split into small ward sections designed to accommodate around 150 wounded men. In reality every Field Ambulance was overstretched. The RAMC men who ran the units were also responsible for transferring men along the evacuation lines or to better equipped medical establishments.

Willie Robinson who was in a bad way was compassionately received by an ordinary RAMC soldier. Private James Carmichael upon the dying soldier's request wrote a letter to his mother back home in Stirling. There is no doubt that Carmichael's intentions were honourable and sympathetic, he believed he was bringing comfort to a dying man, both Rob and I agree upon that. Inadvertently his actions went on to create confusion and ultimately led to Jane Robinson's grief being compounded, it wasn't the fault of the young RAMC man. The actual letter was addressed to a Mrs Robertson, not Robinson, this created logistical confusion during an inquiry that followed. I have no doubt whatsoever the letter was sent to Willie's mother, Jane Robinson. The only way James Carmichael was able to obtain her address would have been from her son Willie, whether by oral communication or from a letter written by her in Willie's possession. Carmichael simply misinterpreted Robertson for Robinson. Below is the full actual transcript of what was to be the first communication regarding the plight of Willie Robinson who mysteriously disappeared in unexplained circumstances. These are the highly emotional words of James Carmichael in the letter to Willie's mother, Jane. Note the directive to Mrs. Robertson, not Robinson.

Dear Mrs Robertson,

You will be surprised to hear from me, I am a complete stranger to you all. I was with your son Willie when he was brought into hospital, and he asked me to send you a few lines, that was on the 22ⁿᵈ March 1918. He was rather badly knocked about, and I stayed with him till he went away. When I saw how ill he was I asked him if he would tell me something about himself, so he said he came from Scotland, and me being a Scotchman my heart warmed to him.

I spoke a great deal to him and tried to keep him up but it was no use, his thoughts were of you. He cried 'Oh Mother Mother', several times. I said Willie have you got any message to send to your Mother. He brightened up and said I send my love and 'God Bless her'. Just send my love, Oh Lord I am going.

I may say it was a very trying time for me but we seem to have strength given from above to bear these trials. We are very busy as you know, and I had another

call to a poor lad and had to leave Willie. When I went back the bearers had taken
him away to another part of the Hospital. Everything possible was done by our
Medical Officers for Willie's comfort and he was so brave and never grumbled.
I think he was pleased to have me beside him, and he had much confidence in
the love of Christ. If you write to me I shall write again. 58th Field Ambulance. I
have much to do, I pray God will comfort you and give you the needed grace and
strength to bear whatever the future holds for you.

   Pte. James Carmichael RAMC.

I found this letter incredibly sad as I know there is more to this story.
The actual letter gives us some clues as to how we can try and solve a
tragic mystery and explain a mother's grief that must have been beyond
comprehension. Willie was severely wounded around the area of Bertincourt
as his battalion was swept westwards towards the former Somme battlefields
from Haverincourt, by the highly mobile German storm-troopers. He is
named upon the Arras memorial over twenty miles north from where he
was initially wounded. The naming of him on the magnificent memorial
confirms that his body was never found and that he has no known grave.
So what did happen to Willie Robinson?

Two inquiries have been held as to try and establish the answer to my
question. The first partly based upon James Carmichael's letter took place
in 1918. It involved correspondence between two senior commanding
officers of separate Field Ambulance units, Willie's mother, Jane and once
again James Carmichael. Other staff officers were also contacted or played
some role in trying establish the truth. A second inquiry was held a century
later in 2018 by yours truly, in my uncompromising style. I was assisted by
Rob whose main job was to keep me on a leash. See what you make of the
conclusions.

The officer commanding No.58 Field Ambulance, Lieutenant-Colonel
F.E. Bissell became concerned after communications from Jane Robinson
reached him regarding the whereabouts and welfare of her son. This
was some time after Willie had vanished. Bissell who acknowledged that
Willie had been brought into his unit was confused as to whether he was
called Robinson or Robertson because of the initial letter. He followed up
the Robertson name theory by contacting an officer from the 7th Border
Regiment after it was claimed a Willie Robertson from that battalion had
been wounded. It was suggested that Robertson had passed through No.58
Field Ambulance. The officer in reply from the Border Regiment revealed

they knew of no Willie Robertson who had served with them. Colonel Bissell then interviewed James Carmichael. The high ranking officer wasn't pleased at the young RAMC chap communicating with Willie's mother but had to accept that Carmichael was telling the truth about what he had written.

Somewhat confused the colonel then realised that Willie must have gone missing. On the day of Willie's disappearance chaos reigned around 58 Field Ambulance who had to move with their Division and move quickly. The Germans were sweeping forward and inflicting devastating casualties upon the British. Carmichael confirms this in his letter stating he was 'very busy'. Colonel Bissell was in the process of ordering an immediate move for his unit when Willie was fighting for his life within it. The bearers moved Willie as Carmichael confirms, but to where? Did they take him and the rest of the wounded with them when they packed up and left? At the same time 149 (Royal Naval) Field Ambulance was preparing to replace No.58 in the same location to cater for their Royal Naval Division soldiers, in effect 149 was moving in where 58 was leaving.

Colonel Bissell communicated officially with the commanding officer of 149. It could have been that in the chaos Willie had been left behind and received by the incoming Field Ambulance. The commander of 149 in a short and rather curt reply remarked he had no knowledge of any such man. He went on to point the finger at two clerks from Bissell's No.58 as responsible for not accurately monitoring what was going on. Later for official purposes upon Willie's service documents it clearly states that he was recorded as 'wounded' and then 'wounded-missing' on the same date March 22nd 1918. The term 'wounded-missing' is unusual and disturbing, however it really does sum-up what happened.

All of these communications were taking place months after Willie had died. Jane in her correspondence clearly believed that her son was still alive and wanted answers, she never got the answers she was looking for. Eventually Jane was notified that Willie was missing, presumed dead. No apologies were given, she knew that someone would have been responsible for not providing the whole truth. Her agony was prolonged and somewhere at the back of her mind she believed her son was still alive in the years that followed. Sadly and tragically Jane slowly came to terms with the fact that Willie had died. Her terrible anguish regarding the fact that her son had no grave ate away at her. Jane knew he really should have received the dignity of a proper burial in consecrated ground. She must have wept many times when reading Carmichael's letter over and over again. The references within it that Willie made directly to her stared right back into her face.

Now here come my theories of what happened to Willie, who was to blame and what if anything can been so many years later. I believe everything that James Carmichael said in his letter was true. Reading between the lines it appears pretty obvious that Willie was close to death when the RAMC man was by his side. Due to his workload the orderly had to leave Willie for a while, when he returned he clearly states that he had been moved to another part of the hospital by the bearers.

Willie had died of his wounds, I don't think there can be any doubt about that. The whole scene within the medical unit would have been chaotic, stressful and confusing as an imminent move was being prepared in extremely testing conditions. Willie's body was more than likely placed on the outside perimeter under a blanket or tarpaulin awaiting a burial party. The RAMC men of No.58 were overstretched beyond their limits, conditions were deplorable. Two priorities were at the fore, to tend to the wounded and relocate as quickly as possible, nothing could be done for the dead at that particular time. Details could be recorded and absolutely should have been but sometimes that was easier said than done.

I believe that Willie was left behind along with several others. In their hurry men of the RAMC hastily dug shallow graves for them and placed them in the ground, that's why 149 couldn't find them. As the war raged on, the makeshift graves would have been destroyed by artillery barrages and Willie became lost forever. The clerks from No.58 Field Ambulance sometimes couldn't logistically deal with casualties who had come in from separate Divisions, Willie had been one such casualty. Having said that Willie's identity discs and possessions would have passed to them. It is interesting to note that no effects were returned to his family.

Willie and his family were terribly let down, they weren't the only ones. Other families had the truth hidden from them simply because the people responsible at the time couldn't cope because of the circumstances they were placed in. I don't blame the clerks, Colonel Bissell or the stretcher bearers. The British Army had been by the time of Willie's death severely weakened by catastrophic losses, especially from 1916 onwards. In 1917 we had lost the majority of our highly experienced soldiers. This placed tremendous strains upon civilian volunteers and conscripts, inevitably standards declined. Soon after the events described Douglas Haig was accepting men at the front in their mid-fifties. Yes, the German advance was stemmed and stopped eventually at a terrible cost and significantly because the enemy had overstretched its logistical lines. Haig who in April 1918 issued his 'Backs to the Wall' directive claimed that he was 'God's Servant'. This was a man who in 1915 personally ordered the use of chemical weapons. During the Boer War he had rounded up women and children to herd into concentration camps, and, let's not forget he signed the death warrants of mentally-ill British soldiers who were executed.

Willie's medals, the 1914-15 Star, the British War Medal and the Victory Medal were all delivered relatively late and separately to his parents between 1921 and 1922 - reigniting their agony. Rob managed to pick up Willie's British War Medal that is responsible for bringing this story of huge historical significance forward. I mentioned earlier if anything could be done regarding Willie's plight. The answer is obviously, no, it is far too late. What we can do in our own hearts and minds is spare a thought for his mother Jane, the words in the letter she received so long ago she took with her to the grave.

David Phillips
Killed in Action
Belgium, August 16th 1917
Aged 22.

THIS is a story that ends with a pilgrimage, a story that has its heart and soul very much in embedded in Wales. Although the life of David Charles Phillips ended abruptly in Belgium so many years ago his cherished memory lived on with his mother and father for a long time thereafter. We begin in the medium sized town of Llanelli, Carmarthenshire, South Wales, where David was born in 1895. Formerly known as Llanelly until 1966, the name was changed to its current spelling as the original was considered as too English sounding. From a practical point of view this put an end to any confusion with another Llanelly – yes, there were two of them in South Wales. The other smaller one being a village that remains and retains the original spelling is situated in the Brecon Beacons near Abergavenny.

Davey was the son of Charles and Elizabeth, who became established well-known local publicans in the town. His father who was actually born in

Birmingham had moved to Llanelli as a young boy with his family. Charles' own father Tom had found work at a local tinplate factory in an industry that dominated the region during the Victorian era, Charlie followed him to the plant when he left school. Local girl Elizabeth Jenkins married Charles Phillips in 1889 and the couple set out to start a family. Liz and Charlie went on to have nine children, amazingly and quite staggeringly six of them died before they reached adulthood. Infant and child mortality rates were high, especially in industrialised regions, to lose six out of nine children was tragically way above the average.

Liz Phillips must have been a tough woman. Born and raised in Llanelli and having lost so many children she decided to take on a pub whilst her husband continued to work at the factory. With three children still to raise, including young Davey she made a success of it. So much so that her husband gave up his job and joined her behind the bar. The couple took on the Oddfellows Inn on Station Road in the centre of town and financially prospered. Liz and Charlie were so resourceful that eventually they managed to purchase their own freehold establishment on Murray Street where they became licensees of the Albion Inn. Stiff competition was all around, several other pubs were also dotted along the same road. Within a town that had a population of around 50,000 people there were 120 pubs at the turn of the twentieth century in Llanelli.

Grammar School boy Davey Phillips grew up in a traditional public house

Davey's parents wanted the best for him, he was a bright boy. Their intrepid endeavours in the licensed trade allowed them to financially invest in his education. David Charles Phillips the son of working-class parents was enrolled at the Llanelli County School for Boys, now Llanelli Grammar School. He returned every evening to the pub in his smart school uniform and never forgot where he came from. I can identify totally with him at that point of his life for I was also once a Grammar School boy from a very humble background.

In South Wales the number of native Welsh language speakers is in a ratio comparison far fewer than of those in the north. Llanelli however has always represented an exception. There have traditionally been more Welsh speakers in the town compared to other areas of South Wales. Charlie and Liz both spoke the language as did their three children, including Davey, who would have developed fluency as he was also taught Welsh at school. In the pubs they ran they met all kinds of folk from mainly working-class backgrounds. Tinplate workers, cowmen, miners, railwaymen, quarrymen and of course Rugby players all frequented the bar. Many Turkish sailors also loved to have a drink when visiting the town. People from other parts of South Wales often referred to Llanelli folk as 'Turks' as so many Turkish sailors passed through there. Llanelli is of course famed for the sport of Rugby with a number of very famous players being born in the town. I can imagine numerous drunken scuffles between the sailors and burly prop-forwards. The banter in the pubs would have been fascinating, some of it discussed in the native language. Davey experienced a slice of it all that grounded him as a young man. He and his family would certainly have been indirectly involved in the most infamous events of the town's history back in 1911.

The Llanelli riots were caused by a mass picket and major civil unrest during a nationwide rail strike. Rebels took over the railway station. Very close by the Oddfellows pub on Station Road was at that time occupied by the Phillips family. It was August 1911, Davey wasn't at school and witnessed absolute carnage. His mum and dad no doubt made themselves a fair profit as the strikers fuelled by anger and readily available alcohol from the multitude of local pubs, turned nasty.

Soldiers from the Worcestershire Regiment were drafted in to help the police control the mob. The deployment of troops was sanctioned by the Home Secretary who gave them the authority to act in whatever means necessary to control the crowds. The 'Riot Act' was reluctantly read by a local official. Soldiers who had been herding the mob around with gleaming fixed bayonets attached to their rifles were ordered to open fire. Two young men were shot dead, a 21-year old tinplate worker and a totally innocent 19-year old youth who was walking out of his garden to see what was happening. In the immediate aftermath the mob went berserk and set fire to the railway wagons. There was an explosion and four other men lost their lives. The incensed crowd then rampaged through the town, smashed up buildings, attacked magistrates and caused chaos leaving behind a huge trail of destruction. The Home Secretary who had sent in the troops and had allowed them to shoot civilians was none other than, Winston Churchill.

Time moved on for Davey and as war was declared he was already being groomed to become a leader of men. The son of publicans was a well-educated young man, intelligent, smart and essentially held very good language skills. He was commissioned into the Royal Welsh Fusiliers as a Second Lieutenant. Liz Phillips the tough, rough diamond pub landlady was so proud that her boy had been made an officer and a gentleman. She probably accompanied him when he went out to buy his own uniform as officers were required to do.

Davey was posted north to the 4th [Denbighshire 1st/4th] Battalion Royal Welsh Fusiliers. This was a Territorial Force unit and consisted of men from North Wales, some of whom had been on the reserve with experience. Many of these lads were agricultural workers or labourers from rural outposts, a large number of them spoke Welsh and would have appreciated their young officer who was fluent in the tongue. In 1915 the 4th Fusiliers had been attached to a London Division and allocated the role of a pioneer battalion. The strong and fit labourers were required to mainly be deployed in groundworks, engineering, trench digging and bridge spanning.

As the war raged on more and more young officers were required as they were falling at an alarming rate. Second-Lieutenant David Phillips was in demand, soon he would be posted to a front line infantry battalion as an attached officer, retaining his Royal Welsh Fusiliers status. Rob explains that he would have been literally sent to where he was urgently required and had no say in the matter. He adds the military command of the time made decisions in their own interests and not always in favour of the individual.

The up and coming young Welsh officer was posted to a very famous regular battalion, the former 2nd/24th of foot, the 2nd Battalion South Wales Borderers. In 1879 during the Anglo-Zulu War in Natal Province, 11 Victoria Crosses were awarded at the defence of Rorke's Drift. A small contingent of British defenders were unbelievably outnumbered by Zulu warriors but held on. The 2nd South Wales Borderers received 7 out of 11 of the Victoria Crosses that day. This action was immortalised in the 1964 film 'Zulu' that some politically correct carrot juice drinking morons have branded as 'racist'. Davey went on to eventually command a whole company of this famous battalion, albeit some years later.

Our young officer arrived in France in February 1917 and was despatched to command a platoon of the Borderers. The men were heavily involved in actions around the Scarpe at Arras before moving north to take part in the Third Battle of Ypres in Belgium. By the late summer the 2nd Borderers had been depleted of officers with a major campaign looming upon the horizon. Davey, the proud Welshman even though only holding the lowest officer position of Second-Lieutenant didn't hesitate when he was requested to take command of 'C- Company'. He took control of around 200 men, some of whom were hardened veterans. The 22-year old former Grammar School boy from Llanelli led his men from the front in the opening phases of the Battle of Langemarck. This position was to the north-east of Ypres, the date was Thursday August 16th 1917.

Weather conditions were dry and humid with an air temperature of around 20-degrees centigrade but the terrain was against the brave advancing Welshmen. Two days earlier a huge amount of rainfall had created mini-lakes in hundreds of shell-holes that pock-marked the ground, many of these were deep enough to completely submerge a human body. The overcast skies and lack of windfall meant the water had not evaporated as the men slogged on forward. Of those hit by shrapnel or bullets some fell directly into the water filled craters. Weighed down by their kit and struggling to move with painful injuries they literally drowned in the shell-holes. Davey Phillips urged his men on, as they approached the ruined remains of Fourche Farm he was hit, the young officer went down in the mud where he took his last breath. The boy from the Albion Inn in Llanelli was lost, yet another brave young victim of war who became cannon-fodder in the slime of Third Ypres.

I made a very emotional visit to the area where Davey fell, ninety years after his death to take part in some documentary film work. The impression made upon me there for an entirely different reason brought home the tragic futility of the waste of human life the First World War was responsible for. I toured the German cemetery at Langemarck where a staggering 44,000 men and boys are laid to rest, 25,000 of them are in one mass grave. These men may have been the enemy and Davey lost his life in an action fighting against them but you can't help feeling huge sorrow when visiting the place. One thing they all have in common with our young Welshman is the fact they too were once human beings thrust into a conflict they hadn't anticipated or requested.

Back at the Albion Inn in Llanelli his mother Liz would no doubt have comforted some of her regulars who had lost their own sons and brothers. Her wisdom, humility and sense of empathy with her officer son serving at the front were always apparent. Then came the crushing news of her Davey's death. At that point in time she had lost seven of the nine children born to her. Husband Charlie, their daughter Lizzie and son Herbie did what they could to stem her tears, this woman's grief was profound, but she was strong, she had proved that so many times, it wasn't over, it simply couldn't be.

Second-Lieutenant David Charles Phillips the young man who wasn't afraid to take responsibility is buried at the Artillery Wood Cemetery close to where he fell. The cemetery in comparison to other Commonwealth War Grave Commission sites is small to medium sized. This divine place holds 1,307 graves of which 807 are identified with individual names. It isn't difficult to find where Davey lies within Artillery Wood. In the 1920's thousands of people made pilgrimages to the former Western Front. Some of these trips were organised as early forms of 'package tours', they offered good value for money. Individual trips could be expensive, time consuming and difficult to organise. This was especially so for those unfamiliar with northern France and Flanders, nobody really was, even the veterans struggled to find their way around. Today there are still striking differences between Britain, rural Belgium and north-eastern France.

Life continued at the Albion Inn, veterans gathered and met for years to talk about their experiences during the war at 'Wipers', their common name for Ypres. Many chairs in such pubs were adapted for the veterans comfort as they struggled with old wounds. Meanwhile, Charlie and Liz saved hard. In the 1920's times were tough, unemployment was high, common people were poor and the pub trade slumped. Charlie returned to work in the tinplate factory as his wife battled on to run the pub. Eventually, ten years after the war had ended they had managed to save enough money to embark upon a special journey, an excursion to see their son Davey…for one final time.

The train journey to London and then on to a channel port with their luggage was difficult enough. Hotels had to be paid for and motor transport arranged upon arrival in Belgium. Armed with their Michelin map the couple eventually arrived at the Artillery Wood cemetery. The Llanelli couple had taken with them a personalised stone tablet as their own sentimental tribute to their beloved son that still stands at the graveside today. I know exactly what it is like to enter the serenity of one of the beautifully kept CWGC cemeteries, however, I have never done so to pay homage to a lost son.

Words cannot describe how the pub landlady felt during her visit and there can be no words that Rob and I would like to suggest regarding the pilgrimage. That very special time remains sacred for eternity and it is not for us to comment upon it. Charlie and Liz eventually retired and both lived well into old age, for them there had been some form of closure that wasn't available to the masses and I am sure they remained eternally grateful for that alone. Davey was awarded the British War Medal and Victory Medal, both of which were received by his parents. The Death Plaque was also despatched to his mother that bore his full name. Liz kept the medals, the whereabouts of them are now not known. The plaque was rescued by Rob and remains a permanent legacy to the young Welsh officer who never wavered and led from the front.

Personally, I found this chapter as a whole very difficult to write, as often as I could I tried to place myself hypothetically in the positions of the women who had to endure incredible grief. Rob brought this chapter forward and he also felt a huge sense of moral responsibility towards everything we have tried to explain. We both sincerely hope we have got it right.

FOREVER SCOTLAND

THERE are many things that stir me with regard to the First World War. I am unashamedly a proud Englishman and the following words from a poem 'The Soldier' I find awesome. These words were written by the tragic war poet Rupert Brooke (1887-1915). The particular words I select from his poem read as follows:

> *If I should die, think only this of me*
> *That there's some corner of a foreign field*
> *That is forever England*

So here I am an Englishman quoting text from an English poet stating 'forever England'. Considering the title of this chapter you may be scratching your heads right now. I do not have a drop of Scots blood within me, no Scottish ancestry whatsoever. My admiration for the sacrifices of Scots soldiers, their bravery, heroism, courage and determination runs very deep. Of all of the nations who sent men to fight in the Great War on the side of Britain no other lost more than Scotland in terms of ratio losses. Varying statistics have been suggested. Some say the Scots lost 25% killed, others 15%, I would say it's somewhere in the middle at around 20% of those who served that actually perished.

Having been involved in remembrance and welfare work in Scotland I have had the opportunities of driving through rural parts of the country many times. It is very noticeable that individual village and small town war memorials to men who fell in the First World War all seem to have something in common. Tragically the modest monuments are in most cases inscribed with the names of too many men, demonstrating a high proportion of deaths.

For the last hundred years or so Scots soldiers, the ones who were kilted are said to have been described as 'devils in skirts' by German soldiers who fought against them in the war. It has been further stated on many, many occasions the Germans feared and respected the 'devils' more than those of soldiers from other nations. I have to say it has never escaped my attention that when certain nasty and difficult assaults had to be undertaken during the war the Scots were detailed to lead the way. I don't think any Englishman would question the courage or bravery of the Scots.

It is interesting to note that a couple of eminent commentators who ply their trade in comfortable British educational establishments, completely disagree with the 'theory' as they put it - that the Germans were fearful of the Scots. The two soaking-wet 'metropolitan historians' just happen to be German themselves, what a co-incidence. Rob and I will let you decide when you have read this chapter.

One in five Scotsmen who left their beautiful land never returned home during the First World War, the highest proportion of all. Many more made it back to Scotland permanently maimed or psychologically distressed as a result of their war service. Rob, who has a lot of Scots ancestry and I the 'Sasanach' now pay tribute to the huge number of brave Scotsmen who fell fighting for the cause of freedom. I had a lump in my throat when I wrote the following words below that we publish right here for the very first time:

We left our crofts and our homes, think only this of us
That there are many corners of foreign fields afore and beyond
That are forever Scotland

William Richmond
Killed in Action
France, July 30th 1916
Aged 19.

THE story of this teenage Scottish warrior and his famous regiment should immediately dispel any doubters or spoon fed 'metropolitan historians' as to the so called 'lack of fear' the Germans had towards the Scots during the Great War. Billy Richmond served with the Royal Highlanders also known by another name, that being the Black Watch. The origins of their identity go back to the early 18th century in the years after the 'Jacobite Rebellion'. King George I authorised General Wade to organise six watch companies to patrol the Highlands of Scotland, they were known in Gaelic as -'Am Freiceadan Dubh' – the dark or black watch. Of the six companies three came from the Campbell Clan, the others from Clan Grant, Clan Fraser and Clan Munro. These no-nonsense and fearsome Clansmen were not to be compromised or ridiculed, the reputation of the Black Watch as a very capable militia was engrained right from its very origins.

The magnificent Forth Railway Bridge is an iconic symbol of Scotland that stands alongside the more modern road bridge, I have travelled many times across the Firth of Forth on these bridges. From the outset of the war the railway bridge transported many soldiers from Fife, southward to Edinburgh. Billy Richmond travelled across the rail bridge for one last time on his journey to the Somme battlefields in France. I connect with Billy in a number of geographical references, for I have walked the ground he once walked upon and taken similar journeys as he did, in peaceful times of course.

Our man was born in Kirkcaldy, Fife, it is a pretty coastal town that I first visited when I was a schoolboy and have revisited several times since. He was one of several children to his parents William senior, a native of Montrose and Helen, nee. Marshall who originally came from Dundee. William the father, was a career soldier, first enlisting into the Royal Scots Fusiliers in 1884 at the age of 18-years old. After completing over eleven years of army service, six of those in the East Indies, a posting that paid big financial bonuses at the pension stage, he left the fusiliers and married Helen in 1896. The couple settled in Kirkcaldy where the former soldier found work as a plasterer's labourer. After having two children, including the eldest Billy, William decided he had to re-enlist, he missed the army life so much and did so in 1902. He went on to see active service in South Africa with the Royal Artillery. Upon leaving again he picked up with Helen where they had left off and had at least four more children with his wife. At the outbreak of the First World War he enlisted for a third time, aged 46. Serving in the Special Reserve of the Royal Scots Fusiliers he never saw active service abroad and remained in the UK on the reserve, probably in a training capacity until after the war was over in 1919.

Billy Richmond the eldest son had a lot to live up to. His father encouraged him to sign-up and join the colours, which he did in 1914. This meant that both father and son were both actively serving during the war. Billy joined the local Fife Territorials, the 7th Battalion Black Watch [Royal Highlanders], he would have known many of the other recruits as they were local to St. Andrews and Kirkcaldy. This battalion was part of 153rd

Brigade and of one the most legendary glorious British Army Divisions of all time, the 51st (Highland) Division. After a period of intense training and induction Billy was sent to France in 1916, in readiness for what was to come, the Battle of the Somme.

The 7th Black Watch fought tenaciously at High Wood, upon the Somme, in one of the fiercest engagements of the entire war. Now I am going to try and paint a picture in your mind's eye of how courageous and fearless Billy and his Black Watch comrades really were. I will start with my own experiences within High Wood that stands slightly aloof above sea-level close to the villages of Longueval and Bazentin-Le Grand. Caterpillar Valley slopes gently away from one of the most eerie and nerve shredding places on earth. Entrance to the public is prohibited, this did not stop me going into the dreaded wood to investigate my curiosity on a number of occasions. Some of my daring experiences are recorded and captured on film. Let me say right here that even today it is a desperately haunting place, the creepiest I have ever visited and it is no surprise as to why. There are over 8,000 corpses within High Wood that have never been recovered, one of those is Billy's. The wood is now thickly grown with all types of greenery, yet upon the haunted ground it is easy to find your way around – without a living soul to bother you.

In 2016, a colleague of mine from the film/media industry and I sneaked into High Wood to record some film footage of me commentating on some of the events of the war that took place there. Risking injury or worse by unexploded ammunition shells that still lie in and around the wood, we persevered. It was a perfectly still and quiet day, with blue skies and no wind factor at all. After around ten minutes or so of film takes, two large trees started to rock fiercely from side-to-side. None of the hundreds of others around them did so, it was physically impossible for it to happen, but it did. On a previous occasion I had volunteered to stay alone on the sunken road that runs down one side of High Wood. As darkness fell, so did the presence of thousands of eyes staring at me, it was terrifying.

I was once told by a reliable source about a famous attack by soldiers of the Black Watch upon High Wood. It followed a similar line to that of the one that Billy was involved in with his battalion. My informant was the son of a former Black Watch soldier. He told me that the flying Scotsmen became soaked to the skin in the pouring rain and bogged down as they made their way up the gentle slope from the valley. The men then decided to remove their sodden kilts and fixed their bayonets. Storming forward, semi-naked on their bottom half's the blood-crazed Scotsmen screamed as they charged towards the German positions. Totally aghast the defenders bolted and ran. Is this a true account of an event that actually happened or the stuff of legend?

On July 30th 1916 after enduring a blisteringly hot afternoon in their trenches, at 18.10 hours 'B' and 'C' Companies of the 7th Black Watch were ordered to attack the wood at its eastern edge, from the direction of Wood Lane. It was still approaching 25 degrees centigrade when the men leapt to the assault. The preliminary bombardment by artillery barrages had failed. German machine-gunners and snipers opened up on the kilted Scotsman as they hurtled towards the wood. Billy was in 'B- Coy' to the right of the two-pronged assault, with 'C'- Coy on the left. 'A' and 'D' companies were in support and were soon called upon. I know exactly where Billy first entered the wood on the eastern perimeter with 200 of his advancing comrades from 'B'- Coy. The machine-gun fire was intense and fanned across the edge of the wood tearing into the bodies of the Scottish warriors.

Inevitably the men dived for cover in shell holes and then in small groups went out in bombing parties taking on the machine-gun positions at point blank range. Desperately they ploughed on but the Germans by then in superior numbers decided to take advantage of their man power and counter-attacked. Billy and his platoon were forced back to the perimeter, then came the order to prepare to die. Rob confirms this wholeheartedly as he realises what the next action would have entailed, he says the Black Watch men would have known that death was almost a certainty. He adds they were determined to take down as many of the enemy as possible, whilst at the same time scaring the life out of the remainder of them.

Like lions the platoon of Black Watch Scotsmen fixed bayonets and charged directly into the overwhelming number of German infantry attackers, confusing and scattering them. I cannot imagine what it would have been like to see three dozen or so screaming, kilted Scots warriors running towards me with their huge bayonets glinting in the sunlight. Hypothetically I wonder how the tartan shortbread munching 'metropolitan historians' would have coped with what I have just described? The Highlanders fought to the death but their actions prevented the collapse of the initiative that was recovered by other Scots soldiers from the Gordon Highlanders the day after. Billy Richmond, the young 19-year old lad from Kirkcaldy died charging at the enemy with fierce and determined courage. The teenager was killed alongside his outnumbered Black Watch comrades. For a critical period of time they wreaked havoc and fear amongst the German infantrymen facing them in larger numbers. To this day Billy

KILLED IN BAYONET CHARGE.

Private William Richmond, Black Watch, who, as reported in our last issue, was killed in a bayonet charge on 30th July. He was the son of Mrs Richmond, East Smeaton Street, Kirkcaldy, and Private Wm. Richmond, who has 31 years' service with the colours, and is now serving with the Royal Defence Corps.

The death of Billy Richmond is reported, the courageous teenage soldier of the 'Black Watch' was killed in action on a bayonet charge.

remains lost on the eastern edge of High Wood, his body lies somewhere beneath the undergrowth.

The local newspaper in Kirkcaldy reported that Billy's mother had been informed of her son's death and described him as - 'A promising young lad'. You really can't help thinking of what went through Billy's mind in the moments before his death. The great tragedy of it is that he probably died unnecessarily, for what was left of his platoon maybe could have escaped out of the wood. However, we are talking about the Black Watch here, their actions prevented positions being completely over-run. The Black Watch officers knew exactly what was expected of them and were aware of the casualties they would have to endure. This reinforces my point that on many occasions Scottish soldiers were used as 'shock troops' who often did the dirty work, demonstrated on so many similar occasions. Rob provided me with some documentation that is out of the ordinary, the 7th Black Watch war diaries comments, nothing unusual about those, however, EVERY single casualty is separately listed by name. It would appear the battalion wanted to record for eternity the horrific suffering they were being exposed to, they fought on and obeyed.

In High Wood the occasional sound of a wild bird singing echoes around the tree tops. A rabbit will occasionally dart across open ground in haste as if being eyed by a sniper. The ghosts of men and boys roam invisibly along several tracks wondering how to escape their eternal confinement. One of those ghosts is Billy Richmond. Let's think about him and try and put him to rest once and for all and ease the spiritual anguish of those who perished alongside of him. Something deep inside tells me that by bringing this story forward and remembering Billy slightly diminishes the never ending and tragic plight of those who still lie within the wood. I certainly, more than certainly felt distant cries for help and eternal salvation when I was there, they were chilling experiences that I will never, ever forget.

Billy's British War Medal and Victory Medal have been beautifully presented in a special case by Rob alongside his dad's medal for service in South Africa and his British War Medal, together with original versions of their cap badges. His death plaque remains within its original cardboard sleeve. The next time I cross the Firth of Forth and reach Kirkcaldy with its shrieking seagulls and calm coastal waters I shall think of Billy. He is lost for eternity somewhere in the depths of just an ordinary French wood, or more to the point an extraordinary French wood. I would not advise or condone anyone to follow in Billy's footsteps. High Wood is not just a place for the faint hearted. The location of this dreadful wood is remote but relatively easy to find. A warning has to be issued regarding High Wood, it is not a safe place. I will once again state there are unexploded devices within its perimeter. Please don't go there.

John Taylor
Killed in Action
Gallipoli, June 28th 1915
Aged 25.

WE now take a journey to the wonders of Castletown, Caithness situated at the very top of Scotland that stands along the A836 close to the Dunnet Bay. Thurso is around five miles to the east and John O'Groats fourteen miles to the west. The tranquillity and beauty of the Highlands of Scotland are breath-taking, against this backdrop a young man named John Miller Taylor was born and raised. He lived with his parents and two elder bothers at the serene sounding Rose Cottage in Castletown, so far, far away from where he would end his days upon a distant shore.

John was born in 1890, I doubt if he was planned. At that time his father Robert was 57-years old and his mother Elizabeth approaching her fiftieth birthday. He had two older brothers, Henry, fifteen years his senior and Robert who was thirteen years older. His home village is within the parish of Olrig, once dominated by the flag quarrying industry. Stone flags from here still pave many streets in London, New York, Paris and Sydney. The ageing Robert Taylor and both John's older brothers all worked as flag quarrymen. This vocation was physically demanding, one that his dad worked in for all of his life, even whilst still in his late sixties. Robert Taylor never retired and worked in the quarry until his death.

The youngest son didn't want to follow in the family tradition and embarked upon a career in tailoring as well as serving a three year stint with a local Territorial Force Battalion of the Seaforth Highlanders (Sutherland and Caithness). John later moved south to the capital city of Edinburgh were he found respectable and meaningful employment with the firm of Christie and Kirkpatrick. Their shop was situated in the south bridge area, close to the old town district. As a promising young tailor John was a smart man about town. He resided in comfortable lodgings on Lauriston Park, the dapper gentleman from the Highlands had everything going for him, his whole life securely established with the future beckoning.

John Taylor was a skilled tailor working in Edinburgh before the war.

Storm clouds were gathering in early August above Edinburgh after a prolonged summer season of hot weather. Dark skies were also descending across Europe as war loomed. The day after Britain declared war on Germany, the sun shone down brightly across the old town district of Edinburgh where John was busy working in the gentleman's outfitters shop. On almost every street corner newspaper vendors were urging people to read all about the war that would be over by Christmas. It was Wednesday August 5th 1914. Buoyed by the news of war many young men wanted to get in on the action, especially the likes of John Taylor, a former reserve territorial soldier who was familiar with army discipline and knew how to handle weaponry. Spurred on by the shouting newspaper boys he didn't hesitate and immediately attested for service on that picturesque Edinburgh summers' day.

John stood above average height for the period at 5'9, he was physically fit, smartly dressed as well as clean and sober making an ideal recruit. Looking at his service papers I made an unusual observation. It appears that upon his attestation his documents were adjusted to state that he would be required to serve for just one year in a Territorial Force Battalion, the locally based 4th Royal Scots (Queen's Edinburgh Rifles). After some discussion Rob and I agree that having previously served he could opt for one year. It was as Rob states a decision of service term that could be extended, primarily though in the interests of the Royal Scots.

The battalion was initially placed upon Scottish Coastal Defence duties and took the time to undergo further training. According to John's service papers he underwent three forms of testing in the months following his attestation to be passed fit for service. This could and I use that word liberally offer an explanation as to why he was attested for only one year in the first instance. In May of 1915, John boarded a train bound for Liverpool where he would arrive for embarkation with his battalion. The 4th Royal Scots were an integral part of the newly formed 52nd (Lowland) Division, comprising of three brigades of four battalions each. All of the men in this Division were Scottish first-line territorials. Many of the lads like John were familiar with the routines of army life through previous territorial reserve experiences. What they were not familiar with was actual warfare.

The first port of call for the men was Alexandria in Egypt, a far cry from the splendours of Edinburgh or the beauty of the Highlands for John Taylor. Conditions in the port city were uncomfortably hot and dirty with a lot of activity constantly keeping everyone upon their toes. The threat of diseases such as malaria had to constantly be monitored in the heat and humidity. A local hospital was bursting to capacity with young soldiers affected by the mosquito bites, many of them would never make it to Gallipoli and succumbed to the dreaded fever. Others were laid up with gonorrhoea contracted from local prostitutes. Dysentery was rife and sunstroke presented a serious problem due to the huge demand for fresh clean water and soldiers failing to take advice about the harming rays of the sun.

It was a period of high drama for John, after setting sail from Alexandria for Gallipoli the vessel upon which he was travelling 'HMS Reindeer' was involved in a night time collision in the Mediterranean with the Royal Naval stores carrier 'SS Immingham'. In the chaos that ensued the Immingham sank, thanks to the coolness of the Royal Scots no loss of life occurred. The whole battalion was praised in an official communication by General Sir Ian Hamilton who acknowledged 300 acts of gallantry referring to the 4th Royal Scots. As far as I am aware no awards or decorations came about with regard to any of those gallant acts.

John Taylor disembarked on the Gallipoli peninsula with his battalion on June 12th 1915. For several weeks a bitter struggle had developed between the Turkish defenders and British, French, Australian, New Zealand and Indian attacking forces. Presiding over much of the actual logistical planning from various points was a man who I have lambasted before as the most foolhardy 'Donkey General' of the entire war. Alymer Hunter-Weston was also deservedly ridiculed as 'Hunter-Bunter'. This very story brought by the humble Private John Taylor and his medal now allows me to go even further. 'Hunter-Bunter' typifies so much about the British High Command during the First World War. Rob hasn't even attempted to hold me back for I consider this handlebar moustache attired buffoon as at best - a drunken, reckless idiot - and at worst a cold-hearted narcissistic butcher.

The Division to which John and his battalion were a part of was commanded by 'Hunter-Bunter's' subordinate, Major-General Granville Egerton. He was appalled at the orders he had to carry out issued by 'Hunter-Bunter' that led to carnage and huge losses of life amongst his 52nd (Lowland) Division. The 156th (Scottish) Rifles, a part of the Division that included the 4th Royal Scots suffered horrifically. An increasingly out of control whisky fuelled 'Hunter-Bunter' had stated that he wanted to 'bloody the pups' – or in other words send the inexperienced Scottish territorials into absurdly and completely ridiculous battle situations. The Scotsmen were pushed into full frontal daylight attacks with very poor or no artillery support. To make matters worse this was often in the searing heat of the middle of the day. The inevitable happened, huge casualties. Sheep farmers, crofters, railwaymen, fisherman, miners and our tailor from Scotland who had volunteered to serve overseas were brutally exposed to certain death in suicidal and unnecessary assaults. These men died for absolutely nothing, nothing at all, it was sheer bloody murder.

Callously the egotistically smug 'Hunter-Weston' acknowledged that he had 'bloodied the pups' after 1300 Scotsmen had their lives literally thrown away. General Egerton was incensed, his anger boiled over, when he complained he was rewarded with a temporary suspension from duties for his dissent. Meanwhile 'Hunter-Bunter' was making crass comments such as this one – 'Casualties? What do I care for casualties? I think that really does sum up this monster. Whilst he couldn't even recognise positional strategy or the logistical supply of fresh water the Scotsmen who had trusted him were dying in their droves. Eventually 'Hunter-Bunter', who had been born in Scotland himself was sent home, away from the comfort of his ship anchored off the shore of Gallipoli. He had never encountered a problem himself getting water for his morning or afternoon tea. Poor 'Hunter Bunter' was evacuated suffering from the effects of dehydration, perhaps due to the endless supply of Scotch whisky that always seemed to find a direct way to his cabin.

John Miller Taylor met his end just over two weeks after he had first landed in the fly-invested hell of Gallipoli. After some pathetic artillery efforts the infantry were once again sent in to face hails of red hot machine-gun bullets. In blisteringly hot conditions water carriers were shot by snipers as the men pushed forward. Often they were mutilated or decapitated by close scale field gun enemy fire. John fell and was laid out stricken, beyond help. The 25-year old tailor who came from the furthest corner of the British mainland died in conditions that to us are totally unimaginable, fighting had been bitter and merciless. Eventually John's rotting corpse was discovered by men from the 2nd Battalion South Wales Borderers. The Welshmen crazed by their ferocious battle experiences had bayoneted to death Turkish soldiers who wanted to surrender whilst screaming for mercy, this was total war. I am sure the Borderers buried John's remains in a makeshift grave before they moved on. John Miller Taylor is commemorated on the Helles Memorial, this tells me that his shallow grave and what was left of him were later totally destroyed by bombardments.

The remoteness of Rose Cottage in the far Highlands was a completely polarised location in comparison as to where John fell. I'm sure that his home and family went through his mind many times in the days before his death. Elizabeth by that time had already been widowed and then lost her youngest son, Castletown had lost another son. The Mediterranean Expeditionary Force at Gallipoli would also go on to lose the campaign that in many opinions, including my own, should never have been entered into in the first place.

Scottish soldiers were sacrificed unnecessarily throughout the First World War and I have provided evidence of that in the past. It brings me back to my comments relating to when I have driven through the remoteness of Scotland itself. As I stopped occasionally to view village war memorials, there were just too many names upon them, far too many. Rob nor I can't change history. I have often been accused of superimposing my passionate opinions with elements of disrespect to certain individuals. Everything I have written here is totally heartfelt. Thanks to a small investment by Rob of just £60 I could write this story for John and his comrades in arms. Their voices were cruelly silenced so long ago.

The modest investment made by Rob was the purchase of John's single Victory Medal, the whereabouts of the remainder of his medals entitlement are unknown, they being the 1914-15 Star and the British War Medal. A little piece of metal we have represents not just John Miller Taylor's legacy it sends out a clear and definitive statement. That very short statement I will unashamedly print below and I know that every single one of the brave Scotsmen who were sent to their deaths would not mind in the slightest how they read below:

'There is and always will be a corner of a Turkish field that will be forever Scotland'.

James Third
Killed in Action
France, July 24th 1915
Aged 20.

OUR journey around Scotland continues with a trip to the small historical town of Cambuslang, Lanarkshire, situated around six miles to the south-east of Glasgow. The featured subject in this story is Jamie Third who was born there in 1895. He was one of four sons to his parents William and Mary, who also had one other child, a daughter, Jamie's little sister whom he adored. His father Willie Third was born in Sligo, Ireland, to a merchant seaman who became a ship's captain, the family moved to Scotland when he was a boy, originally settling in Peterhead.

Jamie was the second born to his parents, Willie had met Mary who was a native of Cambuslang and after marrying her he decided to settle down and start a family in her home town. He became a successful electrical engineer, a sought after and well paid occupation at the time. The family lived in relative comfort within the industrial town that was prosperous for its connections with the iron and steel industry as well as engineering and coal mining. Jamie followed in his father's footsteps and became an apprentice engineer upon leaving school. His prospects for a good life and to eventually attain a decent standard of living were certainly upon the horizon. Looking at a group photograph that includes Jamie it is not difficult to reach the conclusion that he also had the security of a wonderful and loving family background. This young man would certainly have made a good catch for an aspiring bride and I am sure that had he lived, he too would have become a loving family man and father.

At the outbreak of war, Jamie like many other young men of his generation was keen to get in on the action encouraged by the high profile recruitment

Jamie Third pictured third from the right with his family.

drives of the time. Two weeks after the declaration of war Jamie was in Inverness, he had made the journey north to enlist into the 5th (Service) Battalion Queen's Own Cameron Highlanders. The young engineer had no previous military experience and joined this particular battalion that was made up of similar men who had no former service with the colours. Every man of this particular battalion volunteered to fight for a cause and I think I can safely say for the adventures they expected to encounter. Jamie the volunteer was very quickly recognised for his potential and within weeks after his enlistment he was rapidly promoted to Lance-Corporal. Rob and I believe this had something to do with his general practical skills and intelligence as a competent engineer, he was still at that time just 19-years old.

Extended members of his family had also been successful during the course of their lives. A rather bizarre gesture of financial generosity was made by an uncle of Jamie's in a will. The relative who I suspect had been a former soldier himself bequeathed a conditional sum upon Jamie. A particular term of the will is interesting and I wonder if he did the same for two of Jamie's brothers who also went on to serve in the military. William, the eldest joined the Royal Field Artillery and Robert who was only 14-years old when war broke out eventually enlisted into the King's Own Scottish Borderers. The kindly uncle left instructions in his final will and testament that Jamie would receive a considerable amount of money if he complied with his instructions by a certain date. His uncle requested that Jamie had to re-attest for a period of five years full-time service with a further seven on the reserve. His reward would be a £900 – bounty, at the time of me writing this [2018] the figure equates to around £90,000 in modern monetary terms. Now, people sometimes call the Scots 'tight' and having obsessions with money, personally I have always found these assumptions rather unfounded. Regardless of that, I don't really think anyone from a working-class background would refuse such a tempting legacy. Jamie's fixed period to gain this inheritance had an expiry date of February 28th 1915.

This young man was already serving with the Cameron Highlanders when his uncle died. He would have gone to war regardless of whether or not he was accepted for the extended service that would in turn deliver the loot. As a matter of course Jamie set about making an application to re-enlist for the period determined by the terms of the will and who could really blame him. If he completed a five-year stint he would be able to return to civilian life, albeit on the army reserve and pick up his career as an engineer once again, with a hefty sum of money behind him to help provide for his future. As Rob will tell you though, things are not always so straight-forward when it comes to the military powers that be making decisions regarding individuals. This point has been made several times before, the Army has always had its own agenda's to serve its own interests.

The teenage soldier was posted to Bordon camp in Hampshire for preparation and readiness to enter the war on the Western Front in 1915. Lance-Corporal James Elder Third was desperate to get his signature on the forms to ensure he could get his hands on the inheritance, but things were not running as smoothly as he liked. To his credit he was fair and went through the correct procedures. How would the Queens Cameron Highlanders react to what certainly appeared to be one of their own wishing to extend his service purely for financial gain? Was this was a predicament for them? I think to a degree it was, but Rob doesn't and has an interesting theory as to why he holds that viewpoint. Referring to the money once again, I repeat that by the standard value with inflation of 2018 we are talking of £90,000 in modern terms. In 1915 within a volunteer service battalion many of the officers would not have held such financial asset. Rob believes the brass hats considered Jamie for a potential commission to officer status due to his newly established circumstances. Firstly, his wealth and the fact that he had already demonstrated his capabilities as a soldier by earning a rapid fast-track promotion counted in Jamie's favour. All he had to do was go out to war and prove his leadership skills. Rob believes he would of have been granted officer status had he done this and also because of his financial wealth. As it turned out and much to Jamie's relief his application was accepted, just one day before the final deadline. The men at the top had certainly made him sweat.

A happy-go-lucky Jamie had plenty to smile about as he prepared himself for war. He was a long way from home but kept up a warm and regular correspondence with letters to and from his family in Scotland.

Eventually he embarked with his battalion on their first overseas draft to France. Arriving in Boulogne on May 10th 1915 he had departed the day before from Folkestone. It was the first time he had left Britain, Jamie would never return or make it back to his home in Cambuslang, Scotland.

It is a sad fact I have to state that Jamie never really had the opportunity to prove his abilities as a soldier to his superiors. After moving into positions around Festubert where a costly battle had already taken place, Jamie literally found himself in the wrong place at the wrong time. He had been in France for just a couple of months. His battalion had not seen any real battle action at all as summer progressed, their baptism of fire would come in September at Loos. The responsibilities they held during the balmy and often wet French summer of 1915 included assisting with basic engineering works and fortifying trenches and lines of communications, often working alongside the Royal Engineers. Jamie was well suited to the rigours, demands and logistics of organised labour that involved aspects of planning with his background in engineering. He held rank and would have supervised basic works. Army life suited him, in his possession were a number of cheery letters of reply from his own correspondence with his family that he was making on a weekly basis.

Life behind the front lines was not at all idyllic. Men were always in constant danger from enemy artillery fire and accidental incidents. On occasions they also found themselves coming face-to-face with the enemy whilst out on patrols and would end up in fire fights. Working in environments that were downright dangerous with huge stores of ammunition also carried their own risks. The greatest threat to the men toiling on the ground works behind the lines came completely out of nowhere, from the dreaded sniper. Officers and NCO's constantly warned of the dangers of these hidden enemy marksmen whose role was to create fear and disruption amongst their prey. It has to be said that absolutely nobody could be on their guard against these ruthless hunters every single minute of the day or night. A sniper chose his victims with precision and didn't select any particular time to strike.

Jamie had been working and supervising digging parties for well over a week around Festubert from July 15th 1915. The job in hand was going reasonably well but had been slightly hampered by wet weather. There were a small number of casualties suffered as expected mainly due to enemy artillery fire. On the Saturday of July 24th 1915 the Germans were raining down shells upon the working parties, the British gunners were giving more than they got back in return. It was decided to curtail the works until the cover of darkness offered some protection. As the dusk turned into a darkened night sky, the moon rose brightly to eventually become a full moon that shined downwards making the cover of the inky darkness not quite all enveloping. It was still dark enough though for a predator to hide unseen, that predator being the deadly sniper.

Jamie's death was unexpected, ruthless and always alert, the German snipers hit a small number of targets that night. The young Cambuslang engineer being the only one who was killed almost instantaneously. A bullet entered and shattered Jamie's arm then passed through into his chest. As he fell dying whilst more than likely still conscious it took only a short time for him to perish so suddenly without warning. Three more men were seriously injured. Another comrade who had been shot in the knee had to have his leg amputated but died shortly afterwards.

For Jamie it really was all over before it had properly begun. He was just 20-years old when he was picked-off by a highly trained specialist killer. His body was hastily removed from the danger zone and the possessions he held upon his person were carefully packed away. Eventually his personal effects would be returned to his home in Scotland. Touchingly his belongings included nine cherished letters from his family in Cambuslang that he had kept in a specially created letter case. Also upon his person were a metal compass, a cigarette case, hymn book, bible, a birth certificate and four postcards. Jamie was taken by cart to an official burial ground nearby and laid to rest for eternity. He sleeps peacefully now at the Brown's Road Military Cemetery close to where he fell all of those years ago near Festubert.

It is not known what happened to his financial windfall. I assume it is safe to state that his own last will and testament carried by all soldiers would have passed the legacy over to his family. The tragedy of this story in my mind's eye is that an ordinary young man who had everything to live for and had been given a huge beneficial advantage to do so, was denied his future. I have commented so many times on the futility of the war that was meant to end all wars. The sniper who took away Jamie's life was in his own mind just doing a job. It may have just been a job to the marksman but Jamie's death represents the fact that war can be devastatingly cruel.

In the aftermath of Jamie's death both his brothers who also served during the war survived and lived into old age. The same cannot be said for his parents. Jamie's dad was broken-hearted at the tragic death of his engineer son who had followed him into the trade. Willie Third died in 1920, he was 53-years old. A year later Jamie's mother Mary wrote to the military depot at Perth requesting the delivery of her son's 1914-15 Star Medal. An administrative officer responded to the widow and the medal arrived at her home in February 1921. The whereabouts of this particular medal are currently unknown. On December 12th 1921 Mary took receipt of Jamie's other two medals, the British War Medal and the Victory Medal that are now in our safe custody.

Mary Dunn Third also died at the age of just 53 in 1924. The genuine love and family bonds that had tied this family together so closely ended prematurely. There is an old saying regarding money that states -'you can't take it with you when you die'. This story is not primarily about money at all. We have brought to you James Elder Third, a smart and decent young Scotsman who didn't hesitate to volunteer to defend the rights of freedom before he knew of any inheritance that was due to him.

Douglas Cockburn
Killed in Action
France, Apr. 11th 1917
Aged 21.

YOU could easily be forgiven for assuming that a certain place by the name of Monquhitter lies on a sun drenched coastal location overlooking the Mediterranean. In actual fact it is an old parish in Aberdeenshire, six miles east of Turiff. The North Sea coastal town of Peterhead lies just over twenty miles to the west. Monquhitter extends over a rural area that covers around twenty-seven square miles of open country with a history dating back as far as 1670. There are two villages within its boundaries, Cuminestown with a population of around 500 and the smaller Garmond where Dougie Cockburn came from. The whole parish during his lifetime had a population in the hundreds, not thousands. Forty-seven of the men from Monquhitter are named on the local war memorial, they include Dougie, a lot of names for such a sparsely populated area.

The Cockburn family were well known throughout the district. Patriarch, James Cockburn, Dougie's grandfather was a master tailor who had ten children with his wife Jessie. Their five sons all followed suit – pardon the pun – and followed him into the trade. The eldest daughter, Jemima was Dougie's mother, it wasn't a straight-forward relationship between mother and son for one specific reason. Rural Aberdeenshire contained parochial villages, where virtually everyone knew each other, gossip was rife, standards, in particularly moral ones had to at least be seen to be observed. Edwardians as I have previously stated on many occasions liked to hide behind their moral and ethical working class God fearing principals. In reality there really wasn't much if at all any differences between them and us with regard to seeking the pleasures of nature, or as they may have described them, the sins of the flesh.

Douglas Black Cockburn was born out of wedlock on October 31st 1895 at Jemima's family home, Waterloo Cottage, Garmond. There was no doubt as to who the baby's father actually was. James Esson who originally came from the south of the county was a travelling tailor who worked on a freelance basis wherever and whenever he could find employment. He first came to the attention of the Cockburn family when they engaged him on a temporary basis. Jemima at that time was around 15-years old and took a shine to the rugged good looking man several years her senior. Eventually they developed a relationship and became secret lovers, to their credit this enduring carefully orchestrated courtship stood the test of time. It would be a further dozen years on before Jemima fell pregnant with their son Douglas.

James Cockburn the highly respected tailor, church-goer and pillar of the community was deeply angered at the conduct of his eldest daughter and her lover. He feared a scandal and a serious damaging impact to his and the family reputation. Some of the elder members of the community could well have banished themselves from using the services of his trade. Furthermore, they had the potential to encourage others to do so, effectively threatening the very existence of his family business, all because of their viewpoints towards children born out of wedlock.

The ageing tradesman took radical action, he banished his eldest daughter from the family home as she was approaching 30-years old. As for the child it was ordered that he was to remain with the Cockburn's. Douglas was therefore separated from his mother to be raised by his grandparents. Poor Jemima had no say in the matter and had little option but to go and live with her lover James Esson and his family. The young woman moved away from all she had previously known thirty miles or so to the south to the village of Monymusk. Such was the influence of James Cockburn within his trade he made sure that James Esson never operated as a tailor again. Effectively this drastic action removed James from his profession and also from his comfort zone as well. He was forced to take work as a saw miller for the rest of his life.

Determined to make sure that his grandson Dougie would have a successful life and follow in his footsteps as a tailor, James did everything he thought was right for the lad… everything *he* thought was right. Young Dougie was privately educated and that cost money. He was sent to the prestigious Robert Gordon's College in Aberdeen and rubbed shoulders with boys from privileged and wealthy backgrounds. Dougie enrolled there on January 10th 1910, aged 14, after having previously undertaken his studies at Monquhitter public school. Upon completing his studies the young man did what was expected of him and became a tailor.

Not long after the outbreak of war Dougie felt compelled to join up. The region in which he lived had very strong connections with the Gordon Highlanders and especially the Territorial Force of the 1st/5th Battalion. A low localised density of populous meant that many of the lads who went on to serve together either knew each other or were very familiar with the backgrounds of their contemporaries. This battalion in the early days of the war was firmly rooted within the local area, Dougie joined in November 1914.

The original draft went to France in May 1915, some months later they were involved in desperate and horrific fighting at Loos in September, an area I refer to as 'Scotland's Graveyard'. Dougie wasn't with the original detachment, indeed it was some time later that he actually arrived in France on December 5th 1915. Rob offers a credible and interesting explanation as to why. Not all battalion men sailed on the first draft, especially those with a specialist skill. Dougie was a tailor and it is probable that he was involved at some stage in the provision of supply or the manufacturing of kilts for his battalion, this was fairly common with men of his ability. In 1915 many uniforms and especially kilts still had to be provided and it needed specialist personnel attached to the battalion to assist.

In the absence of a service record we can still chart Dougie's movements when he arrived upon the Western Front in France. His first real taste of action occurred in the area of Arras around a location known as the Labyrinth in March 1916. He was also involved in the horrendous actions at High Wood on the Somme in the blistering heat of July 30th/31st of that year. Towards the end of that blood-soaked campaign he was at Beaumont Hamel and witnessed horrific scenes of suffering, slaughter and misery. He was without a shadow of a doubt by that time a seasoned soldier having just turned 21-years of age.

The following year would see the three famous Scottish Divisions, the 9th, 15th and 51st (Highland) thrust into the Battle of Arras. Dougie's battalion formed part of the 153rd Brigade of the 51st (Highland) Division and would go on to perform deeds of exceptional bravery as that campaign went on. I have long been a severe critic of how the Scottish Divisions were handled by the British High Command at Arras with very good reason and much justification. My investigative probing and subsequent documentary film – 'Murder on the Hill' – absolutely slams some of the absurd decisions made that culminated in total madness, spine-chilling incompetence and unnecessary suffering on an horrific scale. Arras was as much a graveyard for Scotland as was Loos, lessons hadn't been learned from there or the Somme in 1916. So many times the Scots were used as 'shock troops' and sent into horrendously suicidal operations at Arras. I will unashamedly state in my opinion that on more than one occasion they were deliberately ordered to die to assess and test the strengths of enemy resources. Worse still, referring here to the 9th Division they were sent to their deaths because of a spiteful resentment towards them by a certain General. Not for the first time I will name and shame this butcher once again, Edmund Allenby was the guilty man who held the smoking gun. You may now be wondering if I am talking about murder. Yes, I am, Scottish soldiers were deliberately murdered in 1917 at Arras by one of their own commanders, who wasn't himself a Scotsman. I am sure this particular statement will have the ears of certain 'metropolitan historians' pricking up as if they were human versions of 'Bugs Bunny'. It bothers me not, they need to watch my documentary.

Dougie Cockburn met his death on Wednesday April 11th 1917 close to Roclincourt not too far away from Arras. Weather conditions were appalling with snow falling, underfoot the terrain was hazardous, slippery and dangerous. The young soldier from the fields of Aberdeenshire found himself trapped along with others of his platoon. Murderous German machine-gun cross fire tore the Highlanders to pieces, Dougie was mutilated and his body was literally shredded apart. He has no grave and is commemorated on the impressive yet hauntingly sad Arras Memorial to the missing, a place where I have shed tears on several occasions.

On the day he died further up the line battalions of Scotsmen were suffering casualty rates around Arras that in some cases were running at 90%. The tactics of attrition some would argue shortened the war, not so in my opinion as I believe they actually extended it. So many times and particularly at Arras Scotsman were thrown against impossible odds. The men of Scotland fought with extreme bravery but the overall casualty

A ruthless German machine-gun team ended the life of Dougie Cockburn.

figures speak for themselves, nobody can argue with me upon that point. I will repeat the Scots lost the greatest percentage of men, maybe I have offered some form of explanation here, but despite the passage of time I will listen to no excuses as to why.

Back in Aberdeenshire Dougie's effects were detailed to be forwarded to Jemima Esson, his mother who had been ostracised by her family and had eventually married her lover, Dougie's father, James. Her grief would have been compounded by the fact that she had missed out upon her son's upbringing through no real fault of her own. Reputations, morals, and down-right selfishness had also denied Dougie the opportunity of embracing his own parents in normal circumstances. The tragedy of this is that he was killed at such a young age, the opportunities for complete redemption therefore were not forthcoming.

A large family such as the Cockburn's extended down the generations and surely some of Dougie's descendants will still live and work in the area of Monquhitter. His full medals entitlement came out of the family possession some time ago. Dougie was posthumously awarded his service medals consisting of the 1914-15 Star, British War Medal and Victory Medal. It is likely his mother had at some point after the war received these medals. I am fairly confident in saying she must have retained some form of communication with her siblings, it is possible with her being the eldest the medals eventually passed to one of them.

Recently Dougie's medals turned up at a specialist military fair in Yorkshire in the hands of a dealer. Rob managed to obtain them at a price slightly below their market value. Perhaps the people of the white rose county had no interest in the artefacts of a Scotsman. These medals have revealed long lost secrets regarding the life and times of Douglas Cockburn and his family. Importantly, simply because of the significance of the date upon which he died I have also been able to express tragedies that are connected to that period. Making a specific point I refer to the date once again, April 11th 1917, one of the darkest days in Scottish military history.

Sometimes there are far more secrets that are attached to what some people would regard as just another set of medals. We can illustrate that point by example through research and the writing of this story corresponding to the the actual history behind the medals. Dougie Cockburn was very ordinary in many ways, yet the dysfunctional circumstances surrounding his birth and upbringing also bring to us crucial historical information. Not only do we refer to the war as a direct result of the acquisition of his medals, for I have been able to bring forward certain social attitudes of a time gone by. Yes, we had so much in common with our Edwardian ancestors and I have always maintained that, yet, things are so very different now. Sometimes certain people refer to the past as being hypothetically a better place. I think Dougie Cockburn's story and the supplementary comments made about his Scots comrades in arms demonstrates how important it is to concentrate on the future. The question also arises as to why did men like Dougie have to die? I somehow can't find the answer to that one, neither can Rob.

Robert Beveridge

Killed in Action
Belgium, Sept. 20th 1917
Aged 24.
Awarded the MILITARY MEDAL in 1917

Robert Beveridge MM - his legacy lives on as he has been immortalised on film and also within this publication.

THE bond I have with Robert Beveridge will remain with me for the rest of my life. Although I obviously never had the privilege of knowing him personally or meeting him face-to-face my connections to him will always remain unbreakable. For almost a century this true Scottish hero had been forgotten. Nowadays, his legacy provides a superb educational resource for many and will continue to do so for generations to come, thanks to the concerted efforts of some very special people. My pride in him is shared by many others, his story is immortalised upon film, his sacrifice and memory no longer forgotten, never, ever.

I will start this particular story in the present century. In November 2006 as my fortieth birthday approached I had already decided to purchase a Military Cross or a Military Medal to a soldier of the Great War, some may say an unusual birthday present to myself. Little did I know when I bought the Military Medal awarded to a young Scotsman by the name of Robert Beveridge that I was about to embark upon a wonderful journey. The roller-coaster ride started when I began to perform the basic research upon the man behind the medal and discovered almost immediately that he had been left off his local war memorial. From that particular point history would be in the making to ensure that Robert's sacrifice would be acknowledged. As it transpired a whole lot more occurred, as we shall discover.

Robert Beveridge was born in 1893 in one of a block of four cottages that made up a hamlet called Masterton in the village of Newbattle close to Newtongrange in Midlothian. This location is just under ten miles to the south-east of Edinburgh city centre. He was the son of William and Elizabeth, the family that was eventually made up of four children was poor and impoverished. Robert's grandfather and his father both worked at the Lady Victoria pit in harsh and uncompromising conditions mining coal. This particular site is now the actual Scottish Mining Museum and gives a realistic insight into what working conditions of the day were really like. When Robert was a young boy his family moved to the village of Broxburn now in West Lothian and took up residency in a tiny cottage at 62 Greendykes Road. A short distance away only about a mile or so up the road is the village of Uphall. The whole area was at the time dominated by the shale oil mining industry, very dirty work for those employed within the job as William was.

Tragedy struck the family when Robert was barely 13-years old. The damp and grimy cottage played its part in the demise of his mother Elizabeth who succumbed to tuberculosis, the scourge of the working classes. She died at the house with no medical help, the stricken mother was just 37-years old. Robert had little option but to follow in his father's footsteps to the 'Paraffin Young' factory at Uphall station. The family desperately needed his income in order just to survive and to help them get on with life the best they could. Robert's two sisters had to combine their work duties in domestic service with those of taking care of their little infant brother Charlie.

As the years passed by William Beveridge himself became sick. Robert and the girls could not afford the services of a local doctor at a time when the NHS didn't exist. In 1914 before the outbreak of the war William suffered the same fate as his late wife and died of tuberculosis, he was just 47-years old. The heartbroken family was then split up. Youngster Charlie went to live with relatives in the village of Rosewell, Midlothian. Robert and his sisters left the house where their parents had both suffered so much, they had little choice. Now the young man had to completely find his own way in life, he moved into lodgings for single men in Uphall. At around this time he decided to join up. The local territorials were recruiting and our man signed on with the 10th (Cyclist) Battalion Royal Scots (Linlithgowshire). He was assigned initially to coastal defence duties from an area not to be confused by names alone that stretched from North Berwick in East Lothian, Scotland, to Berwick in Northumberland, England. The fresh air and outstanding scenery he encountered from those locations I am sure did him a power of good.

As the war raged on reinforcements to front line battalions in France and Belgium became an absolute necessity. The slaughter on the Somme in 1916 had taken its toll upon the regular and volunteer service battalions of the Royal Scots, a regiment that held the distinction of being the premier 'first of foot' of the British infantry. Robert was transferred to the 12th Battalion Royal Scots, a service unit of volunteers from his region, he arrived in France in July 1916. From thereon he became a dedicated soldier and complied with all the tasks set before him. This was quickly acknowledged and his promotion to Lance-Corporal gave him the responsibility of leadership. He didn't let anyone down, he was with guys from his own locality in a foreign land. Robert became a mentor, a leader and ultimately a hero, his men knew that, they depended upon him and trusted him with their lives.

Robert established himself as a true Scottish hero in 1917. He was pitted into the Battle of Arras and came out of that as very much a young man of worthy distinction. In the April of that year he was involved in an action at Greenland Hill that saw a level of suffering amongst Scots and South African soldiers who were a part of his 9th (Scottish) Division that is unprecedented. Rob holds me back here, I want to rant on about what happened to those men and boys, some as young as just 16-years of age and cast the blame. I suppose that I have already previously done that. Rob, in his wisdom was keen to remind me about getting carried away and placed a very sensible emphasis upon me to get on with this story.

The Battle of Arras raged on and one specific strategic position remained the bane of the attacking British forces. It was fought over many times with much blood ultimately being shed, especially by Scottish soldiers. I am referring here to the Chemical Works at Rouex and the adjoining railway station that linked logistical communications for whoever occupied the site. A sixty-metre tower, one hell of an observation point was the key to this position and the Germans held it. To attack such an objective would in the first instance rely upon breaking the rail line of communication and supply, the British had tried many times without success.

On a very hot day in the early June of 1917, the 12th Royal Scots were detailed to take the initiative and attack the lines of communication. Once again the Scottish lads had to do the 'dirty work' against very unfavourable odds. I was at the point of their advance when I visited the location in 2007, the observation tower had obviously gone by then. The terrain there is flat, very flat. Both the railway line and station that still exist today cut straight across open ground, it's like a football pitch with two halves. In 1917 a massive observation point for the Germans gave them two huge angles of visibility, left and right, their machine-guns could sweep from side to side, east to west.

The Royal Scots soon found themselves catapulted into a huge cross-fire, they dug in on the saps of the railway line. Advance parties went out to scare the hell out of the minimal German defensive infantry on the ground. The defenders really didn't need massive flanking support simply because their machine-gun sections were being directed from the observation tower to inflict havoc upon the advancing Scotsmen. Robert took his section out into the middle of the battlefield in an attempt to gain essential reconnaissance information. The Germans in return sent out patrols out to scupper the Scots from gaining the knowledge as to how the tower defences were operating. This meant that attrition would take place between two or more patrols with the Scots attempting to get to where the machine-gun posts were firing from and the Germans trying to stop them. It took place in 'no man's land' somewhere between the railway station and the tower.

Robert and his section soon got pinned down and had to take cover some distance away from their starting point and had to dive into a shell-hole. Then the German patrols came, not just one but numerous ones. In the darkness Robert's section was discovered. The German infantrymen struggled to overcome them with visibility being very poor, desperately the Scots lads held on fighting at times hand-to-hand. Without rations or water they struggled on until they were relieved at dawn. For his actions leading his section in horrendous conditions, Lance-Corporal Robert Beveridge was awarded the Military Medal for his bravery in the field, the date was June 5th 1917.

The former shale oil worker's achievement was recognised not only by the award of his bravery medal. He was almost immediately promoted to the rank of Corporal, giving him further responsibility of permanently commanding a full section of twelve men in battlefield situations. This rank was dangerous to say the least and he could have refused it, he didn't. At that point of the war an infantry section commander was responsible for taking the flank of any attacking situation, he could see from a position from either left or right where his men were advancing. The Germans knew this, they would make special efforts to eliminate the wide man with his two stripes to destabilise and unsettle a wave of force coming towards them. A Corporal controlling his men from a flank had to be taken out as far as they were concerned. It was a dangerous rank for Robert to hold and he knew that. Undeterred he also knew that the boys who relied upon his skill and judgement would get through, Robert believed in himself, as did his officers who trusted his capabilities.

Our hero met his end on a soggy autumn morning in Belgium. Completely devoted to his men Robert led his section into one of the most heroic acts in Scottish military history. His company commander Captain Henry Reynolds deservedly won the Victoria Cross for his incredible leadership on that wet morning. Harry Reynolds knew all of his men, he assured them that victory would be theirs against unbelievable odds, he was right. On that day the 12th Royal Scots overcame their foe. Robert led his section from the flank across open ground that was chewed up by the rain and mud to assault German machine-gun positions covering a high banked railway siding. The Scots with their rifles and grenades had to take out strategic German machine-gun pill-box fortifications dangerously low in the ground ahead of them, they succeeded. Robert fell dying as a result of multiple bullet wounds to the abdomen. His men reached him and removed his pay book and will from his breast pocket before they continued to take out the enemy. In the chaotic scenes that followed the Germans in response launched a huge artillery bombardment. Robert's body was destroyed, he therefore has no grave and remains to this day somewhere in a foreign field.

When I walked through the actual field where he met his death near Frezenberg in Belgium the rain had fallen just before I arrived, as it had done so on that fateful day when Robert was killed. Suddenly the sun came out and shined across the terrain as I looked around alongside the lads who had joined me in the field. The boys I had at my side are some of the guys who helped to make the film of the story of Robert's life, we were all in tears. Those tears turned to smiles as we came together in the aftermath to create Robert's everlasting legacy that he richly deserves.

Danny Metcalfe is a charismatic and likeable Yorkshire lad who dabbles in antiques. I purchased the Military Medal of Robert's from him way back in 2006 as my unconventional birthday present. At that time we both had no idea of the history behind it. Now the pair of us share in what I will describe as an extremely important part of history and Danny to his everlasting credit is very proud to be a part of that. He acknowledges that it is not about us - him or me - it is all about Robert Beveridge. It was Danny who discovered him and brought Robert to me to tell his story that will forever endure, as we shall see.

Spurred on by Robert I decided to make a film about his life. 'A Soldier's Return' (2007), it has sold out. I was ripped off in the end by the American distributors, thankfully though the production has more than made its mark. The team I assembled to make the film were truly magnificent. I wrote and produced the story of Robert's life that culminated in what I will say is the greatest achievement of my life within the media to date. The production cost me more financially to do it than I actually made from it, so what? This film is now in schools throughout Scotland. My platoon section included the superb and well established film cameraman, Ian Livesey who travelled to Scotland, France and Belgium without a budget. Robin Thompson presented and narrated the documentary with consummate skill. Not forgetting the enigmatic Mike Welch who directed and edited utilising his own swashbuckling style to make it happen. Mike, my childhood friend, also created a wonderful soundtrack musical accompaniment to the film entitled – 'A Moment's Goodbye'- He deserves so much credit for that, if you listen to it, you will see why. John Duncan the brilliant Scottish historian also played an essential role portraying his knowledge of the life and times of Robert on-screen.

Now let's go back to the beginning of this story. Robert was left off his war memorial in Uphall for so long… Why? There were 89-names on the memorial at St. Nicholas Church, in the village of Uphall. John Duncan offered the simple explanation as to why our man was left off. There was simply nobody left to put forward his name to place upon the memorial, his family had gone. On September 20th 2007, the day that marked the ninetieth anniversary of Robert's death, everything changed. The Reverend David Black conducted an emotionally charged service at the church that was packed with local residents in honour of Robert Beveridge MM. Robert had his name encrypted upon the war memorial within the church forever more, justice was done. He became the ninetieth name to be included upon the tablet of the wall ninety years to the day he fell so many years before, so far away. I still have the bible that Reverend Black signed personally for me in honour of Robert at the side of my bed. On that day some of Robert's ancestors managed to attend the crowded church, I remember an old man in tears, he was one of Robert's relatives who knew that his long forgotten descendant was at last after so many years, honoured so respectfully.

I am not a fan of politicians, something that may have not escaped your attention as I have wrote this book. There is one man, a true man of the people who has represented his constituents for many years that deserves special mention here. At the time of Robert's memorial service one particular political figure stood tall. Graeme Morrice was then the leader of West Lothian council. This man took a very active interest in Robert as soon as he was made aware of him. Out of respect Graeme paid from of his own pocket the fee to have Robert's name placed upon the church memorial. The film crew team and I had more than our fair share of laughs with this great guy. We indulged in many pints of 'Black Sheep' bitter in the local pub that Robert once frequented in the village of Uphall.

Today we look upon Robert Beveridge's legacy, it is well preserved and forms a very integral part of local life. For that we have to thank people like Tommy Davidson and the organisations that support their local heritage. Tommy was very instrumental in continuing Robert's legacy by helping to organise another fitting tribute to Robert in 2017 that marked the centenary of his death. Another special service was conducted in Robert's honour within the same church. It took place a hundred years after the brave Scotsman perished, thanks to Tommy and his colleagues.

One hundred years after Robert died I completely relinquished any financial rights to the film I made about him with regard to his legacy in Scotland. My conditions to that were straight-forward, and apply only to Scotland. The film can be shown in any educational establishment in that country for all time, simple as that. I remember the premiere of the film back in 2008 on a very wet night in Broxburn. Mike Welch was drunk because he was scared of the Scots, thank goodness they didn't turn up in kilts with flashing bayonets.

Robert Beveridge has concluded this emotional chapter – 'Forever Scotland'. As an Englishman through and through I have been exceptionally privileged to write it and I really do mean that. I normally have the final words on most things, but not this time. Below are my emotionally charged comments, I have to make them. Rob has to remind me that this book is about fifty subjects who thus far have been treated with equal consideration. My feelings given the history and circumstances regarding Robert Beveridge could have created a bias. Rob is right and I hope that I haven't done that. My own personal concluding words regarding this chapter are recorded below. The final paragraph comes thereafter.

'There is not just a field that is forever Scotland, there is a garden of eternity that is forever Scotland. The garden has no soil for bigotry or prejudice, our garden shall grow for humility and for justice. Our sacrifices will forever be for the freedom of all mankind '.

So now we leave this magnificent chapter with the sentiments of my co-conspirator Rob Jackson. I may have written the words in this book but the former Sergeant-Major who pulls me into line has something to say at this point. He tells me he is half-Scottish. I wonder what the Scots lads in this chapter would think if they looked under his kilt! Never mind, his words below provide the ultimate tribute to Robert Beveridge and all of the Scots lads portrayed within this chapter.

'When a man dies his soul becomes immortal. When a righteous man dies his soul becomes immortal and divine, every one of the Scots boys here suffered for righteousness'.

Robert Beveridge's beautifully cased Military medal is with us and open to public display upon request. This true Scottish hero is commemorated on the Tyne Cot Memorial in Belgium and at St. Nicholas Church, Uphall, Scotland.

ON THIS DAY

MANY events of huge historical significance occurred during the First World War that have been extremely well documented and written about over and over again. I could therefore be accused of repeating and following in the footsteps of others as I make reference to certain dates and events from 1914 to 1918. Of course there is a specific reason as to why we have selected this chapter. To continue to provide the fascinating stories of our subjects and to re-examine the background of the historical dates that are connected to them.

Here we really do take a look at history and once again I will be held back by Rob as I strain at the leash to get across what I consider as matters of relevance. Our men featured here find their stories interwoven to a degree with certain exceptional focal points of history. The 'metropolitan historians' who by now must be sick to the back teeth of me will be sharpening their knives I am sure when they have read this chapter. Popular culture sometimes provides people with selective historical material, some of it recorded in writing. As time moves on the information is handed down from generation to generation and contorts as it passes from person to person. Eventually the tales that are told form into what I describe as 'pools of assumption'. Unfortunately some of these pools are very shallow, others so deep that you can never get to the bottom of them.

For those of you who have a knowledge of the First World War I am sure you will understand what I have just said. Both Rob and I hope the guys we feature within this chapter will bring about a greater understanding of what could be the truth. No historian, no matter how eminent he or she may be can consistently guarantee to deliver whole truths. Those who claim they can, and yes, they do exist, should be on the pier at Blackpool dressed up as fortune tellers, or dealing cards in a casino. All great or tragic events can create mythology, confusion, doubt and even suggestions of conspiracy.

Let's see what we can do here to arguably bring about new light to some of the history associated with the Great War. A bold statement of intent but surely by now one that won't surprise you.

Alfred Macklin
Killed in Action
France, Dec. 25th 1914
Aged 33.

> *ON THIS DAY… December 25th 1914 – The Christmas Day Truce? Also, the day when many assumed the war would finally be over, it had hardly began.*

ALFIE Macklin a mature and experienced former regular soldier took absolutely no notice of the waves of optimistic and frivolous comments made by so many as war was declared in August 1914. A huge number of people from politicians to chimney-sweeps were convincing themselves and others the war would be over by Christmas of that year. For some it actually was. Alfie just happened to lose his life on that fateful day. As for the rest of the men fighting on the Western Front, almost another four years of hell lay ahead for those fortunate to make it that far.

There is a widespread and popular belief amongst some that on Christmas Day 1914 the men dug in on the Western Front, British and German, declared a truce or ceasefire. Tales of organised football games between the opposing sides in 'no-man's land' and of soldiers swapping photos and gifts and still are talked about today. Can anyone really believe the war came to a standstill to celebrate one special day? The answer is clear, it didn't. Alfie bears testimony to that. Yes, there were isolated incidents of fraternisation across a long stretch of the front, the odd football may have been kicked about here and there as well. The scale of the 'festivities' that occurred on Christmas Day 1914 have always been exaggerated, sometimes wildly so. Senior British commanders tucked up in their country houses and chateaus miles behind the lines got wind of a small number of friendly exchanges between the British and the Germans. Their reactions were typically unsurprising.

Firm directives were issued by the Generals that should any more similar activities occur then a 'court-martial' would await any such offender, in effect meaning he could be shot. The British Expeditionary Force in

France at that time was commanded by the enigmatic Sir John French. His Christmas was spent in front of a roaring fire, no doubt endless glasses of vintage wine and the finest cuisine comforted the good-time womanising philanderer. Perhaps he even had one of his mistresses on hand to provide him with some further festive cheer! The Corps commanders of the time including French's eventual successor Douglas Haig were also enjoying Christmas. Haig tucked into a hearty dinner with all the trimmings after he had issued instructions that normal routines could be eased for men in quiet sectors across the line. The men as it happened were freezing cold as a heavy frost descended across the ground. Their rations did however include a special tobacco tin, gifts from Princess Mary that contained chocolate and cigarettes. Small comfort but well received by the lads as Sir John puffed away on his expensive cigars.

Alfred Henry Macklin was born in the sleepy old English village of Enford in Wiltshire. The small pretty settlement still boasts a traditional village pub with its thatched roof and a magnificent architectural church. Situated 14-miles north of Salisbury its origins can be traced back to the Iron Age, the Romans also had a small settlement there, Enford is steeped in history. Life was and to a degree even in modern times still is traditional and simple. The small population live life at a pace that we could all envy. Nowadays there is an element of affluence, some properties within the village swap ownership for large sums of money. In Alfie's day things were a little more sedately ordinary. Small homesteads, leafy cottages and winding country lanes snaked around a simplistic part of England where most men and boys worked upon the land.

Alfie's parents William and Emily were both locals. His father worked hard on the land as an agricultural labourer, farm-hand and carter throughout his life, they were very much ordinary people, but maybe the local cider could have had an effect upon William's Victorian morals. His then girlfriend Emily who lived nearby may too have had one or two many swigs of the scrumpy as they romped in the haylofts, eventually she fell pregnant by William. The two had no choice but to get married in those days, she was four to five months along the way to giving birth to Alfie when they tied the knot on May 29th 1881.

More children followed, Alfie's sister Bessie and his four brothers, George, Arthur, Frank and Sid. One other child died in infancy but six made it into adulthood. Alfie like all of his brothers followed in his father's footsteps and upon leaving school at 12-years old having received a rudimentary education, he out went to work in the fields. The pace of life was rather too slow for Alfie, he had seen his father toiling in the countryside for years and decided that he wanted a little more excitement. Ambitious Alfie would have also seen one of two of the local lads set off for war in South Africa at the turn of the twentieth century, one day he hoped that he would do the same and embark upon a career in the military. Alfie was a few inches above the average height for the period and a strapping lad. He was readily accepted into the local infantry of the Wiltshire Regiment aged 20-years old and immediately detailed for a special assignment that was beyond his imagination.

It wasn't to be a direct posting to South Africa as he may well have anticipated. The war against the Boers was coming towards an end in 1902 when Alfie received his first deployment. During the Anglo-Boer War in less than three years the British had taken over 20,000 Boer prisoners of war and quite obviously had logistical problems dealing with them. Many POW camps had been set up around the Cape Colony but were vulnerable to attack. The British with a huge Empire held many overseas territories where they could directly transfer the Boer prisoners to. The island of St. Helena in the South Atlantic was regarded as totally escape-proof. It was surrounded by crashing waves and many miles away from the South American main lands of Brazil and Argentina, only a fool would attempt to abscond. Other destinations for the Boer prisoners included, Bermuda, India and Ceylon [Sri Lanka]. Referring back to St. Helena, this island once held the most famous British captive of all time, Napoleon Bonaparte. The deposed French Emperor was incarcerated there from 1815 for six years until he died on the island in 1821.

Alfie Macklin the farm labourer from rural Wiltshire was duly despatched to Deadwood Prison Camp on St. Helena. He never thought that one day he would become a prison guard. The British have always been condemned for the creation of concentration camps in South Africa during the Boer wars. Women and children were rounded up like cattle and harshly treated within the atrocious camps. On St. Helena the situation was different. The captives were experienced soldiers, horsemen and very capable of causing chaos if control was not maintained. British guards treated their prisoners with respect and allowed certain elements of freedom, likewise the Boers who knew they wouldn't be there forever behaved well, given the odd incident or so. The men were tented across open ground surrounded by barbed wire. British officers in charge of the camp allowed the prisoners as opportunities arose to source local materials and build more accommodating huts. Escape attempts were very few and far between and always failed. Those who were caught were simply put back within the camp without severe punishment.

It wasn't an easy ride for Alfie, he still had to be alert and would have had to exert his authority where and when necessary. The climate of the island could be harsh and cold, long nights on duty were not pleasurable. This was a posting that would have endured long hours of boredom and a longingness to return home. In some ways the place resembles the Falklands and anyone who has served there in modern times will tell you how often they have thought about home when stationed in the South Atlantic.

Alfie's time as a guard lasted just a year, the South African Boer prisoners were repatriated, some of them would go on to fight alongside the British a few years later in the First World War. The young soldier had shown promise, he was tall, strong and could exercise and take discipline. He was also ambitious and wanted to further his military career. On August 4th 1903 he attested with permission into the Coldstream Guards. I believe he signed on for the required period of five years with a further seven on the reserve that would demand an immediate recall to service if required. At the very end of his service period he married his childhood sweetheart Ellen Beatrice Eyres on August 1st 1908 back in his home village. The soldier had returned to settle into family and village life in the loving arms of his sweetheart. Ellen and Alfie celebrated the birth of their son Reginald William Macklin on June 24th 1909, life was bliss. Alfie had returned to work on the land alongside two of his brothers, he was popular, well liked and had everything to live for.

In the late summer of 1914 the Coldstream Guards knew that war was imminent. Even before it was declared they had compiled detailed lists of their reservists for an immediate recall. Without hesitation Alfie was recalled to Windsor, he was in France just

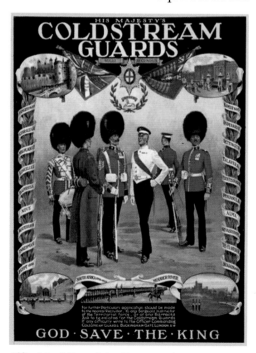

Alfie Macklin originally served as a pre-war regular with the Wiltshire Regiment before becoming a Guardsman with the 2nd Battalion Coldstream Guards.

a week after the declaration, arriving at Le Havre on the night of August 12th 1914, disembarking a few hours later as the dawn arrived on the 13th. There had been precious little time to say goodbye to his wife and child. As previously stated I don't think Alfie promised to be home for Christmas despite what others were saying. He was an experienced military guardsman and Rob an ex-Coldstream man himself is quick to remind me that he was educated in the Guards and took nothing at all for granted. Put an image now into your minds' eye. Picture a strapping man in his early thirties putting his arms around his wife as she stands at their front door on a warm summer day. He kisses her fully on the lips and then cradles her in his arms once more. Then he picks up his little five year old son with both of his strong arms, looks him in the eyes and tells him to look after his Ma until he comes home. The boy smiles and glances at his mum and dad one last time before his father lets him go, young Reggie then scampers back into their little cottage to hide behind a chair. Ellen waves and waves at Alfie until he disappears out of site down the winding lane out of the village… It was the last time she ever saw her husband and childhood sweetheart.

Alfie saw a hell of a lot of action in his short time at the front in Belgium and France in 1914. He was in the absolute thick of everything with the 2nd Coldstream Guards. In August he fought at Mons and was part of the organised retreat in blisteringly hot conditions towards the Marne where he was once again in action. Towards the end of September Alfie was fighting around the Aisne, he was close by when his comrade and pal Fred Dobson went out into 'no-man's land' to rescue the wounded at Chavonne. Fred was decorated with the Victoria Cross for his incredible courage.

In October and November Alfie and his battalion were involved in some fierce exchanges with the Germans around Ypres and Zonnebeke in Belgium where they suffered some appalling casualties. Alfie an original member of the British Expeditionary Force played his part in saving France from capitulation. The 2nd Coldstream Guards amongst others held back the Germans from capturing Ypres, had the enemy done so they would have made for the Channel ports and cut-off the British. The men of the BEF who fought in 1914, regular soldiers have my greatest admiration. These guys were always outnumbered, sometimes very heavily and eventually their ranks declined dramatically due to casualties. Eventually replacement territorials, volunteers and conscripts would follow the depleted 1914 professional British Army. Any 'old contemptible' another name for a 1914 veteran would always modestly say he had just done his job. The particular men of the original BEF were true heroes, every single one of them.

December came and the weather turned miserable, cold and wet as the Coldstream Guards made their way south to take over a sector around La Bassee within the Nord-Pas-de-Calais region. As Christmas Day approached the conditions worsened and temperatures dropped. A heavy frost settled as the dawn broke and the ground started to freeze hard, it was as expected a relatively quiet day. In the distance men could hear Christmas carols being sung. There were no footballs being kicked around this area. The 2nd Coldstream Guards were on their toes and organised their defences as they would do so on any other day. Two companies remained in the trenches, one in support and one providing the night relief, it was very much business as usual. Enemy snipers didn't take a day off to eat mince pies and drink mulled wine as the officers reminded their men, the officers were proved to be right.

Rob and I have discussed the myths and realities of what happened on the Western Front on Christmas Day 1914. From what I have just described the professional Coldstream Guards took no liberties at all and accordingly set themselves up for any eventuality. Both Rob and I believe this was more or less the situation across the whole of the front. Yes, casualties were far fewer that day because all of the artillery units considerably reduced bombardments. This enabled both sides to gather their wounded from 'no-man's land'. These far from unofficial sporadic and opportunistic 'truces' were practical ones, not as many 'metropolitan historians' would have us believe. Organised football games and fraternisation across the whole of 'no-man's land' did not occur on Christmas Day 1914. Yes, there were a few incidences of contact and that news travelled fast down the line, but it was far from a traditional holiday period for the men at the front.

Rob, a father and grandfather himself expressed his sorrow for Alfie's infant son and sighed when he said to me – 'why couldn't the German sniper take a day off'. Alfie Macklin the battle hardened soldier must have been thinking continuously about his wife and little boy at home. He would have pictured in his mind his son gleefully putting his little hand down his Christmas stocking as the candles on the Christmas tree glinted in his eye. In the freezing cold filth of his trench Alfie kissed a letter sent to him from his wife one more time and maybe, just maybe, mumbled the words – 'Merry Christmas my darling'.

German snipers had been specially trained, many of them were former hunters who were used to shooting game. On Christmas Day 1914 they weren't out playing football or exchanging gifts. The ruthless marksmen were gunning down British soldiers like reindeers on a festive Bavarian shooting party. As harsh as it may sound they were doing the job they were ordered to do. There were relatively few casualties that day, Alfie was one of eight Coldstream Guardsmen picked off by cunning snipers whose Christmas gift to each of them was a bullet through the brain, so much for a festive truce.

Alfie had already received the Queens South Africa Medal, despite the fact that he served in the South Atlantic guarding Boer prisoners. He was also awarded the 1914 Star with clasp, the British War Medal and the Victory Medal. Rob paid a hefty premium for all of Alfie's medals simply because he is a 1914 Christmas Day casualty - and because Rob very much wanted this particular story told.

Alfred Henry Macklin, aged 33, was buried in a makeshift grave by his pals on Christmas Day 1914 in a plot close to the brewery at nearby Givenchy. His body was later destroyed by high explosive shells, he now is lost forever. He is commemorated on the Le Touret Memorial to the missing in France. Raise a glass to him this coming Christmas time, let him stick in your mind, remember him.

Fred Lewis
Drowned
near Irish Coast, May 7th 1915
Aged 38.

> **ON THIS DAY… May 7th 1915 – The sinking of the RMS Lusitania with the loss of 1,198 lives, by a German U-boat, the U-20.**

WE have a Mercantile Marine Medal that was issued to Fred Lewis, a waiter who sailed aboard the ill-fated luxury liner the 'RMS Lusitania'. Fred perished when the prestigious ocean-going passenger ship was sunk off the Old Head of Kinsale, close to the Irish coast. This event marked one of the most significantly tragic and catastrophic disasters in history. Almost 1,200 men, women and children were murdered by an act of human aggression compounded by political incompetence that is almost beyond belief. Yes, a German submarine was responsible and that cannot be denied, but the finger of blame will be directly pointed by me at others too, for this was a terrible tragedy that could and should have been prevented.

Fred just happened to have been born in my hometown of Bolton, Lancashire. I am very familiar therefore with where he was raised and I have certainly on many occasions followed in his very footsteps. He came from a very ordinary and close knit working-class family and was one of eight children born to his parents. Fred was the eldest of six who survived into adulthood. His father Thomas married local girl Alice Wardle in 1876. Frederick Lewis was born less than a year after their nuptials in 1877. His dad worked in a traditional industry associated with the town in a local cotton mill as a warehouseman. The family as it expanded continuously moved around the suburbs, from Halliwell, a district that adjoins the one where I was brought-up, to the Haulgh and finally the Breightmet area.

When Fred left school he too found employment in the cotton mill, Bolton at that time had hundreds of mills and securing employment was as easy as falling off a log. There wasn't much excitement working long hours in filthy and often dangerous conditions but Fred persevered until he entered his late twenties. Keen upon bettering himself he decided upon a new career, one that would culminate in his early death. As for the rest of the family, five of the six children continued to live with their parents well into their adult lives. They were all employed in various occupations, the youngest daughter, Fred's sister was a school teacher. His father Tom also later escaped the dreary life of working in a cotton mill and became a clerk with the booming Co-Operative Society.

Fred travelled to Liverpool and joined the world famous and highly respected Cunard Line and trained as a steward and waiter. The ambitious young man took up lodgings at 16 Bankfield Street in Liverpool and lived between there and his family home at 579 Bury Road, Bolton, during the periods when he was not crossing the Atlantic Ocean. By the fire side the wonderful tales he must have shared with his parents and siblings would have been enthralling to them. In 1906 Fred was aboard the 'RMS Carmania'. For those of you who don't have any maritime knowledge the initials 'RMS' denote the definition of Royal Mail Ship, most transatlantic liners carried hefty loads of mail to and from Britain and the United States. The Carmania that made its maiden voyage on December 2nd 1905 was a magnificent vessel. It was once one of the two largest liners in the world until the 'RMS Lusitania' was launched ironically in the same year as Fred first went to sea, 1906. He would go on to make many crossings to New York via Queenstown, along the same route as the ill-fated 'RMS Titanic' would later follow.

After a few years Fred was transferred to the smaller liner the 'SS Ivernia', the initials 'SS' denote Steam Ship. This particular vessel was famous for making the 'immigrant run' from Liverpool to Boston. Fred met many excitable people who were embarking upon the first step towards their new lives, what an interesting time he must have had. When war broke out in 1914 the liners continued to cross the Atlantic despite the presence of German U-Boats prowling around British and Irish coastal waters. After all, they wouldn't dare sink civilian liners, would they? Things were about to change dramatically as the Germans introduced 'unrestricted submarine warfare' – to them all shipping became a target. Was this a deliberate act of aggression and the creation of fear? Not quite as we shall discover as they had their reasons to do so. Fred was overjoyed when he was detailed a post as a second-class waiter upon the Lusitania, the fastest ocean going passenger liner in the world. It could cross the Atlantic in less than five days.

On the afternoon of Friday May 7th 1915 the Lusitania was heading around the Old Head of Kinsale off the southern Irish coast, she had to make a specific nautical manoeuvre to negotiate a course. It was just after half-past one. Fred was his usual busy self. He was serving drinks and luncheon to his passengers in the second-class lounge, rushing to and forth with a smile upon his face as he carried out his duties. The liner straightened its course and was a marvellous sight to behold, especially for one man, the highly skilled commander of the U-20 German submarine, 30-year old Walther Schweiger. Peering through his periscope he sighted the Lusitania square on the starboard side directly within his range. He immediately ordered the release of one torpedo that sped through the waves before smashing into the liner directly beneath the bridge where her Captain, William Turner, was supervising the nautical course she intended to follow.

It was a direct hit but Schweiger knew that it would be unlikely just one torpedo would take the mighty ship down and send her to the bottom of the sea. Before he could order a second release he was stunned to hear the sound of a huge second explosion aboard the Lusitania. He watched aghast as the stricken liner started to sink extremely quickly. Later he was recorded as saying the following:

'I couldn't have fired another torpedo into this mass of humans desperately trying to save themselves'.

Absolute panic gripped the stricken liner as she lurched into the sea. Fred picked himself up and desperately headed for one of the lifeboats on deck. I don't think he even made it to the launching points and if he had he probably wouldn't have been able to get inside one. Only six out of forty-eight lifeboats were actually launched as the ship was heading down to the bottom of the sea very quickly, it took just 18-minutes for her to disappear. One man who did get off though was the Captain, William Turner.

So what caused the fateful second explosion that sent Fred and 1,197 other souls to their deaths? Was it a boiler room blast or a coal-dust ignition? No, it was neither, it was the stores of ammunition being carried within the Lusitania that blew up and sent her down so quickly. This statement I make was suggested at the time but denied by the British authorities who declared that the vessel was carrying nothing more than a limited number of small arms. Rob knows only too well that a cargo of rifles would definitely not explode in such a dramatic way. The denials continued until 1982 when the British finally admitted the Lusitania was carrying stores of highly explosive ammunition. I cannot find any evidence of any compensation being paid out to survivors of the Lusitania, some of whom were still around in 1982. They are all gone now.

The Lusitania was under the direction of the Admiralty at that time and had been given orders to ram U-Boats on sight. She could easily outrun the German submarines, so let's put the perspective of Schweiger into focus. He had his orders and he too was a potential target. The Germans were not fools, they had long suspected that ocean going liners were carrying supplies of arms from Canada and the United States, weapons that would kill and maim their countrymen fighting in France and Belgium.

Chillingly the British Admiralty knew what the passengers on board didn't, I am convinced the Captain of the Lusitania did also. The Germans had warned

Waiter Fred Lewis met his end when the RMS Lusitania was sunk by a torpedo From a German submarine.

time and time again that ocean liners were to be targeted. Now Rob has a question for you. Would you board a ship with your children that was a target for the enemy and was carrying large stores of ammunition? Perhaps there was another reason as to why the Lusitania was targeted and this one really is frightening.

There is compelling evidence the then First-Lord of the Admiralty, Mr Winston Churchill himself was very keen to gain American involvement in the war on the side of the allies. In a letter he ambiguously suggested that vessels sunk by German U-boats may influence American opinion and encourage them to join the war as Britain's fighting ally. There is absolutely no doubt that Churchill knew that citizens of the United States were aboard the Lusitania, men, women and children, 128 of them perished. The Royal Navy was mighty, it could have protected such vessels against the declared unrestricted submarine warfare as they entered home waters. No escort of any description had been offered to the Lusitania. In the aftermath of the sinking British public opinion was raging. Churchill wanted the Americans to show the same depth of feeling regarding the loss of their own citizens who perished upon the mighty liner.

Back in Bolton Fred's family were desperately anxious and waiting for news about him. Had he survived? Was he one of the fortunate 764 people who had scrambled to safety? The newspapers were full of the story, Tom and Alice hoped and prayed, surely there was a chance they would see their boy once more and hear of his tales of exotic travel. Eventually the news came that he was lost, the sea being his grave. The truths were totally denied to them, it was the 'beastly hun' [Germans] that had taken their son, Fred the waiter.

Although the Americans were incensed they did not declare war on Germany for another two years. The German Kaiser, Wilhelm II was keen to keep them out of the war and directly ordered that no further attacks upon ocean liners could be warranted. This decision was eventually reversed when the United States did eventually declare war upon Germany.

So what of Walther Schweiger, the ruthlessly ambitious U-Boat commander. Less than four months later in direct contravention of orders he was responsible for sinking another liner in the south Irish Sea. 'RMS Hesperian' that was acting as a cargo vessel and hospital ship became his victim. Almost a year to the day after the Lusitania went down Schweiger was at it again. The carnage continued as 'SS Cymric' that had recently delivered 17,000 tons of ammunition from America to Liverpool was sent down by his torpedoes. The commander was heavily criticised even by the

Kaiser but was soon forgiven when it was revealed that he was responsible for sinking 49-ships weighing-in at a total of around 185,000 tons. He was awarded Germany's highest military honour, the Pour Le Merite, otherwise known as the 'Blue Max' in recognition of his 'achievements'. Schweiger also later found his grave in the depths of the deep blue sea, he was drowned when the U-88 he was commanding was running from a British warship in the North Sea, 'HMS Stonecrop'. His submarine hit a British mine and he perished aged 32-years old.

Life would never be the same again for the Lewis family, the chirpy waiter had gone forever. I have walked along the road where Fred lived many times, like everyone else in the modern era from Bolton I had been unaware that a man from my hometown had perished on the Lusitania. Fred is commemorated on the Tower Hill Memorial in London. There is no recognition of him in Bolton. Rob and I share the same sentiments regarding his death and those of all the others who suffered and died on that fateful day in history. They were duped, all of them, victims of war, maybe, but duped. The multi-vitamin pill swallowing 'metropolitan historians' may not agree with us. As we have said before make up your own mind, this time to determine as to what you think about this tragic and heart wrenching story.

Edward Betts

Killed in Action
France, Sept. 15th 1916
Aged 33.

ON THIS DAY... September 15th 1916 - Tanks were used for the very first time in history, with disastrous consequences.

EDDIE Betts just happened to be in a certain place at a certain time when history was made. For the very first time in 1916 the tank was deployed into battle and would later become one of the most effective and fearsome weapons ever created. On that very first action the tanks that had been conceived and commissioned into war by the British in less than a two year period, created havoc on the battlefields around Flers-Courcelette in France. It wasn't the enemy that came out worse, it was the British and their tanks who were responsible for killing many of their own men and altering general tactics that resulted in huge casualties to themselves. Two outspoken claims I make here, that I will back–up and those to blame will get another literary lashing. I know the 'metropolitan historians' will be choking on their gluten-free yoghurts at the very comments I have just made. Let's hope this story teaches them something and steams up their round-rimmed spectacles.

The modest fee of £39 – that Rob paid for a solitary Victory Medal to a Norfolk infantryman who was gunned down by the crew of a British tank has brought this highly controversial story to you. Once again reckless incompetence by over-ambitious 'Donkey Generals' and their blood thirsty butcher of a Commander-in-Chief, Douglas Haig, cost the lives of many ordinary civilian volunteer British soldiers. Not surprisingly in the wake of the tragic slaughter there was a 'cover-up' and the truth has never fully surfaced to embarrass those responsible – until now.

Edward Betts came from a very tight-knit and loving family. He was born in rural Norfolk, several miles to the west of Norwich in the rather grand sounding hamlet of Great Melton, populated by less than a couple of hundred people. His father George met Eliza Rachel Abbs and the two fell in love and were married in 1876. George spent his whole life working as a woodman on one of the country estates around the area. Virtually all of the land around Great Melton was owned by Major Edward Henry Evans-Lombe. Almost every resident of the hamlet were tenants of his and worked for him in some capacity as did George, it was employment for life and appreciated by those who worked for the Major.

George and Eliza went on to have ten children, including Eddie, eight survived into adulthood, two died in infancy. As well as having to provide for his immediate family the hard working George spent most of his life making sure his sister who couldn't fend for herself was diligently cared for. Mary Ann Betts, known as Polly was Eddie's aunt who lived with the family, they were all close to her. Auntie Polly was always happy and lively despite being blind from birth. The closeness of the family bond was very strong, they struggled financially but stayed together with the local church also helping to provide assistance for Auntie Polly.

Eddie was one of four boys, he had two elder brothers, George and James and a younger male sibling, Lennie. James and Len became carpenters, Eddie and George went on to be bricklayers, all skilled and handy lads. As time marched on Eddie had to move around Norfolk and Suffolk with his job and often stayed in lodgings, intermittently returning to his family home whenever possible. When war broke out Eddie didn't hesitate to join the colours, he had no previous military experience but as a bricklayer he was fit and strong. The local volunteers of the 9th Battalion Norfolk Regiment readily accepted him into their ranks upon their own formation, he signed on at Britannia Barracks, Norwich in September 1914.

This particular battalion was assigned to the 24th Division, notoriously under-equipped and very short of trained officers and NCO's. From the very beginnings his military service was hampered by critical shortages that he probably hadn't expected. Despite that the camaraderie was always abound, all the recruits were local Norfolk lads and the banter was stimulating. The men began their training with no uniforms and wooden rifles around Shoreham. In June of 1915 and still without rifles clad in makeshift outfits they were transferred to Aldershot for their final training period before they would embark for France. Enthusiastic and hardly prepared in the best way, they were however keen and willing to be deployed. Thankfully their Lee Enfield .303 rifles arrived just weeks before they set sail to France.

Eddie was with the original battalion draft that landed at Boulogne on August 30th 1915. The lads had been together for almost a year having only received compromised training due to shortages and had just received their weapons only the month beforehand. Within a day they arrived at Montcavrel where they would remain for further training until September 21st. The 9th Norfolk's were then rapidly route-marched across northern France and made an exhausting and foot-blistering journey to Bapaume. It was then on to a place known as Lonely Tree Hill close to La Bassee where they were placed in readiness to take part in the Battle of Loos.

With very limited experience and no familiarisation with trench life the Norfolk boys were pitted into a horrendous situation after things had gone badly wrong for the British in terms of casualties. On September 25th the British had suffered appalling losses on the first day of the battle. Commander-in-Chief, Sir John French who could only be contacted by the damaged and unreliable French national telephone system at his HQ was a complete and utter buffoon. He had placed the reserves too far back from the main attacking force, they couldn't be deployed to support the first waves who were pummelled, especially the Scots. The following day as part of the hastily assembled reserves in went the Norfolk's amongst others for a repeat performance of slaughter. There had been no centrally consolidated area where waves of attackers could follow each other. The Germans picked off the British after having enough time to re-organise and smash the delayed assaults. John French's butchers' bill for the 9th Battalion Norfolk Regiment at Loos was 446 killed, wounded or missing out of 1,017 inexperienced volunteers in action for the first time, a 44% casualty rate. The commander, who knew more about frolicking and cavorting with women than he did about military tactics was responsible for other hideous butchers' bills at Loos. Some of the battalions who fought under his wretched command went on to receive 90% casualties.

Eddie Betts must have wondered what he had let himself in for after the nightmare of Loos. Many of his chums had perished in front of his eyes never having fired a shot. His brothers-in-arms had been slaughtered like sheep following deranged instructions from a commander who was replaced soon afterwards… by the one and only Douglas Haig, another butcher of even higher proportions. It would be a full year before the 9th Norfolk's would be thrust into a major battle again, at Flers-Courcelette on the Somme. Haig driven by his wild ambitions had already turned a blind eye to the unbelievable casualties his volunteer soldiers had suffered on the Somme, undeterred he launched yet another insane assault.

On September 15th 1916 a great new weapon would be launched upon the Germans. Haig pushed and pressed hard for its inclusion on the battlefield. It was far from ready, its crews were hardly trained and the decision to deploy it at that time was bordering upon madness. Haig was a reckless old fool, he sent in the tanks and still believed his cavalry who were close by, men on horses, would eventually win this battle. To emphasis my point, yes the tank had to be used and tried but should have been done so later on in the war with better trained crews and on a more modest localised scale. Of the 48 tanks sent out that day, 33 broke down in no time. Not surprisingly 15 remaining machines also suffered further mechanical failures resulting in more breakdowns. This alone more than confirms their use at that time was not properly considered. Even British Leyland cars of the 1970's were far more reliable than the British MKI tanks. Haig never properly considered anything but the blinkered arrogance of attrition at any cost. Even after their breakdowns he still sent what was left of the force into battle with catastrophic results.

These thirty-ton monsters were frightening spectacles to behold, as Eddie would soon find out. The tanks came in two versions, the 'male' adaptation with two cannons and three machine guns and the 'female' variety with six machine guns, they had crews of 6 to 8 that included an officer in command of each machine. Part of the strategic tactics drawn up by 'Donkey Generals' were the creation of 'tank lanes'. This in effect meant that British artillery was forbidden to shell the lanes in order not to damage their own advancing tanks. So the Germans got off lightly for there were precious few tanks to actually go down the lanes, they had all broken down. Henceforth, the relatively unmolested German infantry and their machine guns could sweep across the lanes and beyond inflicting severe casualties upon their British counterparts.

On that fateful day Eddie and his comrades from the 9th Norfolk's were ordered to attack a German stronghold position on a 500-yard front, it was known as the Quadrilateral. Men of the 1st Leicester's were alongside them with the 9th Suffolk's supporting. The advancing soldiers had to go forward in column formation and leave a 100-yard corridor for the three tanks that were detailed to support their advance. It was hoped the tanks would scare the living daylights out of the Germans. Two of the tanks failed to reach the start line, leaving just one machine, yes one tank, to take the initiative.

The remaining solitary tank commander was a young officer, 25-year old Second-Lieutenant Basil Henriques, a public school educated boy who went to Harrow and studied history at Oxford. He had no engineering or mechanical background, yet controlled a huge iron monster of a machine. I suppose it would have been like asking a history teacher without a driving licence to drive the bus to school with his pupils aboard. Henriques was under huge pressure, he was alone with his crew, none of whom had ever been in action in a tank before. Almost immediately the Germans started to blast away at it with their artillery, with many high-explosive shells falling upon the Norfolk lads, close by. The badly positioned tank was totally attracting the wrong kind of attention. Inside the roasting hot, fume-filled iron beast the hopelessly clueless Henriques ordered his driver to reverse 20-yards and head for the start line.

All hell then broke loose as the bungling officer completely out of his depth instructed his driver to advance. The tank and its crew headed straight for a British trench containing men of the 9th Norfolk's and the 9th Suffolk's. What happened next is beyond comprehension. I really can't imagine what went through the minds of the East Anglian lads as they saw the colossal tank trundle towards them, then it started to open fire. The 'female' tank had six machine guns. Desperately some of the men leapt out of the trench and dived for cover in nearby shell-holes, only to become easier targets for Henriques and his motley crew of amateurs. The tank men quite obviously thought they were firing at the enemy. In desperation an officer of the 9th Norfolk's, Lieutenant Crosse, risked his life and dashed out right in front of the tank waving his arms wildly to halt the slaughter. Henriques either overcome with the fumes inside the tank or wide-eyed in a fit of fear eventually acknowledged, his machine turned and then headed off once again in the wrong direction.

The beleaguered Norfolk's had to press on leaving their dead and wounded behind, many of them victims of Henriques' incredibly inexperienced bloody foolishness, one of these victims was Eddie Betts as we will confirm. As the night wore on the next assaulting wave reached the positions the Norfolk's had vacated and were shocked by what they found. Men of the 2nd and 14th Durham Light Infantry discovered the trench and in particularly a number of shell holes full of dead and dying men from the 9th Norfolk's and 9th Suffolk's. The Durham lads had arrived on the scene of carnage in the dark at around 22.30 hrs. Tirelessly until the following dawn these men attended to and removed those they thought could be saved, the dead were left behind, for some, very conveniently so. The 9th Norfolk's suffered 436 casualties that day with 161 confirmed deaths, although this figure rose and is not conclusive. With direct regard to Eddie there is one fascinating clue that tells us he was accidently killed by 'friendly fire' from the tank.

A medal index card that details Eddie's medals entitlement is of standard issue. Rob and I have seen literally thousands of examples of this type of document. The vast majority of men who lost their lives during the war have words attached to their index cards. These words range from the following: 'Killed in Action', sometimes abbreviated to 'K.I.A'. 'Died of Wounds', often shortened to 'D.O.W' or simply 'Died', normally donating death by disease or sometimes accident. Rarely, we may come across the word 'Missing' on a card. Never have Rob and I actually seen the following words placed upon an index card from the First World War, they are – 'Died on Active Service'. These are the words on Eddie's card, it doesn't take a genius to work out what they mean based upon the comments I have just made.

Eddie was killed, aged 33-years old by the friendly fire from the tank and the person writing out the medal index card knew that, he broke with convention to write those words, as Rob suggests. I'm not too sure about that but I am certain that Eddie was killed by the tank's machine guns. If the truth had fully been exposed there would have been some very awkward and embarrassing questions directed at certain people, especially senior officers of the tank corps and of Douglas Haig himself. Basil Henriques came from a powerfully influential family, his reputation was therefore protected. He was later wounded and moved on to a more administrative role regarding tank operations. A number of soppy 'metropolitan historians' have gone out of their way to enhance his credibility by expressing that he served with

The very first use of tanks in history resulted in the British inflicting casualties upon their own men, one of whom was Eddie Betts.

distinction. One or two of these rain-mac wearing egg-heads have acknowledged the incident and commented upon the 'several' casualties that occurred. As previously stated we know the Durham lads spent all night clearing the wounded out of those shell holes that were littered with dead bodies. These were the bodies of men who had desperately leapt to their deaths trying to escape the murderous fire of one of their own tank's six machine guns at close range.

The former bricklayer's body was left to rot where he fell along with all of the others, none of the lads were given burials. He was reported as 'missing' just like the rest of the men butchered by their own side that day. The Norfolk volunteer soldiers are now named upon the Thiepval Memorial, their bodies having being left to disintegrate into the mud where they fell in order to preserve certain reputations. A shocking and deplorable piece of British military history has just hereby been exposed.

As for Basil the calamitous tank commander he later became, Sir Basil Lucas Quixano Henriques CBE, JP. There is no doubt that he was an active philanthropist in the dark East End of London in the years between the two world wars. He set up boys clubs for the deprived Jewish youth of the area, Basil was from Portuguese-Jewish stock. The judge served upon the East London Juvenile Court for 32-years and even had a street named after him in Whitechapel. I have seen no details of any remorse from Basil regarding the events of September 15th 1916 published, although it is fair to say that as a human-being he had to live with the consequences of his actions. I'm not sure, nor would it appear is anyone else as to how he really coped with what he had done.

In the little hamlet of Great Melton there are twelve names on the church war memorial, they include that of Eddie and one of his cousins who also fell during the First World War. This memorial was commissioned by the good-hearted local landowner who also added four more names to it. Incredibly, both his daughters, Albinia and Victoria were widowed during the war, not once, but twice each. Their officer husbands died as a result of the conflict. The ladies remarried two more officers and the same tragic circumstances were astonishingly and tragically repeated. Major Evans-Lombe therefore had four son-in-law's names placed upon on the monument alongside the local lads.

On dark still nights it has been said that a phantom white coach speeds through the hamlet of Great Melton, its passengers being four ghostly women dressed all in white. One more spirit has wandered those narrow leafy lanes for over a century now. Eddie Betts never received true justice, neither did his family. Perhaps only now his ghost will fade away and he can finally rest in peace, for that is the very least he deserves.

Unknown Warrior
Served on the Western Front 1917-18.

ON THIS DAY – April 6th 1917 – The USA declares war on the German Empire.

ONE aspect of this publication is that it has the capability to surprise and here we go off our normal course in order to highlight a very important and totally deserving tribute. Rob and I hereby honour the men of the United States of America, 'the doughboys' who fought and died on the Western Front. Not enough credit has ever been given to these guys, many of whom lie forever at peace and far away from home, this is our opportunity to tell their story.

I am able to write this piece because of Rob's purchase of an Allied Victory Medal issued to an American soldier who served in the First World War. Unlike the British version of the Victory Medal the American ones were not named to the recipients. In the absence of detailed provenance – that many of these medals do not have – dedicated research upon an individual is impossible. This medal was purchased from the United States and came with a photograph, as illustrated, we believe the young man who looks out at you from that portrait is the recipient of the medal. What he is responsible for is allowing us to represent all of his comrades in arms, in particular the ones who never made it back to their homes and loved ones.

The involvement of the United States of America in the Great War was pivotal, in a contradiction of terms I have to say it was both under-estimated and over-estimated, this means I really have some work to do here to explain that statement. We will start with the origins of the actual medal and then build from there. Rob paid a total of £46.86 for the Victory Medal that included shipping and packaging. It was sent from Ashford, Connecticut, a village that lies around 80-miles south-west of Boston and 160-miles or so north-east of New York City. We believe there is a strong possibility the young man in the picture was probably local to that area. As the First World War progressed

This picture of an American 'doughboy' came with the medal featured within the story.

the sleepy village of Ashford with a population at the time of just several hundred inhabitants was a world away from the mud, blood and hell of the Western Front, so many thousands of miles away across a vast ocean.

Ashford, Conneitcut, is situated in Windham County, close to the Mount Hope River within the north-eastern coastal forests. It is a back-water, serene, peaceful and typical of rural America, it's an easy place in which to 'chill-out' around several picturesque local lakes and also easily accessible to two of the major cities of the USA. This is the location we believe our man came from, we don't know his name, his age, his religion or background. Maybe his image can paint some kind of picture in your mind. I will refer to him from hereon as 'doughboy', the name given in affection to the US soldiers who served in the First World War.

Okay, so the first job now is to explain the origin of the term 'doughboy' and where it comes from. There are a number of explanations given by various sources, although there is a common belief the term originates from the Mexican-American war (1846-48). I have read all of the differing theories as to the origin. My belief is it was because of the US Army soldier's uniforms that got covered in dust on the Mexican terrain of that war that gave them the appearance of being covered in dough. The name, just like dough to make bread - stuck.

On Monday April 2nd 1917, President Woodrow Wilson boldly asked a special joint session of the U.S Congress for a declaration of war against the German Empire. Two days later the Senate voted in support and finally on Friday April 6th 1917, war was officially declared. President Wilson, a shrewd and very forward thinking leader had taken a huge gamble, for what he perceived was morally correct. The political advantages for him personally he could see upon a horizon, however, I believe they came second to his virtues. Let's not forget Wilson had won an election only the year before by promising to keep America out of the war, he had some guts and the people of his country realised that. Woodrow Wilson did truly believe in the 'American Dream' of freedom and liberty, he also knew that citizens of the USA would have to die for those principals for the sake of mankind, in a foreign land on a far off continent.

President Wilson didn't come to his decision lightly despite being very heavily pressurised by the British in particular. Winston Churchill a very influential man of his time in both world wars knew of the importance of gaining real U.S combat role support and relentlessly pressed hard for it. Churchill, whose mother was an American herself was extremely tactful and I have to say devious in swaying popular opinion, but more importantly opinion of state. He was certainly behind several controversial and some would say conspiracy elements to get America into both world wars. Whatever I or anyone else may say about him, he was successful in doing so.

The British naval blockade of Germany led them to resume their programme of unrestricted submarine warfare in 1917. Two years earlier they had called it off after the controversial sinking of the ocean liner 'Lusitania'. Almost 1,200 people had died as a result of the destruction of that vessel by a German submarine, 128 of them were U.S citizens. Germany did not want to provoke America in to declaring war. By 1917 the whole situation had changed. Russia had been knocked out of the war releasing hundreds and hundreds of thousands of experienced German soldiers to fight upon the Western Front. The French and British having already suffered horrendous and unsustainable casualties were alarmed at Russia's withdrawal from the conflict. As for the Germans, they were not worried by the American declaration of war against them at that time and believed they could be victorious before the USA could make any real difference. German intelligence knew what everyone else did. America was mighty, strong and powerful but was hopelessly unprepared for war in 1917, the Germans had time upon their side and all they needed to do was exploit it.

The British had declared war back in August 1914 with limited resources but reasonably well prepared for what was to come, despite being heavily outnumbered when they arrived in France and Belgium. By the skin of their teeth they managed to hold on and defy the numerically superior Germans. In 1917, the USA had a very small regular standing army of around 130,000 men scattered across the whole of their vast country. These soldiers would have to be mobilised, organised, trained and relocated to the eastern seaboard for embarkation to Europe. Mass recruitment would also have to be organised to swell their numbers as the British had done previously. The common belief was that it would take around two years to bring the U.S strength to its maximum, I would have to agree with that. By 1919, at least 100 mighty American Divisions could be assembled to smash the enemy, but it was only 1917.

Recruitment wasn't as straight-forward as anticipated. The densely populated areas of the north-eastern part of the USA were particularly targeted. Only a year before the British had handled the Easter Rising regarding Irish independence in Dublin in a highly controversial manner, making martyrs out of many of the ringleaders by executing them. The prime area of U.S recruitment was home to hundreds of thousands of Irish-Americans who resented the British. Nevertheless, the multi-cultural mix of American society swung behind their 'doughboys' and by 1918 they had volunteered in huge numbers. Logistics though still presented the greatest challenge, enthusiasm and patriotism don't win wars.

The first American soldiers had reached France by June of 1917, they had no actual combat experience and although reasonably well-armed many of them had to be equipped with uniforms by the French and British. Chirpy and enthusiastic 'doughboys' had arrived by whatever means could be made available, ocean liners had been requisitioned alongside other vessels. Senior allied commanders looked upon the keen newly arrived Americans as amateurs and to a degree they had a point. The 'doughboys' had to prove their worth, tragically and with a great deal of sorrow I have to say they tried too hard during their first year period at the front. Most of the 'doughboys' were extremely inexperienced, their officers especially so, but they were brave guys. With less than 90,000 men in the field by November 1917 who were only partially equipped to fight they were caught out too many times in their quest to prove themselves. The Germans inflicted many casualties upon them in the stages leading to the summer of 1918. Despite battling in support of the more experienced French and British, the Americans fighting often in clustered groups were too many times relatively easily picked off. The 'doughboys' didn't give up and became more and more determined, skilful and ruthless as time went on.

Commanding the American Expeditionary Force during 1917-18 was General John J. Pershing. He was a self-determined character and a veteran of the 6th U.S Cavalry who had fought the Sioux and Apache tribes in the Indian wars. He was also a veteran of the Spanish-American war. Pershing was an intelligent and robust thinker and had led a chequered life. He had once been a teacher to African-American students. Promotions seemed to come his way faster than those of his contemporaries that often caused resentment, he was the right man for the job on many occasions. Known as 'Black Jack Pershing' his characteristics were somewhat stand-offish, reserved and stern, he knew that he commanded respect because of his demeanour and wasn't afraid to exercise discipline at any given opportunity. His attitude became more focused upon his duties after his wife and three of his four children had been tragically killed in a fire. John J. Pershing was a decent General who genuinely held respect where it was due for those who served under him. He was intelligent, perceptive and didn't suffer fools gladly. From a standing start with a very small force of just 130,000 men Pershing mustered together two million more in just a year and a half, this figure would have more than doubled if the war had continued beyond 1918.

Now I refer back to our 'doughboy'. From the photograph and accompanying paperwork that came from Connecticut here we have a cavalryman. His uniform displays service stripes denoting that he was on the Western Front as it was in 1917 and 1918, also serving at some point in 1919. After some more research I have to suggest that our man served with the mounted 2nd U.S. Cavalry Regiment in Belgium. American victory medals have campaign clasps attached to their ribbons that demonstrate where the individual actually saw battle action. The 'doughboy' we have here had no such clasps. Men of the 2nd U.S Cavalry had been despatched to guard field trains, depots and also had to perform some reconnaissance duties without actually being utilised in battle. Our man still had to cope with being under fire and the constant danger of being maimed or killed. Interestingly the term 'doughboy' has been stated as a reference used by cavalrymen of a different period to describe the dusty men of the infantry.

So maybe our man is technically not a 'doughboy', food for thought.

There is absolutely no doubt the Americans were welcomed when they arrived in France in 1917. Huge crowds of civilians lined the streets and cheered them on when they landed at St. Nazaire. The French by that time had taken a severe mauling in terms of casualties. Many had lost husbands, fathers, sons and brothers in the defence of their homeland. Continuous slaughter was starting to influence mutinous elements within the French armies. The British High Command had also failed to learn from their horrendous campaigns of attrition, Arras in 1917 had been the latest. With many good experienced fighting men still in resource Haig instead of building a huge tactical consolidation ring-fence, continued with his tactics of assault and attrition. Hundreds of the thousands more men were lost later that year at Ypres, Passchendaele and Cambrai. An opportunity of fortifying the front with a wall of steel had been lost. The war had been raging for three years, the British and French military leaders wanted to finish it at all costs. A prospect of continuing as far as 1919 when the Americans would overwhelm the enemy – and effectively win the war - was unthinkable to the brass hats like Haig. Instead he threw in conscripted men in their late forties and fifties and continued slaughtering two generations of ordinary civilian volunteer soldiers.

Pershing learned very quickly, the already physically strong Americans were given tougher training to increase their fighting capabilities. His absolute insistence upon obtaining maximum individual physical output from his men started to pay off. The Americans fought their first major campaign alongside the French at the Battle of Cantigny towards the end of May 1918. They proved their worth and considerably raised the morale of their French allies. General Pershing was very keen to embark upon a strategic and well tactically organised American led assault. In one of the most ground-breaking and innovative moves of the war that set the standards of modern warfare this was carried out. A huge American led campaign at St. Mihiel between September 12th-16th 1918 with the French in support co-ordinated infantry, tank and air attack. From there the Americans caused further serious problems for the Germans at the Argonne. The retreating enemy then began to realise what they would have to face if the war was to go on against formidable U.S orchestrated and ongoing military might.

American successes at St. Mihiel and at the Meuse-Argonne were significant turning points but not completely decisive. French and especially British further involvements in the war were critically important. The USA did not win the First World War, they certainly contributed to its finale. A beleaguered German high command realised that it would only be a matter of time before huge numbers of Americans would flood on to the frontlines to launch similar campaigns. I am of the opinion this fact alone heavily influenced them to eventually sign an Armistice less than two months later.

John Joseph 'Black Jack' Pershing wasn't in favour of the Armistice as it became. He stated the Germans should have been taken all the way back to Berlin and forced to sign an unconditional surrender. Pershing warned that if the whole of the process wasn't handled robustly they would one day return in anger to the Western Front. He was right, just over twenty years later Nazi Germany, embittered by the terms of the Armistice did return with catastrophic and overwhelming ruthlessness.

Our 'doughboy' made it back home, conflicting figures of American casualties, the unlucky 'doughboys' who didn't get back across the Atlantic are questionable. With some consideration I estimate the American war cemeteries of the First World War in France, Belgium and England and the memorials to the missing dead number around 125,000. I believe around 210,000 U.S 'doughboys' were also wounded. These figures represent a huge and gloriously brave loss to a nation that gave the lives of their boys in a relatively very short period of time.

Various sources in the United States often complain and with some justification that the sacrifice the nation made during the First World War has often been overshadowed. Publicity relating to the Second World War and the conflict in Vietnam often takes the spotlight. I really do hope that any American reading this understands that around 125,000 'doughboys' of so long ago lie so far away in foreign fields and will never return home. The boys from New York, Chicago, Boston, San Francisco, Houston, San Antonio, Denver, Tucson, Washington and so many other locations across the USA went to fight on behalf of others for what all decent human-beings believe in, liberty and freedom.

Ahmad

Died
Mesopotamia November 11th 1918
Age Unknown.

ON THIS DAY – November 11th 1918 – The signing of an Armistice between the Allies and the Germans, effectively delivered a conclusion of the conflict on the Western Front.

NOVEMBER 11th upon the calendars of the civilised world represents a day of special significance. It was on that particular date back in 1918 that an Armistice was signed that brought to an end hostilities between Germany and the allied nations that had fought against her. The First World War, a conflict of utter unparalleled devastation especially on the Western Front in France and Belgium was to all intents and purposes finally over. In the very most part it was, however, skirmishes continued in other parts of the world, especially involving the British. By 1919 the war was truly over after the signing of the Treaty of Versailles.

The British Empire and her Dominions had fought a bloody campaign that collectively cost the lives of more than one million of their fighting men. On Armistice Day we come together to remember them and those who fell in other conflicts. We also hold the main service on Remembrance Sunday upon the closest day to November 11th, recognising the Armistice was actually signed upon the Sabbath. Occasionally as a matter of co-incidence the two days actually fall together as they did on the centenary of the signing of the Armistice, Sunday November 11th 2018.

Ahmad was one of 370,000 men who volunteered to join the British Indian Army from the Punjab region, made up of Muslim, Sikh and Hindu soldiers.

Personally, I have attended countless events, parades and commemorations upon those dates throughout my life. I have marched many times alongside veterans and a superb brass band with the 'United Services Veterans Association' of which I hold a life membership. In 2017 I had the honour of being a standard bearer on Remembrance Sunday at Stockton, Teeside, on behalf of another association. I have also been invited to numerous civic functions and made speeches of dedication. Also, as a member of the Jullundur Brigade Association I especially remember the many thousands of Indian soldiers, all volunteers who gave their lives for our cause. The sacrifices these men made have all too often been understated or completely ignored. Here we bring you the story of Ahmad, just an ordinary insignificant man from a desolate area of the Punjab who lost his life. He died on the very day that millions of people in many parts of the world celebrated the end of a war that had taken away so much and changed the world forever.

There are only a few information sources available regarding this soldier, one of those being the fact that he was called Ahmad. We have his service number and the unit in which he served, the name of his father, a man called Nathu and the place where he is commemorated, that's all. Based upon the very basic details we possess my position and duty is to provide essential accuracy where and when I can. Large parts of this story will be based upon the knowledge and experience I hold to provide theoretical and conjectural consistency, Rob assists as always with his own opinions and specialist military knowledge.

First of all we start with Ahmad's sole surviving legacy, a single Victory Medal that Rob purchased from a well-known associate. The medal is in poor condition with its suspender ring and ribbon missing. Over the years it has found its way from the Gujrat region to Scotland, Lancashire and Yorkshire. So here we go, let me do my level best to describe the life of Ahmad, our mysterious soldier.

The recruitment of Indian soldiers had ran at a steady pace, all were volunteers. In the days of the British Empire they were organised upon similar lines as the British with the vast majority of their officers being from England. Typically an Indian volunteer would enlist between the ages of 18 and 23, either before or after serving some form of rudimentary apprenticeship normally associated with agriculture or construction. Many more young Indian men chose a military career simply to avoid a life of poverty. When the war broke out carefully placed recruitment posters often encouraged more enlistment from the huge Indian peasant population.

Support was forthcoming, men volunteered to fight in large numbers.

One of the most predominant regions for enlistment was the Punjab now an integral part of both India and Pakistan. The later was formed in 1947 after British colonial rule. Ahmad was a Muslim who came from the Kotla area around the Gujrat region of the Punjab that is now a part of modern day Pakistan. From the Punjab 190,000 Muslims, 97,000 Sikh's and 83,000 Hindu's volunteered to join the British Indian Army, a considerable proportion of the whole of that force. Brave men from different faiths fought and died side by side right from almost the beginning of the war. The Lahore Division was engaged upon the Western Front in 1914 and arrived before any of the British volunteer battalions.

Ahmad came from a very small and rural community and I suspect his literacy was pretty limited, he would have been able to understand the Koran and learned about reading from there on. The definition of his name means 'much praised'. His father was called Nathu, a particular name suggesting someone hard-working, diligent and independent who gets tasks completed from start to finish. For some unexplained reason I suspect he could have been a carpenter, representing an essential trade. Ahmad may have followed in his father's footsteps explaining why he was selected to join the 3rd Sappers and Miners of the Indian Army who became Divisional Engineers. I think it is likely that Ahmad held a particular skill associated with engineering. Taking a look at the area where he was from, dominated by agriculture and farming it is reasonable to speculate that he had carpentry abilities, hence his selection to an army engineering company. I further speculate Ahmad was in his early twenties when he did enlist with an already existing knowledge of his trade. His service number defines that he attested in the later part of 1915 or possibly early 1916.

From the information relayed so far I believe that Ahmad was not with the original draft of the 3rd Sappers and Miners part of the 3rd (Lahore) Division that arrived in France in 1914. Without doubt he served with the Mesopotamian Expeditionary Force and I believe he joined the Lahore Division before they found themselves stationed within Mesopotamia in 1916. Upon his arrival he was sent to the HQ of the Divisional Engineers joining one of the three engineering field companies of the 3rd Sappers and Miners alongside the one pioneer company of Sikhs. All of these men were originally stationed at Samarra in central Mesopotamia on the banks of the Tigris River north of Baghdad. At short notice he could be deployed anywhere within the country to carry out his duties normally moving to a destination point by night for cover of protection.

So where and what is Mesopotamia? Nowadays the land is called Iraq. An ancient civilisation has existed there for thousands of years between the two rivers of Euphrates and Tigris. The area had been conquered and inhabited by various tribal factions over the centuries. From the sixteenth century until the twentieth it was the Ottoman Turks who dominated Mesopotamia. The Turks were allied to the Germans during the First World War who influenced them very heavily with military advice, support and command. As far as the British were concerned the interests of the land had to be controlled and taken. With enormous influence throughout the middle-east and with some support from certain Arab factions, the British realised that one commodity was absolutely essential to secure. The very commodity you will not be surprised at me revealing was oil. Britain's mighty Royal Navy of the time was becoming virtually oil dependent, Britain wanted and needed the oil.

The vast majority of soldiers deployed in British interests within Mesopotamia were Indian and came from all parts of the sub-continent, some of which are today known as Pakistan, Bangladesh (originally, East Pakistan) and Sri Lanka (Ceylon) after the partitions of the former India in 1947. Rob suggests an interesting theoretical background as to why. He says the British had a history of deploying troops from certain parts of the world to areas where they could cope. Referring here to climate, terrain, disease and a lack of resources he has a point. Colonial soldiers were never treated as equals in the mind-sets of some of those who wielded power. Ahmad certainly didn't have it easy at all. The threat of disease was greater than that of actually being killed in enemy action. Most of the time the climate was incredibly hostile, temperatures regularly exceeded 50-degrees centigrade, conditions in which he had to work in a manual capacity. Fresh water and food supplies were haphazardly distributed when available and road networks were in the most part non-existent. Medical supplies and treatment facilities left more than a lot to be desired as I will later explain. Ahmad certainly had much to contend with, survival would have been his priority.

At this point I will express my own controversial opinions as to why I think the British deployed mainly Indian soldiers to Mesopotamia. Firstly, they knew that confrontations with the Turks were inevitable. Despite what had happened at Gallipoli the British still regarded the Turkish soldiers as inferior warriors and were confident they could be handled by the Indians serving under British officers. Secondly, Great Britain, the island nation had created the largest empire the world had ever seen. How had they achieved such a feat? Using the principal of 'divide and conquer' as far as I am concerned and they were damn good at it. The Indian soldiers of the time came from an India before partition with a huge Muslim population. A large number of Indian soldiers were of the Islamic faith and the Ottoman Turks were themselves Muslims. I don't think co-incidence plays a part when I state the British knew exactly what they were doing. Pitching huge numbers of their colonial Indian Muslim soldiers against fellow Muslims from Turkey was a test of loyalty in more ways than one. The Germans who themselves were of the Christian faith hypocritically encouraged the Turks to create Jihad [holy war] against the British colonial soldiers in Mesopotamia.

After studying official deployment records I know that Ahmad was actually in Mesopotamia after the British had suffered a humiliating defeat at Kut-al-Amara in 1916. The 3rd Sappers and Miners were redeployed to Palestine in the early part of 1918, Ahmad didn't go with them and remained in Mesopotamia. After some long discussions Rob and I have both come to an agreement as to why we think he was left behind although we could be wrong. All three of the possibilities we debated between ourselves are offered to you to form your own opinions.

The first theory is that he developed a serious medical condition or disease and was hospitalised. Medical facilities in the Mesopotamian theatre of war were at best rudimentary and at worse utterly appalling. We both doubt that he would have survived for a prolonged period of time had he contracted a serious illness. Medicines and trained medical personnel were always in short supply and sometimes completely unavailable. If a soldier became sick in Mesopotamia he would be fortunate to survive more than a couple of weeks if not evacuated.

A second possibility is that he was wounded. Again we have to look at the provisions available. The lack of trained physicians meant that operations on injured men, especially within the poorly equipped Indian units were sometimes carried out in what I can only describe as horrendous conditions. At times surgical procedures in some instances were similar to those carried out during the medieval period. Sepsis, infections and gangrene were all common even after relatively minor wounds had been treated. In some instances 'volunteers' had to carry out necessary amputations. Unqualified men were asked to take brave decisions to crudely and clumsily hack-off the infected limbs of their stricken comrades. This was particularly harsh for any Muslim soldier who had to endure such a horror. Without any anaesthetic or morphine available, alcohol was often administered in a desperate attempt to ease the suffering. Muslims on account of their religious beliefs would refuse the alcohol, what they went through is beyond the imagination. No blame here is attached to the Indian medical personnel, for they were so badly equipped and in such short supply of qualified numbers. We both doubt that Ahmad could have been treated and cared for had he been wounded. Several months had passed since the last of his comrades from the 3rd Sappers and Miners had left him behind for Palestine.

This leaves one other theory that we have both agreed upon but can't conclusively prove. It is quite possible that Ahmad was captured and taken as a prisoner of war. The fact that he was a Muslim wouldn't have gone down very well with his Islamic captors and he more than likely would have been severely beaten. As an engineer and one with a skill he may have been regarded as useful, especially if he had been as I have suggested, a carpenter. Prisoner of war camps in Mesopotamia were horrific places but still had to be fenced off with barbed wire fortifications. Ahmad, if he had worked upon them would have been issued with survivable rations. We believe he was literally kept alive because he served a purpose to his captors, this would not last as the war for the Turks was coming to an end in defeat.

Since the early part of 1917 the British had reinforced Mesopotamia with many more soldiers from India and Britain under the skilful command of Major-General Stanley Maude. The commander had captured Baghdad in the March of that year and his men were gaining the upper hand against a determined, stubborn and awkward Turkish resistance. Eventually at the end of October 1918 they were completely victorious when the Turks signed an Armistice. Skirmishing did however continue between local tribal factions, some from over the border in Syria. The war was over in Mesopotamia, so what happened to Ahmad?

Defeated, the Turkish captors had fled, Ahmad was effectively free, without provisions, food and with little water available in a deserted scorched wasteland. The malnourished young man somehow had to reach safety and survive. We believe that he did in a very poor physical state after his months in captivity. His weakened physical health could have left him susceptible to contracting a disease. Not long after the Turks had surrendered Ahmad died, I believe in isolation. By that time medical provisions of all kinds were virtually exhausted but specialist isolation wards had been created. The personnel who worked within them were themselves exposed to the threat of contracting a deadly disease. When patients inevitably passed away at an alarming rate they were gathered together and hastily buried in unmarked mass graves.

Ahmad has no known grave, he is commemorated on the Basra Memorial to the missing. To certain people of the time and others since his sacrifice meant little or nothing at all. He was just another Indian soldier, just 'Ahmad' who died and probably disappeared into a mass grave amongst others. I have only one thing to say to people who may still hold those opinions. Ahmad's life was worth exactly the same as that of any other human being. If he was discarded like a piece of trash then there is nothing I nor Rob can do about that. What we can do and we ask you to do is to just spare one thought for Ahmad on Remembrance Sunday. He was one of around 70,000 men who perished in horrific circumstances from what is now India, Pakistan, Bangladesh and Sri Lanka. All of these men had volunteered to fight for what they were told and believed was right, they were loyal and brave. Ahmad is not and will never be forgotten, his story remains here for evermore, as does his ultimate sacrifice.

DEATH UNBECOMING

THROUGHOUT this publication we have examined the demise of our subjects in often tragic and sometimes harrowing circumstances. The basic human instinct of survival has always been apparent amongst those of whom have fought in wars. Very few men volunteered to fight expecting to die in battle even though they were aware of the inevitable risks. If death did meet any of them quite often it was sudden and unexpected. Even when it was imminent when outnumbered and surrounded, men still fought on to their last breath to survive. For some, tortured in their minds, or wracked with pain, death was a release, it was an escape.

In this final chapter we take a look at five more real people who became victims of the First World War but not as a result of a direct confrontation with the enemy. The men featured are not unique as in the way they met their deaths. Stories of people like our subjects chronicled here are the ones that are never told. I have previously stated on more than one occasion there are no winners in a war, only losers. This chapter should open the eyes of those who think that wars are necessary or others who regard them as glorious. The five guys featured were once just like you or I, you could have walked past them in the street and they wouldn't have warranted a second glance, they were ordinary everyday folk.

We have to make you aware that a couple of stories within this chapter make prominent references to issues relating to the tragic circumstances of suicide. Some of the content is both distressing and shocking.

William Greenwood

Suicide or Murder?
Jan 3rd 1916
Aged 49.

ONE of my favourite activities is walking with my dog, a 'giant' Yorkshire terrier called Jenson, who like me is from Lancashire. From our home in Burnley we often make our way down to the canal where we feed the local ducks, it's peaceful and relaxing for us both. Jenson the 'Yorkshireman' I am sure will always continue to enjoy trotting down the tow-path, for me, things have changed a little. I don't feel as comfortable as I once did these days strolling down the canal-side. Another Yorkshireman has something to do with that.

Bill Greenwood came into this world a complete century before I did in 1866. He was born in Rob's hometown of Leeds, Yorkshire. On a cold and frosty morning his lifeless body was fished out of a canal, apparently he had taken his own life, an inquest was held and a jury returned a verdict of… 'Suicide whilst of unsound mind'. Details of those proceedings will obviously be provided within this story of Bill's life. There will be a second inquest into the tragic circumstances surrounding this man's death, it will be held right here by Rob and myself. I will say that our verdict may shock you. The 'metropolitan historians' will especially accuse me of sensationalism as they chew upon their celery sticks. As ever, we ask you to make up your own minds. There are always two sides to a story.

In a statement of fact here and now, neither I myself or Rob can conclusively prove what we are about to publish. Once again we rely upon our experiences and knowledge and use very considered conjecture to at least try and bring about justice for an ordinary man. In a bold and very

William Greenwood was found face down floating in a canal in highly suspicious circumstances.

controversial statement right here and now we believe he was murdered because of what people perceived as his sexuality and disapproved of it. In the male dominated world of the army of the time volunteer soldiers were being converted into ruthless and merciless killers in readiness for war. Homosexuality of course existed within that environment, it was ruthlessly forbidden and the punishments for those caught were harsh. An immediate jail sentence of a minimum of two years would be handed down to any men who had engaged in sexual acts with each other. Severe beatings were often administered to those who were suspected of being a 'queer' the common term of the day that refereed to gay men. Remarkably, homosexuality was also seen as being unpatriotic on the basis that physical intimacy between two men could not reproduce children to help replace fallen soldiers who had been killed at the front. It was also described as 'Germanic' in an absurd attempt at propaganda that suggested many German men were homosexuals. The practice of homosexuality between consenting adults was illegal until 1967 in the UK. In the military there were undoubtedly many brave men who gave their lives who just happened to be gay, it was their secret.

Bill was a single man, he had never married. His life until the final and shockingly dramatic last part had been mundane. He had achieved relatively little throughout his life but had served for twelve years in the British Army from a young age. On January 1st 1886 he joined the West Yorkshire Regiment and was allocated the service number of 1226. Bill was 19-years old when he made the decision to embark upon what he hoped would be a great adventure. After completing his basic training he was posted to India a year later where he formed part of a garrison to police the area of the north-west frontier. He remained in India for a number of years before transferring to the army first-class reserve in December 1893. Bill was finally discharged as time-expired on December 31st 1898, he had been a very ordinary soldier who hadn't distinguished himself and had never risen in the ranks. William Greenwood was for official purposes rated as third-class, he must have been disappointed and then just got on with life as best he could.

As the years passed by he worked in a foundry as an iron dresser. A low-paid and dirty job that involved the cleaning of moulds and cast iron. By the time war had been declared he had already reached the age of forty-eight. The average life expectancy of a manual worker from an industrialised town or city at that time was between fifty and sixty, Bill was reaching that milestone. Living alone at nearly fifty, never having married and considering what happened in the final part of his life both Rob and I think Bill was a gay man. In September 1914 he went to enlist and I have to say at that time I am very surprised he was accepted on account of his age. Rob is quick to make an observation regarding his attestation. Bill was posted to an infantry battalion the 9th West Riding (Duke of Wellington's), he was an experienced former soldier who would need little or no training that his ageing body could not cope with. There were other essential roles older men carried out within infantry battalions and one of those was being engaged in work at the cookhouse. Potatoes had to be peeled, basic meals had to be prepared and served. Bill was sent to the cookhouse more than likely knowing that he would have been. He was in an all-male environment that we think suited him for his own reasons. The veteran was an experienced man of the world and most likely the oldest soldier in the entire battalion. Bill would have known the routines of discretion, however in the volatile and bawdy conditions of base camps discretion could not offer guarantees of secrecy or safety. Someone, somewhere within this battalion of working-class mill workers, coal miners and railwaymen either knew or suspected he was gay.

It was a very busy time for Bill in the cookhouses of four camps as the battalion, recruited entirely of volunteers from Halifax, Huddersfield and parts of Leeds moved around in preparation for war. In less than a year Bill moved to Wareham, Bovington, Wimbourne and Hursley Park before embarking with the original draft to France in July 1915. Rob hastens to point out that he feels it highly unlikely that Bill actually got involved in any front line duties and would have continued in a role of catering for the nutritional needs of the men.

As a highly experienced former soldier Rob remarks that some of the younger recruits would have seen Bill as something of a kindly uncle figure at the camps. They were away from their mother's for the very first time. 'Old Bill' would have provided a measure of reassurance and there is some evidence from documentation that he got along well with people when engaged in his work at camps in England. Things quickly turned sour for Bill in France. Conditions were not as they had been at camp. Men were stressed, constantly on their guard and had opportunities of dishing out their own methods of justice in conditions that could not always be monitored by officers. At this point I wonder if Bill had mistakenly made an amorous assumption, if so, it led directly to his downfall.

After less than three months at the front Bill was invalided home and sent to the Lincoln War Hospital where he spent a further two months recovering from his injuries. During the period of his time at the front his battalion had been sent from St. Omer in France to an area south of Ypres in Belgium where the men took up trench familiarisation duties. The battalion did not see action until 1916. Bill an old man of his time had received injuries so serious that he had to be evacuated and hospitalised in England. Like the rest of his comrades he had not seen any action with the enemy, so what happened to him?

Bill had suffered a 'rupture' as it was described without any further details. A rupture is often caused by an external impacting force, such as a beating or a sexual assault. A metal or tough leather scabbard is a sheath pouch for a bayonet, a sharp and deadly blade that attaches to the end of a rifle. Both Rob and I believe that Bill was sexually assaulted by having a scabbard inserted through his rectum that in turn caused the rupture. This was a hideous form of unofficial punishment that was administered randomly and cruelly. It was not as uncommon in the trenches as some would like us to believe. Gay soldiers constantly lived in fear of a 'beasting'. Of course had the perpetrators been caught they would have been subjected to the weight of military law regarding this form of torture. Sometimes those in authority such as non-commissioned officers turned a 'blind eye' to this crime, on occasions they administered this appalling cruelty themselves. I suppose the 'metropolitan historians' are now mopping their sweaty brows in disbelief with their eyes watering, yes, 'beastings' happened as sickening and shocking acts of brutality.

Having poured over the accounts of his final months from transcripts delivered at the inquest into his subsequent death less than three months later I am deeply disturbed by my findings. So much so that I asked Rob directly to assist me and hold a second unofficial inquest in to Bill's death. During his period of two months in hospital at Lincoln, Bill became very depressed, his state of mental health deteriorated rapidly and he began to talk of something that may happen to him. Quite obviously he was frightened, however to the authorities he was insignificant, just an old man, of the lowest rank. Hospital beds were needed, he had to go. Some knew the nature of his injuries and cared little about his obvious dilemmas and fears. In mid-December he was duly transferred to the 11th Battalion West Riding Regiment. This was a reserve battalion comprising of older volunteers and ones being marked out for promotion. These men were not particularly tolerant. Frustrated at not being posted to the front they could get passes from their camp at Brocton on Cannock Chase to go out drinking in Walsall and Wolverhampton. The men of the 11th were rough and ready, this is where Bill was sent to the cookhouse upon the base camp.

Within two weeks he was so concerned about what he described was being said about him that he feared for his safety. He also remarked that he could receive ten years in jail if what was being rumoured regarding his conduct by other men in the cookhouse was true. We believe this statement relates directly to acts of homosexual behaviour. Ironically, on the thirtieth anniversary of his very first attestation into the army he made an appointment and was seen by his company officer. It was new Years' Day 1916. The officer clearly didn't rate his complaints as serious enough to conduct an official inquiry. He made some verbal attempts to find out if there was any truth in Bill's claims that came to nothing. He also ordered Bill to put down his concerns in writing, the frightened old soldier did so accordingly. The conclusion on the part of the officer was that the matter was trivial and akin to 'tittle tattle'. He also warned Bill that if he wanted to pursue the complaint he would have to take measures against the accused individuals. The ambiguous and uncaring pompous ass of an officer wasn't interested.

Old Bill's fears and despair heightened as his tormentors laughed and taunted him, even their officer had let them off the hook with what amounted to the bullying of an ageing soldier. Could they now get away with what they perceived as a threat, by murdering the old 'queer' and get away with it? A day later Bill disappeared, on the following day, January 3rd 1916, he was officially reported as 'missing'. In view of the circumstances of his complaint and obvious signs of distress and with some people describing Bill as hallucinating, news of his disappearance didn't come as a surprise. We still have to ask why there is no record of anyone at all making any kind of an effort to find him, including the military police

On the cold Monday morning of January 24th 1916, Bill's body was spotted at 11' o'clock in the morning floating in a canal close to a farm in Newtown, Bloxwich. Several men had made the gruesome discovery at the same time, one of them who gave evidence in court was a coal-miner. He was not asked as to why he or the other men he was with were not at work at the time of the discovery of the body. William Greenwood was dressed in his uniform, although his puttees that wrapped around the lower legs and his cap were missing, his pockets were also empty. He had been missing for almost three weeks.

The official inquest was a very hasty affair and took place just two days later on Wednesday January 26th 1916, at Bloxwich police station. How on earth the police, and other officials could bring together proper evidence as to the circumstances of the death in such a short time has never been explained. It has to be said the police had almost immediately ruled out 'foul-play' and that the inquest would merely be a formality, as it turned out it was. In my opinion it was farcical with no consideration being made to adjourn and examine the facts more precisely.

Mr. J. F. Addison presided, he being the Borough Coroner. Addison heard evidence from just one of those who found Bill's body, miner, William Hancox. He explained that when they spotted the body they went off to inform the police, when they arrived back on the scene the police had already arrived and recovered the body from the water. Inspector Haycock and Police-Constable Vaughn had removed the clothing and discovered the identity disc around Bill's neck confirming who he was. It seems rather odd the police arrived so quickly, there were no forms of telephone or radio communication, they appeared to have arrived at the canal before Hancox and his many pals had actually made it to the station.

Bill's legs were bound loosely by a leather shoelace and his hands by a khaki handkerchief. Both the police officers and the doctor [Dr McDonald] in attendance at the inquest agreed that Bill had bound himself by using his hands to tie the shoelaces around his feet. In a ludicrous statement thereafter they claimed that he had tied the hankie around his hands with his teeth and then jumped into the canal where he subsequently drowned. The only other evidence provided by these men was to confirm that Bill had died as a result of suffocation by drowning and that no other marks were upon his body. They also confirmed that he had been in the water for a prolonged period of time. Private John Hudson a comrade of Bill's stated that he knew of him as having a cheery disposition but that his demeanour had changed since he had left hospital. Hudson also reaffirmed that Bill's fears were unfounded. The nervous soldier in the witness box had a lot upon his shoulders, did he really dare tell the truth?

The shambolic inquest was brought to an end in a hurry with the jury all in agreement. Borough Coroner Addison directed towards the verdict of 'Suicide whilst of unsound mind'. He ridiculously ruled out foul-play upon the grounds that nobody would have bound Bill so loosely and that he intended to drown himself after suffering from hallucinations. In those days suicide was a criminal offence, it could not be punished because the perpetrator was dead. People who had taken their own lives were often not buried in consecrated ground, their bodies were given to local hospital authorities and medical research was performed upon individual corpses, this was standard practice. Bill was buried in Walsall (Bloxwich) Cemetery, he has an official headstone… he is buried in consecrated ground.

So now to our inquest, first of all our verdict – 'Death caused by a person or persons unknown, murder'. William Greenwood was an extremely vulnerable ageing man. He had requested protection from an officer and that had been denied, he wouldn't have gone to ask for help had he not felt it necessary. If he had been subject to fits of hallucinations he would not have been on duty. Bill had obviously just come off-duty and the first thing a soldier of that period did was remove his uncomfortable puttees. He would also have put down his cap and more than likely emptied the possessions of his pockets into his locker or cabinet. All these traits indicate that he was aware of what he was doing as per normal routine. It was a cold and frosty night on only the second day of January in wartime. If he had decided to walk across the frozen Cannock Chase to the canal, a journey in the dark that took quite some time he would have left the camp and either been spotted by a patrol or the duty guard. Bill would have been stopped for being improperly dressed for a start and secondly be asked to explain why he was leaving camp. Yes, he could have sneaked away, do you really believe that he did so with the intention of walking for miles in the freezing night before drowning himself?

Rob suggests Bill was set upon and murdered in a manner that would have left no marks upon the body. There were plenty of experienced men in the camp who could have done this by a method of asphyxiation. Perhaps someone or some others had secrets of their own sexuality to hide? Or more than likely the rampant homophobia that existed at the time within the camp was responsible. The section of canal at Bloxwich was a relatively quiet one where Bill was found floating three weeks after his disappearance. Transport from the base at Brocton camp regularly collected supplies from the canal narrowboats. Bill's body could have been concealed within the transport and at a point dumped into the canal, perhaps initially weighted down. Neither Rob nor I believe for one minute that his body would remain undiscovered within a commercial water canal lane for three weeks.

The notion that he tied his hands together with a hankie using his teeth is ridiculous and almost mythical, it was also claimed that his feet were loosely tied with a shoelace. A sad fact is that the majority of people who make suicide attempts almost immediately regret their deed and try to take evasive action, not always successfully. We cannot accept that a man would throw himself into a canal of water and simply remain still whilst waiting to drown, especially one so loosely bound. We believe at some point he would quite easily have been able to remove the shoelace or the hankie without much of a struggle within the shallow water. Bill was a soldier, a veteran with over a dozen years of experience, an expert with weaponry who had available access to firearms at the base camp. Surely if he had wanted to take his own life he would simply have put a bullet through his brain.

There was no final letter, no mention of suicidal intentions and the whole grotesque discovery of the body and very hastily arranged inquest both seem to throw up more questions than answers. We believe that Bill's hands and feet had been bound by someone else. I further suggest that for a period of time his body had been submerged in the water to allow the lungs to fill with water and conceal the real cause of his suffocation. It was no co-incidence that 'several' men conveniently discovered his body and that the police arrived before it was officially reported. William Greenwood although frightened, distressed and worried did not deliberately throw himself into a canal to drown himself. He was killed by those who could not bear to be alongside the person that he was.

The purchase of Bill's single British War Medal by Rob for a mere -£38 has uncovered one of the most controversial individual stories of a British soldier of the First World War. Importantly we have revealed the deplorable and shocking social attitudes that were practised and endorsed by sections of society at every level, relatively speaking, not so long ago in the twentieth century.

James Wallace Cooper
Killed
France, May 9th 1915
Aged 20.

NOBODY goes to war and expects to be killed by their own side. That is exactly what happened to Wallace Cooper as he was preparing to go into action for the very first time. The young Yorkshireman and some pals who were stood in close proximity to him were killed by a British artillery battery firing defective shells. Not surprisingly there was no admission of guilt in the aftermath of this appalling tragedy and once again the truth was economically delivered. This incident was part of an overall crisis that affected the British at the time and contributed to bringing down an ineffective and useless war-time Prime Minister. Certain decaffeinated coffee swilling 'metropolitan historians' will to a point agree with my comments regarding the political upheaval. The egg-heads will probably splutter uncontrollably choking upon their butter croissants as I fully intend to unmercifully condemn those responsible for what really went on. There is no excuse for what happened to this boy, it makes my blood boil.

James Wallace Cooper grew up and lived in close proximity to the man in our previous chapter, they more than likely crossed each other's paths from time to time walking down the main Harrogate Road in the area of Moortown, Leeds. Cooper is another one of Rob's 'hometown' boys that he is delighted to see has made his way into this book, only just, for the research attached to this story has caused me a couple of sleepless nights. Known as Wallace, his middle name, this created havoc when I was conducting the research. The other two male members of his family, his father and younger brother were also were known by their middle names, henceforth, everything has been double-researched and checked.

Wallace was the middle child of three born to his parents Robert John Cooper, known as John and Betsey, nee. Douglas. He had an elder sister, Lily and a younger brother Henry Douglas Cooper, who was known as Douglas. John the father was a farmer's son and worked on the land as a horseman and agricultural worker. He never actually became a tenant farmer himself and was always a paid employee, relying on seasonal work and having to move around Yorkshire. He met his future wife Betsey whilst employed in the Selby area, she hailed from nearby Osgodby and was herself the daughter of an agricultural labourer. The couple were actually married over thirty miles away in the northern part of Leeds on December 1st 1889. John was 29-years old, his wife four years younger. As newlyweds the couple settled in the Moortown district as John had obtained employment as a carter within the building trade delivering supplies across northern Leeds. The family were poor in what was then a rundown area with a high infant mortality rate. Poverty influenced Betsey's decision to return back to the home of her parents in rural north Yorkshire to give birth to all of her three children, assisted by her mother and sister. Lily, b. 1891, Wallace, b.1894 and Douglas, b. 1896 were all born in Osgodby returning to the family home in Leeds shortly after their individual births where they would all grow up.

Upon leaving school Wallace found work as a jobbing gardener, there were a number of affluent avenues with large individual garden plots not too far away from Moortown that required the services of his labour. The job didn't provide a regular income but it kept Wallace out in the great outdoors and not tied to a mill or a coal mine. His sister had already left home to enter domestic service, an employment option he didn't wish upon himself. Wallace was still a teenager when war was declared, he saw an opportunity of adventure and in August 1914 enlisted into the local territorial battalion known as the Leeds Rifles not far short of his twentieth birthday.

The Leeds Rifles consisted of two battalions the 7th and 8th West Yorkshire Regiment, they were a territorial outfit. A vast majority of those who served with the Rifles were Leeds men, many being old chums or workmates. Not to confuse matters the Leeds Pals were the 15th and 17th Battalions of the West Yorkshire Regiment, volunteer service battalions also consisting of men in the majority from Leeds. The Pals often get more publicity than the Rifles, however, all the Leeds battalions retained their own identities and rivalries recognising their common West Yorkshire Regimental origins. It was an exciting time for Wallace, his initial posting was to Selby, just a few miles from where he was born. From there it was to Strensall and then York. In mid-March 1915 his battalion the 8th were sent to Gainsborough for final preparations with the emphasis being on musketry. A month later Wallace sailed with the original draft of his battalion and landed at Boulogne, France, on Thursday April 15th 1915.

Back in England another Yorkshireman born at Morley close to Leeds was quickly learning what war was all about. Prime Minister Herbert Henry Asquith was constantly being criticised for his rather laid-back and passive attitude to the war in general. Political opponents and rivals of the Liberal party statesman were busy sharpening their knives. Military heavyweights such as the then commander of the British Expeditionary Force, Sir John French and Secretary of State for War the Irish-born, Horatio Herbert Kitchener also held their own concerns regarding his leadership. Asquith, often referred to as 'squiffy' due to his heavy boozing was a politician with his best years behind him. Before the war he had introduced for the very first time rudimentary social security provisions for the unemployed and pensions for the elderly as well as reducing weekly working hours. He had however failed to deal adequately with the issue of Irish home rule and refused to acknowledge the rights of women to the vote. The drunken whisky sodden leader often slurred his words from the dispatch box in the House of Commons, he was out of his depth. Indirectly what happened to Wallace and many of his comrades would lead to Asquith's downfall.

Over in France, Wallace and the Leeds Rifles battalion were making their way across country from Boulogne. The men soon encountered St. Omer, with its beer taverns and brothels before heading towards Hazebrouck.

Their final destination would be Aubers Ridge where they would for the very first time find themselves in a hostile action against the enemy. At dawn on May 9th 1915 the Leeds Rifles were in dugouts awaiting orders to man the parapets. In a controversial reference right here I believe the commanders and in particular Kitchener himself knew beforehand that defeat was inevitable. The claims I will go on to make here will have the 'metropolitan historians' reeling and reaching for their indigestion tablets. So… here I go, Rob is not holding me back.

Wallace Cooper and his comrades would never have known what they were letting themselves in for. All major assaults were normally pre-supported by significant artillery barrages in order to damage enemy defences such as barbed wire and machine gun posts. These bombardments were also essential in order to boost the morale of the infantry who would go into the actual attack. Rawlinson, in charge of IV Corps to which Wallace's battalion were attached was the 'puppet' subordinate of Haig who at the time was commanding the First Army in France. He was well known for scuttling off miles behind the lines to safety as the action commenced, his co-ordination between his artillery officers mattered little. The men in battle had concerns about their equipment, the guns were worn and many of the shells ineffective. Crews handled shells in the main containing shrapnel that would not cut enemy wire as they lacked high explosive output. Even if Rawlinson communicated these concerns to Haig – who already knew of the state of affairs it made no difference. Haig, I believe wanted the action to fail. He was after the position held by his superior Sir John French, one that he would eventually succeed in obtaining. French would take the blame in his eyes, opening up the door for his sly, wily and cunning ambitions.

Haig's ambitions effectively saw him use his men as pawns in a power game. He wasn't alone. Kitchener hated John French and the feeling was mutual. He was a bullish Secretary of State for War and in my opinion Kitchener was an egocentric and hypocritical man. The tragedy of the last story of William Greenwood who was hounded to his death for being gay slaps right at me here. I am convinced Kitchener was himself a homosexual who frolicked in his desires with total impunity. Less than a month before Wallace Cooper was killed at Aubers Ridge the shell crisis and defective guns had been reported to Kitchener, he did nothing, knowing that if it continued John French would take the rap. Haig and Kitchener played the game and cared little for volunteer British working-class soldiers who were butchered. The two powerful men wanted French out, but the old commander would not go without a fight of his own.

Lord Northcliffe, the press baron and David Lloyd George, a powerful politician being the Chancellor of the Exchequer were about to bring about a positive change. The Chancellor held ambitions of ousting Asquith as Prime Minister and both he and Northcliffe were reliably informed by John French of the shell crisis. The British public then got to know about it, Northcliffe had newspapers to sell. This led to Asquith a weak sozzled leader having to compromise his position and form a coalition government. Lloyd George became Minister of Munitions. John French much to Haig's dismay survived a little longer thanks to Lloyd George who Haig despised. By end of 1916, the intrepid Lloyd George, the Manchester born Welshman was Prime Minister, ousting Asquith. As for Kitchener, in my opinion the 'gay' Secretary of State for War like William Greenwood in our previous story had drowned in an 'accident' and Haig had replaced French. Power struggles would continue, especially between Lloyd George and Haig as the war raged on.

Wallace Cooper just a 'pawn' in the game never actually made it into battle. Had he have done so he most likely would have been killed anyway. The strategic and logistical position of the British at Aubers Ridge was ridiculously exposed, they went on to suffer over 11,000 casualties that day on top of the 13,000 suffered less than a month before at Neuve Chapelle. Kitchener and Haig behaved like two poker players each with a good hand in the knowledge they had hundreds of thousands more volunteers from the working classes to follow. Before the action had commenced Wallace along with a small number of his pals, including the famous rugby player of the day, Jackie Tindall, had volunteered to take rations up to the artillery lads who were about to commence with the bombardment. With dilapidated equipment and many 'dud' shells their field commanders had no choice but to open fire as per orders. The worn gun barrels started to send shells off-course and soon the whole of the assault became a disastrous farce. Wallace and his pals dived for cover into a trench still carrying the rations forward.

Rob has managed to obtain an eye-witness account of what happened next from a soldier who arrived on the scene of the trench where Wallace had been sheltering. Quite rightly he is annoyed by the fact the official war diary that many sweet sherry sipping 'metropolitan historians' always consider as totally accurate, does not mention what the eyewitness saw. This does not at all surprise me in the slightest, meanwhile, as the action commenced Kitchener lay tucked up in bed, just after dawn, probably stark naked in the arms of one of his good looking staff officers.

The soldier eye-witness arrived to a scene of devastation. Men of the Aberdeen artillery had just shelled the trench, one soldier was already dead. Another four including Wallace Cooper and Jackie Tindall were so severely injured that nothing could be done for them, they died minutes later in agony, some of them having had their limbs torn off. One man was saved and confirmed the story, however, the war diary didn't make any reference to the incident whatsoever. Wallace Cooper had been killed by his own side whilst trying to get food and rations up to them, what an absolute disgrace and an unforgivable tragedy. The shocking ignorance by authorities who failed to record the truth demonstrates profound contempt and total disrespect that still casts a long dark historical shadow. Wallace Cooper's family and the relatives of his chums were also denied the truth, again, no surprise there.

It was friendly-fire from British guns that killed Wallace Cooper.

I think I have covered who was to blame. In an irony Asquith whilst still Prime Minister went to Haig in 1916 to try and get his son Raymond, a Grenadier Guard, out of the line and into a safe staff job. Haig would have obliged but Raymond would have none of it, he was later killed in action. Asquith never got over the death of his eldest son. Throughout this publication I have always been grateful for the opportunities to express what I believe are extremely significant points of history and Wallace Cooper has allowed me to do that once more. How much of my testimony you go with is entirely your choice, however, one fact remains, Wallace's death was entirely preventable. In the murky and misty world of power ordinary lives are cheap, yes, times have changed for the better and will continue to do so when certain truths are revealed.

Asquith took Great Britain into a war that I certainly believe we should never have entered. He lost one of his own son's. John and Betsey Cooper had two sons. The shambolic events and subsequent lies surrounding their eldest son's death were bad enough. On a rain soaked afternoon during the later stage of Haig's bloody Battle of the Somme, their youngest son Douglas was killed in action whilst serving with the Royal Marine Light Infantry.

Wallace Cooper is buried in the Estaires Communal Cemetery in northern France. Around 45-miles further south his brother rests at peace in the Knightsbridge Cemetery close to Beaumont-Hamel where he fell. Wallace was 20-years old when he was killed, Douglas was 19-years old. Rob clutching a copy of the original war diary that shamefully omits the tragedy that befell Wallace Cooper held his 1914-15 Star, British War Medal and Victory Medal in his hands and stared silently at them. I know Rob just how much this story of one your hometown boys has meant to you.

In one final comment I have to say once again that politicians and power-brokers cause wars. Despite my attitudes and feelings towards Herbert Asquith the former Prime Minister, I do recognise that he too lost a son and that he suffered the same grief as so many others.

George Taylor
Died in Hospital
Bradford, Jan. 18th 1920
Aged 30.

This particular story demonstrates how the devastating effects of the First World War had far-reaching consequences. For hundreds of thousands, if not millions of ordinary families the significances of the conflict were almost never ending. George Taylor died well over a year after the fighting had ended, his wartime experiences we are certain contributed to his premature demise. He became just another victim, one more man of solid social standing who served his local community and was taken in his prime before his time. A further opportunity arises here for me also to provide supplementary aspects of social history relevant to George's life, together with the portrayal of a minds-eye backdrop to what is without doubt an emotional story.

George Robert Taylor was born just before the Christmas of 1889 in Duke Street, Hoyland a small town several miles south of Barnsley in Yorkshire. He entered the world at the home of his grandparents, Robert and Martha Taylor, both of whom were each approaching sixty years of age and still working long hours. Robert was a colliery labourer at the Hoyland Silkstone pit, coal-mining was an absolute way of life to almost the whole of the local community. George's grandmother Martha toiled daily as a seamstress. Old Robert struggled on account of the heavy work and his age so it was no surprise that George's parents also lived under the same roof. His father John was a horse-keeper [underground] at the local pit, placing him in charge of the pit ponies. George's mother Kate worked as a dressmaker to help provide for her baby son and his infant older sister Marian. Three generations of one family lived in a tiny cramped house within a community entirely dependent upon coal-mining. Life was a constant cycle of long working hours, the repetitive chores of keeping the home crisp and clean also had to be incorporated into the monotonous routines, nobody complained, they got on with it.

John Taylor, George's dad was the pit pony man at the Hoyland colliery. Pit ponies had been introduced at almost every British colliery several decades earlier ironically after a disaster had occurred at a pit in Hoyland back in 1838. At that time women and children some as young as six were also sent down the mines. When twenty-six children drowned at Hoyland ponies were then drafted in to replace them throughout the country. The lives of the pit ponies were miserable, dark, cold and very hard going. Despite suffering such hardships they were affectionately treated by the pit men. All of them had individual names. At nearby Cortonwood Colliery, ponies named Nelson, Jerry, Lion, Boxer and Dandy heaved their loads in the same dangerous conditions as their human friends. The average underground working life of a pit pony was four years before they were dispatched to duties above ground where some lasted a further fifteen years. Ponies who became sick or lame rendering them not fit to work were culled. All underground working pit ponies lived beneath the earth only getting fresh air when or if the colliery closed for a holiday. John Taylor had a very responsible job, he always had to make sure his ponies were very well fed in order to sustain their heavy workloads. The horse-keeper had to constantly source high protein food such as hay and maize as well as act as a 'vet' when things went wrong and treatment was required.

As George grew older and started his rudimentary education both his grandparents had passed away. At the age of twelve he also went down the pit to help maintain the family. There was one aspect that was continuously becoming apparent, George was growing. By the time he had reached his late teens he was well above the average height for the period standing at almost six-foot tall. His size and presence marked him out for greater things. George was also a bright lad and this had been recognised. As he reached adulthood he had moved across to Droylsden on the eastern edge of Manchester to take upon a responsible role as a foreman at a colliery. His pal Billy Hufton, the same age as him held a similar position overseen by his father who was the under-manager. The strapping young Yorkshireman also lodged with his chum and the manager in a comfortable house. His duties were to oversee boys carry out the loading and filling of tubs underground. George spoke with a distinctively different accent from the lads he supervised but they daren't make fun of him for that, after all George was a big lad who commanded authority as we will discover as this story moves on.

Back over in Yorkshire George had left his childhood sweetheart behind. Sarah Eliza Bamforth lived only a short distance from his former home in Hoyland. She too was the daughter of a collier. With opportunities limited for young women she like many girls of the time entered domestic service as a servant, her meals and board were provided, together with a pittance of a wage. She would get one Sunday a month off-duty that offered the only opportunity she had to get a train over to Manchester to see her sweetheart. The two lovers couldn't bear to be separated and I am certain without the blessing of her employers she decided to abscond to be with her sweetheart. Sarah packed her bags and boarded a train to be with him for good and headed for Droylsden. The two made plans to marry and spend the rest of their lives together. George had also decided to take advantage of his tall and strapping physique, he wanted to provide his wife-to-be with long-term security. His supervisory role down the darkened pit would help achieve his aim, for he could obtain references to demonstrate that he could handle responsibility and hard physical work. Sarah and George were married two days before Christmas in 1911, just after his 22nd birthday at St. Mary's Church in Droylsden. Career motivated, keen to escape the drudgery of pit life and anxious to get back to Yorkshire, George successfully applied for a position with the Bradford City Police. He was accepted and became a constable within that force.

The life of a policeman wasn't at all easy at any point. The vast majority of constables were from the working-classes. Individual police forces placed the emphasis upon continuity of service and recruited heavily amongst the low-skilled and poorer classes. Men who like George often had to move around from pit to pit in order to secure work were more likely to appreciate long-term employment. The pay of a police constable was low and the opportunities of promotion were limited. More than a quarter of Edwardian police constables never attained any higher rank even after 25-years of service. Benefits outweighed the disadvantages. George had a job for life that included payment if he was sick, outings for his family, social and recreational activities, convalescent homes for poorly officers, social respect, order and regular weekly pay.

George Taylor served with the Bradford City Police before and after the First World War.

He settled with Sarah into a neat little house at 32 Thorpe Street, Bradford in the Shearbridge district an area to the east of the city centre heavily populated by mill workers. PC Taylor would have patrolled his own patch that had numerous back street pubs and taverns, one or two brothels and gambling establishments. His initial military based training lasted around five weeks with the focus being very much upon physical fitness. George was a big man and very able. Police officers of the day placed more emphasis upon learning on the beat and from senior constables who accompanied the new recruits in their early days of service. George would have got to know the local drunks, prostitutes, illegal bookies and petty thieves. At that time a blind-eye was encouraged to leave alone those who were paid to inform upon the more serious criminals. If he so wished George could exercise a high degree of brutality when he considered it necessary to subdue a situation. He would have beaten the living daylights out of anyone he considered to be a threat to public order. Had he himself or one of his colleagues taken any physical abuse the perpetrators would be rounded up and given a severe punishment beating in a locked cell. Not surprisingly there were few assaults against police constables in the Edwardian age.

George recognised the working-classes from where he came from, most policemen of the day did also. Despite their benefits of office they were always complaining about their low pay and lack of promotional opportunities. A lot of constables liked to drink, more than three-quarters of actual dismissals of lower ranking police officers related to being drunk on duty. Their grievances were never far away just like those of the working-class. Threatened with the sack if they dared to join a trades' union by public school educated senior officers, most of them like George with young families to provide for simply carried on. Meals would always be on the table for his wife Sarah and his little girl Connie, his sergeant would remind him of that fact if he decided to have a moan about his pay.

You may be surprised that the role of a policeman was not considered to be deemed as a reserved occupation during the First World War. This meant they could and were conscripted if they hadn't already signed to join-up. Regular police constables were replaced by civilian volunteer special constables, too old to be considered as fit to fight. The regulars who did come back returned to their constabularies if they were not deemed as too far physically disabled. A lot of time, money and resources had previously been invested into them as individuals, furthermore, so many young fit men had been killed or maimed for life that new recruitment drives from 1919 onwards became ever more difficult.

George decided to volunteer in January 1916 as the conscription of able bodied men was being planned. In Bradford the Royal Garrison Artillery had a depot. The strapping police constable was an ideal strong and physical recruit as far as they were concerned, especially to become a member of a heavy gun team of men urgently needed for war service at the front. He was immediately placed on to the reserve and mobilised in June of 1916. Specialist training had to be completed by George, he had to learn every aspect of the mechanisms and operational procedures of the heavy howitzer gun. The constable came through everything all well and good and was posted to 163 Siege Battery who had been stationed in France since the Battle of the Somme. George arrived to commence his active service on the Western Front in November 1917. Within four months he had been promoted to the rank of Bombardier in recognition of his abilities, organisational and leadership skills.

The policeman served with a heavy siege battery, operating 6-inch sixty-pounder guns. These weapons were responsible for inflicting damage upon opposing German artillery, stores and transport systems and were a constant thorn in the side of the enemy. A notoriously difficult unit to research I know that 163 Siege battery was subjected to German artillery gas attacks in January 1918 and suffered a number of casualties as a result. George wasn't identified as one of the more serious gas casualties, however, after some discussion Rob and I believe the gas had a detrimental effect upon his health in the months that followed. It is worth pointing out here that his rank of Bombardier was essential to the continual effectiveness of the unit in general. Rob thinks he may not have received the recuperation or treatment he maybe should have been considered for because of the demands of his rank and responsibility.

As the war raged on the Germans launched their massive offensive in late March and subjected the 163 Siege Battery to further gas attacks as well as aircraft machine-gun assaults. Back home in Bradford, prior to George leaving for the front, Sarah and youngster Connie had moved into a more comfortable house at 37 Thursby Street off the Leeds Road in a better part of the city. It was there within their new home that a terrible tragedy struck. In her mother's arms little Connie died aged just five on June 12th 1918, after complications with a cerebral abscess. This devastating news reached George at the front and he was immediately granted an extended period of home leave to comfort his grief-stricken spouse. Together in mourning they had to arrange the funeral of their only child. With a heavy heart he returned to France in July leaving behind his anxious wife who obviously had seen how the war had affected him, especially after the gassing. She had to come to terms with her overwhelming grief and also the ongoing worry regarding the welfare of her husband.

Two months later George's war was effectively over. He was invalided home with what was described as a back strain in September of 1918. George was sent to Catterick Military Hospital in Yorkshire spending three months confined to bed before being allowed to return home. Both Rob and I suspect his problems were not merely confined to a back strain considering how his health deteriorated so rapidly thereafter. The policeman was finally given an essential discharge in January 1919 on account of his occupation. George returned shortly afterwards to his duties with the Bradford City Police, he wasn't a well man. At some point during the war he had lost all of his teeth and had to wear dentures. These had been misplaced somewhere at the hospital. His sergeant encouraged him to write a letter to have them returned, it was clear that senior officers at the police station knew that George wasn't the man he once was.

Considering his period of hospitalisation prior to his return to duty as a police officer Rob suggests he was given a more comfortable role at the station. This can't be proved but it does help to explain why he developed serious blood circulation problems. If he had held a desk job, sitting down all day wouldn't have helped him as he had already developed another underlying serious health issue, one he wouldn't have anticipated or been aware of. We have to remember that George had once been a very fit man, only three years before. What effect had the gassing left upon him? Did it contribute to his death that occurred less than a year after he commenced his duties as a policeman?

George Robert Taylor saw his health rapidly deteriorate, he became short of breath, started to cough up blood and lost weight. Not long after he turned 30-years old, just after Christmas 1919 he was admitted to the Bradford Royal Infirmary. Less than a month later he died, a man in the prime of his life, so what was the cause of death? Officially he was recorded as dying of: (1) - Malignant Endocarditis and (2) – Pulmonary Embolism. Neither I nor Rob claim to have medical qualifications, however we both agree the first cause incurred a bacterial infection within the heart that could have been caused by poison gas. The second cause indicates a blood clot from his lower regions, possibly one that originated in the calf and moved towards the lungs, no surprise as his circulation was affected by the damage to his heart. To put it another way we both think his death was indirectly caused by the after effects of gas poisoning he had received a couple of years previously in France. Our opinions and modern day verdict weren't considered all those years ago. If certain people had thought what we do then his wife would have been compensated via an increment in pension and George would have been considered as a war casualty. George Taylor wasn't the only man to die after the war as a result of what happened because of the use of chemical weapons. Thousands more perished, some twenty or more years after the war because of that particular hideous form of warfare.

George Robert Taylor is therefore not a casualty of war as far as officialdom is concerned. He does not have a Commonwealth War Graves Commission headstone at the cemetery in Bradford where he is buried. To us, he was very much a victim of war but we realise that professional medical opinion may not confirm our opinions. It's up to you to decide what you think. Sarah Taylor lost her husband and child within just several months. She eventually found happiness once more when she married the local milkman, David Lee at Bradford Holy Trinity Church on October 31st 1922, she was 31, David 36. The woman who had been George's childhood sweetheart and the love of his life died in Bradford aged 74 in 1966. This interesting, emotional and slightly controversial story was brought to you as a result of Rob's £28- purchase of George's silver British War Medal. Just a small piece of metal represents an everlasting legacy to a long forgotten ordinary police constable. A casualty of war? We certainly think so.

Harry Harris

Died of Disease
England, October 30th 1918
Aged 26.

THE story of this man also bears great testimony to a very special group of men who weren't sent to war to directly face the enemy. These intelligent, caring and diligent guys rarely faced bullets, high explosive shells or gas, they were confronted by appalling suffering with the very real possibility of contracting fatal disease. The men of the Royal Army Medical Corps offered hope, salvation, care, compassion and comfort to the wounded, diseased and dying. Rob has a 1914-15 Star, British War Medal and Victory Medal to just one of their ordinary ranked personnel, the man in this story. At the outbreak of war the RAMC only formed sixteen years before in 1898 had a strength of 9,000 men, by 1918 that had swelled to

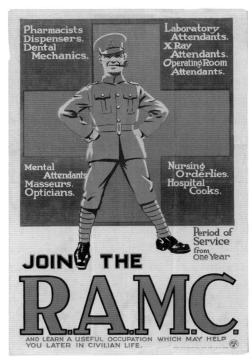

Harry Harris served with the Royal Army Medical Corps, it would ultimately lead to his premature death.

over 100,000. For the very first time the British deployed field ambulances. These were not vehicles, they were fully equipped front line medical units, mobile hospitals manned by around 250 to 300 men with sixty or so horses, several motor ambulances and a chain of line operational staging points. The men of the RAMC worked unarmed and often in extremely stressful and challenging conditions, around 7,000 of them lost their lives whilst serving during the First World War.

Harry Harris was born in Hornsey, north London in August 1892. He was actually christened as George Henry Percy Harris but was known throughout his life as Harry, a version of one of his middle names, Henry.

The reason for this was simple, his dad was called George and it was very common for a son with same first Christian name as his father to be known by his middle name. Harry's dad George Harris originally came from Shoreditch, an overcrowded and impoverished London district. He had done well for himself becoming a skilled upholsterer before marrying a girl from Finchley. George and Mary Harris tied the knot in 1881. Harry the eldest son was born the following year, another son Fred came along in 1894 followed by a daughter May in 1896, the family was complete. Eventually they all settled down into a relatively comfortable life at 11 Watford Road, Stoke Newington in north London where they lived for many years.

Upon leaving school Harry and his brother Fred, two intelligent lads entered into careers within the insurance industry, both becoming clerks. Their sister was sent to a local college to improve her educational skills, family life was bliss with no hardships to blight the futures of the Harris children. Harry was just approaching his 22nd birthday when war was declared, Fred was just over a couple of years younger and still a teenager. The younger brother had already married with his parents and brides parents' permissions to the daughter of a Dutch seaman. Harry was a tall, clean and sober young man. Just a few months after war had been declared and probably under some pressure he decided that he would sign-up and join the colours. Perhaps he had been influenced by the sight of wounded soldiers arriving back from the front to London. He visited the RAMC depot on January 28th 1915 in nearby Haringey and was readily accepted to be accommodated within their ranks. Almost immediately he was deployed for basic military and specialist medical field operational training.

In July 1915 after passing through his courses without any problems or complications Harry was deployed to the Gallipoli peninsula for active service. The British alongside their Empire and Dominion forces from India, Australia and New Zealand and the French were fighting desperately in temperatures often exceeding 40 degrees centigrade. This campaign was turning into a bitter struggle against a determined Turkish resistance. My criticism of the British being there in the first place has already been documented. The men on the ground faced the constant danger of being shelled, machine-gunned or sniped and had to contend with ludicrous command decisions made by 'Donkey Generals' that sent many of them directly to their deaths. A whole host of medical conditions and diseases such as malaria, dysentery, tuberculosis and typhoid manifested daily, in the living boiling hell of Gallipoli, the dangers for everyone were colossal.

Harry worked in trying conditions, a lack of fresh water was always a problem. Dehydration, sunstroke, sickness and diarrhoea, sepsis as well as men with horrendous wounds all had to be coped with in addition to the threat of contracting diseases. All RAMC personnel faced these dangers on a daily basis, those who had to treat desperately ill patients in isolation tents were at even greater risks. After some discussion we have concluded that Harry came into prolonged contact with men suffering from diseases who were being treated and nursed in isolation units. This explains why he was himself evacuated to a hospital ship for immediate embarkation to Britain. He had served for a period of just fifty-two days before he left Gallipoli suffering from dysentery on August 30th 1915. It comes as no surprise to me that Harry contracted this awful condition. During the hottest period of the year, August, rotting corpses that littered the battlefields were consumed by millions of maggots and flies that infested the whole of the peninsula. Dysentery became rife amongst the men and spread with incredible speed as hygiene levels were non-existent. The dry and barren scorched earth where large numbers of dead human beings lay still in death became a paradise for the flies.

On his voyage back to England Harry had developed a further health problem, he had started to cough up blood and mucus. At that point his condition was noted and recorded. After a period in hospital he eventually overcame the uncomfortable and degrading effects of dysentery, however, his consistent cough was getting worse. In January of 1916 he was ordered to be officially medically examined and the results weren't positive at all. The official report clearly demonstrated that a tubercle of the lung was present, the onset of tuberculosis was inevitable. Without hesitation an official discharge had to be administered for Harry who was considered as a risk to others as tuberculosis was contagious. Conveniently for the authorities this discharge would in effect mean that Harry was no longer their problem, he was out of service, out of pay, out of sight and out of mind.

The once fit and healthy young man had no option but to return home. To his dismay he was not reconsidered to resume his former role as an insurance clerk due to his condition. His parents did their level best to care for him as he spent many, many lonely hours shut up in a bedroom. Harry's symptoms gradually increased unfavourably. The persistent cough grew worse and he began to suffer weight loss, night sweats, high temperatures, swelling and loss of appetite. Undoubtedly pressures upon his father George and in particular his mother Mary grew daily. Harry's miserable existence would I suspect have also caused him acute anxiety and bouts of unbearable depression. He suffered and endured monumental physical and emotional turmoil almost beyond the imagination.

This once happy, bright, ambitious and respectable family were witnessing a disintegration of all they had once held dear compounded by a further tragic event on March 1st 1917. Fred Harris, Harry's younger brother who had joined the infantry died of his wounds in France whilst serving with the King's Royal Rifle Corps. He had also been suffering for a period of time and his parents had been made aware of that. In reality George and Mary Harris had both of their much loved and adored sons placed upon a macabre form of 'death-row', the agony they too must have suffered doesn't even bear thinking about. It is probably likely that one or both of them suffered a mental breakdown after the loss of Fred, could things get worse? Yes, they did, Harry deteriorated even further after having endured over a year of suffering.

Ironically as his condition worsened in the April and May of 1917 the authorities officially recognised that his situation could have been caused as a result of his military service. This came at a time when his parents could not or were incapable of continuing to care for their eldest son. The government astonishingly accepted that Harry's war service had only contributed to a degree of 50% as to the tuberculosis he had contracted. I find this absolutely astonishing and to an extent disgraceful. He had first shown the symptoms upon evacuation from Gallipoli and less than six months later he was discharged to fend for himself. Harry obviously contracted the TB whilst treating patients during his war service. The authorities realising that something had to be done to ease the burden upon Harry and his family accepted a partial responsibility. I wonder if his father George was 'means-tested' before they made this preposterous decision.

For Harry there really was little hope, he was becoming immobile. The 50% claim may have, I say may have, allowed some form of payment to Harry that in turn was used to fund his care at a sanatorium in Kent. His parents may also have been expected to financially contribute to help provide for his care at the imposing and grand looking Frimpton Sanatorium. Patients at the institution were encouraged to do gentle exercise in the clean country air, no antibiotics existed at the time to combat the degenerative tuberculosis. For Harry, it was far too late. Had he been admitted earlier closer to the point of his discharge things may have been different. Harry had been cast aside and as a result of that he suffered terribly.

Looking at old photographs of the sanatorium I can picture Harry staring silently alone out of one of the windows overlooking the luscious landscaped gardens. I am convinced he knew that he was going to die, his death sentence had been confirmed over three years before on a hot, filthy and bloody peninsula. He lost his fight for life on October 30th 1918, aged 26-years old and is buried in a churchyard not far from the institution. Harry Harris was robbed of his dignity, youth, his life, the chance to marry, have children and grandchildren, because politicians start wars, it is as simple as that.

Tuberculosis was the scourge of the poor and the working classes during the Victorian and Edwardian eras. The Harris family didn't live in poverty, George the father had worked his way out of it. Even as his sons left for war the last thing he would have worried about was the threat of tuberculosis actually killing one of them. Returning to the subject of Harry's service in Gallipoli I spoke with Rob about his duties. I suggested that his lowly rank of Private was responsible for him taking care of diseased patients who had been placed in isolation. Rob disagrees and says that Harry probably volunteered to look after those particular men. If that was the case it really does show the measure of the young man and further compels the sadness of how he suffered his own eventual fate.

The Royal Army Medical Corps have been overlooked by many in generalised accounts of events that occurred during the First World War. There is absolutely no doubt the roles they played in every theatre of that war were essentially vital. We often hear of tales of immense courage and bravery during war, films are made, books are published and fairy-cake munching 'metropolitan historians' love a good text book tale or two of gallantry. How brave do you have to be to volunteer to care for a human being with a highly contagious disease who is staring death in the face? How much courage is required to comfort that person in their desperate hours of need knowing damn well you may end up in the same condition yourself? I wish I could have asked these questions to the people who decided that it was only a 50/50 probability that Harry died because of his service.

Having lost both of their sons Mary and George Ellis were survived by their daughter May who married a bank manager in 1921. She went on to live a long life in the suburbs until her death aged 92, back in 1989. May had one child, a daughter, Margaret.

Albert Bowey

Suicide
Ripon, England, July 29th 1918
Aged 38.

IT had been a cool July in England back in 1918, the middle of the month had seen heavy showers and even hail. Dawn broke on Monday the 29th to a clear blue sky overlooking a glistening gentle dew upon the ground below as the temperature still struggled to rise. A man awoke that very morning his mind tortured by what he had previously seen during the carnage of war. The draughty barrack room had the stench of stale tobacco smoke and boot polish all around, the man closed his eyes to imagine for one last time his wife and five children anxiously waiting for him at home. His darling sweetheart Rosie was stood upon the doorstep, the kids jostled to get past her out of the narrow front door... their daddy was coming home.

The long silver razor glinted in the sunlight that flooded through the window just behind his bed. He gripped it tightly and raised it towards his neck. With one deliberate slicing movement he cut straight through his throat. He closed his eyes and felt no pain as the warm blood gushed and spurted across his chest, he lay backwards silently resigned to his fate as his demons slowly slipped away forever.

This is the story of Albie Bowey our final subject within this book, it is unequivocally heart wrenching. He typifies the - oh so average man of the time, this is by no means an average story, Albie really does sum up everything - in more ways than one. I defy or dare anyone to criticise what follows. My 'friends' the 'metropolitan historians' as they read on sat comfortably by the side of their tropical fish tanks will be stunned into reaching for large glasses of their 12-year old malts. History has no hiding place or denials within this true story.

Albert Edward Bowey came from Salisbury in Wiltshire. This small historic city can date its origins back to a pre-historic time of around 5,000 years ago. In Norman times the city was named Serum and by 1075 boasted a settlement and cathedral. This was rebuilt and completed in 1334 and still stands today representing a marvellous architectural sight to behold. As time moved on Salisbury became an important centre for the cloth trade. Other small industries such as leather making and the production of cutlery also provided employment. In more recent times the city has been associated very prominently with the military. At the turn of the twentieth century the 2nd Army Corps HQ was set up and many soldiers came to live in the city, this led to a surge in house building as the area started to expand. The surrounding suburbs grew larger when the Army based their Southern Command base in the vicinity. Close by Salisbury Plain became a very well-known operational training location.

Against this backdrop Albie saw the many changes that affected his city. Salisbury was a good place to live and the Bowey family were well known and respected within the local community where they had lived for many generations. Albie's parents were married some time before he was born. William Uriah Bowey tied the knot with domestic servant Mary Herrington on July 15th 1868 at Bower Chalke, her home village several miles to the west of Salisbury. The wedded couple moved to a residence close to the centre of the city and went on to have ten children. Albie was blessed with three older brothers, two elder sisters, one younger brother and three little sisters. Tragically one of them, Beatrice, died aged just 14-years old in 1903. His father William was ambitious, he had always been employed in the grocery trade a vocation he held throughout his lifetime. This hard working man never retired and spent over sixty-years working, starting out as a grocers assistant before eventually gaining retail premises himself as a grocer in his own right. The enterprising William Bowey also went out as a mobile shop vendor across the region, even whilst in his seventies. His large family wouldn't have gone without provisions, William would have seen to that.

Albie was born in 1879 at 60 Brown Street, Salisbury, he witnessed the growth of his small city as the soldiers arrived in their thousands, by that time he had already established himself as a skilled man within the printing industry, a career path he never wavered from. Albie was a compositor, he was responsible for type-setting the actual letters of documents prior to print. This job required a lot of concentration as he had to work in a 'mirror image' capacity reading all the words back-to-front. Albie also had to be quick and nimble fingered. He worked on all kinds of publications before finally becoming employed by the post office. The pay of a compositor was reasonably good. Albie lived with his family well into his adulthood and helped to contribute to the household budget, there was still enough left for him to enjoy himself when he could and Albie certainly knew how to do just that.

The print worker had fallen for a local girl five years his junior. Rosie Porton was a pretty domestic servant in her teens who lived barely a mile away when she caught his eye. I am not sure whether her father, an engineer, approved of their relationship that endured for a number of years. Rosie was only 18-years old when Albie got her pregnant. In the Edwardian period marriage would have been expected between Albie and Rosie, however the teenage mum-to-be was under the age of majority. Anyone below the age of twenty-one was not categorised as an adult and needed parental permission to enter into wedlock. It appears pretty obvious this permission was denied by her father William at the time. Nevertheless, the baby was born, out of wedlock, ironically named after her father and Albie's dad also. William Albert Bowey entered the world on September 12th 1904. He initially lived with his teenage mother and her parents. Despite the disapproval of the Porton family regarding their daughter's relationship with Albie, the father of her child, she continued to keep him close as her lover.

Eventually with everyone's blessing Albie and Rosie were married at her local church, All Saints in East Harnham, Salisbury on March 2nd 1908. The 23-year old bride became Mrs Rose Emily Bowey. Albie, his bride and infant son all moved into their own little house close-by at 12 Old Street very near to where both sets of their own parents lived. Albie's father William ran a thriving grocery shop upon nearby Wilton Road. The compositor continued to work hard in order to support his beloved growing family. He and Rosie had four more children between 1909 and 1916, Kathleen, Frank, Fred and Emma became siblings to their eldest son William. After war had broken out in 1914 Albie became aware of certain events and circumstances regarding local people caught up in the conflict, simply because of the nature of his job. He would have seen official communications and items of news before most people as he was responsible for type-setting those very correspondences. At that time Albie was in secure employment and as a married man entering his late thirties with four children, three of whom were aged five and under, he wasn't required to sign-up for military service.

Nevertheless, I have to say I don't think his wife approved when he felt compelled to commit himself by attesting shortly before Christmas, on December 12th 1915. He was accepted and placed upon the reserve order to be mobilised at the discretion of the Royal Garrison Artillery to whom he had pledged his service. He initially passed a routine medical but it was noted that he required dental work. I have often seen this kind of remark on attestation papers and wondered why teeth problems are recorded and remedial work was deemed as necessary. My curiosity compelled me to ask Rob about this and his knowledge of military life offers an interesting explanation. Rob tells me that any soldier who had or even today has serious dental issues is or was required to have their problem rectified. Military authorities are all too aware that soldiers on active service who encounter serious toothache are unable to function properly. These men are removed from their duties as they could pose risks to their comrades. Soldiers have to be 'dental- fit' in order to be 'battle-fit' as Rob goes on to explain. Henceforth, it would appear that prevention rather than cure in the matter of oral hygiene has always held a high priority regarding military service. As for Albie, he had fourteen rotten teeth removed on the top and bottom sets that were replaced by dentures. I'm not too sure how high the dental treatment standards of the day were, he must have gone through hell having such a daunting procedure.

After undergoing a second medical examination the print man standing at around the average height for the time and also weighing in at the average was recommended for mobilisation, complete with his new smile, thanks to the dentures. I am not too sure that Rosie had a smile on her face when he left for his initial training in early September 1916. She was literally left holding the baby. Their little daughter Emma had been born only five months earlier, four other children aged between two and twelve also had to be cared for. It was fortunate their grandparents from both sides of the family, who all lived within short walking distances, were on hand to assist.

Albie didn't particularly distinguish himself within his training period. He was subjected to the same physical routines of young men half his age and had to comply without any dispensation. Eventually he was deployed to France as a replacement reinforcement to a Heavy Artillery Siege Battery, number 239, the date was June 19th 1917 and 239 who had been in action for several months had already taken a number of casualties. Albie holding the lowest rank of Gunner was quickly pressed into action toiling and labouring on the big sixty pounder gun, handling heavy shells and responding quickly to instructions. There is no doubt at all that he encountered certain disadvantages that didn't necessarily affect his comrades. In the first instance Albie was more than likely the oldest man in the unit, his fitness levels and stamina would have been much less than those of the other men. Expectations placed upon him especially in the heat of battle would have worn him out physically. Secondly, his maturity and experience as an intelligent and skilled man opened up his mind to the very realities of the situations he was facing. Younger lads within his unit shared senses of immortality that weren't appreciated by Albie. The compositor was a thoughtful man who would have constantly been working out his realistic expectations of avoiding serious injury or death.

At some point as his war service continued things started to go very badly wrong for Albie. Within a matter of months he was struggling both physically and mentally, so much so that by the early November of 1917 he had been hospitalised as 'sick'. We can only speculate as to what had happened to Albie based upon the serious future disintegration of his mental health. There was an acknowledgment by the authorities that his war service had directly contributed to his condition. Rob believes that during his relatively short period of service at the front in France something serious happened to him personally. When the heavy guns themselves came under direct fire and attack from the enemy by means of shelling or air attack, the crew teams had to rapidly take cover in makeshift trench-type shelters. There is a possibility that Albie was buried alive when one of the dugouts imploded due to an indirect hit. This has been suggested by Rob as the most terrifying instance that could happen to a soldier, particularly an older soldier. My theory is that Albie the civilian print worker had actually seen one or more catastrophic incidents of horror occur in front of his very eyes. He may have encountered a neighbouring gun battery receive a direct hit. Had that been the case Albie witnessed men literally being blown to pieces, their limbs ripped from their bodies, he could have been splattered with their body parts, organs or their blood. We both agree that Albie experienced an ordeal of horrendous proportions.

The mature volunteer soldier was invalided back to Britain with no apparent physical injuries. After a period of respite and recuperation he was deemed to have made a recovery from his ordeal. In my opinion at some point within his rest period he took leave with his family back in Salisbury and realised exactly everything that he held dear. This would have made him extremely anxious about the prospect of a return to the front. Albie wasn't far off 40-years old with a wife and five children. The mature volunteer had been evacuated from the front suffering from either 'shellshock' or another form of what we know today as post-traumatic stress disorder [PTSD]. He could have been medically discharged but this was 1918. The British were literally running out of volunteer and conscripted soldiers to send to the front. Men who were ten or more years older than Albie were being called-up, guys in their fifties were shockingly sent to war. By this time the whole of the recruitment situation brought upon by reckless slaughter was diabolically absurd.

Towards the end of March 1918 Albie was posted to No.4 Depot Royal Artillery stationed at the huge Ripon military camp in Yorkshire. The older soldier was given basic routines to comply with and monitored as to the state of his general fitness and well-being. Four months later tragedy struck, a tragedy completely unforeseen by those responsible for 116903 Gunner Albert Edward Bowey. Rob is convinced that Albie had been informed that he was being re-posted to the front in France and I have to agree with him. The mature soldier had coped well enough with four months of regular army drills, routines and fatigues at Ripon. There was one thing that absolutely terrified him, the mere thought of going back to the front line to relive the horrors he thought he had escaped from.

I have already described the horrific method of how Albie took his own life. With my head in my hands and with tears rolling down my cheeks I have to pause briefly here……….. In the immediate aftermath of this terrible tragedy Albie's blood drenched body was removed to the military hospital on site. An urgent inquiry was ordered and the shock of what happened reverberated all around the huge military camp. To their credit the officers although they could not deny that Albie had taken his own life, a criminal offence at the time, worked to ensure that his widow and family were accordingly considered. For official purposes only minimal references were attached to the fact that he had committed suicide due to 'temporary insanity'. He was recorded as having died of wounds and was granted that recognition with an official military headstone. After some consultation his widow Rose was granted a pension that related to her husband's actual service and the fact he had five children. In effect he was treated exactly the same as any other casualty of war. These affairs could have been handled differently and the outcome may have been much worse had they been so.

Four days after Albie had taken his own life he was committed by burial back in his home town of Salisbury. The weather had improved considerably and the sun shone brightly on the morning of Friday August 2nd 1918. As Albie's coffin was lowered slowly into his final resting place the children he fathered looked on in stunned silence. Billy aged 14, Kate 9, Frank 6, Fred 4 and Emma 2 were accompanied by their 33-year old mother Rosie dressed all in black. She turned her head briefly to look at the church behind her, the church where she and Albie had married each other after a long and difficult romance ten years before. Her father William held her close as her own mother looked on. Close by Albie's parents William and Mary stared down into the grave as the casket touched the earth below. The devoted grocer and his wife never got over the shock of what happened to their son Albie, they both died within days of each other three years later after 53-years of marriage.

Rosie continued to live at the family home in Old Street and remarried in 1922. Her new husband Harry Clark, a bricklayer was almost ten years her junior. They went on to have one child, a daughter, the family remained at the house, new husband Harry having moved into Albie's old home. I'm not quite sure that Rosie really ever got over the death of her first love. She went on to suffer from a number of health problems and died whilst still in her fifties.

Albie's grave within the churchyard of All Saints in East Harnham, Salisbury attracts visitors who have placed poppy crosses around his headstone. Some are aware that he took his own life due to the stresses of war, now for the first time the extended account of his life and times are hereby published. I encountered his British War Medal and Victory Medal for sale in an online auction site that opened up this very story and the conclusion to this book. What is war really good for? Absolutely nothing. In a final testimony to all of those who like Albie have had their stories told within this publication the simple wording placed at the bottom of Albie's headstone really does bring everything to a respectful conclusion. The words simply read, 'thy will be done'.

Forever now at peace, Albie Bowey.

QUESTIONS & ANSWERS

THROUGHOUT this publication opinions have been expressed in certain terms that may need further explanations. Rob and I have also occasionally disagreed regarding certain aspects of how the overall portrayal of the book should be defined. You may also have been left wondering how the format was eventually concluded. We as individuals have four questions of our own to ask to each other... as follows:

Charles's questions for Rob;

Questions	Answers
How much has your knowledge of the Great War expanded as a result of your work with this book?	You should know judging by the lengths of conversations we have had to participate in regarding the overall subject matter. I now have the confidence to go out and actually talk to the public about the men within this book without fear or prejudice.
You by your own admission have spent so many hours thinking very deeply about the subjects in this book. Have you had many sleepless nights because of your genuine compassion for these men?	The answer is yes. In particular the story of Stanley Edward Hall (Chapter Two) it kept and still occasionally keeps me awake. The reason why is that by referring to certain parts of his story, I thought Christian charity was for all. I didn't realise effectively a cost was attached to it. As a Christian this has had an impact upon the personal understanding of my faith.
How important and significant is the history of the First World War in general?	I feel it is exceptionally important because that very war changed the whole of the world order and brought about enormous global change. The struggles of those who participated in the Great War should never be forgotten.
What are your hopes and aspirations for this book?	It is very important for those who read this book to gain a better understanding of events that actually happened to ordinary everyday people. I hope this tremendously compassionate publication demonstrates to everyone just how pointless war really is.

Rob's questions for Charles;

Questions	Answers
Charles, what on earth is a metropolitan historian? You told me to wait until the end of the book to ask, so now what is the answer?	The term 'metropolitan historian' I coined to describe a certain type of person who has a narrow-minded and blinkered approach to history. These egg-heads are usually ring-fenced within a comfortable or zonal institutionalised environment. Unfortunately many of them are extremely smug and refuse to acknowledge alternative statements of historical importance.
Has the writing of this book eased any of the many issues you have had to deal with over a lifetime regarding the subject of WW1?	This is a difficult question to answer. On numerous occasions I was taken back in my minds-eye to revisit certain tragedies from WW1 that affected me personally. On occasions I felt a spiritual sense of foreboding as if a form of guidance was being pushed in my direction. I believe that a force beyond yonder may have had something to do with the 'issues' you mention.
Considering all of the circumstances leading up to Britain's declaration of war upon Germany in 1914, was it right for the British to go to war?	Definitively, No. It was the greatest mistake in British history. Treaties and declarations of potential support were far too expensive in terms of the loss of a generation. Europe wasn't our problem. Okay, we would undoubtedly have seen a form of a 'Greater Germany' on our doorstep, but in no way as threatening as the one that followed twenty years later..
Are you able to select one story that sticks out more than the rest? If so, why?	Unfortunately no, I have to say that in every instance I made a concerted effort to treat each subject with equal consideration. This created a balanced approach to the work I produced, although some stories were more emotional than others. Essentially and importantly I never held any bias or was swayed by subjects I had previously dealt with in a historical context.

INDEX

ALL of the men featured within this publication are indexed below in the order of their respective stories. The summarised information provided below essentially donates where each of them are either buried or commemorated.

15 **JOSEPH KNOWLES** – 1ˢᵗ (Otago) Battalion New Zealand Expeditionary Force.   103
Born October 29ᵗʰ 1884, Leeds, Yorkshire, England. Son of Thomas and Mary
Ann Knowles. Killed-in-Action, near Bapaume, France, August 25ᵗʰ 1918
– Aged 33. Buried within the L'HOMME MORT BRITISH CEMETERY in
France.

16 **ALAN SMITH - DCM** – 2/7ᵗʰ Battalion West Yorkshire Regiment (Leeds Rifles). 110
Born July 14ᵗʰ 1894, Wakefield, Yorkshire, England. Son of Henry and Mary
Smith. Killed-in-Action, Bucquoy, France, March 28ᵗʰ 1918 – Aged 23. Buried
within the GOMMECOURT BRITISH CEMETERY No.2 in France.

17 **SHARPLES DRIVER – MM and Bar** – 6ᵗʰ Battalion Kings Own Scottish Borderers. 116
Born 1896, Oswaldtwistle, Lancashire, England. Son of Thomas and Isabella
Driver. Killed-in-Action, near Arras, France, May 3ʳᵈ 1917 – Aged 21. No
known grave, commemorated on the ARRAS MEMORIAL in France.

18 **ROLAND CASEMORE – MM** – 1ˢᵗ Battalion West Yorkshire Regiment.   122
Born 1892, Bromley, Kent, England. Son of Henry and Emily Allen
Casemore. Killed-in-Action, near Buissy, France, March 21ˢᵗ 1918 – Aged 26.
Buried with the QUEANT ROAD CEMETERY in France.

19 **WILLIAM MALLIN – DCM, MM** – 2ⁿᵈ Battalion South Lancashire Regiment.   128
Born 1880, Dublin, Ireland. Son of Patrick and Mary Ann (Polly) Mallin.
Killed-in-Action, France/Belgium border, September 1ˢᵗ 1918 – Aged 38.
Buried within the WESTOUTRE CHURCHYARD EXTENSION in Belgium.

20 **GEORGE GRAHAM** – 375 (Siege) Battery, Royal Garrison Artillery.   137
Born 1887, Newcastle-upon-Tyne, England. Son of George J. and Hannah
Graham. Killed-in-Action, near Passchendaele, Belgium, November 7ᵗʰ 1917
– Aged 30. Buried within the BARD COTTAGE CEMETERY in Belgium.

21 **THOMAS HOY** – 1ˢᵗ Battalion Loyal North Lancashire Regiment.   148
Born 1877, Darwen, Lancashire, England. Son of Thomas and Sarah Hoy.
Killed-in-Action, near Ypres, October 31ˢᵗ 1914 – Aged 37. Buried within the
BEDFORD HOUSE CEMETERY in Belgium.

22 **THOMAS DUNLAVEY** – 3ʳᵈ Battalion Scots Guards.   153
Born 1888, Bradford, Yorkshire, England. Son of James and Annie Dunlavey.
Died of wounds at home, November 2ⁿᵈ 1915 – Aged 27. Buried within the
BRADFORD (SCHOLEMOOR) CEMETERY in Bradford, England.

23 **THOMAS BLACK** – 12ᵗʰ Battalion Royal Scots.   159
Born 1880, Linlithgow, Scotland. Son of Esther Black. Killed-in-Action,
Gouy-Servins, France, September 6ᵗʰ 1916 – Aged 36. No known grave,
commemorated on the ARRAS MEMORIAL in France.

32 EDWARD MILLETT – 3/10th Battalion Middlesex Regiment.   217
Born 1891, Clerkenwell, London, England. Son of James and Elizabeth
Millett. Killed-in-Action, Broodseinde, Belgium, October 4th 1917 – Aged
26. No known grave, commemorated on the TYNE COT MEMORIAL in
Belgium.

33 OSCAR HANSSON – 8th Battalion East Yorkshire Regiment.   224
Born 1894, Hull, Yorkshire, England. Son of Oscar Hansson and Marte
Talette Larson. Killed-in-Action, Tilloy-Les-Mofflaines, France, April 9th 1917
– Aged 22. Buried within the TILLOY BRITISH CEMETERY in France.

34 WILLIAM ROBINSON – 9th Battalion West Riding Regiment.   230
Born 1895, Alva, Clackmannanshire, Scotland. Son of William and Jane
Robinson. Died of wounds, France, March 22nd 1918 – Aged 22. No known
grave, commemorated on the ARRAS MEMORIAL in France.

35 DAVID PHILLIPS - 4th Royal Welsh Fusiliers. Att. to 2nd South Wales Borderers. 238
Born 1895, Llanelli, Carmarthenshire, Wales. Son of Charles and Elizabeth
Phillips. Killed-in-Action, Langemarck, Belgium, August 16th 1917 – Aged
22. Buried within the ARTILLERY WOOD CEMETERY in Belgium.

36 WILLIAM RICHMOND – 7th Battalion Black Watch (Royal Highlanders).   248
Born 1897, Kirkcaldy, Fife, Scotland. Son of William and Helen Richmond.
Killed-in-Action, High Wood, Somme region, France, July 30th 1916 – Aged 19.
No known grave, commemorated on the THIEPVAL MEMORIAL in France.

37 JOHN TAYLOR – 4th Battalion Royal Scots.   253
Born 1890, Castletown, Caithness, Scotland. Son of Robert and Elizabeth
Taylor. Killed-in-Action at Gallipoli, June 28th 1915 – Aged 25. No known
grave, commemorated on the HELLES MEMORIAL in Turkey.

38 JAMES THIRD – 5th Battalion Cameron Highlanders.   258
Born 1895, Cambuslang, Lanarkshire, Scotland. Son of Charles and Mary
Third. Killed-in-Action, near Festubert, France, July 24th 1915 – Aged 20.
Buried within the BROWN'S ROAD MILITARY CEMETERY in France.

39 DOUGLAS COCKBURN – 5th Battalion Gordon Highlanders.   263
Born October 31st 1895, Garmond, Aberdeenshire, Scotland. Son of Jemima
Cockburn and James Esson. Killed-in-Action, Roclincourt, France, April
11th 1917 – Aged 21. No known grave, commemorated on the ARRAS
MEMORIAL in France.

To the Father I never knew

Lesley Ronald Norman

Leeds

1932 ~ 2010